STATISTICS

(THE EASIER WAY)

WITH R

SECOND EDITION

http://stewr.com

N. M. Radziwill

ISBN-13: 978-0-9969160-5-9
ISBN-10: 0-9969160-5-9

Cover Design: Morgan C. Benton
Indexing: Athena Benton
Publisher: Lapis Lucera, San Francisco, California.

2nd Edition: August 21, 2017 – celebrating the total solar eclipse across the USA

For a free PDF eBook, please email a copy of your receipt (and preferably, a picture of you and/or your book in a beautiful location!) to the author (nicole.radziwill@gmail.com) with "251 PDF" in the subject line. You will receive a PDF eBook by email AND your picture might show up on the http://qualityandinnovation.com blog. Supplemental videos and classroom materials including slides & videos are available at http://stcwr.com (instructors can request exams and answer keys). For information on distribution, bulk sales, or classroom adoptions contact the author directly with subject line "251 BULK" or on Twitter at @nicoleradziwill.

Part 1 of "Significant" - an XKCD cartoon by Randal Munroe
(https://xkcd.com/882/)

About the Author

Nicole M. Radziwill

Nicole Radziwill is an Associate Professor in the Department of Integrated Science and Technology (ISAT) at James Madison University (JMU) in Harrisonburg, Virginia, where she has worked since 2009. Prior to 2009, she spent nearly a decade hanging out with brilliant astronomers and engineers at the National Radio Astronomy Observatory (NRAO) working on software and systems to make giant radio telescopes work. Her teaching interests include quality, innovation, process improvement, cyber-physical systems, cybersecurity management, predictive analytics, intelligent systems, industrial simulation, technology management, and applied statistics. She has been active in the American Society for Quality (ASQ) since the late 1990's, and in addition to serving as one of ASQ's official "Influential Voices" bloggers at http://qualityandinnovation.com, she was recognized by Quality Progress (ASQ's flagship publication) as one of the society's 40 New Voices of Quality in 2011 and "40 Under 40" in 2016.

Nicole is certified by ASQ as Six Sigma Black Belt (CSSBB) #11952 and Manager of Quality and Organizational Excellence (CMQ/OE) #9583. She was Chair of the ASQ Software Division from 2009 to 2011, and served as a national examiner for the Malcolm Baldrige National Quality Award (MBNQA) in 2009 and 2010 appointed by the National Institute for Standards and Technology (NIST). She has a PhD in Technology Management and Quality Systems from Indiana State University, an MBA from Regis University in Denver, and a BS in Meteorology from Penn State. Nicole is the Editor-in-Chief of *Software Quality Professional*, a peer-reviewed journal that covers quality and improvement in software-intensive systems, including big data, analytics, cybersecurity, artificial intelligence, machine learning, and the Internet of Things (IoT).

Her research uses data science to explore quality systems and innovation in production systems, with a focus on emergent environments for living and learning that incorporate cyber-physical systems, alternative economies, and gift cultures such as Burning Man.

Part 2 of "Significant" - an XKCD cartoon by Randal Munroe
(https://xkcd.com/882/)

Brief Contents

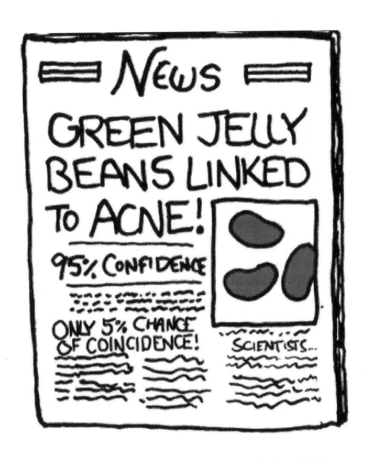

Part 3 of "Significant" - an XKCD cartoon by Randal Munroe
(https://xkcd.com/882/)

Table of Contents

Preface

I've become so tired of reading statistics textbooks that *feel like textbooks*. Why can't someone just write a book that makes me feel like I have a *real live person* sitting next to me, who *cares* about me, who *wants* me to understand this stuff? Why can't someone document some examples in R (my favorite statistical software package) that actually include *all of the steps I need to follow* instead of leaving out one or two critical steps that leave me tearfully troubleshooting for hours? Why can't someone write a cookbook that provides *just enough statistical theory and formulas* so I can understand how the analytical solutions match up with the solutions provided by the statistical software?

That's the kind of book I wanted to recommend for my students. But after years of searching, and a couple more years of trying out books that didn't quite fit, I came to realize that the ideal book I was looking for just didn't exist: if I wanted my students to have a friendly, accessible, affordable, non-threatening textbook... I would have to write it for them. Finally, I started hitting LaTeX and the word processor. *I'll do it*, I committed. It took about three years to get to this point, but late is better than never (I hope).

SO... the purpose of this book is to help you analyze real data – quickly and easily, no fuss no muss – using the R statistical software. Along the way, you'll learn some of the most important fundamentals of applied statistics, which will help you think more critically about the story your data is telling. **My style is to tell you only what I think you need to know to quickly become productive.** I'll provide you with some background, some examples, and an explanation of what each of the commands in R does (and the options you can provide to those commands). I want to give you just enough theory so you know exactly what's going on under the surface, and just enough practice so that you know how to gain insights from your own data.

As a result, this book is NOT intended to be a substitute for a full-length text or course in statistics! You won't learn how to solve homeworky-style problems. However, I've often found that it's easier to get interested in how and why these methods work - and under what conditions - after you've had some success using them, and maybe even working with your own data.

Most importantly, each chapter has been written so that you don't need to be a math or statistics or programming ninja to be able to complete the exercises! Rather than trying to impress you with my slick coding skills in R, **I have purposefully chosen less elegant but more instructive coding strategies**, and I've attempted to show you ALL the lines of code for EVERYTHING that is produced in this book. **I have also been repetitive, on PURPOSE**, so you don't have to remember every single detail from previous chapters to get the job done in a later chapter! I have piloted all the chapters in one or more of my classes, and students in majors ranging from anthropology to business to science to technology have completed the work and provided the feedback that's been used to clarify each chapter.

I wrote this book as the primary text for the undergraduate sophomores and juniors in my introductory applied statistics courses. I was strongly motivated to do this for two reasons: 1) as silent activism against textbook publishers who charge $200+ a pop for very beautiful, glossy statistics textbooks that all of my students are required to purchase, *yet none of my students actually read*, and 2) to give my students just the essential information I think they need to become confident and capable data analysts using the most essential statistics. (At this point, the statistics textbooks tend to become a lot more interesting to *everyone*.)

To be clear, I have nothing against traditional textbooks themselves – or the authors who have labored to create clear, engaging texts with tons of pretty pictures and armies of practice problems. Actually, I admire the authors who spent so much time constructing their vision of a clear, cogent presentation of a subject. (It's not hard for me to admire and appreciate these contributions, since I myself have actually been a part of these teams of authors who have written reasonably awesome, yet expensive, textbooks -- which publishers are now making unconscionable bank with.) I just think traditional textbooks are kind of outmoded and passé. I can find lots of pretty pictures and examples on the web, and I'm not going to flatter myself by thinking that any more than one or two students work practice problems beyond what I cover in class.

I thought it was a sin that my students should pay $200 for a paperweight with a lifetime of just a semester and a resale value of less than 50% of the initial investment. I decided the book that I would create would not be heavy with beautiful and elegant typesetting, or stock photos of cheerful people working on statistical problems, or discussions that took the standard tone of "I am the great textbook, here to confer to you my power and wisdom." Textbooks never admit that some concepts are difficult, or *why* they're difficult. Textbooks aren't conversational, and don't really provide moral support. Textbooks have to be politically correct, which can preclude talking about really intense examples that students usually remember... like whether smoking too much pot is related to lower test scores.

I figured that a textbook that cost only 15-20% of the "standard", and that actually had some useful recipes that students could leverage for semester projects in other classes, might have a little more lasting value and maybe even find a permanent home on my students' bookshelves. That's my dream, at least.

Who This Book Is For

Although originally designed for *my* undergraduate statistics students, I think this book will be useful to you if you are *any* of the following types of people:

- Undergraduate college students in the first semester of applied statistics who are looking for a textbook that does not spend too much time on fluffy explanations of concepts, but rather, presents information in a more direct and less mathematical-ese way

- Professors who want a relaxed, informal book for their intro stats classes that won't cost students $150-$250

- Graduate students who need to use statistics to plan and complete a thesis or dissertation, but don't have that much background in it, and need help NOW

- Early to mid-career data scientists who don't have a PhD in statistics and don't want one, but do want to get more familiar with R, with foundational concepts in statistics, and/or learning how to tell better and more compelling data-driven stories

- Smart, business-savvy people who want to do more data analysis and business analytics, but don't know where to start and don't want to invest hundreds or thousands of dollars on statistical software!

- People who are studying for their Six Sigma Black Belt exam. As a Black Belt myself, a lot of the understanding I've gained has come from the discipline of process improvement, so my treatment of topics naturally tends to reflect what's important for that exam.

- Middle school or high school students who want to collect some original data and do cool science fair projects.

- High school students who are taking regular or AP Statistics classes, and need a little extra help or information (or maybe you want to supplement the in-class instruction you're getting with some understanding of how to analyze real data).

I *do not* assume that you are a programmer. I also do not assume that you are super smart with either computers or statistics, only that you have the motivation to get some data analysis done with R. More about R in the next section. (I won't assume you know things like *how important it is to coerce an object to another form* if a certain algorithm won't work on the object you have. That would be cruel.)

I *do* assume that you already have R installed on your machine, and that you are impatient and just want to figure out how to do some useful stuff so you can start impressing your boss, your teachers, or yourself.

I *do* assume that you have a positive attitude, and that you'd like to learn some statistics and data analysis techniques that you can start using immediately. If you don't have a positive attitude, you should probably not be reading this book. In fact, it's likely that you shouldn't be doing statistics at all. You would be better served to go off and find some topic or some activity that *does* spin up a positive attitude in you. Why? Because you will have more fun. I wouldn't want you to do stats if it wasn't a little fun.

This Book Uses R

All of the examples in this book use the **R statistical software**. You need to download and install the software onto your own machine to be able to use it. Go to the R Project web site at http://www.r-project.org and select the link to "Download R". It will ask you to pick a "CRAN Mirror" so find a site that's geographically close to where you're sitting when you want to install R. For example, I live in Virginia so I might choose a Maryland or Ohio site rather than one in Argentina or Belgium. Data has to travel over geographic distances too, so I want all those mysterious bits and bytes to have to travel the shortest possible distance between where they live and MY laptop. That way, they will arrive as quickly as possible.

This book does not provide help installing R. Why? Simply because every time I have attempted to install R it has been really, really easy, and I don't consider myself an expert at installing anything on my computer. If you can't figure it out yourself, ask a friend (or if you're older, a friend's computer-savvy kid).

Or, you can try to decipher what's in the official R Installation and Administration manual, which can be found at http://cran.r-project.org/doc/manuals/R-admin.html.

How This Book Is Organized

It seems like every non-fiction book has a section in the front that talks about how the book is organized, so I thought I'd be a conformist and do the same. I mean, sure, you could *look* through the rest of the book to see how it's organized, but why do that when I can describe it right here so you don't have to flip through the pages?

- Section 1 talks about **basic concepts** (like variable types, and loading data)
- Section 2 explains how to create **charts, graphs, and plots** that can help you tell the story of your data through visualization
- Section 3 provides **the framework for how to do a research project** using basic applied statistics, including fundamental aspects of theory, and also shows how to structure the story of your data and your results (featuring "Dr. R's 7 Steps")

- Section 4 summarizes **how to create confidence intervals** for several common scenarios, and recommends best approaches to handle the most challenging cases
- Section 5 contains **step-by-step recipes for conducting statistical inference tests,** drawing conclusions, and interpreting your results
- Section 6 contains **recipes for regression** (which is just a fancy word for *finding relationships between variables*), and
- The Appendices provide some helpful reference information.

Inside each section, there's lots of useful stuff, and lots of me rambling about it.

Conventions Used in This Book

Joy in Repetition

Although I have aimed to keep the text as simple and concise as possible, you may notice that there is substantial repetition between sections, especially throughout **Section 5: Statistical Inference**. That's because I also plan to use this text as a reference for myself. When I am doing an inference test, or even a confidence interval, I don't want to have to flip back and forth between chapters to do things like *remember what all those assumptions are that I need to check.* Or how to load the data. When I am doing a Pareto chart, I want to quickly and easily reference all of the most important ways to change colors, line styles, and common options. When I create pie charts, I want to be able to easily and quickly reference all the most important options to the `pie` command. I don't want to have to flip back and forth between sections just because something was covered earlier in the book.

I don't want to pretend like I'm going to remember even the simplest syntaxes, because that's not easy (and gets less and less easy as your age and number of children increase).

My Fonts

Most of the text is written in Calibri 11-point font because I think it's pretty. Inline R code is in 10-point Courier New, whereas chunks of code are 9-point Courier New. Why all the variability? It's totally arbitrary. I just liked it that way, so I did it. Sometimes it looks good, and sometimes it looks less than good. I'm good with that. Sometimes I violate every design principle that exists by using 9-point font next to 8-point font with some 7-point font thrown in below it. But I have a good reason: I want you to be able to see all the output from R without it looking really horrible. You may think this is design heresy, but I call it practical and page-saving.

My R Code

Code that you can type directly into R is written in 9-point Courier New, and indented half an inch from the left margin, like this:

```
defect.counts <- c(12,29,18,3,34,4)

names(defect.counts) <- c("Weather","Overslept", "Alarm Failure",
"Time Change","Traffic","Other")

df.defects <- data.frame(defect.counts)
```

The code above *creates a vector of numbers* in the first line, *establishes names* for what each of those numbers means in the next two lines, and *creates a special object called a data frame* in the last line. I had to use a smaller font size for code that you can type into R so that most of my text and output would show up looking decent on the printed page. Design purists, I give you my apologies up front.

Code that I typed into R and the output that code produced is also recorded in 9-point Courier New, *but is not indented.* **This is important because it always has a leading caret** (that's the ">" at the beginning of each line). This caret is the R prompt, which you will see if you are using the R Console that comes with non-enterprise installations of the software. **<u>DO NOT TRY TO TYPE THE CARET AS PART OF YOUR CODE OR YOU WILL GET ERROR MESSAGES.</u>**

Here is an example:

```
> df.defects
             defect.counts
Weather                 12
Overslept               29
Alarm Failure           18
Time Change              3
Traffic                 34
Other                    4
```

This means that I typed in the command `df.defects` to see the contents of the data frame that I named "df.defects" in R. The rest is what R responded back to me. If I typed in "> df.defects" I would get an error message that looked like this:

```
Error: unexpected '>' in ">"
```

(And for experienced R programmers: YES, I know that some of the R code in here is not optimized, and I know some of my simulations use loops instead of `apply`, and how could I ever possibly do something like that because that's not the best thing to do. You're right. I don't claim to provide elegant code in this book... just readable and/or explained code.)

My R Functions

I also keep many of the utility functions I use frequently on GitHub. You can scan a list of them at `https://github.com/NicoleRadziwill/R-Functions`. Even though the text of these functions is included in this book, you might just want to load the function into your R console without having to cut and paste.

You can use the `source` command in R to load functions that are stored on Github, like this:

```
source("https://raw.githubusercontent.com/NicoleRadziwill/R-
Functions/master/ztest.R")
```

Then, just use the function as you would any other function:

```
> z.test(80,112)
$estimate
[1] 0.7142857

$ts.z
NULL

$p.val
NULL

$cint
[1] 0.6306212 0.7979502
```

My Data

I keep the data I used in the examples in this book on GitHub. You can see a list of it all at `https://github.com/NicoleRadziwill/Data-for-R-Examples`. For data in CSV format, use `read.csv` and the URL for the *raw* data format on GitHub:

```
> mnms <- read.csv("https://raw.githubusercontent.com/NicoleRadziwill/Data-
for-R-Examples/master/Fall%202016%20M%26Ms.csv")
```

For data in plain text format, use `read.table` and the URL that takes you to the *Raw* data on GitHub, like this:

```
> books <-
read.table("https://raw.githubusercontent.com/NicoleRadziwill/Data-for-R-
Examples/master/anova-textbooks.txt",header=TRUE)
```

When lines of code are long and wrap to the next line like this, you should be able to copy the entire statement (without the leading caret), paste it into R, and get it to run. Be careful! Sometimes, lines of code depend on earlier lines of code – if you get red error messages, you may have to re-enter *previous* lines of code to get your current line to execute.

Changes Since the 1st Edition

With thousands of contributing developers, R changes *all the time*. Fortunately, these changes usually mean that tasks get easier as time goes on, and new capabilities are added.

Within days of the release of the 1ˢᵗ Edition, for example, it became *much, much* easier to source functions from GitHub: a seven-step process became a one-step, *one line of code* task. In summary, here are the changes that appear in this 2ⁿᵈ Edition:

- Chapter 1.6 ("Getting Data Into R") and all of the Chapters in Section 2 have been substantially revised; all chapters have been somewhat revised.

- Dr. R's 12 Steps have been consolidated into Dr. R's 7 Steps. The role of the short 7-step solution process is now more fully explained in Chapter 3.3. Tests on regression slopes and intercepts have been adapted to the 7 Stepmethod.

- External datasets are easier to access, and no intermediate downloads to your local machine are required. I no longer use `RCurl`. It's much easier to load functions and data from GitHub or any other location on the web than it used to be.

- I use `shadenorm` sometimes, but also support the use of `polygon` for shading areas under the normal curve and other distributions. There are examples using both methods throughout this book.

- There are headers on each page so you can more easily flip through the book and see what section and chapter you are in, and all equations have been re-rendered.

- I still haven't written an R package for this book because I don't want a package to mask important tasks like acquiring data and acquiring functions from the web.

- I haven't made the transition to teaching starting with `tidyverse` (yet).

How to Contact Me

If I have the time, I am more than happy to address comments and questions about this book, its examples, or problems that you are having working through your own data. I am more likely to have the time to respond to you in between semesters (which means most of December, and May through early August). If you don't hear back from me, don't despair: it just means that your message fell through the cracks, and I'm often either busy or distracted (or just plain scatterbrained), so I might have missed it. Try again. If I don't have the time to answer or explore your query, I'll let you know.

I also invite you to follow me on Twitter - my ID is **@nicoleradziwill** - but be advised, you will also be getting a lot of tweet spam about severe weather, tornadoes, solar flares, coronal mass ejections, and Burning Man. (You may like this.) Also, if there is ever an interesting planetary configuration or an asteroid that is about to impact Earth, you will be among the first to know.

Disclaimer

The purpose of this book is *not* to be mathematically elegant or comprehensive, but to give you enough of what you need to know to be productive - quickly - without leaving you statistically naive. I've included links to longer, more extensive proofs in many places if you want to know more about the mathiness underlying everything in this book. I am not a professional statistician or mathematical purist, but a realist who analyzes data almost daily; I want you to be able to analyze your data too.

Acknowledgements

I would be remiss if I did not mention the people who influenced me to become a person who really likes to use, and teach, statistics. First of all, I am eternally indebted to all the students that test drove my explanations of concepts, and my early drafts of this book. They helped me recognize what can be confusing to learners, and helped me illuminate the things that were actually confusing to *me*. I'm also thankful to my teaching assistants Andy Duong, Meghan Mooney, Aimee Cunningham, Cassidy Moellers, and Chris Miller who helped me in the initial stages of piloting the new approaches and creating new course materials.

Dan Teague of the North Carolina School of Science and Math in Durham, NC was my first statistics teacher and deserves a lot of credit. He was brave enough to explain to the group of 14- to 17- year olds in my class nearly two decades ago that statistics is just a game of exploring variation in n-dimensional vector space. I was smitten. Bob Ryan of the 1990's statistics department at Penn State deserves some credit for *keeping* me hooked. He was one of the executives of Minitab, a company he founded with his wife at the time, totally down to earth, and told cheesy (yet "good" to me!) jokes in class. The jokes made me want to keep doing applied statistics. (Yes, I can be that easily influenced.) Plus, he made all of us buy Lyman Ott's applied statistics book, which I still have, and still use. Mike Hayden of Indiana State University also deserves a mention and much gratitude. His recipe for executing and documenting a statistical hypothesis test (which he calls "Hayden's 16 Steps") influenced me greatly, and certainly snuck into my own recipes and approach, even forming the basis for "Dr. R's 7 Steps" which are a theme within this book. I am also eternally grateful to him for helping me *really understand* what setting your alpha level is all about... balancing cost and risk. And ethical considerations... but I added that last part.

I am also thankful for H. M. Schey's book *Div, Grad, Curl, and All That: An Informal Text on Vector Calculus*. Had I not possessed that book as an undergrad, I never would have passed my vector calculus course, which was essential for my major (meteorology). The book you're reading now is in many ways a tribute to this author's style... especially the subtitle, "an informal text on applied statistics."

I also appreciate the support and feedback from the Department of Integrated Science and Technology (ISAT) at James Madison University (JMU) in Harrisonburg, Virginia, especially my colleagues Anne Henriksen and Morgan C. Benton. Anne and I have had many discussions about how to teach introductory statistics in an integrated way (that embraces thinking about social context) for the past few years, and she helped me identify some really important typos in some of the early versions of my chapters. My partner and co-conspirator Morgan provided extensive technical, moral, and emotional support throughout the entire process of preparing this book, including extremely geeky conversations exploring things like the possible relationship between P-Values and the observer effect in quantum physics... and pointers to all of the XKCD cartoons. And Netflix. And many hours of fantastically blissful and enjoyable research, for which I have much gratitude.

SECTION 1: BASIC CONCEPTS

- Categorical and Quantitative Data
- Formatting Your Data for R
- Measures of Central Tendency and Variability
- Probability and Probability Distributions
- Using the Normal Model

1.1 Intro to R: Installation, Working Directories, & Packages

Objective

The purpose of this exercise is to get R installed on your computer, set your working directory, check out some basic concepts with a quick "Hello World!" exercise, and practice loading in a new package. By the end of this exercise, you'll have gained a rudimentary understanding of R and its potential.

Background

The R statistical software is a tool for analyzing and visualizing data. It was designed in 1993 as a prototype to see how a statistical computing platform might be built. Today, R has become more than just a simple testbed. It's a widely used, collaborative, open source environment for statistical modeling and data analysis.

The R programming language is based on the S language (a statistical language based around functions and the concept of objects). R is an *interpreted* language, which means that it interprets plain text and numerical values input by the user. For example, if you type in 2+2 at the caret prompt in the R console, the interactive R session will reply with 4. It's a calculator! The fact that R is an interpreted language makes coding at the command prompt very approachable; whatever you type in, you can see the results immediately when you press the `Enter` key. R handles all sorts of things, from classical statistical tests to data cleansing and advanced analysis. If you have some data and want to do something with it, R more than likely has a solution for you.

Part 1: Installing R

To start with R, first we have to download it from the web.

1. Go to the website http://www.r-project.org/. This is the home base for everything R, including manuals, FAQs, screenshots, and code repositories.

2. On the left-hand side of your screen, click on "CRAN". This will take you to a page titled "CRAN Mirrors".

3. On the page "CRAN Mirrors", scroll down until you see the heading "USA". Underneath this heading you'll find lots of links. Each link allows you to download R, so no matter which one you press, you'll go to the R download page. Click on one that's close to you geographically: this will take you to a page called The Comprehensive R Archive Network (that's what CRAN stands for).

4. On that page, click the link that matches your operating system. This will take you to a page titled "R for (your operating system)".

5. There, do one of the following:
   - For Mac OS: click on "Download R for Mac OS". After that, select the link that ends in the file format ".pkg".
     - ❖ Note: If your browser informs you that this file may harm your computer, select "keep".
   - For Windows: click on "Download R for Windows". After that, click on the link titled "base". Then, click "Download R for Windows".
     - ❖ Note: If your browser informs you that this file may harm your computer, select "keep".

6. Once your package/file has downloaded, navigate to your operating system's Downloads folder. From here, double click on the file/package and follow the on-screen instructions to install R. A shortcut for R should be created on your desktop if you are running Windows, or your applications folder if you are running Mac OS.

Part 2: Getting and Setting Your Working Directory

Now that you have R installed on your computer, you can set your *working directory*. This is the place R will look to find data, functions, and other resources on your computer. You can change your working directory to point R to *any location* on your local machine, depending on which local directory contains the data, functions, or other files you want to import into R.

1. Open up R by clicking on the Icon that was created for you in Part 1. An R coding environment should pop up. You'll see some introductory text and a caret (">") which is R's way of telling you it's ready to do your bidding.

2. The first thing we want to do is find out *where the working directory is already set.* You want to set it to a place that's convenient for you. To get your current directory, type `getwd()` and press Enter.

3. Your working directory will display below where you typed `getwd()`. I recommend creating a folder titled R in the default working directory (you'll do this outside of R, either in the "Finder" application on Macs, or through the "Computer" option that you see when you click the Windows start button). Navigate to it by typing

   ```
   setwd("/your/directory/name/goes/here/R")
   ```

   If you wish to change your working directory entirely, find a directory that you like and use `setwd` to specify the path to that directory.

4. If all is successful with the step above and you type `getwd()` once again, you should see the directory you just specified. Your working directory has now been set!

5. Double check by typing `dir()` -- after which you should see the contents of the directory you'd like R to point to.

Part 3: A Very, Very Simple Hello World! Exercise

Now that your working directory is set, let's do a simple "Hello World!" Exercise to become more familiar with R syntax.

1. In your R terminal, type the following and press `Enter`:

   ```
   x <- ("Hello")
   ```

2. Type `x` and you should see `[1] "Hello"`. In the step above, we assigned the word `Hello` to a variable `x` by using the assignment operator `<-` which looks like a left-pointing arrow. Note that any *string*, which is a series of characters containing non-numeric values, must be contained in quotes.

3. Once again in your terminal, type the following and press `Enter`:

   ```
   y <- ("World!")
   ```

4. Type `y` and you should see `[1] "World!"`. This time, we assigned the word `World!` to a variable y.

5. Now let's combine these two words and store them to a new variable that we'll call `z`. Type the following and press enter:

   ```
   z <- paste(x,y)
   ```

6. You will see `[1] "Hello World!"` after typing `z` at the caret. The paste command combined the contents of the variables `x` and `y` that you defined previously.

Part 4: Installing Packages

One of the best things about R is that it's a highly versatile environment. It allows you to download packages to do all sorts of stuff like create awesome graphs, tables, and maps, and it can also help you mine and analyze data. **Bringing new packages into your R environment is something you will do often**. This is a three-step process. First, you have to figure out which R package will provide the functionality that you need. For example, if you want to use R to acquire data from Facebook, you might type "package to download

Facebook data in R" into Google. A search might produce many R packages that provide similar functionality, so you'll have to install the one that looks best; try it out to see if it's what you're looking for. If not, search for a different package and start over.

Let's say our search tells us that the `Rfacebook` package might provide us with what we need. The second step in the three-step process is to install this package (that is, download the code to our machine) from a CRAN mirror (one of the many repositories around the world that provide us with an up-to-date collection of all of the publicly downloadable R packages).

1. While in your R console, navigate to a dropdown menu titled `Packages` (Windows) or `Packages & Data` (Mac). Click on `Install Package(s)…` (Windows) or `Package Installer` (Mac). Alternatively, just type this on the R command line, replacing `package_name` with the actual name of the package you want to retrieve (being very careful to get the capitalization and spacing right):

```
install.packages("package_name")
```

2. A window should appear that says something along the lines of "Please select a country". Select a location that's *geographically close* to you. That way, the bits and bytes won't have to flow all the way around the globe to get to your machine, and the installation process will probably be quicker. (Since I live in Virginia, I typically choose the Ohio or Pennsylvania sites.)

3. After selecting your country, you should see a long list of libraries. For Mac users, you may need to click on `Get List` to see the list (make sure `CRAN (binaries)` is selected from the dropdown menu above before clicking `Get List`).

4. Navigate down until you see `Rfacebook`. Highlight it, and click `OK` (Windows) or `Install Selected` (Mac) **For Mac users, make sure to check the "Install Dependencies" box. It will save you A LOT of hassle later.** This will download your selected library. Note that you can download more than one library at once.

To load the library that you just downloaded into *active memory* so you can use it, type:

```
library("Rfacebook")
```

This will load in the selected library. As with downloading libraries, you can load multiple libraries as well (but we recommend that you just do one at a time). Now that you have the package installed on your local machine, you should never have to install it again. However, *every time you launch the R environment, you'll have to use the* library *command* for each package that you want to use during that session.

Now What?

Congratulations! You've now downloaded R and started working within the R environment. Over time, you'll see how versatile and cool R is, and how it can empower you as a programmer and data analyst. You're now ready for some more advanced exercises, or to begin exploring the useful examples at R Bloggers (http://www.r-bloggers.com).

You can also search Google to find different flavors of the "Hello World!" exercise that other new R learners have tried. See if you can expand your code to do something more interesting, like prompt you to enter your name from the keyboard using the scan() function and have R say hello to you by name.

1.2 Why I Love R

Objective

The purpose of this chapter is to give you a sense of why I use the R Statistical Software daily, wherever and whenever I can. On Valentine's Day in 2012, I decided that I would publicly declare my love for my favorite software package. Here is that declaration.

Preamble

My valentine is unique. It will not provide me with flowers, or chocolates, or a romantic dinner tonight, and will certainly not whisper sweet nothings into my good ear. *And yet – I will feel no less loved.* In contrast, my valentine will probably give me some routines for identifying control limits on control charts, and maybe a way to classify time series. I'm really looking forward to spending some quality time today with this great positive force in my life that saves me so much time and makes me so productive.

Today, on Valentine's Day, I am serenading one of the loves of my life – R. Technically, R is a statistical software package, but for me, it's the nirvana of data analysis. I am not a hardcore geek programmer, you see. I don't like to spend hours coding, admiring the elegance of the syntax and data structures, or finding more compact ways to get the job done. I just want to crack open my data and learn cool things about it, and the faster and <u>more butter-like[1]</u> the better.

Here are a Few of the Reasons Why I Love R

- **R did not play hard to get.** The first time I downloaded R from http://www.r-project.org, it only took about 3 minutes, I was able to start playing with it immediately, and it actually worked without a giant installation struggle.

---

[1] http://qualityandinnovation.com/2009/01/24/the-butter-test/

- **R is free.** I didn't have to pay to download it. I don't have to pay its living expenses in the form of license fees, upgrade fees, or rental charges (like I did when I used SPSS). If I need more from R, I can probably download a new package, and get that too for free.

- **R blended into my living situation rather nicely, and if I decide to move, I'm confident that R will be happy in my new place.** As a Windows user, I'm accustomed to having hellacious issues installing software, keeping it up to date, loading new packages, and so on. But R works well on Windows. And when I want to move to Linux, R works well there too. And on the days when I just want to get touchy feely with a Mac, R works well there too.

- **R gets a lot of exercise, so it's always in pretty good shape.** There is an enthusiastic global community of R users who number in the tens of thousands (and maybe more), and report issues to the people who develop and maintain the individual packages. It's rare to run into an error with R, especially when you're using a package that is very popular.

- **R Is very social; in fact, it's on Facebook.** And if you friend "R Bloggers" you'll get updates about great things you can do with the software (some basic techniques, but some really advanced ones too). Most updates from R Bloggers come with working code.

- **Instead of just having ONE nice package, R has HUNDREDS of nice packages.** And each performs a different and unique function, from graphics, to network analysis, to machine learning, to bioinformatics, to super hot-off-the-press algorithms that someone just developed and published. (I even learned how to use the "dtw" package over the weekend, which provides algorithms for time series clustering and classification using a technique called Dynamic Time Warping. Sounds cool, huh!) If you aren't happy with one package, you can probably find a comparable package that someone else wrote that implements your desired functions in a different way.

- (And if you aren't satisfied by those packages, **there's always someone out there coding a new one.**)

- **R helps me meditate.** OK, so we can't go to tai chi class together, but I do find it very easy to get into the flow (a la Mihaly Csikzentmihalyi) when I'm using R.

- **R doesn't argue with me for no reason.** Most of the error messages actually make sense *and* mean something.

- **R always has time to spend with me.** All I have to do is turn it on by double-clicking that nice R icon on my desktop. I don't ever have to compete with other users or feel jealous of them. R never turns me down or says it's got other stuff to do. R always makes me feel important and special, because it helps me accomplish great things that I would not be able to do on my own. R supports my personal and professional goals.

- **R has its own journal (http://journal.r-project.org).** Wow. Not only is it utilitarian and fun to be around, but it's also got a great reputation and is recognized and honored as a solid citizen of the software community.

- **R always remembers me.** I can save the image of my entire session with it and pick it up at a later time.

- **R will never leave me.** (Well, I hope. It was really crushing that one time *Java* left me. It was in the mid-90s, and I had spent about a year with Java 1.0 and was really starting to get productive, at a time when the language was fresh and new and amazing. But Sun deprecated all of my favorite classes and methods in Java 1.1, and it hit my productivity and my heart so deeply, I've just never gone back to Java... even though the language is much better behaved now, and has a lot more people holding it to standards.)

The most important reason I like R is that I *just like spending time with it*, learning more about it, and feeling our relationship deepen as it gently helps me analyze all my new data. (This is seriously geeky – yeah, I know. At least I won't be disappointed by the object of *MY* affection.)

1.3 Variables and the Case Format

Objective

Before you analyze your data, prepare charts or graphs, or do statistical tests, it's important to gain a sense of what that data is all about. What's the *story* behind the data? How *good* is it? Why do I *care* about what research questions I'm asking? The purpose of this section is to introduce you to some conceptual approaches for understanding your data before you load it into a software package like R for further analysis. You will:

- Learn the difference between categorical and quantitative variables
- Learn how to make categorical variables out of quantitative raw data
- Find out the difference between independent and dependent variables
- See how to characterize your data in terms of the 5 W's (and 1 H)
- Be introduced to the concept of a *case*, and why it's important to prepare your raw data in case format so that a statistical software package can understand it

When I was in school, going through my first few classes on statistics and data analysis, I was really frustrated by all of these classifications of variables. I mean, why do you have to know this stuff? It just seemed like worthless memorization. What I discovered later was that *the type of data you have available* **dictates** *what you can do with it.*

Would you like to prepare a scatterplot and maybe perform a linear regression to generate a predictive model? Well, OK, as long as you have two quantitative variables (which are preferably both continuous). Want to do a one-way Analysis of Variance (ANOVA)? No problem, as long as you have multiple collections of quantitative variables, and you can split them up into groups using one of the categorical variables you've collected. Want to construct a bar plot? OK, but you'll need categorical data or else you should be preparing a histogram instead. Want to calculate your average grade? No problem, if your grades have been measured quantitatively, but you'll have a hard time computing your average hair color (a categorical variable). Knowing the types of variables you're working with is not only essential to prevent you from going down unproductive dead ends, but also, it will help you decide what data structures to use if you need to do more advanced programming to facilitate your data analysis.

Categorical and Quantitative Variables

A categorical variable places an observation in one (and only one) category chosen from two or more possible categories. An observation can't be in more than one category at the same time! If there is no ordering that can be done between the categories, the variable is *nominal*, whereas if there is some intrinsic order that can be assigned to the categories, those variables are *ordinal*. Here are some examples of categorical variables:

- Your **gender** (Male, Female, or Other)
- Your **class** in school (Freshman, Sophomore, Junior, Senior, Graduate)
- Your **performance status** (Probation, Regular, Honors)
- Your **political party** affiliation (Democrat, Republican, Independent)
- The **color** of some object (red, orange, yellow, green, blue, purple)
- What **type of degree program** someone is in (BS, BA)
- Your **hair color** (blonde, brown, red, black, white, other)
- What type of **pet** someone has (cat, dog, ferret, rabbit, other)
- The result of someone's **performance in a game** (win, lose)
- **Race** (Hispanic, Asian, African American, Caucasian)
- **Machine settings** (Low, Medium, High)
- **Method of payment** (Cash, Credit)

(Only two of the above examples are clearly ordinal, one is possibly ordinal if you know how the groups are assigned, and the rest are nominal. Can you pick out the ordinal variables?)

Quantitative variables, in contrast, are measured as numbers. Here are some examples of quantitative variables:

- Your **age**
- The number of **siblings** you have

- The number of **spouses** you've had
- The number of **children** you have
- Your weekly, monthly, or annual **salary**
- Your monthly **rent or mortgage payment**
- The **mass** or **weight** of an object
- The **number of speeding tickets** you've received
- The **speed** you were going when you got each ticket
- Your cumulative or most recent **GPA** (measured on a continuous scale from 0.0 to 4.0 or 5.0, depending on your school)

Just because a value is sampled as a number doesn't mean it's automatically a quantitative variable! For example, here are some numbers which are actually categorical variables in disguise:

- Your **social security number** (yeah, can't add or subtract those... logically)
- The **outcome of a game** where you have won (1) or lost (0)
- The **boarding class** on your airplane ticket (1, 2, 3, or 4)
- Which **group you were assigned to** for a team project in one of your classes (1,2, 3, 4, or 5)
- Your **level of agreement** with a particular statement (measured on a *Likert scale* where 1=disagree, 2=slightly disagree, 3=neutral, 4= slightly agree, and 5=agree)

Sometimes researchers will treat values measured on a Likert scale as quantitative, and create scatterplots or do inference tests that require quantitative variables. Purists, like mathematicians, think this is a terrible practice (although researchers who use this approach typically argue that the mean of values measured on a Likert scale has meaning to them). I tend to side with the mathematicians on this one.

There are Different Kinds of Quantitative Variables

Quantitative variables can be classified further as being on the *interval* or *ratio* scales of measurement. With interval data, you can perform logical operations between them, and you can add and subtract them, but you can't reasonably multiply or divide them. Temperature measurements are on the *interval* scale, because although you can tell which of two temperatures is higher or lower, and you can say that 80 degrees is 10 degrees warmer than 70 degrees, you can't say that 80 degrees is exactly twice as warm as 40 degrees. Length and time are quantitative variables on the *ratio* scale of measurement: a distance of two miles is exactly twice as long as a distance of one mile.

Fortunately, these distinctions are not so important if you're just trying to figure out what statistical tests you can use, given that you know you have quantitative data.

Discrete and Continuous Data

Values that variables take on can also be classified as discrete or continuous. For example, when you roll a six-sided die, it can only take on one of six values (1 through 6). Categorical data is, by its nature, discrete. Continuous variables can take on values anywhere within an interval of possibilities. *Distributions* can also be discrete or continuous. It's easy to tell whether a distribution is discrete or continuous by **checking to see whether it's smooth or spiky**. Note that in the discrete distribution below, variables can only take on values that are numbers between 0 and 10. In the continuous distribution, variables can take on values *anywhere* within the interval from 0 to 10.

Discrete Distribution

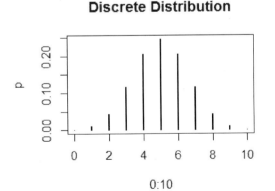

Continuous Distribution

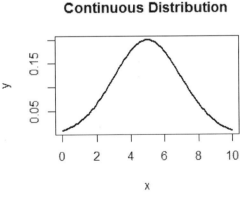

Here is the R code that produced the distributions you see here:

```
par(mfrow=c(1,2)) # Set up plot area with one row and two columns
p <- dbinom(0:10,size=10,prob=0.5)
plot(0:10,p,type="h",lwd=2,main="Discrete Distribution")
x <- seq(0,10,length=100)
y <- dnorm(x,mean=5,sd=2)
plot(x,y,type="l",lwd=2,main="Continuous Distribution")
```

Independent and Dependent Variables

This characterization describes *how you plan to use* your categorical and quantitative variables; it does not tell you anything about the variables themselves.

A *dependent* variable is one that you've decided to predict from other (*independent*) variables. As a result, independent variables are sometimes called *predictors*, and dependent variables are sometimes called *response* variables. If you have only one predictor and one response variable (that is, one independent variable that you use to predict one dependent variable), and both are quantitative, the dependent variable will be the one plotted on the vertical (y) axis.

Because this label describes how you're *using* your data, you can generate multiple predictive models from one dataset and change what variables you're treating as independent and dependent. Here are some examples of what you can do:

- Use **simple linear regression** to predict one quantitative dependent variable based on the values of one quantitative independent variable

- Use **multiple linear regression** to predict one quantitative dependent variable based on the values of two or more quantitative independent variables

- Use **logistic regression** to predict one categorical dependent variable based on the values of one or more quantitative (or categorical) independent variables

Recoding Quantitative Variables into Categorical Variables

Sometimes it is useful to generate categorical variables from the quantitative values you have collected. This process is called *recoding*. For example, say you want to do a study to see whether top performing students smoke fewer cigarettes than students who don't do as well. How do you determine which students are the high performers, and which students are not? Perhaps you might ask them if they're in an honors program or not, but the criteria for getting into an honors program is different from school to school. Also, there may be lots of high performing students who have chosen not to enroll in an honors program due to schedule constraints, program requirements, or other unrelated factors. One way to get around this challenge is to gather information about student performance in terms of a *quantitative variable* and then recode that variable to a categorical variable after the data is collected.

For example, you may decide that cumulative GPA is a reasonable measure for student assessment. You go out and ask 200 students to tell you their cumulative GPA (so far). You end up with a wide variety of values! A substantial fraction of students in your sample didn't do so well, and they are reporting cumulative GPAs between 0.5 and 1.8. However, there were also quite a few students whose GPAs were greater than 3.7 (something you didn't expect). How do you decide which students are the high performers? Since you have so many, you may decide that a cumulative GPA of 3.7 is a good threshold to set.

But what would happen if, in your sample of 200 students, you didn't have very many *at all* who achieved a cumulative GPA greater than 3.7? You might look through your data and say well, it might be more reasonable (for this group of students) to set the threshold at a cumulative GPA of 3.5. Or maybe you will decide to set the bar a little lower, at 3.2. It all depends on what kind of data you collect.

The nice thing about collecting quantitative data wherever you can is that *you always have the flexibility to decide on the boundaries for your categories later!* What would have happened if you decided, before the fact, that a "high performer" was someone who had a cumulative GPA greater than 3.8? Then, you went out and collected data, and *only* asked students if their GPA was greater than 3.8 (thus, you collected that data as a categorical variable). When you reviewed the data you had collected, you found out that *no students reported a cumulative GPA greater than 3.8!* In this case, your research study would be dead in the water. SOL, and not in the educational-standards sense. You would have to start over... and you probably wouldn't be happy about it.

You *lose information* when you recode quantitative variables into categorical variables. As a rule, it's always best to collect data as quantitative when you can, and reserve the privilege of creating categorical variables from your quantitative values later.

To recode a quantitative variable into a categorical value, just 1) decide on the boundaries for your categories, and 2) assign each quantitative variable into a category. You can revise your recoding as often as you need to. It's a great superpower to have.

A Simple Characterization of Metadata Using the 5 W's (and 1 H)

Metadata is data that tells you more about data. What this means, in real people terms, is that it can be useful to talk about *how* you collected your data and *why* you collected your data so that people in the future will know how (and whether) to use the beautiful data resources that you have painstakingly prepared. Think of metadata as your way to ensure your legacy in the realm of personal time travel: some data analyst in the future, who finds the data that you collected, will try to determine whether he or she can use that data for *their* own unique purposes. And you can help them. Some of the questions you will want to answer for them (what I call the "5W/1H questions") are:

- **Who**: *There are two parts to answering this question!* First, who are your data about? The data can be about a person, a group of people, an object or class of objects (e.g. computers, machines, or a particular type of computers or machines), a type of animal, or maybe even an inanimate object like a lake or pond (where you might be collecting information about water quality or other aspects of the environment). Second, who is collecting the data? A future researcher will treat data collected by an elementary school student much differently than he or she would treat data collected by a scientist or a professional in industry. Be sure to establish your qualifications for collecting the data, and in what context you are applying your skills. You may even want to include contact information in case anyone has a question about your data.

- **What**: What is your data about? What types of data are you collecting about whatever subject you identified when you answered the "who" question? I like to provide a subjective overview about each of my variables here, sometimes articulating which are categorical and which are quantitative, the enumerations of each of the possible categories, and whether I recoded some quantitative data to get some of the categorical variables.

- **When**: When were your data collected? This is particularly important if you wish to look at changes in the values of a variable that occur over time (for example, measurements of CO_2 in the atmosphere if you are studying global warming). Also, values collected earlier in time will be subject to the limitations of the less advanced sensors or technologies that are used to collect the measurements.

- **Where**: In what location(s) did you collect your data? Sometimes, this can be as easy as collecting a geographical marker (for example, a latitude and longitude) for each item in your sample. Or, you might just describe the location that is associated with all of your data, for example, the city, country, or organization within which your data was acquired.

- **Why**: For what original purpose did you collect your data? What were the objectives of your study? This will help a future researcher understand the assumptions and limitations that you were aware of at the time the data were collected.

- **How**: How were the data collected? You might want to explore what instruments you used to measure the values for each variable, or what sampling strategies you used to ensure a random sample where the observations are independent. If you obtained your data from an archive (or from multiple archives), be sure to include the locations of the archives, so that someone in the future will potentially be able to retrieve the source data directly from the same location you did.

Why is it important to describe these things? First and foremost, because if you don't do it at the point of data collection... *you'll probably forget*. If you're young, or if this data is important to you, you might be thinking "no way... I'm not going to forget." But you will. I've collected so much data over the past two decades that when I go back and look at an old dataset, I have to remind myself what I was thinking about the first time I worked with it. So, metadata provides a way for my *past self* to communicate with my *future self* and help her be more productive.

Second, while you're analyzing your data, you may need to enlist the help of friends, colleagues, or other smart people on the internet who can help you troubleshoot the issues you're having analyzing your data in a software system like R. People won't be able to help you if you can't provide them with useful information about your data, how you got it, and what you've done with it already. So be ready to exchange metadata and a step-by-step history of what you've done with (and to) your data with any person (or bot; yes, we're almost there) who may be able to provide help.

Third, *reproducibility* is becoming a more and more significant issue in the sciences. What this means is that if you've done an experiment once, you should be able to collect the data and analyze it again, and draw pretty much the same conclusions. However, this is much easier said than done. There's a huge volume of published research in the academic literature, but not all of it can be reproduced - even by the researchers who designed and executed the initial studies!

The Wikipedia page on reproducibility (http://en.wikipedia.org/wiki/Reproducibility) includes a section on "noteworthy irreproducible results" which, though sparse, includes the famous "cold fusion" case from the late 1980's. Although this would have represented a huge breakthrough in our ability to produce energy, the experiment was not reproducible and could not be verified. Also, because the results could not be reliably reproduced, further studies to explore the technological potential of cold fusion were impossible.

Finally, when you encounter data that's *new to you* that someone else has collected, it is always useful to ask yourself the 5W/1H questions to get a better sense of what that data is all about. Also, thinking about the data will help you understand how to structure the data for analysis in R or another statistical software system using cases (described below).

Case Format

I've found that the most challenging aspect of gathering data is making sure that you format your results so that a statistical software package will actually be able to do something with it. Here are some heuristics (rules of thumb) to help you format your data. In your mind, picture a spreadsheet with rows, columns, and cells where you will enter each element of your data.

- Each of the columns should contain ONE AND ONLY ONE variable
- Each of the rows should contain ONE AND ONLY ONE "who" from your sample
- The total number of rows should equal n, the number of items in your sample

For example, if you are collecting information about the distributions of colors and defects in a bag of M&Ms, it's very easy to produce a spreadsheet that looks like this:

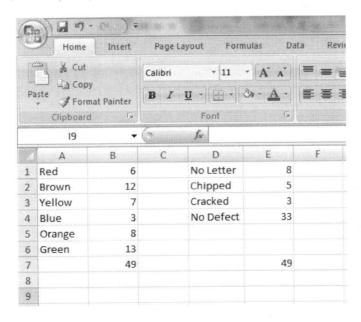

However, **_this is bad_**! If you try to upload data in this format into a statistical software package, it won't know what to do. It's not in *case format*. After you answer the 5W/1H questions, you'll know that that answer to "Who are your data about?" is "the M&Ms." Each

21

case (or row) in your properly formatted data should be about one (and only one) "who" - which, in this case, is one M&M. Each row should contain data about one (and only one) of the M&Ms in your sample. In contrast, **here's what properly formatted data, organized as cases, looks like:**

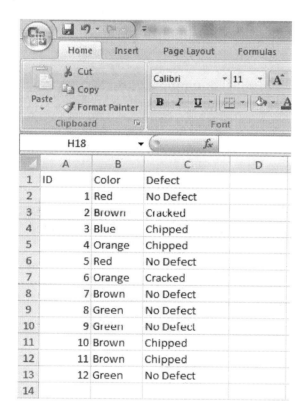

Notice how each row contains data collected from one M&M. Also, we didn't include any *summary* information or descriptive statistics in our spreadsheet - for example, the total number of items in our sample (49) that's been tallied in the previous example. Our statistical software can very easily produce any of this summary information, so we don't need to add it up ourselves. We have been consistent in labeling the values from our categories so that our statistical software will be easily able to compile the values (that is, we didn't say "Red" in one place and "RED" in another - R will treat those as two completely different values).

Other Resources

- Confused about recoding quantitative variables into categorical variables? Read this: https://drive.google.com/open?id=1ryRmLuR7Rr_rxKRJahTs6pq0d0N7Hs22v69NJ8y4wU4
- Here is a web-based game that lets you guess whether a variable is categorical or quantitative: http://mathnstats.com/applets/Categorical-Quantitative.html
- Here's a useful article on continuous quantitative vs. categorical data: https://eagereyes.org/basics/data-continuous-vs-categorical
- Jeff Good of UC Berkeley has written "A Gentle Introduction to Metadata" at http://www.language-archives.org/documents/gentle-intro.html
- A catalog of R resources for reproducible research is available at http://cran.r-project.org/web/views/ReproducibleResearch.html
- There is even a Coursera class where you can learn all about reproducible research! Find it here: https://www.coursera.org/course/repdata

1.4 Central Tendency and Variability

Objective

A probability distribution (or "distribution" for short) describes the possible outcomes for an event, and how likely each of those outcomes are. When characterizing a distribution of categorical or quantitative values, the things you typically want to know are: 1) where's the center of it, 2) how fat or thin is it, and 3) does it have any unusual characteristics (e.g. is it skewed to the right or left, or does it have more than one hump, or is it asymmetric). **"Central tendency" is a fancy sounding phrase that just means:** *if you have a whole bunch of values, what's in the middle (and what does "middle" even mean)?* Measures of variability (e.g. variance and standard deviation) tell you how fat or thin your distribution is. This chapter covers these two basic topics, including how to compute them analytically and how to compute them in R. Distribution shapes are covered in the chapter on histograms.

Who cares about such a simple topic? Well, just knowing the values for the mean, median, and mode, coupled with the variability information provided by the variance and standard deviation, you can get a sense of the shape of your distribution. You can also sometimes get a sense for what proportion of your observations fall within various bounds. Also, many of the statistical inference tests you perform are related to *figuring out if you really know where the center of a particular distribution is located*. If you read fancy proofs, you'll hear the term "Expected Value" quite a lot. What they mean is: *the value we think is in the middle of all the possibilities.* That's all. This chapter covers the first two of these basic topics, including how to compute them analytically and how to compute them in R. Distribution shapes are covered in the chapter on histograms.

Mean (Arithmetic)

The arithmetic mean identifies the midpoint between all the values in a dataset of numbers, even if there isn't an observed value *at* the midpoint. It is calculated by adding up all of the values, then dividing by the total number of observations. Finding a mean in R is simple, because you can pass values directly to mean *or* give it a vector or data frame selection:

```
> mean(c(1,2,3,4,5,6,7,8))
[1] 4.5
> x <- c(1,2,3,4,5,6,7,8)
> mean(x)
[1] 4.5
```

The arithmetic mean is not the *only* variety of mean that can be used to express central tendency! The geometric mean and harmonic mean are also potential measures if your quantitative data is on the *ratio* level of measurement (and, for the geometric mean, if your values are positive). The geometric mean characterizes the *average growth rate* between values, and is often used in financial applications. The harmonic mean characterizes an *average rate*. I've never used the geometric or harmonic means for data analysis personally, though, so I can't provide any recommendations beyond noting that you *can* potentially use these.

Median

The median identifies *the observation* that sits at the midpoint between all the observations in a dataset. If there are an even number of observations, the median is computed as the arithmetic mean of those two observations that sit at the midpoint. Like mean, you can pass values directly to median *or* give it a vector or data frame selection. Here are some examples in R:

```
> median(c(1,2,3,4,5,6,7,8,9))
[1] 5
> median(c(1,2,3,4,5,6,7,8,9,10,11,12))
[1] 6.5
```

As long as the values in a dataset can be *ordered*, you can find the one (or two) observations that sit at the midpoint, and thus find the median. You can compute a median for all kinds of variables... except categorical variables that are nominal. As an example, you can't compute the median of several M&M colors (because that's a categorical variable at the nominal level of measurement) but you can compute the median of several scrabble tile values (because those letters can be ordered). Because of its versatility, there are many inference tests that can be done to compare the medians of datasets.

Mode

The mode identifies the *most frequently observed value* in a dataset. Unlike the median, calculation of the mode is not precluded by the level of measurement. For example, it's possible to determine:

- The mode of M&M colors in a bag (that is, the most frequently observed color)
- The mode of Scrabble tiles still left in the bag (that is, the letter or letters that have the most tiles available)
- The mode of customer satisfaction responses (that is, which item between "Strongly Dissatisfied" and "Strongly Satisfied" was most frequently selected)
- The mode for daily high temperatures in summer (that is, which high temperature occurs most frequently)

These illustrate what the mode looks and feels like for nominal, ordinal, interval, and ratio level data, respectively. The only one you have to be careful with are modes for ratio level quantitative variables, because sometimes the mode is just not meaningful. As an example, think about what your data might look like if you're measuring how much people weigh. If you're collecting that data in pounds to the second decimal place, it's likely that your data looks something like this, with no repeated values:

145.59   220.31   197.63   105.25   118.80   145.14   170.28   166.37

It would be really unlikely for the mode to be meaningful in this case: we might not have any numbers that are observed more than once, making the "most frequently appearing observation" an absurd notion. **Bottom line: if you have ratio level data, check to make sure the *mode* is *meaningful* before you report it.** It's actually pretty easy with R to determine if a mode is "meaningful" or not. Here's an example where the mode is clearly meaningful. First, we pull 100 <u>r</u>andom numbers from a **<u>uni</u>form** distribution between 1 and 10. (This is just like rolling dice, only we're working with a 10-sided die where each of the numbers 1 through 10 is equally likely to appear. That's the purpose of the `runif` function.)

```
> x <- round(runif(100,1,10))
> x
  [1]  7  8  1  3  5  4  3  3  4  3  3  7  2  4  1  7  2  7  8  9  6
 [22]  1  7  2  1  5  2  1 10  8 10  3  3  5  3  7  4  9  6  1  2  4
 [43]  5 10  8  1  5  3  2  3  1  8  7  4  4  6  7  7  9  3  6  2  9
 [64]  5  2  3  4  1  8  5  5 10 10  8  7  6  5  7  8 10  9 10  4  7
 [85]  2  7  6  9  8  9  5 10  9  2  1  6  8  3  6  5
```

Now, let's add up how many 1's, 2's, 3's and so forth we got using the random number generator by invoking the `table` command. The top row represents the numbers from 1 to 10, and the bottom row includes the counts of how many of those random numbers were generated by `runif`. Using `sort` arranges the numbers so that the lowest frequencies appear first, and the higher frequencies appear later.

```
> y <- sort(table(x))
> y
x
 6  9 10  4  1  2  8  5  3  7
 8  8  8  9 10 10 10 11 13 13
```

Here are the commands we can use to pull out which elements of x appear most frequently (`mode.names`) and how many times they appear (`max(y)`). As long as you store your sorted table in a variable called `y`, you will be able to use these commands to identify the mode (or modes, because you can have more than one) and the observation count that corresponds to that maximum value.

```
> mode.value <- max(y)
> mode.value
[1] 13
> mode.names <- names(y[y==max(y)])
```

```
> mode.names
[1] "3" "7"
```

This also works if your values are categorical (at the nominal level of measurement). Imagine that you own a restaurant specializing in New Mexican cuisine. You want to find out how your customers prefer the chile on their burritos: red, green, or Christmas. Here's a way to simulate that data from 100 customers:

```
> x <- sample(c("RED","GREEN","CHRISTMAS"), 100, replace=TRUE)
> x
  [1] "GREEN"     "RED"       "RED"       "RED"       "CHRISTMAS"
  [6] "RED"       "GREEN"     "CHRISTMAS" "CHRISTMAS" "GREEN"
 [11] "GREEN"     "RED"       "CHRISTMAS" "CHRISTMAS" "CHRISTMAS"
```

The mode can be determined the same way as in the previous example:

```
> y <- sort(table(x))
> names(y[y==max(y)]) # these are the modes
[1] "RED"
> max(y) # we just have one mode... how many customers preferred red?
[1] 35
```

What about the case where the mode is meaningless? Well, that's what would have happened if we didn't round our randomly sampled numbers between 1 and 10. Try this, and you'll see a mode that's not meaningful at all:

```
> x <- runif(100,1,10)
> y <- sort(table(x))
> max(y)
[1] 1
> names(y[y==max(y)])
  [1] "1.08012562571093" "1.12060043844394" "1.17615319066681"
  [4] "1.18749733804725" "1.39209767919965" "1.41802837909199"
  [7] "1.4363781651482"  "1.62966463225894" "1.63671832019463"...
```

What's the frequency of our mode? One. Just one observation. That means EVERY SINGLE ONE of the values we generated is the mode. A hundred values, a hundred modes. **If *everyone* is an important mode, then *no one* is an important mode.** The mode, in this case, is meaningless as an indicator of central tendency.

Relationships Between Mean, Median, & Mode

If you have a collection of quantitative values, and you know the mean, median, and mode, there are a lot of things you can figure out about the shape of your distribution. As a result, these measures of central tendency are like *clues* that you can use to draw a picture of the distribution in your head:

- The mode is always at the highest point of the distribution... the peak.
- If the distribution is skewed to the left, meaning that it has a tail stretching out along the left side of the x-axis... the median is pulled to the left.
- If the distribution is skewed to the left, the mean is also pulled to the left. But all it takes is one or two outliers to really really pull that mean even farther to the left. The mean is much more sensitive to outliers than the median.
- If the distribution is skewed to the right, meaning that it has a tail stretching out along the right side of the x-axis... the median is pulled to the right.
- If the distribution is skewed to the right, the mean is also pulled to the right. But all it takes is one or two outliers to really really pull that mean even farther to the right. The mean is much more sensitive to outliers than the median.
- In a symmetric distribution like the normal, the mean, median, and mode are all lined up together at the peak of the distribution. The most frequently observed value (mode) is the same as the average value (mean). Exactly 50% of the observations are below the mean, and 50% of the observations are above the mean, putting the median at the same spot as the mean.

In summary, here are the measures of central tendency that can be applied to the various variable types and levels of measurement:

Variable Type	Level of Measurement	Ways to Represent Central Tendency
Categorical	Nominal	Mode
	Ordinal	Median
Quantitative	Interval	Arithmetic Mean, Median, Mode
	Ratio	Arithmetic Mean, Median, Mode, Geometric Mean, Harmonic Mean

Variance

The variance represents how spread apart the values in your distribution are, and as a result, characterizes *how fat or thin* the distribution will be when plotted. To get the variance, you need to know all of the values in your dataset. You use them to calculate variance like this:

1. First, **find the arithmetic mean** of all the values.
2. **Find the squared deviations**: Take each value one at a time, and subtract the mean (which gives you negative numbers for all values that are *below* the mean, and positive numbers for all values that are *above* the mean) and then square whatever you get (that is, multiply it by itself). This makes all the values positive.
3. Now **divide the total of all those squared deviations you just figured out by one less than the number of observations**. (Why don't we just use the actual number of observations, and take the average? Because that would be *biased*... but more on that later when we talk about Bessel's correction.)

The equation that represents variance looks like this. Variance is represented by σ^2, and n is the number of observations. The sum is over all elements of your dataset (from the first one through the nth one), and you're adding up the squared differences between each value and the overall mean:

$$\sigma^2 = \frac{1}{n-1} \sum_{i=1}^{n} (y_i - \bar{y})^2$$

Variance is also very easy to figure out in R, as long as you have your data arranged in a vector (or can extract a vector out of a data frame). For simplicity, let's just use the values that are stored in *x* - the ones we got from sampling 100 random numbers between 1 and 10:

```
> var(x)
[1] 6.556027
```

Standard Deviation

Take the square root of the variance, and you'll get the standard deviation:

$$\sigma = \sqrt{\frac{1}{n-1} \sum_{i=1}^{n} (y_i - \bar{y})^2}$$

This is also dead easy to do in R using the sd command. Of course, if you have the variance handy, you can just take the square root of that to get the standard deviation and it all works out the same:

```
> v <- var(x)
> sqrt(v)
[1] 2.560474
> sd(x)
[1] 2.560474
```

Bessel's Correction: Why We Divide by (n-1)

If you Google around to find equations for calculating the variance and standard deviation, sometimes they tell you to divide by the total number of observations n, and other times they tell you to divide by (*n-1*). Oh no!! Which one should you believe? What do you do? And which one does R do?

- **Which one should you believe?** Believe the (n-1) version. It's more accurate, especially when the sample size is small.
- **What do you choose when you have to calculate it yourself?** If you calculate variance and standard deviation yourself, be sure to use the (n-1) version.
- **Which one does R use?** Fortunately, R uses the (n-1) version for both the variance and the standard deviation... so you can trust R.

What's the Rationale for Bessel's Correction?

The smaller your sample, the less likely you are to *realistically* capture the magnitude of the variance in a distribution. It takes a lot of observations to get a good sense of the true spread-outed-ness of values within a distribution!

But to determine the variance and standard deviation, you have to know the mean of the *entire population* (or at least have a good idea what it is). You're only guaranteed to estimate this well if you have a really big sample. So with an ordinary sized sample, you're not going to capture *all* of the variance that's really there. You need to bump up your estimate to account for the variability that you can't see. And since this is always true for sample sizes that are 2 or more...

$$\frac{1}{n-1} > \frac{1}{n}$$

...that means if you use the (*n-1*) version, you'll be making your estimates of the variance and standard deviation *just a little bigger*. The bigger the sample size *n* gets, the closer the *biased* estimator (where you divide by *n*) will be to the *unbiased* estimator (where you divide by *n-1*). **Unbiased is better.** This adjustment improves your variance estimate tremendously, and your standard deviation estimate *almost* as tremendously.

Other Resources

- Did you know there are guidelines on how to report central tendency and variability in APA style research papers? Details are provided here: http://statistics-help-for-students.com/How do I report central tendency and dispersion data in APA style.htm #.VQtgtI7F-o0
- Find out more about Bessel's correction (n-1 in the calculation of the variance and standard deviation) at http://en.wikipedia.org/wiki/Bessel%27s_correction
- A really nice, intuitive explanation for Bessel's correction with graphs is here: http://www.physics.ohio-state.edu/~durkin/phys416/Fall2011/LectureExtras/besselfactor.pdf

1.5 Descriptive Statistics

Objective

Sometimes, you want an easy way to quantitatively summarize the characteristics of a collection of data, whether that information comes from an experiment, an archive, a survey, or some other kind of source. *Descriptive statistics* provide simple summaries about the sample you have collected, and complement charts and graphs that provide an additional representation of the data. With descriptive statistics, you are not attempting to draw any conclusions about the data: you are just presenting what the data shows, *prior to any analysis*.

Descriptive statistics are often supplemented by measures such as skewness and kurtosis, which describe the basic state of the distribution, or basic charts and graphs, such as histograms, boxplots, scatterplots, and contingency tables, which are covered in **Section 2: Charts, Graphs, and Plots.**

Data Acquisition

First, let's load some data from the National Oceanic and Atmospheric Administration (NOAA) severe weather data inventory at http://www.ncdc.noaa.gov/swdi. We're going to choose our data, download it to our local machine, unzip it, and then make sure R is looking in the right directory. Finally, we can examine *descriptive statistics* on our data.

After going to the main SWDI page, I clicked on the option for "Bulk Download" and then "HTTP". This took me to http://www1.ncdc.noaa.gov/pub/data/swdi/ which is a directory listing for several CSV files. (I notice that all the files have a .gz extension, which means that I need to *unzip* the file I download before I can use it. To be able to handle .gz files, I have to download a utility program that unzips this particular kind of zipped file. Since I use a Windows machine, I first downloaded and installed a program called 7-Zip from http://download.cnet.com). Then, I navigated back to the SWDI repository and downloaded `tvs-201407.csv.gz` to my local machine, unzipped it, and saved the resulting `tvs-201407.csv` file to my `C:/Temp` directory. This is a document containing all the Tornado Vortex Signatures (TVS) in the United States during the month of July 2014. Now I can read the data into R:

```
setwd("C:/Temp")
tvs <- read.csv("tvs-201407.csv",header=TRUE,skip=2)
```

Because the first two lines of the data file contain comments (they start with a #, and so are ignored by R), the `skip=2` argument tells R to read in my CSV data, *but only after skipping those first two extraneous lines*. Now, I can take a look at what's in the file:

```
> head(tvs)
      X.ZTIME        LON      LAT WSR_ID CELL_ID CELL_TYPE RANGE AZIMUTH
1 2.01407e+13  -91.53766 41.34569   KDVN      M7       TVS    46     250
2 2.01407e+13  -94.51676 40.24530   KMCI      J1       TVS    46      13
3 2.01407e+13  -88.06882 41.52247   KORD      W7       TVS    19     210
4 2.01407e+13  -94.79196 40.04702   KMCI      C1       TVS    33     356
5 2.01407e+13  -87.99919 41.58894   KORD      W7       TVS    14     207
6 2.01407e+13  -91.13138 41.24971   KDVN      S7       TVS    33     229
  AVGDV LLDV MXDV MXDV_HEIGHT DEPTH BASE TOP MAX_SHEAR MAX_SHEAR_HEIGHT
1    34   83   83           4    26    4  30        29                4
2    32   52   52           3    17    3  20        18                3
3    37   50   53           2     7    1   8        46                2
4    32   31   70          14    18    2  20        33               14
5    41   56   56           1     6    1   6        63                1
6    33   53   53           3     6    3   9        26                3
```

What is this data about? It looks like the first column contains a timestamp, and the second two contain the longitude and latitude of the observed TVS (a place where Doppler radar detected a likely tornado). WSR_ID is the name of the radar station that reported the observation. CELL_ID provides a way for us to distinguish between tornadoes associated with different thunderstorms. CELL_TYPE indicates that we are looking at TVS observations, so this value should be the same for all rows. RANGE and AZIMUTH tell us where the TVS was observed, relative to the radar, and the remaining values tell us physical parameters about the tornado signature. The information we will be interested in gathering descriptive statistics for are the DEPTH of the tornado signature (in thousands of feet), the TOP of the tornado signature (also in thousands of feet), and the MAX_SHEAR (or maximum wind shear, in meters per second). Since we are only interested in a subset of the data, let's construct a smaller data frame containing only those values that are of interest to us. This creates a new data frame, sub.tvs, which consists of all rows from tvs, and just these three named columns:

```
sub.tvs <- tvs[,c("DEPTH","TOP","MAX_SHEAR")]
```

Descriptive Statistics with summary

Once we have our data in the proper format, we can generate descriptive statistics using the summary command:

```
> summary(sub.tvs)
      DEPTH            TOP          MAX_SHEAR
 Min.    : 5.00   Min.    : 5.00   Min.    : 10.00
 1st Qu.: 7.00    1st Qu.: 9.00    1st Qu.: 24.00
 Median :10.00    Median :13.00    Median : 30.00
 Mean    :12.34   Mean    :15.57   Mean    : 38.03
 3rd Qu.:17.00    3rd Qu.:21.00    3rd Qu.: 42.00
 Max.    :63.00   Max.    :69.00   Max.    :283.00
```

The descriptive statistics that are displayed are:
- The **minimum** value observed for this variable in the dataset
- The **first quantile** (also called Q1); 25% of the observations are BELOW this value and 75% of the observations are ABOVE this value
- The **median**; an actual observation within the dataset indicating that 50% of the observations are BELOW this value and 50% are ABOVE this value
- The **mean**; a number characterizing the center of the distribution that is obtained by finding the average value across all the observations
- The **third quantile** (also called Q3); 75% of the observations are BELOW this value and 25% of the observations are ABOVE this value
- The **maximum** value observed for this variable in the dataset

Descriptive statistics can give us a quick indication of some of the characteristics of the distribution: for example, if the mean is far greater than the median (to the right of it on the probability distribution), we know that the distribution must be skewed to the right. Similarly, if the mean is far less than the median (to the left of it on the probability distribution), we know that the distribution must be skewed to the left. One limitation of the `summary` command in the base R package is that it doesn't give you really useful and critical descriptive statistics like the standard deviation, variance, and mode (the most frequently observed value in the set of observations). Fortunately, you can compute those separately, but you have to do each variable one at a time:

```
> sd(sub.tvs$DEPTH)
[1] 7.19
> var(sub.tvs$DEPTH)
[1] 51.7
```

To obtain the mode, first cut and paste the following code to load in the `mode` function:

```
mode <- function(x) {
        uniq.vals <- unique(x)
        uniq.vals[which.max(tabulate(match(x, uniq.vals)))]
}
```

Alternatively, you can `source` it from GitHub directly:

```
> source("https://raw.githubusercontent.com/NicoleRadziwill/R-
Functions/master/mode.R")
> mode(c(2,3,4,4,4,4,5,6)) # Check to make sure it works
[1] 4
```

Now you can use that function on your data:

```
> mode(sub.tvs$TOP)
[1] 7
```

Some of these limitations can be overcome by using an alternative approach: the `stat.desc` function which is part of the `pastecs` package.

Descriptive Statistics with `stat.desc` **from the** `pastecs` **Package**

If you don't have it already, first `install.packages("pastecs")` and call it into memory using `library(pastecs)`. Then, the following commands will work:

```
> options(scipen=100)
> options(digits=3)
> stat.desc(sub.tvs)
                  DEPTH        TOP  MAX_SHEAR
nbr.val        1532.000   1532.000   1532.000
nbr.null          0.000      0.000      0.000
nbr.na            0.000      0.000      0.000
min               5.000      5.000     10.000
max              63.000     69.000    283.000
range            58.000     64.000    273.000
sum           18905.000  23850.000  58260.000
median           10.000     13.000     30.000
mean             12.340     15.568     38.029
SE.mean           0.184      0.205      0.631
CI.mean.0.95      0.360      0.401      1.238
var              51.724     64.179    610.432
std.dev           7.192      8.011     24.707
coef.var          0.583      0.515      0.650
```

Since `stat.desc` likes to use scientific notation, the first two commands allow you to set the number of significant digits you want to see. In addition to the basic descriptive statistics provided by summary, `stat.desc` shows you:

- The **number of observations** as `nbr.val`
- The **number of null observations** as `nbr.null`
- The **number of "not available" (NA) observations** as `nbr.na`
- The **range** of values (that is, how far it is to get from the minimum observed value to the maximum observed value) as `range`
- The **sum** of all values as `sum`

- The **standard error** of the mean (`SE.mean`) indicates how precisely you can know the true mean of the population, given only what you have in your sample. It accounts for the sample size and the scatteredness (or dispersion) of the dataset.
- The **width** of the 95% confidence interval as `CI.mean.0.95` (meaning that the mean minus this value indicates the lower bound of your confidence interval, and the mean plus this value indicates the upper bound of the confidence interval)
- The **variance** of all the values, which gives you an indication of how scattered or dispersed they are, as `var`
- The **standard deviation**, which is the square root of the variance and indicates pretty much the same thing as the variance, as `std.dev`
- The **coefficient of variance**, which is the standard deviation divided by the mean, and also gives a sense of how scattered or dispersed the observations are, as `coef.var`

Here is a summary of the arguments that you can use to generate descriptive statistics:

Argument to `stat.desc`	What it does
`basic=TRUE`	Include number of observations, number of nulls, number of NAs, min, max, range and sum
`desc=TRUE`	Include median, mean, standard error of the mean, width of the confidence interval, variance, standard deviation, and coefficient of variation
`norm=TRUE`	Include measures for skewness and kurtosis
`p=0.99`	Specify the width of the desired confidence interval (e.g. 99%)
`options(digits=3)`	Specify the number of significant digits to display (e.g. 3)
`options(scipen=999)`	Specify a "penalty" to use when determining whether scientific notation (e.g. 1E+03 or 1000); higher values incur greater penalty, and a 999 will prevent use of scientific notation almost entirely

Descriptive Statistics with the `xda` Package

If you don't have it already, first `install.packages("xda")` and then when it's available on your machine, call it into memory using `library(xda)`. As long as you have a data frame loaded, you can use the `numSummary`, `charSummary`, and `bivariate` commands to extract descriptive statistics about your data. (There is also a `plot` function, but it doesn't perform reliably.) I've included a couple examples on the R-Bloggers site at http://www.r-bloggers.com/using-xda-with-googlesheets-in-r/.

Other Resources

Here are some other resources to help you understand the concepts in this chapter and explore the severe weather datasets that were obtained:

- This article discusses the difference between *descriptive* and *inferential statistics*: https://statistics.laerd.com/statistical-guides/descriptive-inferential-statistics.php
- This article and online quiz will help you get a better handle on definitions: http://study.com/academy/lesson/what-is-descriptive-statistics-examples-lesson-quiz.html
- This applet can be used to explore descriptive statistics on simple datasets: http://www.rossmanchance.com/applets/Dotplot.html
- Find out more about the meaning and detection of Tornado Vortex Signatures (TVS) at http://en.wikipedia.org/wiki/Tornado_vortex_signature
- More information about the data in the TVS datasets can be found here: http://www.ncdc.noaa.gov/swdiws/csv/nx3tvs
- There is an R package to access data directly from the SWDI. Find out more at http://cran.r-project.org/web/packages/rnoaa/vignettes/swdi_vignette.html
- The complete NEXRAD radar data archive can be accessed at http://www.ncdc.noaa.gov/nexradinv/
- Comprehensive documentation for the pastecs package, which does a lot more than just descriptive statistics, can be accessed from this location: http://cran.r-project.org/web/packages/pastecs/pastecs.pdf

1.6 Getting Data Into R

Objectives

Before you can manipulate and analyze data, first you have to load it into R. The purpose of this section is to introduce you to techniques for acquiring data and manipulating data structures in R. You will:

- Learn how to get, set, and explore working directories with `getwd` and `setwd`
- Learn how to open a file on your local machine using `read.csv` and `read.table`
- Learn how to retrieve data that is accessible on the web using a URL
- Learn how to retrieve data that is stored in spreadsheet format on Google Docs (using Jenny Bryan's amazing `googledocs` package)
- Inspect data using `head, tail,` and `str`
- Understand why it's important to be aware of data types and data structures as you're acquiring data from different kinds of sources

Step 1: Getting, Setting, and Viewing Contents of the Working Directory

The concept of the working directory is fundamental to R. Basically, R can only be pointing to (and looking at) one directory on your machine at any given time. Much of the time, your data will be stored on your local machine, and you need to load it into R so you can manipulate and analyze it. If you want to find out which directory R is looking at right now, "get your working directory" by typing `getwd()` - I'll show you what it looks like when I do it on my machine:

```
> getwd()
[1] "C:/Users/User/Documents"
```

When you execute this command on *your* machine, you may or may not be pointed to the same directory that's displayed above. The first step will be to tell R where you want it to look for datasets. I have a "work in progress" directory called R on my D drive where I keep some datasets, so that's the location I want to "set my working directory" to:

```
setwd("D:/R")
```

Then, you can find out what's in that directory by typing `dir()`:

```
> dir()
 [1]  "AHP"
 [2]  "alcdata1.csv"
 [3]  "astro-data.jpg"
 [4]  "Bill Project"
 [5]  "ccc.xls"
 [6]  "Ch0-EthicalAI-v2.txt"
 [7]  "Ch0-EthicalAI.txt"
 [8]  "Class M&M Data.csv"
 [9]  "college-admissions.csv"
[10]  "creating-an-84x10xwhatever-array.txt"
[11]  "Data for Examples"
[12]  "Fall 2016 M&Ms.csv"
[13]  "FCMgraph.jpg"
[14]  "GeYan_ChangePointAnalysis.pdf"
[15]  "ie479.txt"
```

The displayed files are stored as a data frame, so you can capture these values and use them in your programming later. For example, let's do this using a variable called `my.dir`:

```
> my.dir <- dir()
> head(my.dir)
[1]  "AHP"                  "alcdata1.csv"
[3]  "astro-data.jpg"       "Bill Capehart Project"
[5]  "ccc.xls"              "Ch0-EthicalAI-v2.txt"
> my.dir[6]
[1]  "Ch0-EthicalAI-v2.txt"
```

Once you know where your data is located, there are many methods to import it into R:

- If your data is stored as TXT, CSV, or XLS and listed in the directory contents displayed on your screen, go to **Step 2 Option A** to import it into R,
- If your data is online as a **Google Spreadsheet**, go to **Step 2 Option B**
- If your data is on **GitHub**, go to **Step 2 Option C**
- If your data is online but at **another URL**, go to **Step 2 Option D**
- If you just want to use **R's built-in data sets**, go to **Step 2 Option E**
- If you want to load **JSON** data, go to **Step 2 Option F**

...and follow the instructions. I tend to store and retrieve my data as CSV (comma-separated variables) files, and keep notes in TXT format. I do data entry, editing, and cleaning in Excel, but then save the contents as CSV for import into R. Everyone has different preferences.

Step 2 Option A: Loading Data from a TXT, CSV, or XLS file on Your Machine

When you first install the base R package, you are provided with several rudimentary commands to import data, including `read.table` (to bring in observations that are separated by spaces or tabs) and `read.csv` (to bring in observations that are separated by commas). I have a text file with data in it called `x.txt` that contains observations of M&M candies. If I open the file with a text editor, the variable names are in the first row, and the observations are in subsequent rows:

student	id	color	defect	hour	minute	weight	total.number
1	1	1	2	10	48	50.14	57
1	12	1	4	10	49	50.14	57
1	23	1	2	10	49	50.14	57
1	34	1	4	10	49	50.14	57
1	45	1	4	10	50	50.14	57
30	34	1	4	10	42	48.3	49
30	3	1	4	10	44	48.3	49

Because the observations are separated by tabs, the columns do not appear aligned in the text editor, but R will know which observations correspond to which variables. Use `read.table()` to import the data, use `head()` to make sure it's been imported correctly, and use `str()` to see what variable types are contained in the dataset. We use `header=TRUE` to declare that the first row of our file contains *variable names*.

```
> my.data <- read.table("x.txt",header=TRUE)
> head(my.data)
  student id color defect hour minute weight total.number
1       1  1     1      2   10     48  50.14           57
2       1 12     1      4   10     49  50.14           57
3       1 23     1      2   10     49  50.14           57
4       1 34     1      4   10     49  50.14           57
5       1 45     1      4   10     50  50.14           57
6      30 34     1      4   10     42  48.30           49
> str(my.data)
'data.frame':   2884 obs. of  8 variables:
 $ student     : int  1 1 1 1 1 30 30 30 30 30 ...
 $ id          : int  1 12 23 34 45 34 3 10 22 43 ...
 $ color       : int  1 1 1 1 1 1 1 1 1 1 ...
 $ defect      : int  2 4 2 4 4 4 4 2 4 4 ...
 $ hour        : int  10 10 10 10 10 10 10 10 10 10 ...
 $ minute      : int  48 49 49 49 50 42 44 46 49 51 ...
 $ weight      : num  50.1 50.1 50.1 50.1 50.1 ...
 $ total.number: int  57 57 57 57 57 49 49 49 49 49 ...
```

Importing data from CSV is very similar, only the raw data is separated by commas:

```
"sg","V1","V2","V3","V4"
"sg1",1.397,1.349,1.278,1.279
"sg2",1.397,1.399,1.397,1.311
"sg3",1.397,1.288,1.29,1.828
```

This data is contained in a file called `xbar-r-subgroups.csv` which is a tiny file that contains data I collected while starting a control chart exercise. We use `read.csv()` to pull it into a variable called `cc.data` (for "control chart data") in R:

```
> cc.data <- read.csv("xbar-r-subgroups.csv",header=TRUE)
> head(cc.data)
   sg    V1    V2    V3    V4
1 sg1 1.397 1.349 1.278 1.279
2 sg2 1.397 1.399 1.397 1.311
```

```
3 sg3 1.397 1.288 1.290 1.828
> str(cc.data)
'data.frame':    3 obs. of  5 variables:
 $ sg: Factor w/ 3 levels "sg1","sg2","sg3": 1 2 3
 $ V1: num   1.4 1.4 1.4
 $ V2: num   1.35 1.4 1.29
 $ V3: num   1.28 1.4 1.29
 $ V4: num   1.28 1.31 1.83
```

To load an Excel file like this one, you have to obtain the `xlsx` package first:

```
install.packages("xlsx")
library(xlsx)
```

Fortunately, the process for importing is identical to the previous two methods. Just use `read.xlsx` instead of `read.table` or `read.csv`.

[Note: The `xlsx` package depends on the `rJava` package, which *also requires that you have a functioning version of Java on your machine and IN YOUR PATH.* If you don't know what this means, or how to make both of these things happen, then I'd stick to saving your files as CSV or TXT and using the other import methods. I am not providing an example of this because I don't have Java, `rJava`, or `xlsx` installed on my machine, and I try not to use Excel for anything other than data cleaning.

Step 2 Option B: Loading Data from Google Spreadsheets

To import data stored in the cloud on Google Spreadsheets, there are **three options**. The easiest option, if you own the Google Spreadsheet, is to publish the data to the web as a CSV file, and then load it in directly using `read.csv`. For example, I have a data set at this long URL (which you should be able to load it up from your R console as well):

```
> fitts <- read.csv("https://docs.google.com/spreadsheets/d/e/2PACX-
1vQzmp_ok7b5sQTlJrdrYxE7NvsnStN1qkDCpWoAOnoPKzIE9izqWAcfLgQRy4LcejKwredCe0yF
VdR3/pub?gid=106072055&single=true&output=csv")
> head(fitts)
   subject equipment task size.cm distance.cm response.time.ms
```

1	Sarah	PC	1	0.5	1	965
2	Sarah	PC	1	0.5	1	966
3	Sarah	PC	1	0.5	1	931
4	Kyle	PC	1	0.5	1	953
5	Kyle	PC	1	0.5	1	892
6	Kyle	PC	1	0.5	1	935

Publishing data to the web is a two-step process:

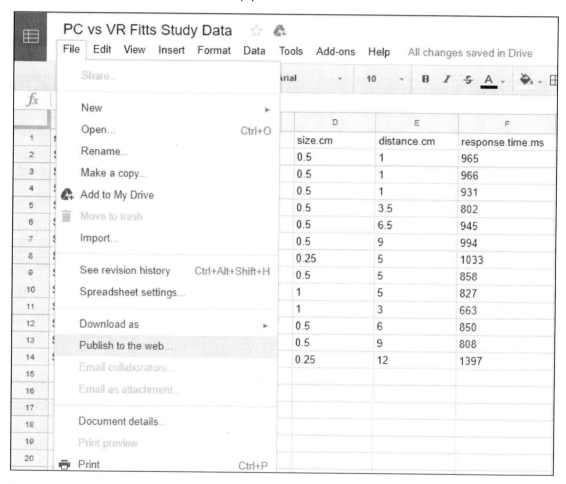

First, go to `File -> Publish to the Web`. This will take you to a second screen where you will choose which spreadsheet to publish, and the target format (.CSV):

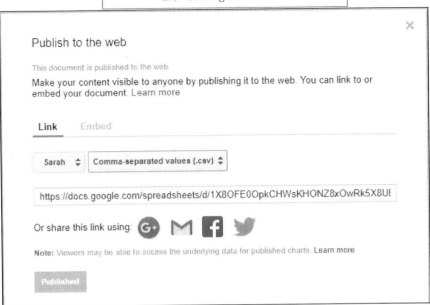

The second option is to open the data in Google Drive and download a copy of it to your local machine. You do this by going to

```
File -> Download As -> Comma-separated values (.csv, current sheet)
```

Remember what directory you used to store the file, because you will need to make sure you set your R working directory to that location before using `read.csv` to import.

Your third option is to use Jenny Bryan's `googlesheets` package. First download and wake it up in R, using the `dependencies=TRUE` argument which will also download the additional packages this one depends on:

```
install.packages("googlesheets", dependencies=TRUE)
library(googlesheets)
```

I want to load the M&M data that's in the Google sheet at this URL. Paste it into your address bar so you can see the data:

```
https://docs.google.com/spreadsheets/d/1tykXpknyrpu25Z6kWM55iVxKihV2ZkLhuj4Z
DyCV7w8/
```

We need to know the DOCUMENT KEY to pull this data into R. This is the long, unintelligible sequence of letters and numbers in the URL after you see "/d/". The first thing we have to do in R is to create a variable to store this document key:

```
ss.key <- "1tykXpknyrpu25Z6kWM55iVxKihV2ZkLhuj4ZDyCV7w8"
```

Next, we make a connection between R and this googlesheet:

```
my.gs <- gs_key(ss.key)
```

Finally, we can use that connection to import the data and create a data frame called mnms in R. *If it works, you should see indications of progress displayed:*

```
> mnms <- as.data.frame(gs_read(my.gs))
Accessing worksheet titled 'Sheet1'.

Downloading: 4.3 kB
Downloading: 4.3 kB
Downloading: 12 kB
Downloading: 12 kB
Downloading: 13 kB
Downloading: 13 kB
Downloading: 13 kB
Downloading: 13 kB     No encoding supplied: defaulting to UTF-8.
Warning: 1 parsing failure.
 row col    expected actual
1402  id an integer      C

Warning message:
Missing column names filled in: 'X9' [9]
```

Finally, use the head command to make sure the data actually showed up.

```
> head(mnms)
  student id color defect hour minute weight total.number X9
1 allenrj  1    BL      L   10     48  50.14           57 NA
2 allenrj  2    BL      N   10     49  50.14           57 NA
3 allenrj  3    BL      L   10     49  50.14           57 NA
4 allenrj  4    BL      N   10     49  50.14           57 NA
5 allenrj  5    BL      N   10     50  50.14           57 NA
6  Pinoja  4    BL      N   10     42  48.30           49 NA
```

[**Note 1**: Even though it seems like you might be able to simplify the import code, for example by encoding the document key directly inside the `gs_key` command, or maybe by mashing them all together instead of having them on separate lines... it doesn't usually work.]

[**Note 2**: Sometimes, security issues prevent the `googlesheets` commands from working. If you are having problems, try typing this to authenticate: `my_sheets <- gs_ls()`]

Step 2 Option C: Loading Data from GitHub

In addition to being an excellent environment for source code configuration management, GitHub (http://github.com) is also a place where you can store changing versions of datasets. All of the data that I use for examples in my books can be found in my GitHub data directory at https://github.com/NicoleRadziwill/Data-for-R-Examples. We will load in a CSV file and a plain text file as examples. First, you need to find the URL that corresponds to the raw data by drilling down into the file you want to obtain, and then clicking the "Raw" button on the right-hand side of the page. If I drill down into `comp-temps.csv` (which contains three months of temperature observations from two recording stations in Virginia), the URL that appears is https://raw.githubusercontent.com/NicoleRadziwill/Data-for-R-Examples/master/comp-temps.csv.

You can cut and paste this URL into the address bar to see the data yourself. Next, obtain the data like this. The `head` command displays the first six rows, so you can make sure it imported correctly:

```
> url <- "https://raw.githubusercontent.com/NicoleRadziwill/Data-for-R-
Examples/master/comp-temps.csv"
> temps <- read.csv(url)
> head(temps)
  id       date cho shd diff
1  1 20140601  75  73    2
2  2 20140602  81  80    1
3  3 20140603  83  81    2
4  4 20140604  88  84    4
5  5 20140605  81  78    3
6  6 20140606  81  77    4
```

You can also do it in one line by replacing your file name, in quotes, within `read.csv()` – but I like to create a new variable to store my URL to make my code cleaner and easier later, if (and when) I have to reload my data or start a new R session.

Step 2 Option D: Loading Data from a URL

Perhaps your data is stored on the web somewhere (like in the UCI Machine Learning Repository at `http://archive.ics.uci.edu/ml/datasets.html`), and you can see it in your web browser and want to get it into R. Be sure to note whether the first row contains variable names (if so, use `header=TRUE`) and whether the observations are separated by commas (`read.csv`) or spaces or tabs (`read.table`). For example:

```
> machine <- read.csv("http://archive.ics.uci.edu/ml/machine-learning-
databases/cpu-performance/machine.data",header=TRUE)
> head(machine)
  adviser   X32.60 X125  X256 X6000 X256.1 X16 X128 X198 X199
1  amdahl   470v/7    29  8000 32000     32   8   32  269  253
2  amdahl  470v/7a    29  8000 32000     32   8   32  220  253
3  amdahl  470v/7b    29  8000 32000     32   8   32  172  253
4  amdahl  470v/7c    29  8000 16000     32   8   16  132  132
5  amdahl   470v/b    26  8000 32000     64   8   32  318  290
6  amdahl 580-5840    23 16000 32000     64  16   32  367  381
```

Step 2 Option E: Using One of R's Canned Datasets

If you just want to try out some of the techniques in this book, you might not want to go through the struggle of collecting, recording, cleaning, or simulating data. Fortunately, R has hundreds of built-in datasets that you can use. *Not all of these datasets are created equal.* In fact, basically none of them have identical data structures, so it is extremely important to inspect the data (Step 3) before you try anything interesting. For example, to get Edgar Anderson's famous `iris` data, just do this:

```
> data(iris)
> head(iris)
  Sepal.Length Sepal.Width Petal.Length Petal.Width Species
1          5.1         3.5          1.4         0.2  setosa
```

2	4.9	3.0	1.4	0.2	setosa
3	4.7	3.2	1.3	0.2	setosa
4	4.6	3.1	1.5	0.2	setosa
5	5.0	3.6	1.4	0.2	setosa
6	5.4	3.9	1.7	0.4	setosa

To see what additional datasets are available, type `data()`.

Inspecting Data with `head`, `tail`, and `str`

Each time we retrieve and import data, it's important to check and see if it actually showed up in R. The `head` command, which you've seen several times now, returns the first six elements of the data structure (or, for a data frame, the first six rows). The `tail` command displays the *last* six:

```
> tail(iris)
     Sepal.Length Sepal.Width Petal.Length Petal.Width  Species
145           6.7         3.3          5.7         2.5 virginica
146           6.7         3.0          5.2         2.3 virginica
147           6.3         2.5          5.0         1.9 virginica
148           6.5         3.0          5.2         2.0 virginica
149           6.2         3.4          5.4         2.3 virginica
150           5.9         3.0          5.1         1.8 virginica
> tail(mnms)
       student id color defect hour minute weight total.number X9
2879   boltzjr 37     Y      L   11     54  48.53           52 NA
2880   boltzjr 38     Y      N   11     54  48.53           52 NA
2881   boltzjr 39     Y      N   11     55  48.53           52 NA
2882   boltzjr 40     Y      N   11     55  48.53           52 NA
2883   boltzjr 41     Y      N   11     55  48.53           52 NA
2884 nicho2nx  5      Y      N   11     50  47.34           54 NA
```

The `str` command tells us what the *structure* is of the data we just imported. This includes 1) the data type of each variable in our data structure, and 2) the structure of the *container* within which our data is sitting. Knowing these structures is important because R commands are written to be compatible with certain structures and data types, but not with others. For example, this tells us that the iris dataset is a data frame (which looks like an Excel spreadsheet) containing 150 observations, and each observation has 5 variables (four of which are numeric or quantitative, and one of which is a `Factor`, or categorical):

```
> str(iris)
'data.frame':   150 obs. of  5 variables:
 $ Sepal.Length: num  5.1 4.9 4.7 4.6 5 5.4 4.6 5 4.4 4.9 ...
 $ Sepal.Width : num  3.5 3 3.2 3.1 3.6 3.9 3.4 3.4 2.9 3.1 ...
 $ Petal.Length: num  1.4 1.4 1.3 1.5 1.4 1.7 1.4 1.5 1.4 1.5 ...
 $ Petal.Width : num  0.2 0.2 0.2 0.2 0.2 0.4 0.3 0.2 0.2 0.1 ...
 $ Species     : Factor w/ 3 levels "setosa","versicolor",..: 1 1 1 1 ...
```

The structure is also a critical part of your overall approach and troubleshooting strategy. If your analysis code is not working, the first two questions to ask are:

- Has my data been imported correctly (that is, does it exist in R)? (Use `head` or `tail`)
- Are my data structures what I expect? (Use `str`)

A more in-depth look at R data structures (vectors, lists, matrices, arrays, and data frames) and the data types that make up those data structures (logical, numeric, integer, complex, character, and raw) is provided in the next chapter.

Step 2 Option F: Accessing Real Repositories with APIs, JSON, and `rjson`

Often, data is not *stored* on the web but is *accessible* from the web. You just have to know how to get it, and how to deal with the data format that you are served. It is not uncommon for organizations to offer access to their databases *if you know a little programming*. They will publish Application Programming Interfaces (or APIs) that provide you with objects and methods to get to their data. Two common data formats are eXtensible Markup Language (XML) and JavaScript Object Notation (JSON). This section covers the JSON format and how to obtain data in JSON format through the R console, using the `rjson` package. (You can explore XML on your own, if you like.) Be sure to install `rjson` first!

This example uses the Weather Underground API which is documented online at http://www.wunderground.com/weather/api/. To use it, you first have to register to gain access and get what's called an "API Key". Services like this often want to make sure that *you are a real human*, and not just a bot who will overload their system with requests for information.

I used my key to obtain a weather observation from San Francisco, and stored the JSON file on GitHub. You can cut and paste the URL below into a browser address bar, and see what the raw data looks like. To pull it into R, use this two-step process:

```
> json.file <- "https://raw.githubusercontent.com/NicoleRadziwill/Data-for-
R-Examples/master/example.json"
> json.data <- fromJSON(paste(readLines(json.file), collapse=""))
> str(json.data)
List of 2
 $ response          :List of 3
  ..$ version        : chr "0.1"
  ..$ termsofService: chr
"http://www.wunderground.com/weather/api/d/terms.html"
  ..$ features       :List of 1
  .. ..$ conditions: num 1
  ..
```

The `fromJSON` command reads input in JSON format and automatically converts it into a data structure that is accessible from within R. This is a complicated data structure that consists of lists embedded within other lists!

Additional Resources

- Although we don't use it much in this book, you can also import space-delimited or tab-delimited data into R using the read.table command. This works well if you are opening a file on your local machine, or retrieving tabular data from GitHub, or retrieving data that has been published in text format from Google Spreadsheets.
- If you use RStudio, selecting "Import Dataset" should be all you need, but more info is at https://thepracticalr.wordpress.com/2017/01/31/importing-data-into-r-part-ii/
- The `readstata13` package can be used to import data from the Stata package.

- For more information about the `iris` data, and the hundreds of R examples that use this data, search for "iris data in r" in Google. When I did the search, it returned 685,000 results.

- Datacamp has a good page on data import mechanisms, and includes things like importing files with observation delimiters that are not spaces, tabs, or commas, importing JSON and XML formats, and importing files from other statistical packages (e.g. Minitab, SAS, and SPSS): https://www.datacamp.com/community/tutorials/r-data-import-tutorial#gs.BCWn7ys

1.7 PDFs and CDFs

When an outcome is random, how do you mathematically describe the scope of all possibilities? You can do this by characterizing the distribution of all those possibilities as a probability density function (PDF). For discrete variables, it's called a probability mass function (PMF). The PDF illustrates: *how frequently do you observe certain values?* The cumulative distribution function (or CDF) complements the PDF, and provides additional information. It shows what proportion *of all observations* will be less than or equal to a certain value. When you think of the normal distribution as a bell curve, you're thinking about the PDF.

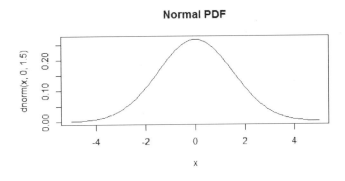

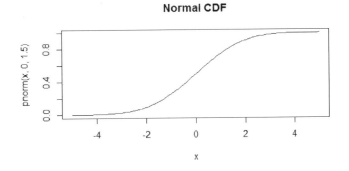

```
> x <- seq(-5,5,0.1) # Generate a sequence of x-values from -5 to +5
> par(mfrow=c(2,1)) # Plot them as 2 rows in 1 column
> plot(x,dnorm(x,0,1.5),type="l",main="Normal PDF")
> plot(x,pnorm(x,0,1.5),type="l",main="Normal CDF")
```

A probability density just tells you, for any given x-value, the long-run relative frequency of seeing a particular outcome occur. The CDF is the integral of the PDF:

$$\int_{-\infty}^{\infty} PDF = CDF$$

Because integration means to *add up all the areas* underneath a function, we can think about it this way. Pretend you are a tiny person standing in front of a bell curve that looks like the normal PDF. You and the normal PDF are on a stage, and there's a stage curtain hanging on rings along the top edge of the stage. We're going to start at x=-4 and walk along the x-axis towards the right, all the way to x=+4. As we do, we're going to *hold the curtain and pull it* as we walk. How much of the area under the normal PDF are we covering as we walk by? Let's *visually integrate* to construct the CDF:

- When you just start walking, and you go from x=-4 to x=-2, you're only capturing a tiny bit of the area under the normal PDF. The y-values on the CDF start at 0, because you have not covered any of the area under the normal PDF yet. The y-value at x=-2 will be about 0.16, since that's how much area we have covered by the time we have walked to x=-2.
- As you walk from x=-2 to x=0, you're capturing the area at a *faster and faster rate*. By the time you get to x=0, you have captured 50% of the area under the normal PDF. The slope on the normal CDF thus increases to reflect that we're capturing the area faster. The y-value of the normal CDF at x=0 is 0.5, to reflect that we have captured half the area.
- As we keep walking to the right, from x=0 to x=+2, we are capturing area at a slower rate. The slope of the CDF begins to decrease. When we get to x=+2, the y-value on the CDF will be 0.84, reflecting that we have covered 84% of the area under the normal PDF by this point.
- Finally, as we walk from x=+2 to x=+4, we are adding area at a much, much slower rate. The slope on the normal CDF decreases to reflect that. By the time we've

walked all the way across the stage, we have covered 100% of the area under the normal PDF, and the y-value on the normal CDF levels off at 1.0.

The probability density function, then, represents the *rate of change* of the cumulative distribution. It is the *derivative* of the CDF. If you know the equation of either the PDF or the CDF, you can determine the equation for the other function by integrating or differentiating, respectively.

You can *visually differentiate* a CDF by pretending you're a tiny person walking from the leftmost position on the x-axis to the rightmost position. All you have to do to create a PDF is to eyeball the slope of the CDF, and plot that value on the y-axis of the PDF you are creating. The area under a PDF is, by definition, 1. **The range of values on the y-axis of the CDF is always 0.0 to 1.0. This is a very convenient property** that enables us to create *inverse transform equations* to generate random numbers from any target distribution we want. Fortunately, there are several functions built into R which make it super easy to work with PDFs and CDFs. All you need to know is the value of the parameters that uniquely specify any given distribution. The normal distribution is fully specified by its mean (which shows where the center of the distribution is at) and standard deviation (which shows how spread out the values are).

R Command	What it does
`rnorm(n,mean,sd)`	Generates n **random variates** selected from a normal distribution with specified mean and standard deviation
`dnorm(x,mean,sd)`	Plots the **PDF** from a collection of values x (which represent various points along the x-axis) centered at the specified mean, and with the specified standard deviation
`pnorm(x,mean,sd)`	Plots the **CDF** from a collection of values x (which represent various points along the x-axis) centered at the specified mean, and with the specified standard deviation
`qnorm(area,mean,sd)`	Finds the quantiles, or **Inverse CDF**. If you know an area under the normal PDF to the left of a particular x-value, this command helps you find the number of standard deviations

above or below the mean where the x-value that forms that boundary sits. (In conjunction with a random number generator, this function can you generate random numbers that were pulled from a distribution with characteristics that you specify.)

Common Distributions

There are PDF and CDF functions for *many* common distributions in R. Each of them works just like rnorm, dnorm, pnorm, and qnorm, only you need to know the parameters that uniquely specify that other type of distribution. For example, the exponential distribution is uniquely specified by just one parameter: the *mean* of the distribution.

Here are several (but not all) of the distributions built into R that you can use:

Distribution	R Functions
Beta	pbeta, qbeta, dbeta, rbeta
Binomial	pbinom, qbinom, dbinom, rbinom
Cauchy	pcauchy, qcauchy, dcauchy, rcauchy
Chi-Square	pchisq, qchisq, dchisq, rchisq
Exponential	pexp, qexp, dexp, rexp
F	pf, qf, df, rf
Gamma	pgamma, qgamma, dgamma, rgamma
Geometric	pgeom, qgeom, dgeom, rgeom
Hypergeometric	phyper, qhyper, dhyper, rhyper
Logistic	plogis, qlogis, dlogis, rlogis
Log Normal	plnorm, qlnorm, dlnorm, rlnorm
Negative Binomial	pnbinom, qnbinom, dnbinom, rnbinom
Normal	pnorm, qnorm, dnorm, rnorm
Student's t	pt, qt, dt, rt
Uniform	punif, qunif, dunif, runif
Weibull	pweibull, qweibull, dweibull, rweibull

Additional Notes

Remember that a discrete distribution (the ones that look like a landscape of spiky towers sitting along your horizontal axis, separated by spaces, which represents the probability that a discrete random variable is equal to some value), is technically called a *probability mass function* (PMF), and not a PDF. In case you ever run into the term "PMF" in your reading, know that it's essentially the same thing as a PDF, only for discrete outcomes.

Other Resources

- There is an amazing list of many probability distributions on Wikipedia at http://en.wikipedia.org/wiki/List_of_probability_distributions. In addition, each statistical distribution (e.g. normal, uniform, Weibull) has its own Wikipedia page that includes PDFs, CDFs, and a wealth of other information about that distribution. These are fantastic pages and I encourage you to get to know them.

- There is a fantastic interactive PDF/CDF explorer that you NEED to play with at http://www.che.utah.edu/~tony/course/material/Statistics/18_rv_pdf_cdf.php

- A comparison of the `qnorm()` and `pnormGC()` commands is here: http://cran.r-project.org/web/packages/tigerstats/vignettes/qnorm.html

1.8 Z-Score Problems with the Normal Model

Objective

Lots of data in the world is naturally distributed *normally*, with most of the values falling around the mean, but with some values much less than (and other values much greater than) the mean. When your data is distributed normally (or when you invoke the Central Limit Theorem), you can use the normal model to answer questions about the the entire population. That's what we'll do in this chapter. You will learn about:

- The N notation for describing normal models
- What z-scores mean
- The 68-95-99.7 rule for approximating areas under the normal curve
- How to convert each element of your data set into z-scores
- How to answer questions about the characteristics of the entire population

The Normal Model and Z-Scores

The normal model provides a way to characterize how *frequently* different values will show up in a population of lots of values. You can describe a normal model like this:

$$N(\mu, \sigma)$$

Here's what you SAY when you see this: "The normal model with a mean of μ and a standard deviation of σ." There is no way for you to mathematically break this statement down into something else. It's just a shorthand notation that tells us *we're dealing with a normal model here, here are the two values that uniquely characterize the shape and position of that bell curve.* To produce that bell curve requires an equation (called the *probability density function* or pdf):

$$f(x, \mu, \sigma) = \frac{1}{\sigma\sqrt{2\pi}} e^{-\frac{(x-\mu)^2}{2\sigma^2}}$$

This may look complicated at first, but it's not. The left-hand side says that the normal model is a function (f) of three variables: x, μ, and σ. Which makes sense: we have to plot some value on the vertical (y) axis based on lots of x-values that we plug into our equation, and the shape of our bell curve is going to depend on the mean of the distribution μ (which tells us how far to the right or left on the number line we should slide our bell curve) and the standard deviation σ (which tells us how fat or skinny the bell will be... bigger standard deviation = more dispersion in the distribution = fatter bell curve). When the mean is 0 and the standard deviation is 1, this is referred to as the *standard normal model*. It looks like this, and was produced by the code below.

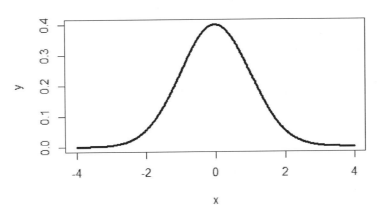

```
x <- seq(-4,4,length=500)
y <- dnorm(x,mean=0,sd=1)
plot(x,y,type="l",lwd=3,main="Standard Normal Model: N(0,1)")
```

The first line just produces 500 x values for us to work with. The second line creates 500 y values from those x values, produced by the dnorm command (which stands for "density of the normal model"). Because dnorm contains the equation of the normal model, we don't actually have to write out the whole equation. Now we have 500 (x,y) pairs which we can use to plot the standard normal model, using a type of "l" to make it a line, and a line width (using `lwd=3`) to make it a little thicker (and thus easier to see) than if we used a line width of only one pixel.

The z-score tells us *how many standard deviations above or below the mean* a particular x-value is. You can calculate the z-score for any one of your x-values like this:

$$z = \frac{x - \mu}{\sigma}$$

The z-score describes what the difference is between your data point (x) and the mean of the distribution (μ), scaled by how skinny or fat the bell curve is (σ). The z-score of the *mean* of your distribution, then, will be zero - because if x equals the mean, x - μ will be zero and the z-score will be zero. So, ALWAYS:

- Positive z-scores are associated with data points that are ABOVE the mean
- Negative z-scores are associated with data points that are BELOW the mean

Consider an example where we're thinking about the distribution of several certification exam scores: the ASQ Certified Six Sigma Black Belt (CSSBB) exam from December 2014. Let's say, hypothetically, that we know the population of all scores for this exam can be described by the normal model with a mean of 78 and a standard deviation of 5:

$$N(78,5)$$

There are a LOT of things we know about the test scores simply by knowing what model represents the data. For example:

- The test score that is one standard deviation _below_ the mean is 73 (which we get by taking the mean, 78, and *subtracting* one standard deviation of 5). This test score of x=73 corresponds to a z-score of -1.
- The test score that is one standard deviation _above_ the mean is 83 (which we get by taking the mean, 78, and *adding* one standard deviation of 5). This test score of x=83 corresponds to a z-score of +1.

- The test score that is two standard deviations _below_ the mean is 68 (which we get by taking the mean, 78, and _subtracting_ two times the standard deviation of 5, which is 10). This test score of x=68 corresponds to a z-score of -2.

- The test score that is two standard deviations _above_ the mean is 88 (which we get by taking the mean, 78, and _adding_ two times the standard deviation of 5, which is 10). This test score of x=88 corresponds to a z-score of +2.

- The test score that is three standard deviations _below_ the mean is 63 (which we get by taking the mean, 78, and _subtracting_ three times the standard deviation of 5, which is 15). This test score of x=63 corresponds to a z-score of -3.

- The test score that is three standard deviations _above_ the mean is 93 (which we get by taking the mean, 78, and _adding_ three times the standard deviation of 5, which is 15). This test score of x=93 corresponds to a z-score of +3.

Let's say YOU scored an 85. (There's no way to actually know this, because the certification administrators don't reveal any information about the CSSBB exam beyond whether you passed it or not.) What's your z-score? It's easy to calculate:

$$z = \frac{x - \mu}{\sigma} = \frac{85 - 78}{5} = 1.4$$

A z-score of +1.4 means that your test score was 1.4 standard deviations _above_ the mean of 78. There is also other information that we can find out by knowing what normal model represents the scores of all test-takers.

For example, we know that a very tiny portion of the test-takers (in fact, only 0.3%) scored either above a 93, or below a 63. We can also show that your score of 85% was better than 91.9% of all test-takers. But how??

The 68-95-99.7 Rule

The *area* under the normal curve reflects the *probability* that an observation will fall within a particular interval. **Area = Probability!** There are a couple simple things that you can memorize about the normal model that will help you double-check any problem solving you do with it. Called the *empirical rule*, this will help you remember how much of the area under the bell curve falls between different z-scores. First, think about how the normal model is *symmetric*... if you fold it in half (from left to right) at the mean, the curve is a mirror image of itself. The right half of the bell is exactly the same shape and size as the left half. (The code to produce these charts is below the images.)

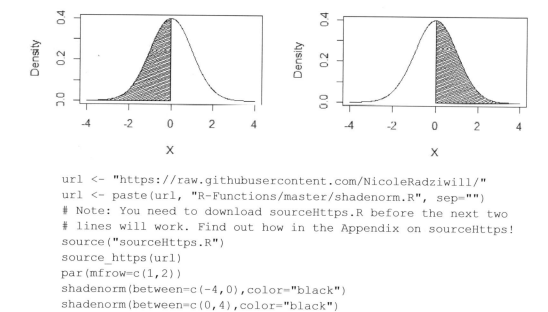

```
url <- "https://raw.githubusercontent.com/NicoleRadziwill/"
url <- paste(url, "R-Functions/master/shadenorm.R", sep="")
# Note: You need to download sourceHttps.R before the next two
# lines will work. Find out how in the Appendix on sourceHttps!
source("sourceHttps.R")
source_https(url)
par(mfrow=c(1,2))
shadenorm(between=c(-4,0),color="black")
shadenorm(between=c(0,4),color="black")
```

Because the total area under the normal curve is 100%, this also means that 50% of the area under the curve is to the *left* of the mean, and the remaining 50% of the area under the curve is to the *right* of the mean. **The 68-95-99.7 Empirical Rule provides even more information:**

- 68% of your observations will fall between one standard deviation below the mean (where z = -1) and one standard deviation above the mean (where z = +1)
- 95% of your observations will fall between two standard deviations below the mean (where z = -2) and two standard deviations above the mean (where z = +2)
- 99.7% (or pretty much ALL!) of your observations will fall between three standard deviations below the mean (where z = -3) and three standard deviations above the mean (where z = +3)

Here's what those areas look like. You read "P[-1 < z < 1]" as "the probability that the z-score will fall between -1 and +1".

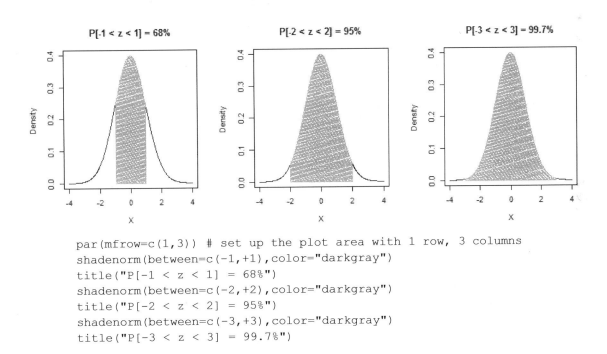

```
par(mfrow=c(1,3)) # set up the plot area with 1 row, 3 columns
shadenorm(between=c(-1,+1),color="darkgray")
title("P[-1 < z < 1] = 68%")
shadenorm(between=c(-2,+2),color="darkgray")
title("P[-2 < z < 2] = 95%")
shadenorm(between=c(-3,+3),color="darkgray")
title("P[-3 < z < 3] = 99.7%")
```

These graphs show that:

- There is a *probability of 68%* that an observation will fall between one standard deviation below the mean (where z = -1) and one standard deviation above the mean (where z = +1).

- There is a *probability of 95%* that an observation will fall between two standard deviations below the mean (where z = -2) and two standard deviations above the mean (where z = +2)

- There is a *probability of 99.7%* that an observation will fall between three standard deviations below the mean (where z = -3) and three standard deviations above the mean (where z = +3)

When data are distributed normally, there is only a VERY TINY (0.3%!) chance that an observation will be smaller than whatever value is three standard deviations below the mean, or larger than three standard deviations above the mean! **Nearly all values will be within three standard deviations of the mean.** That's one of the reasons why you can use the z-score for a particular data point to figure out just how common or uncommon that value is.

The chart for the 68-95-99.7 rule as presented on Wikipedia is shown on the next page (it's from http://en.wikipedia.org/wiki/68%E2%80%9395%E2%80%9399.7 rule). From the 68-95-99.7 rule, we can estimate what proportion of the population will have scored below our certification score of 85, compared to the normal model with the mean of 78 and the standard deviation of 5, or N(78,5).

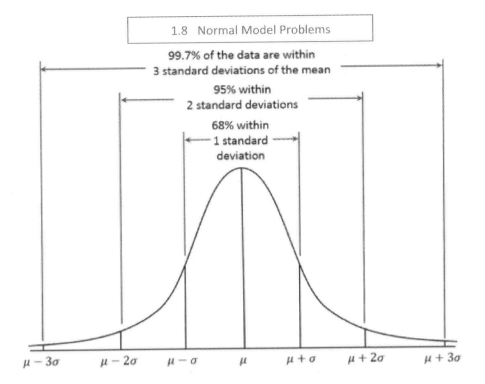

The 68-95-99.7 Rule is Great, But Prove it to Me

When you *integrate* a function, you are computing the area under the curve. So, if we integrate the equation for the normal model between z=-1 and z=+1, we should get an area of 68%. Let's do that. First, we start with the equation of the normal probability distribution function:

$$f(x, \mu, \sigma) = \frac{1}{\sigma\sqrt{2\pi}} e^{-\frac{(x-\mu)^2}{2\sigma^2}}$$

Then simplify it using the *standard normal model* of N(0,1) which is centered at a mean (μ) of 0, with a standard deviation (σ) of 1. (This just means plug in 0 for μ and 1 for σ.) You get:

$$f(x) = \frac{1}{\sqrt{2\pi}} e^{-x^2/2}$$

Now, let's integrate it from a z-score of -1 to a z-score of +1 to find the area between those left and right boundaries. We can pull the first fraction outside the integral since it's a constant:

$$\frac{1}{\sqrt{2\pi}} \int_{-1}^{+1} e^{-x^2/2} dx$$

How do we integrate this expression? My solution (since I'm not a mathematician) is to look at a table of integrals, or use Wolfram Alpha at http://www.wolframalpha.com. All we need to do is figure out how to evaluate the stuff on the right side of the integral, then multiply it by one over the square root of 2π. I'll show you what I typed into Wolfram to make it determine the integral for me:

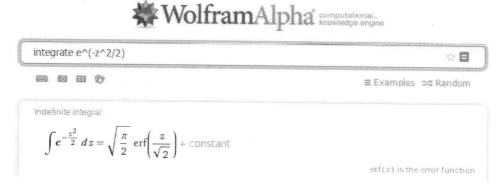

The evaluated integral contains something called $\texttt{erf}$, the "error function". This is a special function that (fortunately) Wolfram knows how to evaluate as well. Let's plug the result from evaluating this integral back into our most recent expression. That vertical bar on the right-hand side means "evaluate the error function of x over the square root of 2 using x=1, then subtract off whatever you get when you evaluate the error function of x over the square root of 2 using x=-1".

$$\frac{1}{\sqrt{2\pi}}\sqrt{\frac{\pi}{2}}\ erf\ \frac{x}{\sqrt{2}}\bigg|_{-1}^{+1}$$

We can simplify all the stuff on the left-hand side of `erf` because they are all constants... it reduces to a very nice and clean 1/2. So we just need to take the difference between evaluating the error function at x=1, and evaluating the error function at x=-1, and then chop it in half to get our answer. Wolfram will help:

All we had to do was type in `erf(1/sqrt(2))` and Wolfram evaluates the right hand side of our expression at x=1, giving us approximately 0.683. If we do this again using x=-1, we'll get a value of -0.683. Now let's plug it all in together:

$$=\frac{1}{2}(0.683-(-0.683))=0.683$$

The area under the standard normal curve between -1 and +1 is 0.683, or 68.3%... nearly the same value that we get from our "rule of thumb" 68-95-99.7% rule! You can try this same process to determine the area under the normal between -2 and +2, or between -3 and +3, to further confirm the empirical 68-95-99.7% rule for yourself.

Calculating All of the Z-Scores for a Data Set

There may come a time where you would like to easily compute the z-scores for each element in a data set that's normally (or nearly normally) distributed. You *could* take each value individually and use this equation to compute the z-scores one by one:

$$z = \frac{x - \mu}{\sigma}$$

Or you could just enter your data set into R:

```
scores <- c(81, 91, 78.5, 73.5, 66, 83.5, 76, 81, 68.5, 83.5)
```

And then have it compute all the z-scores for you at once, using the `scale` command:

```
> scale(scores)
              [,1]
 [1,]   0.36689321
 [2,]   1.70105036
 [3,]   0.03335393
 [4,]  -0.63372464
 [5,]  -1.63434250
 [6,]   0.70043250
 [7,]  -0.30018536
 [8,]   0.36689321
 [9,]  -1.30080321
[10,]   0.70043250
```

Do these values make sense? Let's check. The mean of our test scores is around 78, so all the scores above 78 should have positive z-scores, and all the scores below 78 should have negative z-scores. We see by examining the original data that scores 1, 2, 3, 6, 8, and 10 are all above the mean, and so should have z-scores that are positive. The output from scale confirms this expectation. We can also see that the third value of 78.5 is just slightly above the mean, so its z-score should be very tiny and positive. It is, at 0.0333.

Using the Normal Model to Answer Questions About a Population

For this collection of examples, we'll use real exam scores from a test I administered last year. You can get my CSV-formatted data directly from GitHub as long as you have the appropriate URL:

```
all.scores <-
read.csv("https://raw.githubusercontent.com/NicoleRadziwill/Data-for-
R-Examples/master/compare-scores.csv",header=TRUE)
```

If the code above has successfully found and retrieved the data, you should be able to see the semester when the students took the test (in the `when` variable) and the raw scores (stored in the `score` variable) when you use `head`. There are 96 observations in this dataset, the score is numeric, and the semester is a factor (categorical variable) with three levels:

```
> head(scores)
  when score
1 FA14  45.0
2 FA14  55.0
3 FA14  42.5
4 FA14  37.5
5 FA14  30.0
6 FA14  47.5
> str(scores)
'data.frame':   96 obs. of  2 variables:
 $ when : Factor w/ 3 levels "FA11","FA14",..: 2 2 2 2 2 2 2 2 2 2 ...
 $ score: num  45 55 42.5 37.5 30 47.5 40 45 32.5 47.5 ...
```

First, we should check and see whether the scores are approximately normally distributed. We can do this by plotting a histogram, and by doing a QQ plot which (if are scores *are* nearly normal) should show all of our data points nearly along the diagonal. QQ plots and tests for normality are covered more extensively in Chapter 2.8.

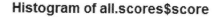

Histogram of all.scores$score

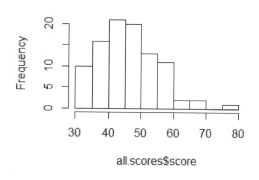

all.scores$score

Normal Q-Q Plot

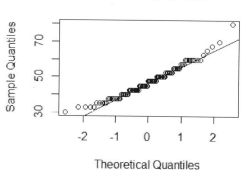

Theoretical Quantiles

```
par(mfrow=c(1,2)) # set up the plot area with 1 row, 2 columns
hist(all.scores$score)
qqnorm(all.scores$score)
qqline(all.scores$score)
```

The histogram is skewed a little to the right, but it's nearly normal, so we can proceed. To figure out what normal model can be used to represent the data, we need to know the mean and standard deviation of the scores:

```
> mean(all.scores$score)
[1] 47.29167
> sd(all.scores$score)
[1] 9.309493
```

Rounding a bit, we should be able to use N(47.3,9.3) (or "the normal model with a mean of 47.3 and a standard deviation of 9.3") to represent the distribution of all our scores. Using this model, we can answer a lot of questions about what the population of test-takers looks like. Looking at the histogram, we can see that a score of 50 is about in the middle. **What proportion of students got below a 50?** We can answer this question by determining the area under N(47.3,9.3) to the LEFT of x=50. It looks like this:

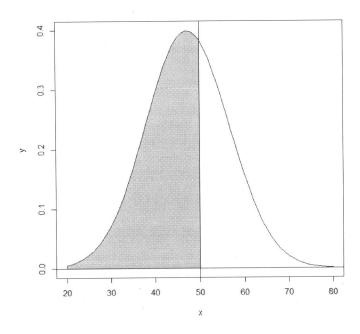

Here's how the shaded chart above was produced:

```
> x <- seq(20,80,1)
> y <-  dnorm((x-47.3)/(9.3))
> plot(x,y,type="l")
> abline(h=0);abline(v=50)
> which(x=="50")  # This tells us where to drop the vertical line
[1] 31
> polygon(c(x[0:31],rev(x[0:31])), c(rep(0,31),rev(y[0:31])),
col="lightgray")
```

Since the mean is 47.3, we know that a test score of 50 is TO THE RIGHT OF THE MEAN. The z-score associated with 50 is going to be *positive*. How positive will it be? Well, since the standard deviation is 9.3, we know that the test score which is one standard deviation above the mean will be 47.3 + 9.3 = 56.6. Our test score of 50 is just a little bit above the mean, so we can estimate our z-score at +0.3 or +0.4. That means the area under the normal to the left of x=50 will be greater than 50%, but not much greater than 50%. Even before we do the problem, we can estimate that our answer should be between 55% and 65%.

To definitively determine the area below the curve to the left of x=50, we use the pnorm function in R. **The pnorm function ALWAYS tells us the area under the normal curve to the LEFT of a particular x value** (remember this!!) So we can ask it to tell us the area to the left of x=50, given a normal model of N(47.3,9.3):

```
> pnorm(50,mean=47.3,sd=9.3)
[1] 0.6142153
```

We can predict that 61.4% of the test-takers *in the population* received a score less than 50%. This means even though our data set only includes students from a couple of semesters of *my* class, we've found a way to use this sample to determine what the scores from the *entire population* of students who took this test must be! As long as my students are representative of the larger population, this should be a pretty good bet.

(But what if you don't have R? Don't worry, you can still use "Z Score Tables" or online Z Score Calculators to figure out the area underneath the normal curve. Z Score Tables are available in the back of most statistics textbooks. Let's do the same problem we just did, AGAIN, using tables and calculators.)

Let's do this problem with a Z Score Table. First Rule of Thumb: **ALWAYS PICK A Z SCORE TABLE THAT HAS A PICTURE OF THE NORMAL CURVE ON IT.**

- The table at http://www.stat.ufl.edu/~athienit/Tables/Ztable.pdf HAS a picture. Use this kind of table!

- The table at http://www.utdallas.edu/dept/abp/zscoretable.pdf DOES NOT HAVE a picture. DO NOT USE these kinds of tables.

It's best to use Z Score Tables that have pictures so you can *match the picture representing the area under the curve you're trying to find* with the picture. To find the area under the curve, you need a z-score. The z-score that corresponds with a test score of x=50 is

$$z = \frac{x - \mu}{\sigma} = \frac{50 - 47.3}{93} = 0.29$$

When we look at the picture we drew, we notice that the shaded portion is bigger than 50% of the total area under the curve. When we look at the picture at the Z Score Table from http://www.stat.ufl.edu/~athienit/Tables/Ztable.pdf, we notice that it does NOT look like what we drew:

Standard Normal Probabilities

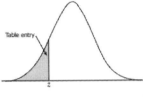

Table entry for z is the area under the standard normal curve to the left of z.

z	.00	.01	.02	.03	.04	.05	.06	.07	.08	.09
-3.4	.0003	.0003	.0003	.0003	.0003	.0003	.0003	.0003	.0003	.0002
-3.3	.0005	.0005	.0005	.0004	.0004	.0004	.0004	.0004	.0004	.0003
-3.2	.0007	.0007	.0006	.0006	.0006	.0006	.0006	.0005	.0005	.0005
-3.1	.0010	.0009	.0009	.0009	.0008	.0008	.0008	.0008	.0007	.0007
-3.0	.0013	.0013	.0013	.0012	.0012	.0011	.0011	.0011	.0010	.0010
-2.9	.0019	.0018	.0018	.0017	.0016	.0016	.0015	.0015	.0014	.0014
-2.8	.0026	.0025	.0024	.0023	.0023	.0022	.0021	.0021	.0020	.0019
-2.7	.0035	.0034	.0033	.0032	.0031	.0030	.0029	.0028	.0027	.0026
-2.6	.0047	.0045	.0044	.0043	.0041	.0040	.0039	.0038	.0037	.0036
-2.5	.0062	.0060	.0059	.0057	.0055	.0054	.0052	.0051	.0049	.0048
-2.4	.0082	.0080	.0078	.0075	.0073	.0071	.0069	.0068	.0066	.0064
-2.3	.0107	.0104	.0102	.0099	.0096	.0094	.0091	.0089	.0087	.0084
-2.2	.0139	.0136	.0132	.0129	.0125	.0122	.0119	.0116	.0113	.0110
-2.1	.0179	.0174	.0170	.0166	.0162	.0158	.0154	.0150	.0146	.0143
-2.0	.0228	.0222	.0217	.0212	.0207	.0202	.0197	.0192	.0188	.0183
-1.9	.0287	.0281	.0274	.0268	.0262	.0256	.0250	.0244	.0239	.0233
-1.8	.0359	.0351	.0344	.0336	.0329	.0322	.0314	.0307	.0301	.0294
-1.7	.0446	.0436	.0427	.0418	.0409	.0401	.0392	.0384	.0375	.0367
-1.6	.0548	.0537	.0526	.0516	.0505	.0495	.0485	.0475	.0465	.0455
-1.5	.0668	.0655	.0643	.0630	.0618	.0606	.0594	.0582	.0571	.0559
-1.4	.0808	.0793	.0778	.0764	.0749	.0735	.0721	.0708	.0694	.0681
-1.3	.0968	.0951	.0934	.0918	.0901	.0885	.0869	.0853	.0838	.0823
-1.2	.1151	.1131	.1112	.1093	.1075	.1056	.1038	.1020	.1003	.0985
-1.1	.1357	.1335	.1314	.1292	.1271	.1251	.1230	.1210	.1190	.1170
-1.0	.1587	.1562	.1539	.1515	.1492	.1469	.1446	.1423	.1401	.1379
-0.9	.1841	.1814	.1788	.1762	.1736	.1711	.1685	.1660	.1635	.1611
-0.8	.2119	.2090	.2061	.2033	.2005	.1977	.1949	.1922	.1894	.1867
-0.7	.2420	.2389	.2358	.2327	.2296	.2266	.2236	.2206	.2177	.2148
-0.6	.2743	.2709	.2676	.2643	.2611	.2578	.2546	.2514	.2483	.2451
-0.5	.3085	.3050	.3015	.2981	.2946	.2912	.2877	.2843	.2810	.2776
-0.4	.3446	.3409	.3372	.3336	.3300	.3264	.3228	.3192	.3156	.3121
-0.3	.3821	.3783	.3745	.3707	.3669	.3632	.3594	.3557	.3520	.3483
-0.2	.4207	.4168	.4129	.4090	.4052	.4013	.3974	.3936	.3897	.3859
-0.1	.4602	.4562	.4522	.4483	.4443	.4404	.4364	.4325	.4286	.4247
-0.0	.5000	.4960	.4920	.4880	.4840	.4801	.4761	.4721	.4681	.4641

This particular Z Score Table ONLY contains areas within the tails. The trick to using a Z Score Table like this is to recognize that because the normal distribution is symmetric, the area to the LEFT of z=+0.29 can be found by taking 100% of the area, and *subtracting* the area to the LEFT of the z-score at z=-0.29 (what's in the area of the tail). Using the Z Score Table from http://www.stat.ufl.edu/~athienit/Tables/Ztable.pdf, we look in the row containing z=-0.2, and the column containing .09, because these add up to our computed z-score of 0.29. We get an area of 0.3859. But we're looking for an area greater than 50% (which we know because we drew a PICTURE!), so we take 1 - 0.3859 to get 0.6141, or **61.4%.**

Let's say we don't have a Z Score Table handy, and we don't have R. What are we to do? You can look online for a Z Score Calculator which should also give you the same answer. I always use Wolfram. There are so many Z Score Calculators out there... and only about half of them will give you the right answers. It's really sad! But Wolfram will give you the right answer, and it also asks you to specify what area you're looking for using very specific terminology. I can ask Wolfram "What's the area under the normal curve to the left of z=0.29?" like this:

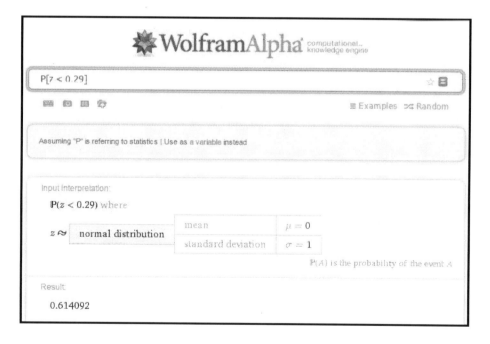

The area is 0.614, or 61.4% - the same as we got from the Z Score Table and the `pnorm` calculation in R.

Let's Do Another Z Score Problem

Say, instead, we wanted to figure out what proportion of our students scored between 40 and 60. That means we want to find the area under N(47.4, 9.3) between x=40 and x=60. For these examples, we will use the `shadenorm` function described in Appendix H. You can load the shadenorm function with this line of code:

```
source("https://raw.githubusercontent.com/NicoleRadziwill/R-
Functions/master/shadenorm.R")
```

If we draw it, it will look like this:

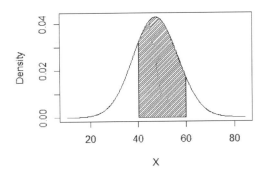

```
shadenorm(between=c(40,60),color="black",mu=47.3,sig=9.3)
```

To calculate this area, we'll have to take *all the area to the left of 60* and subtract off *all the area to the left of 40*, because `pnorm` and Z Score Calculators don't let us figure out "areas in between two z values" directly. So let's do that. Graphically, we'll take the total area in the left graph below, and subtract off the area of the right graph in the middle, which will leave us with the area in the graph on the right:

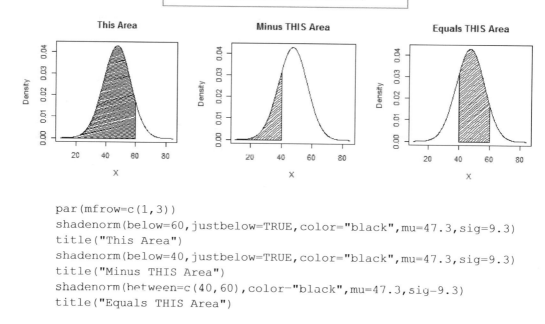

```
par(mfrow=c(1,3))
shadenorm(below=60,justbelow=TRUE,color="black",mu=47.3,sig=9.3)
title("This Area")
shadenorm(below=40,justbelow=TRUE,color="black",mu=47.3,sig=9.3)
title("Minus THIS Area")
shadenorm(between=c(40,60),color="black",mu=47.3,sig=9.3)
title("Equals THIS Area")
```

Fortunately, we can look up areas under the normal curve very easily with the `pnorm` command in R. We'll do it using two terms. The first term (to the left of the minus sign) finds all of the area to the left of x=60, and the second term (to the right of the minus sign) finds all of the area to the left of x=40. We subtract them to find the area in between:

```
> pnorm(60,mean=47.3,sd=9.3) - pnorm(40,mean=47.3,sd=9.3)
[1] 0.6977238
```

We can *also* do this in Wolfram as long as we know how to ask for the answer (see next page). All of the methods give us the same answer: 69.7% of all the test scores are between x=40 and x=60. I would really have preferred that my class did better than this! Fortunately, these scores are from a pre-test taken at the beginning of the semester, which means this represents the knowledge about statistics that they come to me with. Looks like I have a completely green field of minds in front of me... not a bad thing.

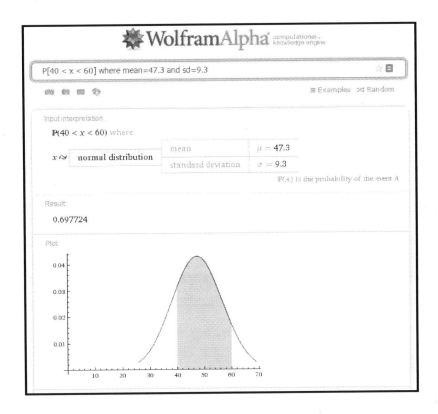

Let's Go Back to That Problem from the Beginning

So in the beginning of the chapter, we were talking about an example where WE scored an 85 on a certification exam where all of the test scores were normally distributed with N(78,5). Clearly we did well, but we want to know: what percentage of all test-takers did we score higher than? Now that we know about `pnorm`, this is easy to figure out, by drawing

```
shadenorm(below=85,justbelow=TRUE,color="black",mu=78,sig=5):
```

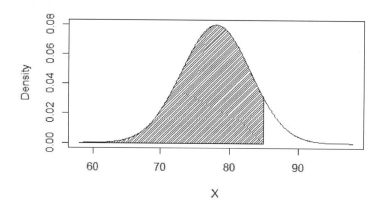

From the picture, we can see that we scored higher than at least half of all the test-takers. Using `pnorm`, we can tell exactly what the area underneath the curve is:

```
> pnorm(85,mean=78,sd=5)
[1] 0.9192433
```

Want to double check? Calculate the z-score associated with 85 for this particular normal distribution, head to Wolfram, and ask it to calculate P[z < whatever z score you calculated].

You Don't Need All the Data

In the examples above, we figured out what normal model to use based on the characteristics of our data set. However, sometimes, you might just be *told* what the characteristics of the population are - and asked to figure out what proportion of the population has values that fall above, below, or between certain outcomes. For example, let's say we are responsible for buying manufactured parts from one of our suppliers, to use in assemblies that we sell to our customers. To work in our assembly, each part has to be within 0.01 inches of the target length of 3.0 inches. If our supplier tells us that the population of their parts has a mean length of 3.0 inches with a standard deviation of 0.005

inches, what proportion of the parts that we buy can we expect to *not be able to use*? (This has implications for how many parts we order, and what price we will negotiate with our supplier.)

To solve this problem, we need to **draw a picture**. We know that the length of the parts is distributed as N(3.0, 0.005). We can't use parts that are shorter than (3.0 - 0.01 = 2.99 inches), nor can we use parts that are longer than (3.0 + 0.01 = 3.01 inches). This picture is drawn with `shadenorm(below=2.99,above=3.01,color="black",mu=3,sig=0.005)`:

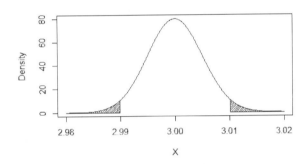

What proportion of the area is contained within these tails, which represent the proportion of parts we won't be able to use? Because the normal model is symmetric, as long as we can find the area under the curve inside *one* of those tails, we can just multiply what we get by two to get the area in *both* of the tails together.

Since pnorm always gives us the area to the *left* of a certain point, let's use it to find out the area in the left tail. First, let's calculate a z score for x=2.99:

$$z = \frac{x - \mu}{\sigma} = \frac{2.99 - 3.00}{0.005} = -2$$

Using the 68-95-99.7 rule, we know the area we're looking for will be about 5% (since 95% of the area is contained *inside* z=-2 and z=+2). Let's look up to see what the area is *exactly*, multiplying by 2 since we need to include the area in both tails:

```
> pnorm(-2) * 2
[1] 0.04550026
```

We can also ask `pnorm` for the area directly, without having to compute the z score. Notice how we give `pnorm` the x value at the boundary of the left tail, since we know `pnorm` gives us everything to the left of a particular x value:

```
> pnorm(2.99,mean=3,sd=0.005) * 2
[1] 0.04550026
```

All methods agree. Approximately 4.5% of the parts that we order won't be within our required specifications. If this was a real problem we were solving for our employer, though, the hard part would be yet to come: how are we going to *use* this knowledge? Does it still make sense to buy our parts from this supplier, or would we be better off considering other alternatives? Should we negotiate a price discount? Solving problems in statistics can be useful, but sometimes the bigger problem comes after you've done the calculations.

Now What?

Here are some useful resources that talk more about the concepts in this chapter:

- My favorite picture of z-scores superimposed on the normal model is here. Print it out! Carry it with you! **Memorize it!** http://en.wikipedia.org/wiki/Standard_score
- http://en.wikipedia.org/wiki/68%E2%80%9395%E2%80%9399.7_rule
- If you want to know more about the normal model, Wolfram has an *excellent* page that goes into depth at http://mathworld.wolfram.com/NormalDistribution.html

Notice that in *all* the examples from this chapter, we've a model of a population to answer questions about the population. If we're only able to select a *small sample* of items from our population (usually less than 30), we aren't going to be able to get a really good sense of the variability within the population. We will have to *adjust* our normal model to account for the fact that we only have limited knowledge of the variability within the population: to do that, we use the *t distribution*.

SECTION 2: CHARTS, GRAPHS, AND PLOTS

- Describe Distributions of Quantitative Data
- Show the Relationship of Parts to a Whole
- Characterize Relationships Between Independent and Dependent Variables
- Present Categorical Data as Contingency Tables
- Determine Whether Your Data Are Normal or Nearly Normal

2.1 Bar Charts/Bar Plots

Objective

To create a bar chart/bar plot in R with the `barplot` function using *categorical data*, which is a collection of numbers that represent *frequencies* (or *counts*) of events or outcomes that fall into different groups or categories. [**Note**: If you are trying to display distributions of *quantitative* data, choose a histogram instead. <u>Bar charts are for *categorical* data only. BAR CHARTS ARE NOT THE SAME AS HISTOGRAMS!</u>]

Background

A bar chart uses rectangular segments to visualize categorical data. The lengths of the bars are proportional to the values they represent, and the bars can be oriented vertically or horizontally.

- Bar charts can be an especially suitable alternative to a pie chart when there are *many* categories to be compared. For me, it is never pleasant to examine a pie chart that has more than 10 slices, because the slices just overwhelm me.
- Good bar charts are labeled nicely, with a clear description of *the categories that are being counted* on the horizontal (x) axis, and a label on the vertical (y) axis that indicates *whether frequencies or counts are displayed*.
- Membership into each category should be *mutually exclusive*. That is, you don't want an observation to appear in multiple bars.
- You will always have to consider whether a pie chart or a bar chart is a better way to display your data. If you are trying to illustrate a collection of items that naturally add up to 100%, a pie chart may be appropriate. However, if there are multiple categories where it may be difficult to distinguish which slice is bigger (such as one observation of 28% and another observation of 29%) a bar chart may be more appropriate. When small variations between categories should be communicated to your audience, bar charts are typically more effective than pie charts in presenting your data.

- If you want to display your data in terms of TWO categorical variables, choose a *segmented bar chart* (described in a separate chapter).

Even More Caution: There is a BIG DIFFERENCE between a bar chart and a histogram! Even though a bar chart *looks* really similar to a histogram at first glance, take a close look at what kind of data is on the horizontal (x) axis. In a bar chart, the horizontal axis lists *categories*. In a histogram, the horizontal axis will contain *ranges of numbers* that represent a continuum (e.g. 0-10, 10-20, 20-30 and so forth). Also, in a bar chart, there will be some *space between the bars* indicating that the categories are separate from one another - whereas with a histogram, there will be *no space between the bars!* The bars will be very cozy in a histogram, mashed up against one another like they're at a crowded party, whereas the bars in a bar chart need a little more breathing room, and thus are distanced from one another.

If You Counted Your Observations Already

For small data sets, you may have already tallied up your observations, and you don't need to load a whole file in to create your bar chart. Here is an example of data generated by opening one package of regular M&Ms to look at the distribution of colors, working with your data as a vector. I counted 12 blue ones, 6 brown ones, 8 green ones, and so forth:

```
mm.counts <- c(12,6,8,10,6,7)

names(mm.counts) <- c("blue","brown","green","orange",
"red","yellow")
```

Note that even though I called my variable `mm.counts`, you can call your variable whatever you want. Just be sure to use that variable name in all future commands. For example, if you call your variable `snakes`, you want to make sure all future commands use that variable name, e.g. `names(snakes)`.

We can also create a NEW variable to store the color names, so that we can use them to make colored bars in our bar chart that correspond to the M&M colors. I'm going to cal this new variable `mm.colors`:

```
mm.colors <- c("blue","brown","green","orange","red","yellow")
```

Now, you can check to make sure that your data was entered correctly:

```
> mm.counts
  blue  brown  green orange    red yellow
    12      6      8     10      6      7
```

The barplot command knows how to plot data that's in this format. Type in this code to produce your bar plot:

```
barplot(mm.counts)
```

If you want the bars to be colored, add a list of colors using the `col` argument:

```
barplot(mm.counts,col=mm.colors)
```

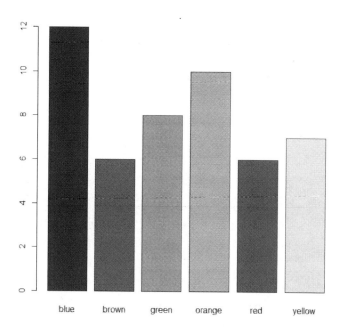

If You Need R to Count Observations for You

In most cases, you will have tens or thousands of observations – it would be impractical to count all of them. I have a file containing data from 1922 M&Ms that my students examined over two semesters. Tallying up how many colors and defects are in that data set would take forever if you had to do it manually, but fortunately, there's an easier way with R so long as the data has been recorded in case format with ONE CASE PER ROW. First, load my data, which is published to the web from Google Spreadsheets. I gave it the name mnms:

```
> mnms <- read.csv("https://docs.google.com/spreadsheets/d/e/2PACX-
1vQ9TZaUrqBc3lDW8OM7bliJa-
ECiQTkLu6An3kSmnp36rM11gEI6SZOOMHsFjojPL9xKvzLBzhI3S6G/pub?gid=0&single=true
&output=csv",header=TRUE)
```

In the case above, I've published my M&M data to the web as a CSV file. The argument "header=TRUE" means that the *first row* of my data file contains *variable names*. Once this command is executed, I'll have a data frame called mnms that contains seven variables. The first four are student (who logged the observation), id (the order I pulled the M&Ms from the bag; first M&M pulled would be "1"), color, and defect. I have six color codes (BL = blue, BR = brown, G = green, Y = yellow, O = orange, R = red) and four defect codes (N = no defects, C = cracked or chipped, L = letter is missing or improperly printed on the M&M, and M = multiple defects).

Finally, each student collected information about the entire bag to use later in the semester. The variables full.bag.weight and empty.bag.weight record the weight, in grams, before and after M&Ms were consumed; total.number reflects the number of M&Ms in the bag upon opening

The next step is to attach the file so you can refer to the variable names directly (that is, you can plot color instead of mnms$color, or defect instead of mnms$defect):

```
attach(mnms)
```

To produce a barplot, the barplot command needs to ingest a table. Here's what a table of colors looks like on its own:

```
> table(color)
color
 BL  BR   G   O   R   Y
311 240 375 420 319 257
```

To generate the barplot, just feed `barplot` that table:

```
barplot(table(color))
```

Let's define our list of colors as a variable so we don't have to retype it again and again:

```
> my.colors <- c("blue","brown","green","orange","red","yellow")
```

To add colors, just add a `col` argument, which will color the bars from left to right:

```
> barplot(table(color),col=my.colors)
```


Adding Labels

And now we can add some labels so the chart could tell the story about what we found in our bags of M&M on its own:

```
> barplot(table(color),main="My M&M Color Distribution",xlab="M&M
Colors",ylab="Number of M&Ms in Bag",col=my.colors)
```

The result of this `barplot` command is shown below; the colors of the bars correspond to the actual M&M colors in the order we listed them. If you don't want to display colors, and would prefer that all the bars are gray, leave out the `col=mm.colors` argument. There are also more color schemes you can use in these charts, even though for this problem it makes sense to use the actual M&M colors. To explore this, try replacing `col=my.colors` in the barplot command with:

- `col=c("red","blue")`
- `col=rainbow(7)`
- `col=heat.colors(7)`
- `col=topo.colors(7)`
- Try adjusting the number 7 in the top three lines and see what happens

My M&M Color Distribution

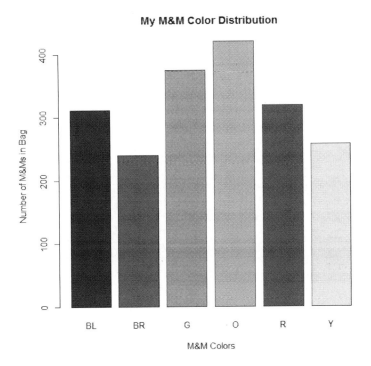

Conclusions

Bar charts, like pie charts, are used to visualize the distribution of proportions (or counts) of observation in categories. Whether you use counts or proportions on the vertical (y) axis for a given data set, your bar charts will look exactly the same! However, if you are using proportions, the bar chart has a different name - it's called a **relative frequency bar chart**. You can create one of those using `barplot(table(color))/sum(table(color))`. As with all of the examples in this chapter, you can feed any categorical variable to the `barplot` command.

There are many optional arguments that you can add to your bar chart using `barplot`, some of which you've seen in the examples above. Here are my favorites:

Option	What it does
`main`	Specify a main title to be displayed above chart
`xlab`	Specify text to describe the x-axis
`ylab`	Specify text to describe the y-axis
`col=mm.colors`	Sets the color palette to the colors that you have designated in the vector `mm.colors`
`names.arg=c("first name","second name")`	Instead of labeling the x-axis with the categories from the raw data, this argument enables you to set up new labels for the bars, which can be useful if you are generating a bar chart from data within a data frame
`legend.text=TRUE`	Adds a box with a legend to the plot
`horiz=TRUE`	Orients the display of the bars horizontally instead of vertically
`border="black"`	Give each bar a border (any color will work)
`density=10`	Makes shaded bars instead of solid (I like to choose values between 8 and 22 here)

Other Resources:

- http://en.wikipedia.org/wiki/Bar_chart
- http://www.forbes.com/sites/naomirobbins/2012/01/04/a-histogram-is-not-a-bar-chart/ - A Histogram is NOT a Bar Chart! From *Forbes*. See, they think so too.
- The Pareto Chart (Chapter 2.7) is another kind of bar chart where the bars are ordered so that the most commonly represented category appears on the leftmost side of the plot.

2.2 Histograms

Objective

To create a histogram in R with the `hist` function using *quantitative data*, which is a collection of numbers that represent *frequencies* (or *counts*) of events or outcomes that fall into different bins. Each of the bins has a quantitative lower bound, and a quantitative upper bound. [**Note**: If you are trying to display categorical data, choose a bar chart instead. Histograms are for *quantitative* data only. HISTOGRAMS ARE NOT THE SAME AS BAR CHARTS!]

Background

Like a bar chart, a histogram uses rectangular segments to visualize data, but in a histogram, the data used to put the observations into groups (or bins) is all quantitative. The lengths of the bars are proportional to the values they represent, and the bars can be oriented vertically or horizontally. To reflect that a histogram contains *continuous* quantitative data, the bars are mashed up really close to one another, like they're all passengers on a packed subway car. In contrast, there's a little bit of breathing room drawn between the bars on a bar chart because each of our categories are *discrete*. (To hear this discussion again, but *from the perspective of the bar chart,* read the chapter on bar charts.)

Histograms are used to visualize *distributions* of quantitative values. Distributions can be characterized by **shape**, **center**, and **spread**:

- The shape is usually described by one or more of these words: **unimodal** (meaning one hump or most frequent value, which is called the mode), **bimodal** (two humps), **uniform** (where all values have the same probability of being observed in the dataset), **skewed right** (meaning there's a tail that extends to the right, towards higher values), **skewed left** (with a tail that extends to the left, towards lower values), and **symmetric** (meaning you can fold the distribution in half, and you'll get mirror images) or **asymmetric** (meaning you can't fold it to get mirror images). There are pictures of various distribution shapes on the next page.

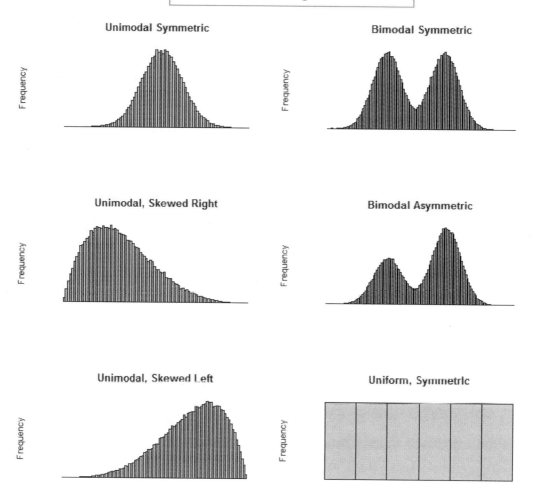

Here are some common histogram **shapes**. All of these distributions were generated using simulated data. The code that produced the simulated data and the plots can be found at the end of the chapter.

- **Center** just refers to where the *middle* of the distribution lies. Often, the mean or median are used to describe where the center is. But in the case of a bimodal distribution, it may be more useful to describe the distribution in terms of where the modes can be found. For a uniform distribution, it's really not as useful to describe the center, although you can report the mean of the data set.

- **Spread** indicates the variability and extent of your data... in short, how spread out it is. You can describe spread in terms of variance or standard deviation (the square root of the variance). Another way to report spread is with range, which is the distance between the smallest value in your dataset to the largest (just subtract the minimum from the maximum). (In other contexts, such as electronics and photography, we call the ratio of the largest to the smallest value *dynamic range*).

Creating a Histogram

Generating a histogram is extremely easy. (This example will use simulated data, but if you have your own data stored in a CSV or text file, you can load that into a data frame first, and then create a histogram from your data.)

First, let's generate some data by randomly sampling 5000 values from a beta distribution with shape parameters $\alpha=5$ and $\beta=2$. The beta distribution takes on many shapes, and when you specify your shape parameters like this, you'll end up with a unimodal distribution that's skewed to the left:

```
x <- rbeta(5000,5,2)
```

Before we create the histogram, let's take a look at the data by pulling up some descriptive statistics with the summary command, then we'll calculate the standard deviation using sd, and the variance using var. Note that the standard deviation is just the square root of the variance.

```
> summary(x)
   Min. 1st Qu.  Median    Mean 3rd Qu.    Max.
 0.1138  0.6223  0.7451  0.7202  0.8427  0.9990
> sd(x)
[1] 0.1627699
> var(x)
[1] 0.02649405
```

Although we'll need to plot our histogram to describe the shape of the distribution, we can tell from the descriptive statistics that this distribution is skewed to the left: the median is at 0.7451, but the mean is *slightly pulled to the left* at 0.7202 indicating that there's a tail on the left. The spread of our data can be described by the standard deviation, which is approximately 0.162, and the range, which is (0.9990 - 0.1138) = 0.8852.

The simplest way to create your histogram is by using `hist(x)`, which will produce this:

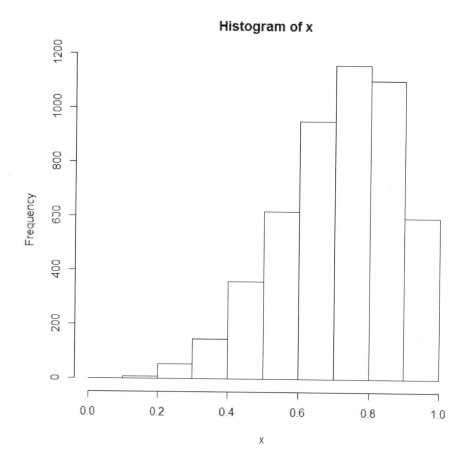

But there are all sorts of enhancements that we can use to make our histogram more descriptive, and prettier. One thing I like to do is to plot my histogram in terms of *density*

instead of frequency. Frequency (the number of times you observe a value in a particular bin) will depend on your sample size, whereas density does not. By plotting the histogram in terms of density, we can then draw a pretty curve on top of our data which shows the *kernel density estimation*. (Those are just fancy words that describe one process for trying to estimate the continuous distribution that a discrete data set represents.)

Here is a histogram using frequency (on the left), and one using density (on the right). The plot on the right has a density curve added to make it prettier. The first command sets the **p**lot **ar**ea to 1 row and 2 columns. The second command plots the histogram on the left. The third command plots the histogram on the right, using the freq=FALSE argument to tell R not to plot the histogram in terms of frequencies. The final line adds a curve on top of the second histogram using the lines command: the density of x will be plotted with density(x), the **l**ine **ty**pe will be "dotted", and we'll make the **l**ine **wid**th a little thicker (3 pixels) to make it easier to see:

```
par(mfrow=c(1,2))
hist(x, col="gray", xlab="Our Randomly Sampled Values",
     ylab="Frequency of Occurrence", main="Frequency")
hist(x, col="gray", freq=FALSE, xlab="Our Randomly Sampled
     Values", ylab="Density", main="Density")
lines(density(x),lty="dotted", lwd=3)
```

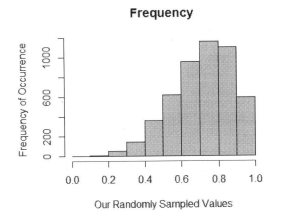

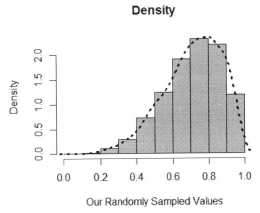

There are many optional arguments that you can add to your histogram using `hist`, some of which you've seen in the examples above. Here are my favorites.

Option to `hist`	What it does
`main`	Specify a main title to be displayed above chart
`xlab`	Specify text to describe the x-axis
`ylab`	Specify text to describe the y-axis
`breaks=10`	Sets the number of bins to whatever number you specify. I've noticed that R doesn't do this well every single time, so if you don't like your histogram at first, try a different number here.
`col="purple"`	Sets the color of the bars. You can name a color directly, use a hexadecimal code, or specify a color palette which will make each of your bars a different color.
`freq=FALSE`	Plot in terms of density, not frequency

Supplemental R Code

Here's the code that was used to simulate the data and generate the six plots at the beginning of this chapter displayed on the top of p. 92:

```
# This line sets up a plotting area that has 3 rows and 2 columns
par(mfrow=c(3,2))

label <- "Unimodal Symmetric"
# Randomly sample 100000 times from the normal distribution with mean
# of 0 and standard deviation of 1:
x <- c(rnorm(100000,0,1))
# Now plot the histogram in gray, with 100 bars, erasing all axis labels
hist(x,col="#cccccc",breaks=100,axes=FALSE,xlab="",main=label)


label <- "Bimodal Symmetric"
# Randomly sample 100000 times from the normal distribution with mean
# of 0 and standard deviation of 1, then again from the normal
# distribution with mean of 4 and standard deviation of 1 (so they have
```

```
# distinctly different peaks). Mash all the data together to form x.
x <- c(rnorm(100000,0,1),rnorm(100000,4,1))
# Now plot the histogram in gray, with 100 bars, erasing all axis labels
hist(x,col="#cccccc",breaks=100,axes=FALSE,xlab="",main=label)

label <- "Unimodal, Skewed Right"
# Randomly sample 100000 times from the beta distribution (which is sort
# of normal looking, but is skewed according to its shape parameters).
# The shape parameters here are alpha=2 and beta=5, meaning it will be
# skewed to the right.
x <- rbeta(100000,2,5)
# Now plot the histogram in gray, with 100 bars, erasing all axis labels
hist(x,col="#cccccc",breaks=100,axes=FALSE,xlab="",main=label)

label <- "Bimodal Asymmetric"
# Randomly sample 60000 times from the normal distribution with mean
# of 0 and standard deviation of 1, then 100000 times from the normal
# distribution with mean of 4 and standard deviation of 1 (so they have
# distinctly different peaks, and so the first peak is not as high as
# the second peak). Mash all the data together to form x.
x <- c(rnorm(60000,0,1),rnorm(100000,4,1))
# Now plot the histogram in gray, with 100 bars, erasing all axis labels
hist(x,col="#cccccc",breaks=100,axes=FALSE,xlab="",main=label)

label <- "Unimodal, Skewed Left"
# Randomly sample 100000 times from the beta distribution (which is sort
# of normal looking, but is skewed according to its shape parameters).
# The shape parameters here are alpha=5 and beta=2, meaning it will be
# skewed to the left.
x <- rbeta(100000,5,2)
# Now plot the histogram in gray, with 100 bars, erasing all axis labels
hist(x,col="#cccccc",breaks=100,axes=FALSE,xlab="",main=label)

label <- "Uniform, Symmetric"
# Randomly sample 100 million times from the uniform distribution with
# minimum of 0, and maximum of 6. We had to sample it a lot in order to
# give the plotted distribution that nice smooth plateau-like form.
x <- runif(100000000,0,6)
# Now plot the histogram in gray, limiting the extent of the x-axis
# to between 0 and 6 so that only our values show, with 7 bars, erasing
# all axis labels
hist(x,col="#cccccc",xlim=c(0,6),breaks=7,axes=FALSE,xlab="",main=label)
```

Other Resources:

- This interactive histogram explainer released in July 2017 is beautiful:
  https://tinlizzie.org/histograms/#
- http://en.wikipedia.org/wiki/Histogram - simple but elegant
- http://www.forbes.com/sites/naomirobbins/2012/01/04/a-histogram-is-not-a-bar-chart/ -
  A Histogram is NOT a Bar Chart! From *Forbes* magazine
- You can read more about kernel density estimation at
  https://chemicalstatistician.wordpress.com/2013/06/09/exploratory-data-analysis-kernel-density-estimation-in-r-on-ozone-pollution-data-in-new-york-and-ozonopolis/

2.3 Segmented Bar Charts

Objective

To create a Segmented (or "Stacked") Bar Chart in R with the `barplot` function. This uses *categorical data*, which is a collection of numbers that represent *frequencies* (or *counts*) of events or outcomes that fall into different groups or categories. You need to have your data organized in terms of TWO categorical variables for this to work, e.g. in a contingency table.

Background

A segmented bar chart, like a plain-old-ordinary bar chart, uses rectangular segments to visualize categorical data. The lengths of the bars are proportional to the values they represent, and the bars can be oriented vertically or horizontally.

- A segmented bar chart has *one bar* for each level of a particular categorical variable (called a "segment" of the sample).
- The segmented bar chart is a *frequency* distribution. Segmented bar charts are usually scaled so all of the bars reach the 100% mark on the vertical axis.
- The information contained in *one* of the bars is called a **conditional distribution**, because it's the distribution of observed cases for which the *condition* of an additional categorical variable having a given value is met.

Data Format

To create a segmented bar chart, all you need is a **contingency table** containing counts of data organized by at least two categorical variables. The following examples are based on M&M data stored within a CSV (comma separated variable) file published to the web, and the *first row* of my data file contains *variable names*. The first four variables are: `student`, `id` (the order I pulled the M&Ms from the bag; first M&M pulled would be "1"), `color`, and `defect`. I have six color codes (BL = blue, BR = brown, G = green, Y = yellow, O =

orange, R = red) and four defect codes (N = no defects, C = cracked or chipped, L = letter is missing or improperly printed on the M&M, and M = multiple defects).

Creating the Contingency Table

Load the data set containing 1922 M&Ms from this URL. So that you can get practice calling variables inside datasets, we will not use the `attach` command with this example:

```
> mnms <- read.csv(https://docs.google.com/spreadsheets/d/e/2PACX-
1vQ9TZaUrqBc31DW8OM7bliJa-
ECiQTkLu6An3kSmnp36rM11gEI6SZOOMHsFjojPL9xKvzLBzhI3S6G/pub?gid=0&single=true
&output=csv,header=TRUE)
```

The `table` command is used to generate a contingency table from the data frame. I'm going to call my **M&M** **c**ontingency **t**able `mm.ct` so I can distinguish it from `mnms`:

```
        mm.ct <- table(mnms$color,mnms$defect)
```

If I were to read out loud what the code on the right-hand side says, I would say "I am creating a contingency table whose rows will be the `color` data from the data frame named `mnms`, and whose columns will be the `defect` data from the data frame named `mnms`." I am creating a contingency table with the (`rows`,`columns`) that I specify as an argument to `table`.

The dollar-sign notation means that I am accessing a variable *within* a data frame. For example, `mnms$color` means that I want the `color` data from the data frame named `mnms`. Whenever you see notation in R in the form `data.frame$variable` this means that you want to access the variable named `variable` which is part of the data frame called `data.frame`.

When you display the contingency table, it will look like this. Using the data set with 1922 M&Ms, you can see that we observed 10 M&Ms that were both blue and chipped, 268 orange M&Ms with no defects, and so on.

```
> mm.ct
```

	C	L	M	N
BL	10	96	7	198
BR	7	82	7	144
G	10	115	13	237
O	26	115	11	268
R	22	72	18	207
Y	17	76	7	157

Producing the Segmented Bar Chart

First, decide whether you want to create a segmented bar chart for the data in the COLUMNS of your contingency tables, or the data in your ROWS. In our contingency table that we called mm.ct, defects are in the columns, and colors are in the rows. As a result:

- If you choose COLUMNS, you will be producing a segmented bar chart showing the distribution of colors by defects.
- If you choose ROWS, you will be producing a segmented bar chart showing the distribution of defects by color.

If you choose **COLUMNS**, you will produce the bar chart by creating a table of proportions (prop.table) from the COLUMNS (that's what the number 2 is for) of the contingency table called mm.ct, like this:

```
barplot(prop.table(mm.ct,2))
```

You can add all kinds of nice arguments to this to make the chart prettier. For example, we can define colors and labels:

```
mm.colors <- c("blue","brown","green","orange","red","yellow")

barplot(prop.table(mm.ct,2),main="Distribution of M&M Colors by
Defect Category",xlab="defect",ylab="percent",col=mm.colors)
```

produces this segmented bar chart:

Distribution of M&M Colors by Defect Category

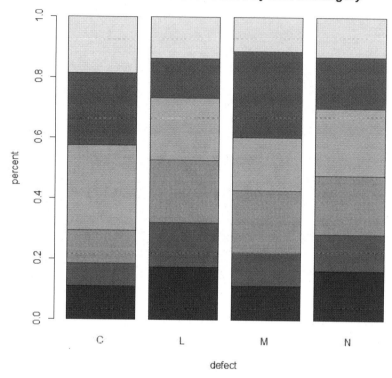

If you choose **ROWS**, you will produce the bar chart by creating a *table of* proportions (`prop.table`) from the ROWS (that's what the number 1 is for) of the contingency table called `mm.ct`. Only in this case, we have to *transpose* the table of proportions using the `t` command to make it all work:

```
barplot(t(prop.table(mm.ct,1)))
```

You can add all kinds of nice arguments to this too. For example, this code...

```
barplot(t(prop.table(mm.ct,1)),main="Distribution of M&M Defects
by Color",xlab="color",ylab="proportion",ylim=c(0,1.4),
col=mm.colors,legend=TRUE,names.arg=mm.colors)
```

...produces a segmented bar chart with a little extra space at the top that the legend can fit nicely into:

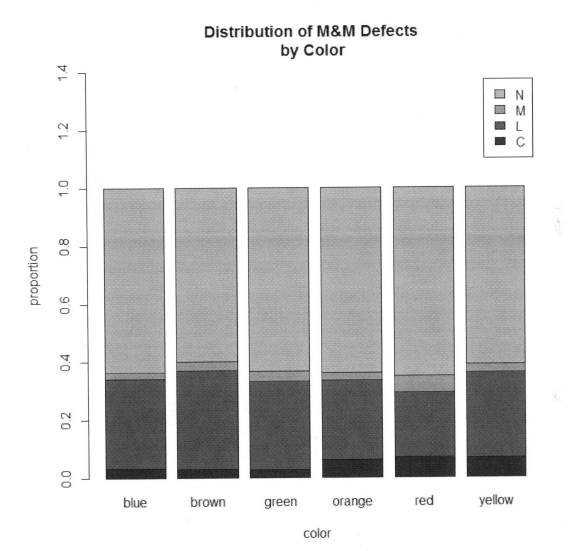

There are many optional arguments that you can add to your bar chart using `barplot`, some of which you've seen in the examples above. My favorites are the following:

Option	What it does
`main`	Specify a main title to be displayed above chart
`xlab`	Specify text to describe the x-axis
`ylab`	Specify text to describe the y-axis
`col=mm.colors`	Sets the color palette to the colors that you have designated in the vector `mm.colors`
`names.arg=mm.colors`	Instead of labeling the x-axis with the categories from the raw data, this argument enables you to set up new labels for the bars, which can be useful if you are generating a bar chart from data within a data frame
`legend=TRUE`	Adds a box with a legend to the plot
`horiz=TRUE`	Orients the display of the bars horizontally instead of vertically
`density=10`	Makes shaded bars instead of solid (I like to choose values between 8 and 22 here)

Segmented bar charts are used to visualize *conditional distributions*, which show the distribution of one variable for only the cases that match a condition. For any contingency table that describes counts or proportions in terms of two categorical variables (that is, a two-way table), one segmented bar chart can be constructed for *each* of the two categorical variables.

Other Resources

- Examples: http://betterevaluation.org/evaluation-options/stacked_graph
- The ggplot package makes beautiful bar plots, and lets you stack the bars in different ways. Find out more here: https://thepracticalr.wordpress.com/2016/11/11/make-a-bar-plot-with-ggplot/

2.4 Box Plots

Objective

Box plots provide an alternative to histograms, providing a way to visualize the distribution of a quantitative variable while accentuating some of the features of the dataset (like outliers, the interquartile range or IQR, and the median). We'll talk more about each of these features in this chapter.

Background

To demonstrate the similarity between box plots and histograms, and also to explain concepts like the IQR and illustrate how they "pop out" on a box plot, we'll simulate data that represents the daily high temperatures for some midlatitude location on 40 randomly sampled days of the summer. Say we know that this particular location has an average high temperature of 76 degrees Fahrenheit, which is approximately normally distributed, with a standard deviation of 9 degrees Fahrenheit. We can generate simulated data using the `rnorm` command, which generates a vector of <u>r</u>andom numbers sampled from a particular **norm**al distribution:

```
temps <- rnorm(40,mean=76,sd=9)
```

We can ask R to provide us with some descriptive statistics about the data we've just randomly generated. First, we'll get the header of our 40-element vector using the `head` command, and then we'll ask for a `summary` of the descriptive statistics, followed by the "five number summary" that we obtain using the `fivenum` command. Your numbers will be different, because you'll have different simulated data, and that's OK – it will have the same statistical properties as the data here.

```
> head(temps)
[1] 92.74207 70.75555 96.99872 78.41796 70.17173 69.74209
> summary(temps)
   Min. 1st Qu.  Median    Mean 3rd Qu.    Max.
  62.85   70.26   75.42   76.41   80.61   97.45
> fivenum(temps)
[1] 62.84572 70.23287 75.41800 80.70212 97.44665
```

From the head command, we can see that our first randomly generated temperature was approximately 92.7, the next one was around 70.8, and so forth. The `summary` command tells us the minimum value in our dataset, the temperature at which the first quartile (Q1) is located, the median, the mean, the temperature at which the third quartile (Q3) is located, and the maximum value in our dataset. The five number summary doesn't label its output, but in order from left to right it tells us the minimum, the first quartile, the median, the third quartile, and the maximum value in our dataset. (The `fivenum` command leaves out the mean, which the `summary` provides.)

What do all these values mean?

- The **minimum** is the smallest value in our dataset.
- The **first quartile (Q1)** represents the point at which 25% of our observations fall *below* that value (and thus 75% of our observations are *above* that value).
- The **median** represents the point at which 50% of our observations fall *below* that value (and thus 50% of our observations are *above* that value).
- The **mean** represents the average value of all our observations. If our distribution is perfectly symmetric, the mean and the median will be the same. If our distribution is *not* symmetric, the mean will be pulled in the direction of the tail more dramatically than the median. You can think of it this way: consider a distribution of all of the ages of people in your class or workplace. Now, imagine that one person (obviously an outlier) joins your group, and he or she is 100 years old. The average age of your colleagues is going to be pulled significantly higher, whereas the median will stay about the same (because that just indicates that 50% of the observations are below that value, and 50% of observations are above - and we've only added one observation).
- The **third quartile (Q3)** represents the point at which 75% of our observations fall *below* that value (and thus 25% of our observations are *above* that value).
- The **maximum** is the largest value in our dataset.

The boxplot, however, gives us even *more* information -- by showing us the *interquartile range,* or IQR, of our data. The interquartile range is the distance between the first and third quartiles, and contains 50% (half) of all our observations:

$$IQR = Q3 - Q1$$

Because we know that 25% of our observations are below Q1, and another 25% of observations are above Q3, this implies that exactly half of our observations - 50% of our observations - will fall between Q1 and Q3. And that's the purpose of the *box* in the box plot: to clearly show the space within which half of our values lie, while clearly showing us the median (indicated by a heavy line somewhere near the middle of our box).

But that's not all! The boxplot also gives us *more* information in the form of a *lower limit* and an *upper limit*! These values provide a heuristic (or rule of thumb) to use when we're trying to determine whether we have any *outliers* in our dataset, and if so, which values they are. The conventions for calculating our lower and upper limits are:

Lower Limit = Q1 - 1.5 x IQR

Upper Limit = Q3 + 1.5 x IQR

Values below the lower limit are outliers. Values above the upper limit are outliers. (**Note**: R provides you the option of *changing* this equation, and thus changing the lower and upper limits you plot on your boxplot, by using the `range` argument to the `boxplot` command. Don't do this!!! Ever!!! People are *used* to seeing boxplots that have been constructed with one and a half times the size of the IQR. If you change that value, their perception of how your data is distributed may not be accurate. So the only reason I could think of that you might want to change this range is if you were deliberately trying to manipulate peoples' perception of your data. *Like I said before... don't do it.*)

Now that you know what all the components of a box plot are, it should be easy to see how a box plot and a histogram are *similar*, but how a box plot communicates far more information about the contents of your data set. We will use the simulated high temperature data that we generated earlier to generate a boxplot *and* a histogram, and see how they compare. The boxplot is tilted horizontally to enable direct comparison:

Box Plot of Summer High Temps

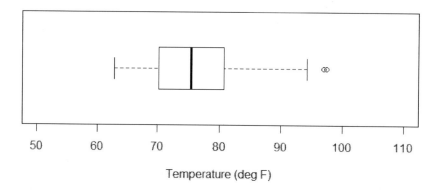

Histogram of Summer High Temps

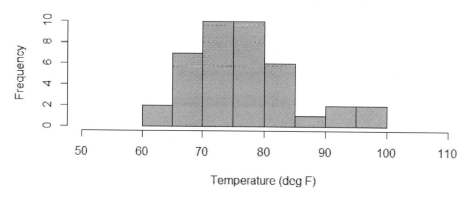

Here is the R code that set up the graphics window to plot both the box plot and the histogram one on top of the other:

```
par(mfrow=c(2,1))
boxplot(temps,main="Box Plot of Summer High Temps",ylim=c(50,110),
    xlab="Temperature (deg F)",horizontal=TRUE)
```

```
hist(temps,main="Histogram of Summer High Temps",col="darkgray",
      xlim=c(50,110),xlab="Temperature (deg F)")
dev.off() # only when you're ready to shut down your graphics window
```

The first command, `par`, sets up the plot area so it's configured with 2 rows and 1 column. This will make the first plot we generate show up on top of the graphics window, and the second plot will show up at the bottom of the graphics window. Next, we issue the `boxplot` command that generated the box plot on top. The `main` argument lets us place a title on our plot, the `ylim` argument controls our display so it only shows values between 50 degrees and 110 degrees, and the `horizontal` argument tilts our box plot on its side (by default, the box plot is oriented vertically).

Finally, we create a histogram using the `hist` command. The `main` argument lets us set a title, `col` controls colors, allowing us to specify that each of the bars on the histogram should be shaded dark gray, `xlim` controls our display so it only shows values between 50 degrees and 110 degrees, and `xlab` lets us place a label on our x-axis.

Here is an overview of what information is provided by the `fivenum` and `summary` commands in R, versus what values are denoted on the `boxplot` when it's graphed:

	Min	Lower Limit: Q1 - 1.5(IQR)	Q1	Median	Mean	Q3	Upper Limit: Q3 + 1.5(IQR)	Max
`fivenum`	✓		✓	✓		✓		✓
`summary`	✓		✓	✓	✓	✓		✓
What's Marked on Box Plot		✓	✓	✓		✓	✓	

Drawing a Box Plot with Comprehensive Labeling

For this example, we will simulate some more data to use for preparing the box plot. This data generation example is taken from the documentation for the `ddply` command, which is contained inside the `plyr` package (a package that lets you manipulate your data structures in highly sophisticated and totally useful ways that we won't cover in this book):

```
dfx <- data.frame(
    group - c(rep('A', 8), rep('B', 15), rep('C', 6)),
    sex = sample(c("M", "F"), size = 29, replace = TRUE),
    age = runif(n = 29, min = 18, max = 54)
)
```

This example creates a data frame called `dfx` with three variables, each of which forms one of the columns of the data frame: `group`, `sex`, and `age`. The group variable is created by replicating the letter A 8 times, then following it with 15 instances of the letter B, then ending with 6 instances of the letter C. The `sex` variable is created by asking R to perform a random sample of the values M and F, representing male and female, and to do it 29 times with replacement (meaning that we can continue to randomly select M's and F's as long as we want... we won't run out of them). The `age` variable is created by randomly selecting 29 values from a uniform distribution that ranges from the lowest value of 18, to the highest value of 54. (Note: "runif" isn't a conditional statement that tells R to "run if" some condition is met. It stands for **r**andom **uni**form... a way to generate randomly selected variables from a uniform distribution.)

The data will look something like this (remember that YOUR data will be different, because every time you simulate data, you'll get values that are unique to your simulation):

```
> head(dfx)
  group sex       age
1     A   M 23.08501
2     A   F 52.94904
3     A   F 49.78979
4     A   M 35.36636
5     A   M 42.78087
6     A   M 37.13228
```

Generating a box plot with labels takes a little bit of a trick, but it's not that hard to do. First, we have to create our box plot labels out of the data from the five number summary, which works as long as we don't have any outliers:

```
my.labels <- round(fivenum(dfx$age),digits=2)
```

Next, we create the box plot out of the age variable within the dfx data frame:

```
boxplot(dfx$age, horizontal=TRUE, ylim=c(10,60),
        col="lightgray", add=FALSE, main="Distribution of Ages")
```

And then finally, we add text to the box plot that specifies our critical points on the diagram, so that the box plot is a much stronger device for effective communication of the story behind our data:

```
text(x = my.labels, y = c(1.15, 1.25, 1.25, 1.25, 1.15),
     labels = my.labels)
```

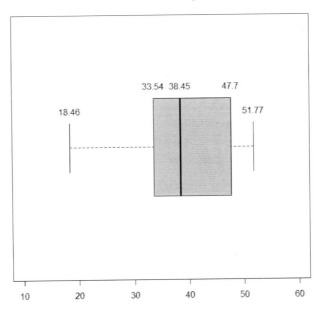

Distribution of Ages

By specifying values for y, we are telling R to plot our labels slightly above the horizontal line that goes through the center of our box plot. The first and last values will be printed slightly above that line, and the middle three values will be printed much further up.

The box plot is also sometimes called a "box and whiskers" plot, where the "whiskers" end at the lower limit and upper limit. It's easier to see why they might be called whiskers if the box plot is drawn horizontally, and enhanced with some very bad art, as in this rendition of the summer high temperatures boxplot that you saw earlier in this chapter:

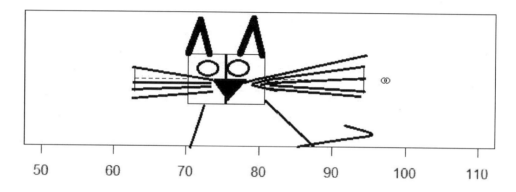

Other Resources:

- How to find the interquartile range (IQR) from a small dataset, analytically: http://www.wikihow.com/Find-the-IQR
- This post shows you how to label *outliers* in your R boxplot: http://www.r-statistics.com/2011/01/how-to-label-all-the-outliers-in-a-boxplot/

2.5 Comparative Box Plots

Objective

Box plots are a fantastic way to visualize the distribution of a quantitative variable, especially since they so clearly indicate the first and third quartiles, the median, and any outliers that are significant within the distribution. However, it can be even *more* useful to compare many distributions to one another, which is very easily accomplished by placing multiple box plots alongside each other.

Loading Your Data

This data is available at a Google Spreadsheets URL that has been published to the web as a CSV (comma separated values) file. We'll store it in a variable called `allscores`, and we use the `header=TRUE` argument to indicate that the first row of our file contains our variable names:

```
> allscores <- read.csv("https://docs.google.com/spreadsheets/d/e/2PACX-
1vQJO9vcBjLbsubNGniH8GIKZ3iUTwPJPJhFQpTT-m6PAxCrpujB2s5Cvpf-
JG7awtt0FblV3xiTp8i0/pub?gid=0&single=true&output=csv",header=TRUE)
> head(allscores)
  group  pre  post   diff
1     1 45.0  47.5    2.5
2     1 65.0  65.0    0.0
3     1 52.5  40.0  -12.5
4     1 65.0  52.5  -12.5
5     1 60.0  52.5   -7.5
6     2 55.0  35.0  -20.0
```

This file contains test scores, one taken at the beginning of the semester (`pre`) and an identical one taken at the end of the semester (`post`). We want to see how much the students have improved – or not – during the course. We've also split the students up into three groups (`group`), and we want to take a look at whether there are performance differences between those groups. These are all things we can begin to investigate with comparative box plots, which can be created in two distinct ways.

Option 1: Give `boxplot` a List of Distributions

Now I can refer to my data as "`allscores`" and ask `boxplot` to give me adjacent boxplots of pre and post test scores. Although you can specify as many groups of quantitative variables as you like, separated by commas, the simplest way to create a boxplot is to provide just one or two groups, as in the following two examples:

```
> par(mfrow=c(1,2))  # make 2 plots appear on the same 1 row
> boxplot(allscores$pre)
> boxplot(allscores$pre,allscores$post)
```

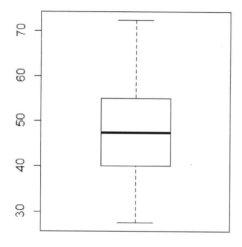 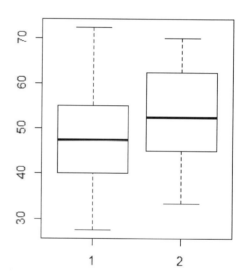

This is OK, but there are no labels on the first chart, and in the second, my pre-test scores are labeled "1" and my post-test scores are labeled "2". I'd like to change that. In addition, I'd really like to add titles (`main`) and make my y-axis range from zero to 100 so I can see how my distributions compare to all possible test scores (`ylim`). Ideally, I could add some color to the boxes to be able to tell them apart a little easier (`col`). Combining all of these possibilities, I can create a boxplot that tells the story of my data a little more effectively:

114

```
dev.off()  # reset graphics window so it stops plotting two per row

boxplot(allscores$pre,allscores$post,
        main="Statistics Pre-Test Score Distributions",
        xlab="Groups",ylab="Pre-Test Scores",
        names=c("Pre-Test","Post-Test"),
        ylim=c(0,100),col=c("lightgray","darkgray"))
```

This boxplot looks much better:

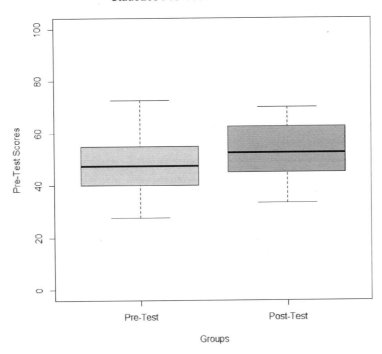

Statistics Pre-Test Score Distributions

Option 2: Give `boxplot` a Quantitative Variable Split by a Categorical Variable

Alternatively, we can ask `boxplot` to plot the distributions of score differences (`diff`), but separate them according to `group` (or any other categorical variable), using the data in `allscores`. Before plotting, we also need to tell R that there is an *order* to our groups.

115

Group 1 needs to appear before Group 2, and Group 2 needs to appear before Group 3. Let's start with that last task first:

```
allscores$group <- ordered(allscores$group,
    levels=c("1","2","3"))
```

Making the group variable an `ordered` factor ensures that the boxes will be displayed in the order we intend. Now, let's create a new chart with all three groups plus a title (`main`), labels (`xlab` and `ylab`), a vertical axis that ranges from -35 to +35 (`ylim`), and colors (`col`):

```
boxplot(diff~group,data=allscores,
    main="Score Improvements in Groups",
    xlab="Groups",ylab="Score Improvements",
    ylim=c(-35,35),col=c("white","lightgray","darkgray"))
```

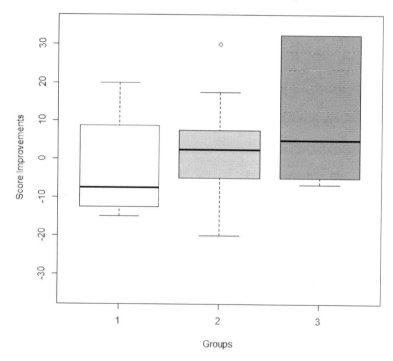

Score Improvements in Groups

You can also tilt the whole plot so that the distributions are oriented horizontally. This can be useful because it gives meaning to "skewed to the right" or "skewed to the left":

```
boxplot(diff~group,data=allscores,
        main="Score Improvements in Groups",
        xlab="Groups",ylab="Score Improvements",
        ylim=c(-35,35),col=c("white","lightgray","darkgray"),
        horizontal=TRUE)
```

Score Improvements in Groups

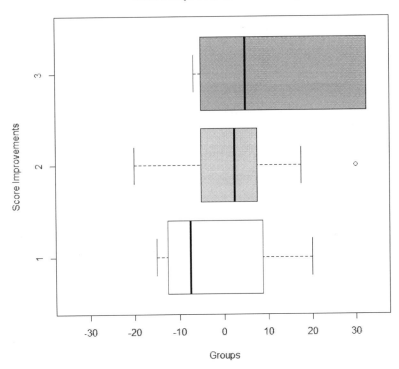

Our charts show that the median improvement for Group 1 isn't actually an improvement... test scores *decreased* overall, even though this distribution is skewed towards higher values. Fortunately, the median score differences are positive for Groups 2 and 3, and there were fewer sinking scores in Group 2 than Group 3. There is *much* more variation in Group 3, and the distribution is somewhat skewed towards higher scores. In Group 3, 50% of the measured improvements were between -4 and 32.5 (the interquartile range). By now, you're probably wondering what the difference is between Groups 1, 2, and 3... and the answer is *class **attendance***. The students in Group 1 were absent most frequently, and the students in Group 3 had fantastic attendance. Group 2 only had two or three absences. As you can see, it looks like Group 3 performed the best... but we would have to do a Two-Sample t-test or One-Way Analysis of Variance (ANOVA) to know for sure.

Other Resources:

- There are some more good examples of code that produces these boxplots at
  http://msemac.redwoods.edu/~darnold/math15/spring2013/R/Activities/BoxplotsII.html
- http://statsmethods.wordpress.com calls them "Side by Side Boxplots" and provides great examples. One of those can be found at
  https://statsmethods.wordpress.com/2013/05/10/617/
- One of my favorite sites, R Bloggers, has some great (and complex) examples at
  http://www.r-bloggers.com/box-plot-with-r-tutorial/

2.6 Pie and Waffle Charts

Objective

Sometimes, you need to be able to display data that clearly shows how *parts* of your data relate *all* of your data. In this chapter, you will learn how to create a pie chart in R from a collection of numbers that represent *frequencies* (or *counts*) of events or outcomes that fall into different categories. Unfortunately, it is really easy to create bad pie charts, so you'll also learn how to create a *waffle chart* as an alternative.

About Pie Charts

A pie chart is a circular plot divided into sectors, or *slices*. Each slice of the pie should be proportional to the amount of observations in that category.

- Again: It is really easy to create *bad pie charts*. Be careful.
- **The observations in all of the slices must add up to 100%.** If the percentages in all your slices add up to *less than* 100% or *greater than* 100%, you have a very bad (and misleading) pie chart. Pie charts are meant to display proportions of a whole, and nothing else.
- Good pie charts adhere to the **Area Principle.** This means that each slice of the pie has an area that corresponds to the percentage of the total number of observations that make up that slice. *If 25% of your observations fall into one category, that category should make up exactly a quarter of the pie.* No more, no less.
- Good pie charts are labeled nicely. I like when pie charts show very clearly both the *counts* of an item in a particular category, as well as the *percentage* of the total number of observations in that category.
- Membership into each category should be *mutually exclusive.* That is, you don't want an observation to appear in multiple slices.
- You will always have to consider whether a pie chart or bar chart is a better way to display your data. If you're trying to illustrate a collection of items that naturally add up to 100%, a pie chart may be appropriate. If there are multiple categories and it

may be difficult to distinguish which slice of your pie is bigger (e.g. one observation is 28% and another is 29%) a bar chart may be more appropriate. When small variations between categories should be communicated to your audience, bar charts are typically more effective than pie charts in presenting your data.

I've seen a lot of reports that use snazzy looking 3D pie charts (usually created in Excel), but usually, creating a 3D pie chart is a *bad idea*. That's because <u>a 3D pie chart will rarely, if ever, conform to the area principle.</u>

If You Counted Your Observations Already

To create a pie chart, all you need is a vector (or array) of numbers. Typically, this vector will contain *counts* of something in different categories. Here is an example of data generated by opening one package of regular M&Ms to investigate the distribution of colors, working with your data as a vector:

```
mm.counts <- c(12,6,8,10,6,7)

names(mm.counts) <- c("blue","brown","green","orange",
"red","yellow")
```

Note that even though I called my variable `mm.counts`, you can call your variable whatever you want. Just be sure to use that variable name in all future commands. For example, if you call your variable `snakes`, you want to make sure all future commands use that variable name, e.g. `names(snakes)`. Now, you can check to make sure that your data was entered correctly:

```
> mm.counts
  blue  brown  green orange    red yellow
    12      6      8     10      6      7
```

How many M&Ms total were in the bag? Looks like 49 of them:

```
> sum(mm.counts)
[1] 49
```

Now it's time to generate the pie chart. I usually *create the labels first*, which requires that I compute the percentages from the counts (to two decimal places), then plot the pie chart:

```
percents <- round(mm.counts/sum(mm.counts)*100,2)
my.labels <- paste(names(mm.counts)," ",percents,"%",sep="")
```

(Try typing `percents` and `my.labels` into your R session at the caret prompt just to make sure there is information stored in each of those variables before proceeding to `pie`.)

```
pie(mm.counts,labels=my.labels,main="My M&M Color
Distribution",col=names(mm.counts))
```

My M&M Color Distribution

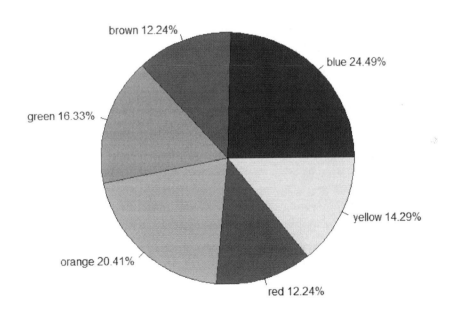

When I set the variable `my.labels`, the `paste` command lets me mash the names of each category together with the corresponding percents. I have to put the blank space in between the names and the percents to override the default behavior, which puts two or three spaces in between. Once the percents are calculated and the labels are set up, to produce the pie chart, all that's needed is the `pie` command. The `labels` option allows you to specify what words are attached to the slices of your pie. The `main` option lets you set a title. The `col` option allows you to specify what colors to use – in this case, we are telling pie to use the names of each category as colors. That will ensure that our slice representing the blue M&Ms is blue, the slice representing the brown M&Ms is brown, and so forth! The `sep=""` option makes sure there is ONLY one space between each of the labels. If you omit it, you will notice that the spacing looks a little too pronounced.

If You Need R to Count Observations for You

Alternatively, you may have your data in case format (meaning you haven't added up all the data, but you still want to create a pie chart). Let's use my CSV (comma-separated values) file containing data from 1922 individual M&M candies, which has been published to the web from Google Spreadsheets. Open it like this:

```
> mnms <- read.csv("https://docs.google.com/spreadsheets/d/e/2PACX-
1vQ9TZaUrqBc3lDW8OM7bliJa-
ECiQTkLu6An3kSmnp36rM11gEI6SZOOMHsFjojPL9xKvzLBzhI3S6G/pub?gid=0&single=true
&output=csv ",header=TRUE)
```

Now that you have the M&Ms data loaded into the `mnms` variable, you can ask R to tally up all of your color counts using `table`:

```
> table(mnms$color)

  BL  BR   G   O   R   Y
 311 240 375 420 319 257
```

Using this information, we can create `mm.counts` and set `names(mm.counts)`. However, we need to be careful setting the color names because B, BR, G, O, R and Y *will not be interpreted as colors by R* even though that's how we had our raw data coded. We have to use the full name of each color and make sure we specify them in the same order that they appeared in the `table` output:

```
mm.counts <- as.vector(table(mnms$color))
names(mm.counts) <- c("blue","brown","green","orange","red","yellow")
percents <- round(mm.counts/sum(mm.counts)*100,2)
my.labels <- paste(names(mm.counts)," ",percents,"%",sep="")
```

And finally, generate the pie chart:

```
pie(mm.counts,labels=my.labels,main="My M&M Color Distribution",
    col=names(mm.counts))
```

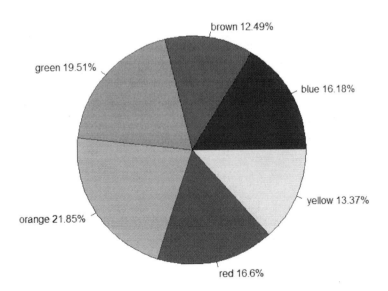

My M&M Color Distribution

There are many options that you can add to your pie chart, such as:

Option	What it does
`main`	Specify a main title to be displayed above chart
`xlab`	Specify text to display where x-axis should be
`col=`*type*`(length(mm.counts))` with n=a number between 1 and 10	Sets color palette for slices in pie chart (in place of *type* use `heat.colors(n)` for reds and oranges, `rainbow(n)` for ROYGBIV, `terrain.colors(n)` for earthy greens into grays, or `topo.colors(n)`
`labels=c("Label 1","Label 2")`	Sets up a list of names for each of the slices
`clockwise=TRUE`	Arranges the slices in a clockwise order, instead of counterclockwise, which is the default
`density=10`	Makes shaded slices instead of solid

If you don't want percents in the labels, just omit the `labels=my.labels` option from your R command.

Pie charts can be useful to visualize the distribution of proportions of an observation between categories, but only if 1) the slices adhere to the **Area Principle,** 2) the slices **add up to exactly 100%,** and 3) there **are no slight variations between slices** that are not easily distinguished on the pie chart. It is very easy to create bad, misleading pie charts. They should be used with care and caution.

Waffle Charts

Waffle charts are an alternative to pie charts that still enable you to communicate how parts of a data set are related to the whole. First, install it and wake it up:

```
install.packages("waffle",dependencies=TRUE)
library(waffle)
```

The `waffle` package consists of one command: `waffle`. To create a waffle chart, you need is a vector of values with a list of names attached to each value.

We will create a waffle chart from the same M&M data we just used to create the pie charts. Since there are so many M&Ms, let's make each square on the waffle equal 10 M&Ms, and set the waffle chart to 10 rows:

```
waffle(mm.counts/10, rows=10, colors=names(mm.counts),
       title="M&M Colors", xlab="1 square=10 M&Ms")
```

You can play around with changing the number of rows and the scaling factor to make your waffle chart even prettier.

M&M Colors

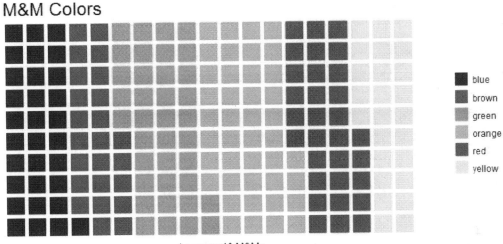

1 square=10 M&Ms

Other Resources:

- http://en.wikipedia.org/wiki/Pie_chart
- http://eagereyes.org/techniques/pie-charts contains a great example of a BAD pie chart – can you find it, and can you identify *why* it's so bad?
- http://blog.revolutionanalytics.com/2009/08/how-pie-charts-fail.html - How Pie Charts Fail
- Find out more about waffle charts and the `waffle` package at http://rud.is/b/2015/03/18/making-waffle-charts-in-r-with-the-new-waffle-package/

2.7 Pareto Charts

Objective

To create an ordered bar chart with cumulative frequencies (a Pareto Chart) from a collection of *frequencies* (or *counts*) of events or outcomes that fall into different categories. To produce the Pareto Chart, the `pareto.chart` function from the `qcc` package can take either 1) a vector (or array) of total counts, or 2) a contingency `table` containing counts.

Background

A Pareto Chart is a sorted bar chart that displays the *frequency (or count)* of occurrences that fall in different categories, from greatest frequency on the left to least frequency on the right, with an overlaid line chart that plots the *cumulative percentage* of occurrences. The vertical axis on the left of the chart shows *frequency (or count)*, and the vertical axis on the right of the chart shows the *cumulative percentage*.

- Primary types or sources of defects
- Most frequent reasons for customer complaints
- Amount of some variable (e.g. money, energy usage, time) that can be attributed to or classified according to a certain category

The Pareto Chart is used to separate the "vital few" from the "trivial many" using the Pareto principle (or "80/20 Rule"). According to this heuristic, in many systems, approximately 80% of consequences will result from only 20% of causes. The goal in Pareto analysis is to identify those critical concerns so they can be prioritized and addressed.

Option 1: If You Counted Your Observations Already

To create a Pareto Chart, you need a vector (or array) of numbers. Typically, this vector will contain *counts* of the defects (or causes for a certain outcome) in different categories. Here is an example of data generated by surveying 50 people to ask "What are the top 2 reasons you are late to work?" The available answers were 1) bad weather, 2) I overslept, 3) my alarm didn't go off, 4) I was confused by the time change to/from Daylight Savings Time, 5) traffic was bad, and 6) other.

You can work with your data as a vector like this:

```
defect.counts <- c(12,29,18,3,34,4)

names(defect.counts) <- c("Weather","Overslept", "Alarm Failure",
"Time Change","Traffic","Other")
```

Note that the *order of the counts* must be the same as the *order of the name labels*! For example, there were 12 reports of being late due to bad weather, 29 reports of being late due to oversleeping, 18 reports of being late due to alarm clock problems, and so on.

Next, install the qcc package (if you have not already) and create the Pareto Chart:

```
> install.packages("qcc",dependencies=TRUE)
> library("qcc")
> pareto.chart(defect.counts)
```

```
Pareto chart analysis for defect.counts
                 Frequency Cum.Freq.  Percentage Cum.Percent.
  Traffic             34        34         34          34
  Overslept           29        63         29          63
  Alarm Failure       18        81         18          81
  Weather             12        93         12          93
  Other                4        97          4          97
  Time Change          3       100          3         100
```

The chart that this code generates is shown at the top of page 129.

Option 2: If You Need R to Count Your Observations for You

More often, you will have a large file of observations in case format, and you'd like to create a Pareto Chart but you need R to tally up your observations. Since the pareto.chart function takes a contingency table as an argument, this method is also easy. The example below uses data from 1922 M&Ms published to the web as a CSV file. First, load the data into the variable `mnms`:

```
> mnms <- read.csv("https://docs.google.com/spreadsheets/d/e/2PACX-
1vQ9TZaUrqBc31DW8OM7bliJa-
ECiQTkLu6An3kSmnp36rM11gEI6SZOOMHsFjojPL9xKvzLBzhI3S6G/pub?gid=0&single=true
&output=csv ",header=TRUE)
```

And then, invoke the `pareto.chart` command on a contingency table for the variable you're interested in examining:

```
> pareto.chart(table(mnms$color))
```

```
Pareto chart analysis for table(mnms$color)
      Frequency  Cum.Freq.  Percentage Cum.Percent.
   O  420.00000  420.00000   21.85224    21.85224
   G  375.00000  795.00000   19.51093    41.36316
   R  319.00000 1114.00000   16.59729    57.96046
  BL  311.00000 1425.00000   16.18106    74.14152
   Y  257.00000 1682.00000   13.37149    87.51301
  BR  240.00000 1922.00000   12.48699   100.00000
```

The chart that this code generates is shown at the bottom of page 129. There are many options that you can add to your Pareto Chart, as well:

Option	What it does
`main`	Specify a main title to be displayed above your chart
`xlab`	Specify a label to display on the x-axis
`ylab`	Specify a label to display on the y-axis
`col=`*type*`(length(defects))`	Sets the color palette to use for the bars in the bar chart (in place of *type* use `heat.colors` for reds and oranges, `rainbow` for ROYGBIV, `terrain.colors` for earthy greens/grays, `topo.colors` for deep blues)
`cex.names=0.5`	Shrinks the fonts on the category labels (values in 0.5-0.8 range usually best)
`las=1`	Controls orientation of labels on axes (1=all horizontal, 2=all vertical, 3=perpendicular to axes)

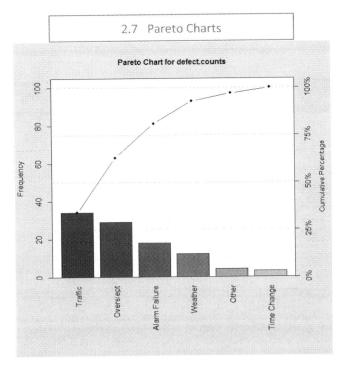

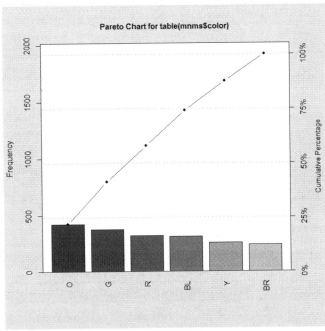

Here's what the options do in the example at the bottom of the page:

- First, `pareto.chart` creates a Pareto Chart out of the data provided
- Then `main` sets the main title of the graph to be "My Pareto Chart"
- The `xlab` option labels the x-axis with "Reasons"
- The `ylab` option labels the y-axis with "Frequency"
- The `cex` option shrinks the fonts on the x axis to 60% (or 0.6) of original size
- The `las=1` option orients the category labels horizontally instead of vertically
- And the color scheme is chosen from the `topo.colors` palette, with one color for each of the 6 categories in our original dataset

Next, I like to add a horizontal line at the cumulative percentage of 80%. I can place an A-B Line (which is just a funny way to say "line" in R) horizontally (that's what the `h=` is for) at the 80% mark on the rightmost scale. I choose red for the color, and set a line width of 4 with `lwd=4`. For a thinner line, I would pick `lwd=2`. Here is the code that does that; the chart appears on the next page.

```
> pareto.chart(defect.counts,main="My Pareto Chart",
xlab="Reasons",ylab="Frequency",cex.names=0.5,
las=1,col=topo.colors(6))
```

```
Pareto chart analysis for defect.counts
              Frequency Cum.Freq.  Percentage Cum.Percent.
  Traffic          34       34         34         34
  Overslept        29       63         29         63
  Alarm Failure    18       81         18         81
  Weather          12       93         12         93
  Other             4       97          4         97
  Time Change       3      100          3        100
```

```
> abline(h=0.8,lwd=4,col="red")
```

The Pareto Chart brings immediate focus to which reasons are part of the "vital few" and thus should receive attention first. By dropping a vertical line from where the horizontal line at 80% intersects the cumulative percentage line, this chart shows that traffic, oversleeping, and alarm failure are the most critical reasons that people in our survey are late for work. Our problem-solving activity might use the "5 Whys" technique or create an Ishikawa/ Fishbone Diagram next to determine the root causes of those reasons.

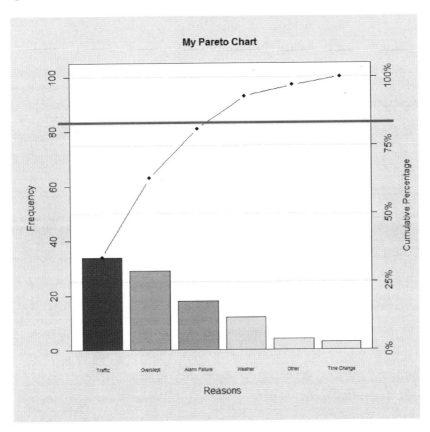

Other Resources:

- http://en.wikipedia.org/wiki/Pareto_chart
- http://en.wikipedia.org/wiki/Pareto_principle
- http://www.dmaictools.com/dmaic-analyze/pareto-chart
- http://stackoverflow.com/questions/1735540/creating-a-pareto-chart-with-ggplot2-and-r
- http://rgm2.lab.nig.ac.jp/RGM2/func.php?rd_id=qcc:pareto.chart

2.8 QQ Plots and Tests for Normality

Objective

QQ plots help you get a quick sense of whether or not the data you have collected are *normally distributed*. This is significant because if you *have* collected some data that are nearly normal (e.g. test scores, GPAs), you can use the normal model and z-scores to answer questions like "What percentage of students performed better or worse than me?" This chapter shows how to construct and interpret QQ plots, and do statistical tests to verify whether your data are normally distributed.

Background

The *normal probability plot*, also called a *QQ Plot* (short for quantile-quantile plot) gives you a quick visual diagnostic that reveals whether the data are distributed normally - or not. This plot compares each point in your data set to where those points *would be* in an idealized, perfectly normal distribution with the same mean and standard deviation as your data set (called the "theoretical quantiles"). As a result, we look for a *general pattern of linearity*.

- **If all of the data points lie along the y=x diagonal line or close to it, then each of the points in your sample are close to where they *would be* in a perfectly normal distribution** - suggesting that your distribution is nearly normal!
- If the distribution is skewed to the right (that is, if the tail of the distribution stretches to the right), the data points will track linearly above the line on the left-hand side of the QQ plot, and then will veer sharply upward on the right-hand side of the plot. (The plot looks sort of like a backwards C.)
- If the distribution is skewed to the left (that is, if the tail of the distribution stretches to the left), the data points will veer sharply upward on the left-hand side of the QQ plot, and then will track linearly above the line on the right-hand side of the plot. (The plot looks sort of like an upside-down C.)
- If the data are bimodal, you'll see an "S" pattern.

- When points fall above the line, it means "there are MORE data elements over here in this region than we would expect... for example, outliers."
- When points fall below the line, it means "there are FEWER data elements in this part of the distribution than we would expect."

Let's say I have a collection of all the wind speeds that were observed for a full year near where I live. I want to check and see if the distribution of wind speeds is normal. When I look at the distribution of speeds, it looks *kind of* normal, but it's skewed to the right, and I'd like to find out whether it *really is* normal. I've loaded my data into R using the `read.table` command, which creates a data frame, and `hist` to produce the histogram:

```
> wx <- read.table("https://raw.githubusercontent.com/NicoleRadziwill/Data-
for-R-Examples/master/kshd-2013.txt",header=TRUE)
> hist(wx$WDSP,col="gray",xlim=c(0,15))
```

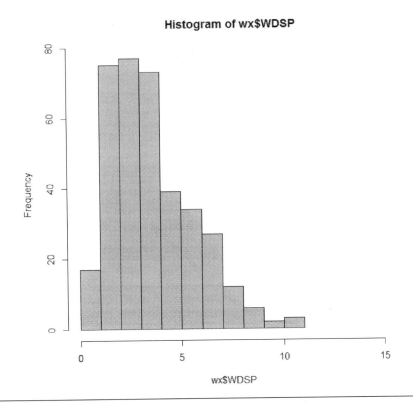

Histogram of wx$WDSP

Creating the `qqplot` with Base R

Are the wind speeds normally distributed? We create a `qqplot` to make this determination.
A `qqplot` can be generated from a variable in a data frame, OR just from data that you enter
directly into an array. Any of these will work (as long as you plug in *your* file names or data):

```
mydata <- read.table("your-data-file.txt or URL",header=FALSE)
mydata <- read.csv("your-data-file.csv or URL",header=FALSE)
mydata <- c(1,2,3,4,5,6,7,8,9)
```

The top one assumes that your data set is in a text file and the top row *does not* contain
variable names (if it docs, change `header` to equal `T` for true). The second one assumes that
your data set is in a CSV file and the top row *does not* contain variable names (if it does,
change `header` to equal `TRUE` for true). The third one *does not* use a data file, but instead
just assumes that you've entered all the data you collected yourself.

Our observational data is already in the wx data frame, in the variable WDSP. There are two
lines of code needed to create a `qqplot`. Remember that we're looking for a *general pattern
of linearity* which will suggest that the data arc normally distributed:

```
qqnorm(wx$WDSP)
qqline(wx$WDSP)
```

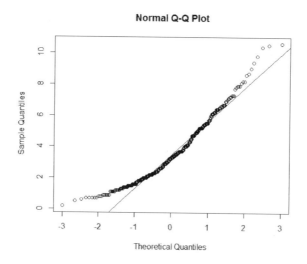

The qqplot shows that the data *do not appear to be normally distributed* – the pattern of points is bowed in the middle, and especially in the tails of the distribution, there are pretty clear deviations from normality. We sort of knew this in the beginning, though... the histogram shows us that the distribution is skewed to the right.

What would a qqplot look like if the wind speeds were *definitely* normally distributed? Let's simulate some data to compare to the wind speeds. We use the rnorm command to get **r**andom **norm**ally distributed numbers. Do this to get 365 simulated wind speeds (the same number of real wind speeds we have in our wx dataset) and generate the qqplot:

```
sim.speeds <- round(rnorm(365,mean=4,sd=2),2)
par(mfrow=c(1,2))
hist(sim.speeds,breaks=12,xlim=c(0,15),ylim=c(0,100),
     main="Simulated Wind Speeds - N(4,2)",col="gray")
qqnorm(sim.speeds)
qqline(sim.speeds)
```

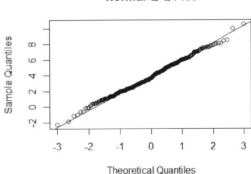

The question we have to ask when we're looking at the qqplot is this: "is there a *general pattern of linearity* evident in this plot?" In this case the answer is yes, because so many of the data points are close to the diagonal line. There are a few points at the far left and far right that deviate from the linear pattern, though. If you're concerned about this, you can take it one step further and perform a statistical test called the Shapiro Test to determine whether the data are normally distributed.

Shapiro Test

In this Shapiro test, the *null hypothesis* is that the data are distributed normally. The alternative hypothesis is that the data are *not* distributed normally. It is common to reject the null hypothesis that the data are normal when the p-value is less than 0.05, so we can see here that the simulated speeds *are* normally distributed (big p-value) but the observed wind speeds are *not* normally distributed (tiny p-value).

```
> shapiro.test(wx$WDSP)

        Shapiro-Wilk normality test

data:   wx$WDSP
W = 0.94234, p-value = 1.032e-10

> shapiro.test(sim.speeds)

        Shapiro-Wilk normality test

data:   sim.speeds
W = 0.99568, p-value = 0.4136
```

Creating the `qqplot` **with** `ggplot2`

There's another way to visualize the QQ plot that may help you conceptualize its meaning: plot the data distribution and the "perfect" distribution in the margins of the QQ plot. To do this, we use the snazzy graphics packages `ggplot2` and `ggExtra`. First, we have to install them and wake them up:

```
install.packages("ggplot2",dependencies=TRUE)
library(ggplot2)
install.packages("ggExtra",dependencies=TRUE)
library(ggExtra)
```

This process requires three steps: 1) create a data frame containing the simulated (nearly normal) wind speeds and the observed wind speeds, 2) create a `ggplot` object called `p`, and

3) construct the plot with a call to ggMarginal, which uses the ggplot object to create a plot with our original distributions visible. Notice how this generates a QQ Plot with the same bowed pattern we encountered earlier.

```
> df <- data.frame(sim.speeds,wx$WDSP)
> p <- ggplot(df,aes(x=sort(df$sim.speeds),y=sort(df$wx.WDSP))) +
geom_point()
> ggMarginal(p + theme_gray(), type="histogram", fill="steelblue",
col="darkblue")
```

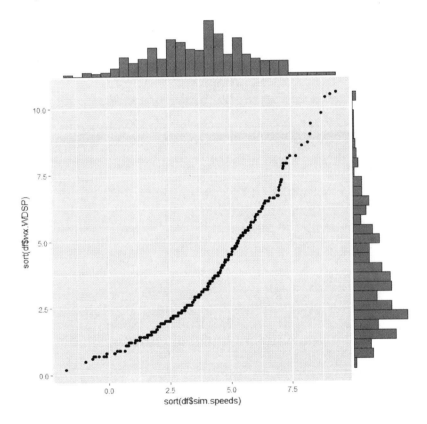

Finally, what would a plot like this look like if the data were *nearly perfectly* normally distributed? Based on what we know about the QQ plot concept, the line should be almost perfectly straight. Let's test that by generating and plotting simulated data:

```
> perfect.x <- rnorm(10000,mean=10,sd=2)
> perfect.y <- rnorm(10000,mean=10,sd=2)
> df <- data.frame(perfect.x,perfect.y)
> p <- ggplot(df,aes(x=sort(df$perfect.x),y=sort(df$perfect.y))) +
geom_point()
> ggMarginal(p + theme_gray(), type="histogram", fill="steelblue",
col="darkblue")
```

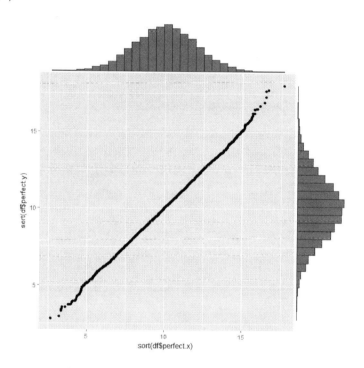

Other Resources:

- http://en.wikipedia.org/wiki/Normal_probability_plot
- http://www.pmean.com/09/NormalPlot.html -- this site provides many examples of patterns you could see in normal probability plots, what they indicate, and what you should be cautious about
- http://stat.ethz.ch/R-manual/R-patched/library/stats/html/shapiro.test.html - R documentation for the Shapiro-Wilk test of normality

2.9 Scatterplots, Covariance, and Correlation

Objective

To create scatterplots (scatterplot grids) from **two different continuous quantitative variables**, and evaluate the scattered-ness of the points using *covariance* and *correlation*.

Background

The simplest form of a scatterplot shows points scattered in two dimensions. The variable on the horizontal x-axis is the *independent variable*, or *predictor*, and the variable on the vertical y-axis is the *dependent variable*, or *response*. Each point is plotted as an (x, y) pair. Here is a scatterplot with average daily temperature as the independent variable, and dewpoint (the temperature below which water vapor starts to condense) as the dependent variable. Each point is plotted as a (TEMP, DEWP) pair. We will use the same weather data set that we did in the last chapter to produce this chart:

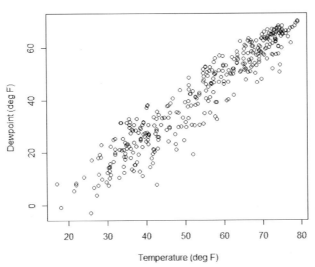

Dewpoint vs. Temperature

```
> shd.wx <-
read.table("https://raw.githubusercontent.com/NicoleRadziwill/Data-for-R-
Examples/master/kshd-2013.txt",header=TRUE)
> plot(shd.wx$TEMP,shd.wx$DEWP,main="Dewpoint vs. Temperature",
xlab="Temperature (deg F)",ylab="Dewpoint (deg F)")
```

You can get a sense of the scattered-ness of the points by finding their *covariance* and *correlation*, which describe the relationship between two continuous quantitative variables:

- Quantitative variables are positively related if, when one increases, the other one also increases.
- Quantitative variables are negatively related if, when one increases, the other one decreases.

Correlation is computed *using* the covariance, so they're closely related. Both covariance and correlation indicate whether variables are positively or negatively related to one another. Correlation, however, *also* tells you the *extent* to which the variables change with respect to one another.

Covariance is computed like this: for the first point in your data set, compute the difference between the x coordinate of that point and the *mean* of all the x coordinates, then do the same for y and multiply those two values together. Then, do that for all the rest of the points! Add up the n products that you computed. Then, when it's all added up, divide by one less than the total number of points (n - 1):

$$cov(x, y) = s_{xy} = \frac{\sum_{i=1}^{n}(x_i - \bar{x})(y_i - \bar{y})}{n - 1}$$

The **correlation coefficient**, r, can be calculated by taking the covariance of the data (s_{xy}) and dividing it by the standard deviation of the x coordinates (s_x) multiplied by the standard deviation of the y coordinates (s_y):

140

$$r = \frac{S_{xy}}{S_x S_y}$$

The correlation coefficient ranges between -1 (perfect negative correlation) and +1 (perfect positive correlation) EXCEPT if all the points lie perfectly along a horizontal or vertical line. Why? Because on a horizontal line, s_y is zero, and on a vertical line, s_x is zero. Since you can't divide by zero, you can't compute a correlation coefficient for points lying exactly on a horizontal or vertical line. Next, we will calculate covariance and correlation for a small data set, both analytically and by using the R commands that make it easy for us. First, we generate some data. I did this manually, because I wanted the scatterplot to have a correlation coefficient of nearly +1, because those are the prettiest (in my opinion):

```
> i <- 1:10
> xi <- c(1,2,3,4,5,6,7,8,9,10)
> yi <- c(.8,2.1,2.9,3.8,5.3,6,6.9,8.1,9.3,9.9)
> xbar <- mean(xi)
> ybar <- mean(yi)
> xi.minus.xbar <- xi - xbar
> yi.minus.ybar <- yi - ybar
> xdiff.x.ydiff <- xi.minus.xbar * yi.minus.ybar
```

Here is the scatterplot of our (x_i, y_i) points, generated with `plot(xi,yi)`:

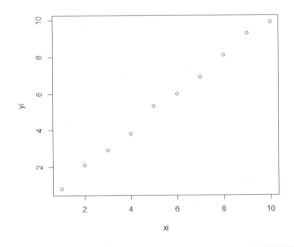

Now it's time to compute the covariance and correlation coefficient, which we can do easily because we've already computed the difference between each x coordinate and the mean of the x's (xi.minus.xbar) as well as the difference between each x coordinate and the mean of the y's (yi.minus.ybar). For each point i, we multiplied these two values together to get xdiff.x.ydiff. Now let's look at them in a data frame:

```
> calc.df <- cbind(i,xi,yi,xi.minus.xbar,yi.minus.ybar,xdiff.x.ydiff)
> calc.df
        i xi   yi xi.minus.xbar yi.minus.ybar xdiff.x.ydiff
 [1,]   1  1 0.8         -4.5         -4.71        21.195
 [2,]   2  2 2.1         -3.5         -3.41        11.935
 [3,]   3  3 2.9         -2.5         -2.61         6.525
 [4,]   4  4 3.8         -1.5         -1.71         2.565
 [5,]   5  5 5.3         -0.5         -0.21         0.105
 [6,]   6  6 6.0          0.5          0.49         0.245
 [7,]   7  7 6.9          1.5          1.39         2.085
 [8,]   8  8 8.1          2.5          2.59         6.475
 [9,]   9  9 9.3          3.5          3.79        13.265
[10,]  10 10 9.9          4.5          4.39        19.755
```

To find the covariance, we can do this (the expression on the far right is the R code that we will use with our data to perform the calculation):

$$cov(x, y) = s_{xy} = \frac{\sum_{i=1}^{n}(x_i - \bar{x})(y_i - \bar{y})}{n - 1}$$

Doing it in R, we get:

```
> sum(xdiff.x.ydiff)/9
[1] 9.35
```

But there's an easier way! R will generate the covariance just with the cov command. All we have to do is supply it with the vectors containing the original coordinates for our points:

```
> cov(xi,yi)
[1] 9.35
```

142

You can see that we got the same values when we used the equation, and calculated each of the pieces of the covariance, as we did when we just asked R to compute it for us from our data. Now that we have the covariance, it is also easy to compute the correlation coefficient. We just divide the covariance by the standard deviations in x and in y. Similar to the covariance, R also provides an easy way to compute the correlation coefficient straight from your data using the `cor` command. The results you get from the manual calculation, and from asking R to do it for you, will be the same:

```
> cov(xi,yi)/(sd(xi)*sd(yi))
[1] 0.9983961
> cor(xi,yi)
[1] 0.9983961
```

Data Format

For the rest of the examples in this chapter, we'll use the data frame of daily weather observations reported throughout 2013 from the Shenandoah Valley Airport (SHD) near Harrisonburg, Virginia. You may already have it loaded as `shd.wx`; if not, do this:

```
> shd.wx <-
read.table("https://raw.githubusercontent.com/NicoleRadziwill/Data-for-R-
Examples/master/kshd-2013.txt",header=TRUE)
```

Each column contains one variable, and there are 365 rows (one for each day of the year). They are arranged in order, with January 1st on the 1st row, and December 31st on the last.

```
> head(shd.wx)
  YEARMODA TEMP DEWP   STP VISIB WDSP MXSPD  MAX  MIN PRCP
1 20130101 43.3 25.8 971.2  10.0  5.4   8.9 47.8 37.8    0
2 20130102 38.5 29.4 973.3  10.0  1.5   5.1 42.3 32.0    0
3 20130103 32.0 19.2 978.0  10.0  1.4   7.0 42.6 21.9    0
4 20130104 34.6 17.4 978.5  10.0  3.6   8.9 45.9 26.2    0
5 20130105 36.0 17.9 981.0  10.0  3.4   8.0 48.2 25.9    0
6 20130106 40.6 26.9 976.8   9.9  3.8   9.9 47.1 31.1   NA
```

I want to check the **str**ucture of my data (using `str`) to make sure that I have some quantitative variables to work with (since scatterplots require quantitative variables).

Indeed, there are many variables that are of integer (`int`) and number (`num`) type:

```
> str(shd.wx)
'data.frame':   365 obs. of  10 variables:
 $ YEARMODA: int   20130101 20130102 20130103 20130104 20130105 20130106
20130107 20130108 20130109 20130110 ...
 $ TEMP    : num   43.3 38.5 32 34.6 36 40.6 40.6 36.9 39.1 46.1 ...
 $ DEWP    : num   25.8 29.4 19.2 17.4 17.9 26.9 26.1 23.8 30.5 29.6 ...
 $ STP     : num   971 973 978 978 981 ...
 $ VISIB   : num   10 10 10 10 10 9.9 10 10 10 10 ...
 $ WDSP    : num   5.4 1.5 1.4 3.6 3.4 3.8 2.2 3 2.9 2 ...
 $ MXSPD   : num   8.9 5.1 7 8.9 8 9.9 12 13 13 8.9 ...
 $ MAX     : num   47.8 42.3 42.6 45.9 48.2 47.1 44.8 56.3 62.8 57.2 ...
 $ MIN     : num   37.8 32 21.9 26.2 25.9 31.1 30.7 24.1 25.3 29.3 ...
 $ PRCP    : num   0 0 0 0 0 NA 0 0 0 0 ...
```

Let's also add a categorical variable, `season`, to enhance our scatterplot later by making the points for each season look different. Using equinoxes and solstices and season boundaries, and knowing which seasons correspond to which rows of `shd.wx`, I did it like this:

```
season <- rep(NA,365)
season[1:79] <- "winter"
season[80:171] <- "spring"
season[172:263] <- "summer"
season[264:354] <- "fall"
season[355:365] <- "winter"
```

Now, armed with a 365-element vector called season that contains season names, I added it onto the end of the `shd.wx` data frame using the `cbind` ("**c**olumn **bind**") command:

```
> shd.wx <- cbind(shd.wx,season)
> head(shd.wx)
  YEARMODA TEMP DEWP   STP VISIB WDSP MXSPD  MAX  MIN PRCP season
1 20130101 43.3 25.8 971.2  10.0  5.4   8.9 47.8 37.8    0 winter
2 20130102 38.5 29.4 973.3  10.0  1.5   5.1 42.3 32.0    0 winter
3 20130103 32.0 19.2 978.0  10.0  1.4   7.0 42.6 21.9    0 winter
4 20130104 34.6 17.4 978.5  10.0  3.6   8.9 45.9 26.2    0 winter
5 20130105 36.0 17.9 981.0  10.0  3.4   8.0 48.2 25.9    0 winter
6 20130106 40.6 26.9 976.8   9.9  3.8   9.9 47.1 31.1   NA winter
```

Preparing Your Scatterplots

You can generate a scatterplot to show the relationship between *any two quantitative variables*. The simplest plot is generated by typing `plot(x,y)`, like we did at the beginning of the chapter, where `x` and `y` represent the vectors of x coordinates and y coordinates for your points. In the next example, we will create a scatterplot of dewpoint versus temperature, color code each point by season, and then add a legend. To create the first scatterplot, we will set our **p**lot **ch**aracter (`pch`) based on the season (`shd.wx$season`) variable by first converting it to an integer (using `as.integer`). We will also specify a title using `main`, and labels for the x-axis (`xlab`) and y-axis (`ylab`):

```
> plot(shd.wx$TEMP,shd.wx$DEWP,pch=as.integer(shd.wx$season),
col=as.integer(shd.wx$season),xlab="Average Daily Temperature",
ylab="Dewpoint",main="Dewpoint vs. Temperature (SHD 2013)")
> legend("bottomright",inset=c(0.02,0.02),legend=c("fall","spring",
"summer","winter"),pch=c(1:4),col=palette()[1:4])
```

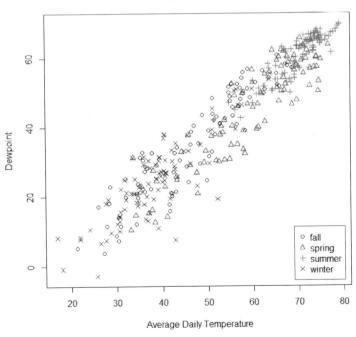

(This looks nice, but here's the problem: *which plot character corresponds to which season?* We need to know this in order to create a legend that's accurate. To double check, just type `as.integer(shd.wx$season)` into the R console, and you should be able to match up the appropriate correspondence. It can be tricky though, so be careful!)

If I wanted to change the colors, I'd do it in this very inelegant (but easy to understand) way, by adding a new column that contained the colors I want to plot. I'll use gray for winter, green for spring, red for summer, and orange for fall:

```
season.color <- rep(NA,365)
season.color[1:79] <- "gray"
season.color[80:171] <- "green"
season.color[172:263] <- "red"
season.color[264:354] <- "orange"
season.color[355:365] <- "gray"
shd.wx <- cbind(shd.wx,season.color)
```

I'll plot all points as plot character 15 (the solid square). Notice that I'm telling the `plot` command to use the color that is specified for each individual point in the `season.color` variable, and I have to tell R specifically that these are *names*, not numbers, to be plotted correctly. That's why I use the `as.character` modifier to the `season.color` variable.

The legend is plotted with the second line, using the command of the same name. You can tell R to place the legend in the `topright`, `bottomright`, `topleft`, or `bottomleft`, and since I don't like my legends to be flush with the edges of the scatterplot, I use the `inset` argument to create a little space.

The most important thing to remember with the `legend` command is that the descriptors that you use in the `legend` argument *must be in the same order* as the colors that you specify in the `col` argument. So we can tell just by reading the code below that `fall` corresponds to `orange`, `spring` corresponds to `green`, `summer` corresponds to `red`, and `winter` corresponds to `gray`.

(Even if you can't see the colors in the black and white version of this book, you should still be able to reproduce the code and try it for yourself.)

```
> plot(shd.wx$TEMP,shd.wx$DEWP,col=as.character(shd.wx$season.color),
pch=15,xlab="Average Daily Temperature",ylab="Dewpoint",
main="Dewpoint vs. Temperature (SHD 2013)")
> legend("bottomright",inset=c(0.02,0.02),legend=c("fall","spring",
"summer","winter"),pch=15,col=c("orange","green","red","gray"))
```

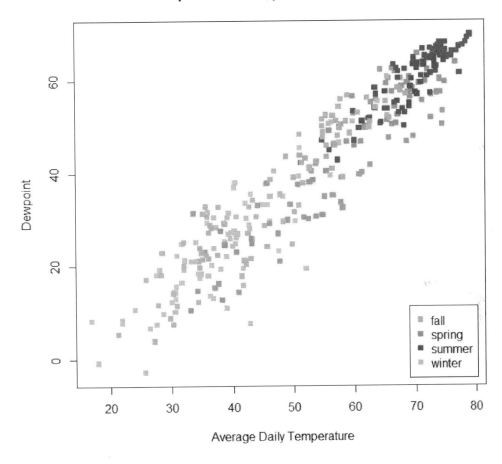

Even though I only used a few of the available plot characters in the examples above, there are many more you can choose from. Just set `pch` to the number below the symbol to use that symbol.

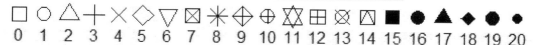

The plot characters above were generated using this code:

```
> plot.new()
> par(usr=c(-1,21,0,1))
> for (n in 0:20) { points(n, .5, pch=n, cex=2); text(n, .45, n) }
> box()
```

Here's a summary of some options that you can add to your scatterplot:

Option to plot	What it does
main	Specify a main title to be displayed above chart
xlab	Specify text to display where x-axis should be
ylab	Specify text to display where y-axis should be
pch=15	Selects the "plot character" - see the image below for a picture of pch 0 through 20
cex=2	Controls the size of the plot character. Values larger than 1 make each point bigger than the default, whereas values smaller than 1 make each point smaller than the default.

The Scatterplot Matrix

In the examples above, we only examined the relationship between two of the quantitative variables in the data set: average daily temperature and dewpoint. But what if we're just in the beginning stages of exploring our dataset, and we want to find out quickly whether there are relationships between the variables that we should examine further? Fortunately, there is a command called pairs which we can use to generate pairs of scatterplots. Using pairs can get unwieldy if you have lots of variables, so let's only plot pairs of scatterplots for all row, but only the first 10 columns, in shd.wx:

```
pairs(shd.wx[,1:10])
```

From just a quick glance, some patterns are evident in the `pairs` display. First, there is a clear linear relationship between average daily temperature and dewpoint, average daily temperature and maximum (`MAX`) and minimum (`MIN`) temperatures, and dewpoint and maximum and minimum temperatures. There is also an interesting relationship between visibility (`VISIB`) and wind speed (`WDSP`): as wind speed gets higher, the visibilities tend to increase, although low wind speeds are associated with the full range of visibilities. Also, there is a clear nonlinear relationship between day (`YEARMODA`) and average daily temperature. Temperatures are higher in the middle of the data set (during the days that correspond to summer) and they are lower at the beginning and end of the data set (during the days that correspond to winter).

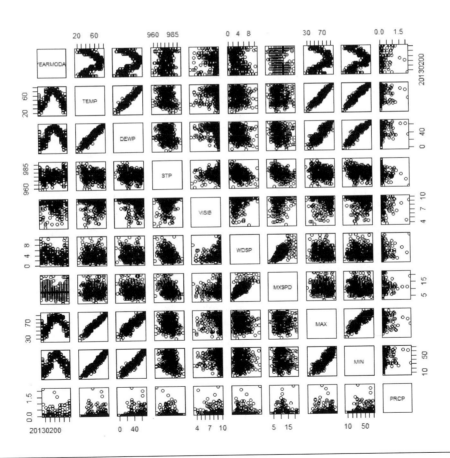

Other Resources:

- The "official" name for the correlation coefficient we talked about in this chapter is the Pearson Product-Moment Correlation Coefficient. There is a great Wikipedia page on the correlation coefficient at http://en.wikipedia.org/wiki/Pearson_product-moment_correlation_coefficient, which also includes this fantastic image below showing the wide variety of scatterplot shapes that are associated with different scatterplot shapes:

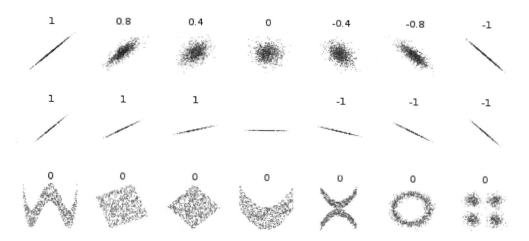

- Why is the correlation coefficient always between -1 and +1? Stackexchange has a nice little proof of why this will always be the case (calculus required): http://math.stackexchange.com/questions/564751/how-can-i-simply-prove-that-the-pearson-correlation-coefficient-is-between-1-an
- Virtual Nerd has a nice video about how to make scatterplots manually: http://www.virtualnerd.com/pre-algebra/linear-functions-graphing/scatter-plot-best-fit-lines/scatter-plots-predictions/scatter-plot-example
- You can also create prettier scatterplot matrices using functions in the lattice and car packages in R. Details about how to use those can be found here: http://www.statmethods.net/graphs/scatterplot.html

2.10 Contingency Tables/Marginal & Conditional Distributions

Objective

Contingency tables display the *frequencies* and *relative frequencies* of observations, which are classified according to **two categorical variables**. The elements of one category are displayed across the columns; the elements of the other category are displayed over the rows. This chapter shows you how to draw simple contingency tables, *and* more complex (beautiful) contingency tables! Fortunately, it is just as easy to create both kinds in R.

Simple Contingency Tables with `table`

There is already a built-in function in base R to construct contingency tables. To see this in action, let's load in some M&M data. I have a CSV (comma-separated values) file containing data about 1922 individual M&M candies:

```
> mnms <- read.csv("https://docs.google.com/spreadsheets/d/e/2PACX-
1vQ9TZaUrqBc3lDW8OM7bliJa-
ECiQTkLu6An3kSmnp36rM11gEI6SZOOMHsFjojPL9xKvzLBzhI3S6G/pub?gid=0&single=true
&output=csv ",header=TRUE)
```

Check to make sure the data has loaded correctly, using the `head` command:

```
> head(mnms)
  student id color defect full.bag.weight empty.bag.weight total.number
1  alborb  1    R     N        49.36            1.02            55
2  alborb  2    BR    L        49.36            1.02            55
3  alborb  3    G     N        49.36            1.02            55
4  alborb  4    R     C        49.36            1.02            55
5  alborb  5    R     N        49.36            1.02            55
6  alborb  6    BL    N        49.36            1.02            55
```

Now, you can create a contingency table using the `table` command. The first argument points to the categorical variable that will appear over the *rows*, and the second argument indicates which categorical variable you want to span the *columns*:

```
> table(mnms$color,mnms$defect)

      C    L   M    N
BL   10   96   7  198
BR    7   82   7  144
G    10  115  13  237
O    26  115  11  268
R    22   72  18  207
Y    17   76   7  157
```

More Fancy Contingency Tables with `CrossTable`

Since your data is already loaded into R and stored in the `mnms` object, it is easy to make an *even more beautiful* contingency table by using `CrossTable` in the `gmodels` package. Before you start, be sure to install the new package using `install.packages("gmodels")` and call its functions into active memory using `library(gmodels)`.

The simplest contingency table is actually prepared using lots of arguments to `CrossTable`, where we have to turn off several of the features (don't worry, we'll turn them on later in this chapter). In contrast to the simple display produced by `table`, this one contains the row totals in the rightmost margin, and the column totals on the bottom margin.

```
> CrossTable(mnms$color, mnms$defect, prop.t=FALSE, prop.r=FALSE,
prop.c=FALSE, prop.chisq=FALSE, chisq=FALSE)


   Cell Contents
|-----------------------|
|                     N |
|-----------------------|


Total Observations in Table:   1245

              | mnms$defect
mnms$color  |          C |          L |          M |          N | Row Total |
------------|-----------|-----------|-----------|-----------|-----------|
          B |         83 |         20 |         21 |        224 |        348 |
------------|-----------|-----------|-----------|-----------|-----------|
         BR |         39 |         13 |         14 |         89 |        155 |
```

```
-------------|----------|----------|----------|----------|----------|
         G |    36   |    13   |     6   |    97   |   152   |
-------------|----------|----------|----------|----------|----------|
         O |    88   |    25   |    17   |   185   |   315   |
-------------|----------|----------|----------|----------|----------|
         R |    44   |     5   |     5   |    80   |   134   |
-------------|----------|----------|----------|----------|----------|
         Y |    38   |    11   |     8   |    84   |   141   |
-------------|----------|----------|----------|----------|----------|
Column Total |   328   |    87   |    71   |   759   |  1245   |
-------------|----------|----------|----------|----------|----------|
```

If you store the output from `CrossTable` to a variable (I'll call it `m`) you can directly access the frequencies (with `m$t`), row proportions (with `m$prop.row`), column proportions (with `m$prop.col`), and table proportions (with `m$prop.tbl`). Each row adds up to 100% with `m$prop.row`, and each column adds up to 100% with `m$prop.col`:

```
> m <- CrossTable(mnms$color, mnms$defect, prop.t=FALSE, prop.r=FALSE,
prop.c=FALSE, prop.chisq=FALSE, chisq=FALSE)
> m$prop.row
     y
x           C          L          M          N
  B   0.23850575 0.05747126 0.06034483 0.64367816
  BR  0.25161290 0.08387097 0.09032258 0.57419355
  G   0.23684211 0.08552632 0.03947368 0.63815789
  O   0.27936508 0.07936508 0.05396825 0.58730159
  R   0.32835821 0.03731343 0.03731343 0.59701493
  Y   0.26950355 0.07801418 0.05673759 0.59574468
> m$prop.col
     y
x           C          L          M          N
  B   0.25304878 0.22988506 0.29577465 0.29512516
  BR  0.11890244 0.14942529 0.19718310 0.11725955
  G   0.10975610 0.14942529 0.08450704 0.12779974
  O   0.26829268 0.28735632 0.23943662 0.24374177
  R   0.13414634 0.05747126 0.07042254 0.10540184
  Y   0.11585366 0.12643678 0.11267606 0.11067194
```

Here's what the table looks like with several other options included:

```
> CrossTable(mnms$color, mnms$defect, prop.t=TRUE, prop.r=TRUE, prop.c=TRUE,
prop.chisq=TRUE, chisq=FALSE)
```

```
Cell Contents
|-----------------------|
|                     N |
| Chi-square contribution |
|           N / Row Total |
|           N / Col Total |
|         N / Table Total |
|-----------------------|
```

Total Observations in Table: 1245

mnms$color	mnms$defect C	L	M	N	Row Total
B	83	20	21	224	348
	0.822	0.767	0.067	0.661	
	0.239	0.057	0.060	0.644	0.280
	0.253	0.230	0.296	0.295	
	0.067	0.016	0.017	0.180	
BR	39	13	14	89	155
	0.082	0.434	3.013	0.319	
	0.252	0.084	0.090	0.574	0.124
	0.119	0.149	0.197	0.117	
	0.031	0.010	0.011	0.071	
G	36	13	6	97	152
	0.409	0.533	0.821	0.203	
	0.237	0.086	0.039	0.638	0.122
	0.110	0.149	0.085	0.128	
	0.029	0.010	0.005	0.078	
O	88	25	17	185	315
	0.303	0.406	0.052	0.258	
	0.279	0.079	0.054	0.587	0.253
	0.268	0.287	0.239	0.244	
	0.071	0.020	0.014	0.149	
R	44	5	5	80	134
	2.143	2.034	0.913	0.035	
	0.328	0.037	0.037	0.597	0.108
	0.134	0.057	0.070	0.105	
	0.035	0.004	0.004	0.064	
Y	38	11	8	84	141
	0.020	0.134	0.000	0.045	
	0.270	0.078	0.057	0.596	0.113
	0.116	0.126	0.113	0.111	
	0.031	0.009	0.006	0.067	
Column Total	328	87	71	759	1245
	0.263	0.070	0.057	0.610	

If you set the `chisq` argument to TRUE, this will also appear below your table:

```
Statistics for All Table Factors


Pearson's Chi-squared test
------------------------------------------------------------
Chi^2 =  14.47214     d.f. =  15     p =  0.4900641
```

With a p-value that's so high (anything above 0.05 is considered "high"), we fail to reject the null hypothesis of the Chi-square test of independence, which is that the two categorical variables are independent of one another. There is no relationship between the color of the M&M, and whether or not it has defects, based on our current data set.

Here is a summary of some arguments you can pass to `CrossTable`:

Aspect of Experiment	Description
prop.t	When set to TRUE, the number of observations in each cell divided by the total number of observations in the entire contingency table will be reported.
prop.r	When set to TRUE, the number of observations in each cell divided by the total number of observations in the row will be reported.
prop.c	When set to TRUE, the number of observations in each cell divided by the total number of observations in the column will be reported.
chisq	When set to TRUE, a Chi-square test of independence will be conducted on your data, and the value of the test statistic χ^2 and the P-Value will be reported.
prop.chisq	When set to TRUE, the contribution of each cell to the test statistic χ^2 will be reported. (Add up all of these values within the contingency table, and you should get the value of the reported χ^2).
expected	When set to TRUE, this value will include the frequencies that each cell will have IF the two categorical variables are independent of one another. (This is extremely useful if you are performing a Chi-square test of independence analytically, using the formula for computing χ^2).

Marginal Distributions

Embedded within each contingency table, there are exactly two *marginal* distributions: one distribution for each of the total observed frequencies for each of the two categorical variables. They are called marginal distributions because they include the totals displayed on the edges (or *margins*) of the contingency table: the row totals on the rightmost margin, and the column totals on the bottom margin. With the M&M data, that means:

- There is one marginal distribution of colors. We can produce a barplot that shows us the frequencies or relative frequencies of all the colors that we observed - not taking defects into consideration at all.
- There is one marginal distribution of defects. We can produce a barplot that shows us the frequencies or relative frequencies of all the defects that we observed - not taking color into consideration at all.

Visualizing marginal distributions in R is simple too:

```
> count.colors <- table(mnms$color); count.defects <- table(mnms$defect)
> par(mfrow=c(1,2))
> barplot(count.colors,main="Marginal Distribution of Colors")
> barplot(count.defects,main="Marginal Distribution of Defects")
```

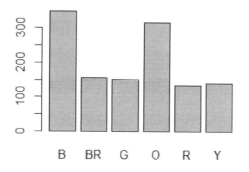

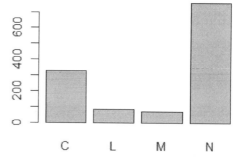

Conditional Distributions

Embedded within each contingency table, there are also *many conditional distributions*: that is, the distribution of how frequently one of the categorical variables is observed *given that* you specifically set the other categorical variable to assume one specific value. Because you're setting a *condition* that one of the categorical variables is taking on a specific value, each of the distributions is called a *conditional* distribution. <u>Here are all of the conditional distributions you can produce from the M&M data:</u>

- The distribution of colors for all M&Ms that are **C**hipped or Cracked
- The distribution of colors for all M&Ms that have **L**etter defects
- The distribution of colors for all M&Ms that have **M**ultiple defects
- The distribution of colors for all M&Ms that have **N**o defects
- The distribution of defects over all the **B**lue M&Ms
- The distribution of defects over all the **BR**own M&Ms
- The distribution of defects over all the **G**reen M&Ms
- The distribution of defects over all the **O**range M&Ms
- The distribution of defects over all the **R**ed M&Ms
- The distribution of defects over all the **Y**ellow M&Ms

It's easy to visualize one of these conditional distributions by pulling out a subset of the mnms data frame that matches the desired condition, and then plotting the variable of interest. For example, on the left we see the *distribution of defects for all green M&Ms*, and on the right, we see the *distribution of colors for all chipped or cracked M&Ms*:

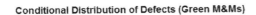

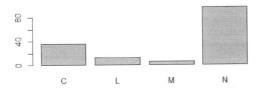
Conditional Distribution of Defects (Green M&Ms)

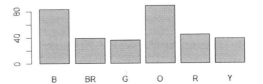
Conditional Distribution of Colors (Chipped/Cracked)

157

Here is the code that produced the barplots above:

```
> defects.for.greens <- table(mnms[mnms$color=="G",]$defect)
> colors.for.chippedorcracked <- table(mnms[mnms$defect=="C",]$color)
> par(mfrow=c(1,2))
> barplot(defects.for.greens,main="Conditional Distribution of Defects
(Green M&Ms)")
> barplot(colors.for.chippedorcracked,main="Conditional Distribution of
Colors (Chipped/Cracked)")
```

Let's examine the line of code that pulls out the distribution of defects for the condition that the M&Ms are green:

```
defects.for.greens <- table(mnms[mnms$color=="G",]$defect)
```

There are three things going on here, and each of them is underlined separately. The element in the middle pulls out all the rows where `color` is equal to G. Since there is nothing after the comma, that means that when we are pulling out the rows that are equal to G, we are also pulling out *all* of the columns. The `$defect` portion at the end tells R that we're *really* only interested in the values contained within the `defect` column. And finally, the `table` command adds them all up, to give us only the total number of defects in each category for all of those green M&Ms.

Now What?

- This resource shows how to make publication-quality contingency tables:
  https://cran.r-project.org/web/packages/expss/vignettes/TablesWithLabelsInR.html
- Find out more information about `CrossTable` at http://www.inside-r.org/node/89238
- I also found this fantastic paper that describes how one researcher is exploring alternative (and hopefully better!) ways to visualize categorical data. In addition to being an interesting read, it demonstrates alternatives like the mosaic:
  http://www.datavis.ca/papers/koln/kolnpapr.pdf
- The `vcd` and `vcdExtra` packages provide more sophisticated ways to display categorical data: http://www.datavis.ca/courses/VCD/vcd-tutorial.pdf

SECTION 3: FOUNDATIONS FOR YOUR RESEARCH

- The Difference Between Experiments and Observational Studies
- A 6+ Methodology for Planning and Answering Research Questions
- The Central Limit Theorem (and why it's important)
- Samples, Error, and P-Values... and a Word of Caution!

3.1 Randomness, Sampling, and Sampling Strategies

Objective

One of the most fundamental aspects of using inferential statistics to draw conclusions about a population is the concept of *randomness*: to get valid results; you need to make sure you have a *random* sample of cases that's *representative* of the population you want to study. In this chapter, you will learn:

- What randomness really is
- How probability is related to randomness
- The difference between a *sample* and a *population*
- The difference between *sample statistics* and *population parameters*
- What it means to generate a *representative* sample
- Some techniques for collecting random, representative samples, and (hopefully) avoiding *bias*

What is Randomness?

What does it mean to be *random*? When I ask this question in class, I typically hear things like *when something is haphazard*, or *when something is unplanned or unexpected*, or *when you do something without thinking about it*, or crazy and erratic behavior. When you think about randomness this way, it's kind of overwhelming. How can you possibly get a handle on a process that's so wild and unpredictable?

But there's a more precise definition of randomness in statistics. Because although random events are *individually* not predictable, it's often possible to determine what will happen collectively over many events. For example, every time you roll a fair, six-sided die, you will get a 1, 2, 3, 4, 5, or 6. *Each roll is random, because you don't know what you're going to get from roll to roll!* But if you roll that die a hundred times or a thousand times, you'll see that the distribution of possible values is uniform; that is, you will roll each number with approximately the same frequency. Don't believe me? Let's try it. You don't have to sit around rolling a die a zillion times though... we can make R do it (using a process called *simulation*).

People are NOT good random number generators. Here's an interesting exercise you can do if you have a group of people available: have them all close their eyes, and select a number from 1 to 4 at random. Tally up the number of people who choose 1, all the people who choose 2, and so on. Then create a bar plot showing the distribution of people who chose each category. (But before you read any further... COLLECT THIS DATA WITH A GROUP OF PEOPLE!! I want you to collect your own data so you can see what happens.)

Let's imagine that we did this in a room with 26 students. Only 2 picked a "1", 5 students picked a "2", another 13 selected "3", and the remaining 6 students chose "4" as their random number. Here's how you can look at the distribution in R. (If you're plotting your data, be sure to change the numbers in the first line.)

```
choices <- c(2,5,13,6)
barplot(choices, ylab="Frequency", names.arg=c(1,2,3,4))
```

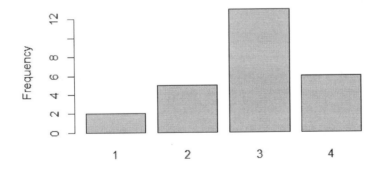

What you'll notice is that *the most frequent value people tend to choose* is a 3. People are hard-wired to favor the numbers slightly above the middle of the possible values, when they're "randomly" selecting on the interval from 1 to 4! One guy decided he was going to test this concept, but instead let people pick between 1 and 20, just to see if the "favoritism to the right of middle" pattern was consistent. What happened? You can see his results at http://scienceblogs.com/cognitivedaily/2007/02/05/is-17-the-most-random-number/.

I've been doing this test in all of my classes for the past several years, and I think there's only been one time that people did not overwhelmingly "randomly" choose the 3. People are just notoriously bad at generating random numbers, so if you really want to randomize something, you're going to have to enlist the help of a Table of Random Numbers (there are *many* of these online... just Google for one) or a computer program that uses techniques like the Linear Congruential Generator (LCG).

I didn't realize that having an understanding of randomness like this, and knowing that people are very bad random number selectors, could ever have practical application in my life until last year. We were on our way to Burning Man in Nevada, which is an annual gathering of about 70,000 people who get together to celebrate art, technology, and freedom of expression. Everyone drives in on the same two-lane road, but once you get to the Black Rock Desert (the site where everyone camps), traffic is funneled into 12 lanes. Morgan was driving, and traffic (at that point) was moving pretty quickly, but we knew that was probably going to be short lived - the year before, we'd sat in the entry line for about 12 hours. He said "Quick, you know about statistics. Which lane should I get in?"

It was then that I remembered how bad people are at randomly selecting stuff. "Go all the way to the left!! Get in Lane 1!" I figured that everyone would be favoring lanes 6 through 9, so if we went all the way to the left, we'd have the shortest line.

As soon as we sorted ourselves into the 12 lanes, traffic slowed down to a halt. A couple hours later, still in stopped traffic, there was a huge rain and hail storm that lasted for several more hours. The Black Rock Desert is actually the dry lake bed from the ancient Lake Lahontan, and although a few centimeters of water tend to collect on the playa during the winter, it's bone dry all spring and summer. *Any rain, even a seemingly innocuous sprinkle, means you can't drive.* If you tried to drive, your wheels would get stuck in the wet playa, which quickly acquires the consistency and other unfortunate properties of wet concrete. You can see pictures of the rainy miserable mess (and all the stuck people) at http://www.skellington.com/bman/bm2014/storm.html.

As a result of the storm, the Burning Man gates were closed for about 24 hours. We had to stay in our vehicle for a long time. When the playa started to dry out later the next afternoon, we met some people who were a few lanes to the right of us. They had brought out a Chinese tea set, and some teas that one of them had just purchased in China a few weeks earlier, to share with all of us. As we were sitting around our Oolong talking about the storm, they asked us what time we'd gotten stuck the night before. "About 2:30AM," we told them.

They were shocked! "We've been here since about 10PM!" Long story short: they had chosen a more favored "random" lane, and because ours wasn't as psychologically favored, we ended up saving a few hours of wait time. This is a great concept to remember next time you're in a long line waiting for your favorite festival or event to begin (Burning Man included!)

Probability is the *Long Run Relative Frequency* of an Event

What's the probability of flipping a coin and getting heads? You probably intuitive know that it's 50%... because about half the time you'll get heads, and the other half, you'll get tails. But what if you only flip the coin 10 times? Are you going to get exactly 5 heads, and exactly 5 tails? Most likely, no. What if you flip the coin 100 times? How about 1000 or 10000 times? The more times you flip the coin (that is, generate an event) the more likely you will be to observe that the frequency of heads (that is, the number of times that you observe heads) approaches 50%.

Random events are *individually* not predictable (that is, every time we flip the coin, we're never sure whether we'll get a head or a tail) but over a *long run* of many, many, many flips we can be pretty sure that heads will turn up half of the time. As a result, the *probability* of flipping heads is 50% (or, alternatively, 0.5). **The Law of Large Numbers (LLN)** says that when you look at all of your outcomes from a multitude of trials, the results will converge on some expected value - even when the individual outcomes are random.

Samples and Populations

The *population* of all of the possible coin flips that could ever occur, in the history of history, is pretty large. In fact, it's infinitely large, given a universe where you have a lot of time (and coins available to flip). To study the outcomes associated with the random nature of coin flips, we have to choose a *sample* that's smaller than the size of the entire *population* of coin flips.

It would take a really long time to study the entire population of coin flips. Similarly, in a large *population* of people (like all of the people who live in your home country) it would take a long time to study each and every one of those people (a process called a *census*) - but it takes a lot less time and energy to infer things about those people by studying a smaller *sample*. The great benefit of performing statistical inference tests is that they let us get a sense of what happens in a *large population* just by observing outcomes within much *smaller samples*. As a rule, samples are ALWAYS smaller than populations, and your sample size must be selected so that your results will be statistically meaningful.

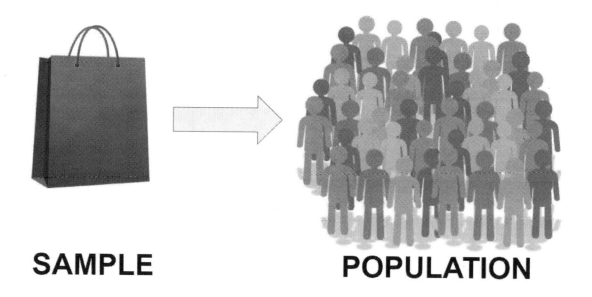

SAMPLE   POPULATION

For many statistical inference tests to work, in addition to making sure your samples are *large enough,* you even have to make sure that your samples are *small enough* – that they contain fewer than 10% of the members of the total population. To make it easier to remember when you're looking at equations, we choose different variable names to represent whether a value is from a sample or from the larger population:

Description	Sample or Population?	Symbol
Mean of a quantitative variable	Sample Statistic	$\bar{x}$
	Population Parameter	μ
Standard deviation of a quantitative variable	Sample Statistic	s
	Population Parameter	σ
Variance of a quantitative variable	Sample Statistic	s^2
	Population Parameter	σ^2
Proportion of an outcome occurring	Sample Statistic	$\hat{p}$
	Population Parameter	p
Proportion of an outcome *not* occurring	Sample Statistic	$\hat{q}$
	Population Parameter	q

If you see a **BAR** or a **HAT** on top of a variable, that's a big clue that you are looking at something measured within a **sample**. The way I remember this is that you can't take everyone in a population *to* a bar, nor can you put a hat on top of everyone's head in a population (it would be too expensive). But you might be able to take everyone in your *sample* to a bar, or put a hat on each person's head in your sample.

Typically, a **bar** also indicates that the variable represents an average of some kind. (If you see a variable with *two bars* on its head, you're dealing with an average *of averages*.) Also, you always refer to the values that pertain to samples as *sample statistics*, and refer to values that pertain to populations as *population parameters*. Remember the alliteration! S goes with S, and P goes with P. _There is no such thing as a sample parameter. There is no such thing as a population statistic._ Also, for the most part, _it's impossible to really KNOW population parameters._ That's why we have to use samples to make guesses about the characteristics of the population parameters.

There's an appendix at the end of this book that shows you how to type letters with bars and hats over them. This is a really useful trick to be familiar with, because there are no fonts that just have x-bar or p-hat natively available. Alternatively, you can use a LaTeX generator like http://www.sciweavers.org/free-online-latex-equation-editor and type `\widehat{p}` to get a p-hat, or `\overline{x}` to get an x-bar. (I like to render my symbols using the 18-point Mathpple font using this system.)

A Representative Sample

It's important to select a random sample from a population, but it's equally important to select a _representative_ sample. This means that your sample should have characteristics that are similar to those of the entire population. Here's an example. In January 2015, a friend of mine posted to Facebook that the 114th Congress in the United States had just started their work together. He noted that this group was _the most diverse Congress to date_ in the United States! 80% were Caucasian, 80% were men, 92% were Christian, 99% were heterosexual, and 50% were millionaires. (Yikes, that's a lot of diversity!)

If we wanted to take a random sample of people in the United States, would selecting the members of the 114th Congress be a good idea? Heck no! Even if we could be sure that we selected these people at random from the population of U.S. citizens, we'd be introducing _bias_ into our sample because there are far more people who are not Caucasian, definitely a lot more women, people representing many more religions (or even no religion), people who have different sexual orientations, and... far fewer millionaires. Unfortunately.

The members of the 114th Congress are definitely **not** a _representative_ sample of the population of the United States.

Common Sampling Strategies

So now that we know what it means to be random and representative, how do we pick the right people (or things) from a giant population to ensure that we have a nice workable sample to study? Fortunately, there are several approaches you can use. Some are better than others, depending upon the context of your population and the specific 5W/1H for your study. Here are some possibilities:

- **Simple Random Sample (SRS):** In a simple random sample, each member of a population is equally likely to become part of the sample. For example, if I wanted to select a simple random sample of 100 students from the 20,000 students currently enrolled at my University, I would assign each of them a number (from 1 to 20,000) and then use a random number generator to select 100 random numbers. I would survey the students whose numbers matched the ones picked by my random number generator.

- **Systematic Sampling:** This is where you choose every nth member that you encounter within the population. In the example above, where we are trying to randomly select 100 students from my University, we would first calculate the *sampling fraction* by taking n=100 and dividing it by the population size. This gives us 0.005, or 1 in 200. We would start with student #200, and then select student #400, and then include every 200th student from there on out to create our sample. A similar (but not as robust) way to do systematic sampling is to select every nth person who is a potential candidate for the sample (e.g. every 3rd person who walks by, every 20th item that comes off the manufacturing line, every 5th service call that comes into my company).

- **Stratified Sampling:** Sometimes, SRS and systematic samples don't do a good job at generating a representative sample. In the University case, I might want to make sure that there are enough members from each of the classes (freshmen through graduate students) in my sample. To accommodate this, I would first *stratify* my population into groups, based on those classes, then perform an SRS within each of these groups.

- **Cluster Sampling:** This approach is similar to stratified sampling, but is often more natural when the population is already broken up into different groups. Frequently, the clusters are different physical or geographical areas, organizations, or periods of time. Within each cluster, you generate a simple random sample or a systematic sample, then you combine all the results together to get your full sample. For example, if you wanted to look at differences in study habits between students in the College of Business and the College of Technology, each of those colleges would represent a cluster. If you wanted to study the eating habits of students who live on campus, you might consider each dorm as a cluster, and select a simple random sample from the residents within each of the dorms.

- **Convenience Sampling**: Sometimes, I like to poll my students so we can get some data for in-class examples. I might ask them whether they agree or disagree with a particular political issue, or how many hours of sleep they get each night, or how much money they spend each week on food. Am I getting a random, representative sample of all students at our University? No way. I'm not even really getting a random or representative sample of all of the students in our particular department. But the students are there, in the class, and we need data! Hence the convenience sample. <u>You should be very wary of using a convenience sample to generate any meaningful conclusions</u>. But sometimes, it's all you can get.

- **Voluntary Response Sampling**: When a researcher asks subjects to opt-in to a study, the composition of the sample depends on the people who choose to participate. For opinion polls, you'll tend to get people who feel very strongly (for good or ill) about a particular subject, and you won't hear from people who are basically ambivalent. For studies that require a greater investment of time or energy from the participants, you might only attract people who are available during those days or hours. This can be a problem. Where it's *not* a problem is in situations where you have to find people with a certain characteristic to participate in an experiment: for example, people with a particular disease. If you are running a clinical trial to find out whether a new drug or a new form of therapy is effective, you need to make sure everyone in your sample has that disease. You compensate for the voluntary nature of the participation by ensuring that all of your subjects are randomly assigned into experimental groups, and that they don't know who is receiving the treatment and who is receiving a placebo (or is otherwise in a control group). This is OK as long as you are doing an experiment – which we don't cover in this book.

Preventing Bias

The reason it's important to get as random and representative a sample as possible is that you're trying to avoid *bias*. Bias occurs when your data collection approach systematically favors certain outcomes over others. (Remember the 114th Congress? Clearly, the composition of the members indicates that they *might just possibly* be biased towards decisions that favor white Christian men who are millionaires.)

Sometimes bias can be unintentional. For example, what if you decided to conduct a survey by phone, and obtained a random sample of land-line numbers in your area? There would probably be a lot of older people and senior citizens in your sample (I mean, who do *you* know who still has a land line? Everyone I know uses their mobile as their primary phone number.) Or maybe you've created a survey using Google Forms, and you're going to post it on your Web page so that people can find it and complete it. Your outcomes will be biased towards people who encounter your page, but even more fundamentally, people who have the Internet access in the first place and are *able* to get to your online survey.

Other times, bias can lead to huge embarrassments. During the 1936 presidential election, *Literary Digest* (which was a very popular magazine at the time) published the results of its opinion survey, which predicted that Alfred Landon would win in a landslide over Franklin D. Roosevelt. The magazine had conducted a similar opinion poll for the past several elections, and had correctly identified who the next President would be based on the results. They were noteworthy in that they directly sampled millions of people, and thanks to their accuracy, had earned a lot of credibility!

For the 1936 poll, the *Digest's* sampling strategy involved randomly sampling from phone lists, then sending mailers (which needed to be returned to the *Digest*) asking voters who would receive their vote. But the designers of the survey hadn't considered that at that time, only upper-class and upper-middle-class people even *had* telephones. This was a relatively new technology! And in the first election after the Great Depression, the economy was the key issue for voters, especially for those in the lower and middle classes who overwhelmingly favored Roosevelt. *Literary Digest* ended up with a sample strongly biased in two different ways:

- **Undercoverage**: Because the sampling strategy overwhelmingly favored upper and upper-middle class voters, it was impossible to proportionately include the opinions of voters in other economic classes. Although *Literary Digest* generated a random sample, it was certainly not a representative sample.

- **Non-Response Bias**: Although 10 million people received the mailers, only 2.4 million returned them. As a consequence, the results would be limited to those who felt strongly about participating, or perhaps those who could even afford the postage to return their survey. (Granted, due to the initial selection bias, this latter possibility would be less likely.)

Both of these are forms of **selection bias,** meaning that there's a problem in how the sample was generated. You can also have **voluntary response bias**, in which the participants in your study self-select and typically only engage if they're interested in (or passionate about) what you're investigating.

Something similar happened in the 2016 Presidential election between Democratic contender Hillary Clinton and Republican Donald Trump. Although pre-election polls and exit polls put Clinton firmly in the lead, these polls may have suffered from something called **biased nonresponse**, which means people who decline to participate in a survey are markedly different than those who are willing to participate.

In addition to selection bias, there are other sources of bias that can be attributed to an inadequate measurement process. For example, **response bias** can arise if the questions you ask your survey participants are worded improperly, or lead your respondents to a particular answer. You can also introduce **social desirability bias** by asking questions that people are hesitant to answer, for example, about illegal or embarrassing activities. Bias is always an issue, and it's your job to craft your sampling strategy and design your survey in a way that minimizes it. You'll probably never end up with a sample that's not biased in some small way, so be sure you record your thoughts and state those potential sources of bias when you describe the assumptions and limitations of your study. Convenience samples are *usually* biased; voluntary response samples are *always* biased.

Now What?

Before you actually embark upon selecting your sample, you'll need to determine the proper *sample size* so that your results will be statistically significant. The chapter titled "Calculating Appropriate Sample Sizes Using Power Analysis" will help you do this. In the meantime, here are some places you can visit online to learn more about the concepts in this chapter.

- Find out more about biased nonresponse in the 2016 Presidential election at https://www.qualtrics.com/blog/biased-nonresponse-polls-missed-2016-election-mistakes/.
- Here's a nice overview of the terms and concepts associated with sampling, prepared by the Web Center for Social Research Methods: http://www.socialresearchmethods.net/kb/sampterm.php
- One of the best resources I've found to learn more about sampling strategies - and by best, I mean THIS IS ONE OF THE BEST RESOURCES I'VE EVER SEEN IN MY LIFE - is at http://dissertation.laerd.com/sampling-strategy.php
- More information about the *Literary Digest* story can be found at http://www.math.upenn.edu/~deturck/m170/wk4/lecture/case1.html
- Wikipedia has a great page on sampling bias at http://en.wikipedia.org/wiki/Sampling_bias
- I also like this article on "Elements of Sampling" because it's written on behalf of a professional society, and illustrates how sampling can have practical applications for real people in their real jobs (in this case, accounting auditors): http://www.nysscpa.org/cpajournal/2004/1104/essentials/p30.htm

3.2 Experiments vs. Observational Studies

Objective

I review a *lot* of project proposals... some from students, some from professionals. Because I've been teaching statistics for several years now, I've developed some pet peeves about the way people talk. One of my pet peeves is how carelessly people tend to use the word *experiment*, as in, "for our experiment, we did [this thing that is totally not an experiment]". In this chapter, you'll be introduced to the difference between an experiment and an observational study, and learn some of the characteristics of experiments that have been designed well. Here are the most important things to remember about the difference between experiments and observational studies:

- The presence of the words *effect*, *affect*, and *influence* in a research question suggest that the investigator wants to explore a *causal relationship*, and should choose an experiment to explore the question
- Observational studies, in contrast, can only uncover a *relationship*, *association*, or *pattern* observed within and between variables
- Correlation describes how, and whether, pairs of quantitative variables are related to one another. As a result, both experiments and observational studies *may* uncover correlation, but as a rule, I don't like to formulate research questions that ask "Is there a correlation between... [these things I'm studying]?" Unless you're examining correlation coefficients, you're probably not exploring the correlation between two quantitative variables.

Experiments

In an experiment, the researcher <u>*manipulates*</u> the environment in some way. He or she sets up one or more *treatments*, and randomly assigns subjects either into a *control group* (that doesn't receive any of the treatments) or a group that receives a treatment. Sometimes, there is only one control group and one treatment group. Other times, there is one control group and several treatment groups. Measurements are taken on variables of interest before the treatment, sometimes during the treatment, and then after the treatment to see if an independent variable has some sort of effect on a dependent (or response) variable.

Here are some examples of experiments:

- An investigator wishes to determine whether a new painkiller is effective. He or she randomly distributes each of 200 subjects into the control group (who will receive a placebo) and two treatment groups: one that receives a lower dose of the painkiller, and one that receives a higher dose of the painkiller. The patients do not know who is receiving the placebo, who is receiving the lower dose, and who is receiving the higher dose. Level of pain is measured at the start of the experiment, and again after each patient is treated for three days. The researcher wants to determine which dose of the painkiller, if any, results in relief for the patients.

- A group of students wants to design a paper airplane that can fly the farthest. They design an experiment to explore the effect of several control parameters (paper type, wing length, body width, body length, number of paper clips attached, and wing shape) and two noise parameters (whether there is a draft, and who is the operator) on the response variable, which is number of seconds in flight. They determined that wing length and body length influenced the flight duration to the greatest extent.

- A chef at a local restaurant is interested in knowing whether people in his or her city prefer an old recipe over a similar (but new and improved) recipe. They conduct a taste test at the local supermarket, and ask every 4th person who walks by if they would try a sample of each of the two foods, and rate which one they prefer. Based on the results, they may or may not change how they cook that entree at their restaurant.

- A team of web designers has staged A/B Testing to determine whether visitors to their site complete sales transactions more often based on the design that's presented to them. They want to identify which of the two designs maximizes the click-through rate to get to the ordering process.

<u>A controlled experiment is the *only* way to establish a cause and effect relationship between two variables!</u> So if your research question asks what *effect* or *impact* one variable has on another, whether one variable *affects* another, or whether a change in one *influences* changes in the other, this indicates that you should be performing a controlled experiment.

If you do not have a control group, if you have not randomly assigned subjects to groups, and if you are not manipulating the environment of your subjects or participants in any way... <u>then you are *not doing an experiment*</u>! Instead, you are probably performing an *observational study*.

To begin understanding how experiments are designed and conducted, there are some basic definitions that are important to know. Here is a story that weaves together all of the definitions in context, and the table that follows provides a summary of the definitions.

You want to do an experiment to find out what will make the whites in your laundry brighter and cleaner looking. You have several white socks and t-shirts that you can use in this experiment, so the **experimental units** are articles of clothing. There are several **factors** that you are going to vary: the type of detergent, the temperature of the water, and the length of the cycle. Each **factor** has some **factor levels**: you will try two different brands of detergent, the temperature of the water can be hot, warm, or cold; and the length of the cycle can be short (28 minutes) or long (54 minutes).

To serve as the **control group**, you will wash the clothes the way you normally do (the way that, you feel, just doesn't get them white enough). This involves using Brand A with warm water and a short cycle. The different **treatments** you will try involve various combinations of brand, temperature, and cycle length. Because you don't care about the difference between the socks and the t-shirts (in fact, you only need to use two kinds of clothing because that's what you have available in your house), you will consider type of clothing as your **blocking** variable. You want to block out the effect of any variation that might occur by having both t-shirts and socks as experimental units. You will measure the whiteness of your clothing scientifically, using a spectrophotometer and the ASTM whiteness index (http://www.axiphos.com/WhitenessPrimer.pdf).

Aspect of Experiment	Description
Experimental Unit	An experimental unit may be one person, one machine, one plant or animal, or one object. This represents who or what is manipulated during the experiment.
Control Group	A group of subjects or participants in an experiment that do not receive a treatment. Their environment is not manipulated by the researcher in any way.
Randomization	This is the practice of randomly assigning subjects to a control group or a treatment group. There are many different techniques for doing this, just like there are many different sampling strategies available.
Factor	A controlled independent variable. The values of each factor are set by the person doing the research.
Factor Level	The specific values that each factor may assume.
Treatment	A "recipe" created by combining factors at specific levels.
Blocking	Sometimes, the researcher doesn't care about the effects of a particular factor, so it gets *blocked* out.
Blind	The participants in the experiment do not know whether they are receiving the treatment or not. The researcher, however, does know who is in what group.
Double Blind	The participants in the experiment do not know whether they are receiving the treatment or not. The researcher ALSO does not know who is in what group.
Placebo	A knowingly ineffective "treatment" given to subjects in the control group, in an attempt to blind them from whether they are receiving a treatment or not. This can reduce the possibility of introducing bias into an experiment.
Replication	Instead of just applying a treatment to one experimental unit, you can apply it to several to get a better sense of the variation in the response variable.
Hawthorne Effect	Even in well-designed experiments where blinding and/or placebos are used, human subjects may unwittingly change their behavior, simply because they're aware of being observed! The name comes from a series of experiments to explore improving worker productivity at the Hawthorne Works factory complex, near Chicago, in the 1930's.

Observational Studies

If you're just trying to figure out the *relationship* between different variables, or whether there is an *association* between different variables, then an observational study can be appropriate. In an observational study, you just take measurements and gather other observations, and look for relationships. You *don't* manipulate variables in the environment at all.

Observational studies can be *prospective* (meaning that participants are tracked or followed into the future) or *retrospective* (meaning that you're looking back on data that was collected in the past). A study where you're using archived data to look back into the past, even when you're using that data to compare to measurements or observations you're making in the present, is still considered a retrospective study. Of course, observational studies don't *require* that you look into the past, or that you track subjects into the future. Perhaps you just want to create a survey now, and find out whether there is a relationship or association between two or more population parameters. This type of observational study, called a *sample survey*, relies on self-reported values and often includes assessing the opinions of individuals and groups.

In *prospective* studies, the subjects are followed *longitudinally* (that's a big word that's actually simple - it just means *over a span of time.* So for example, if you kept track of your grades over the course of your education and examined them for patterns, you could say that you conducted a longitudinal study of your academic performance). Here are some examples of *prospective* observational studies:

- A group of women with similar exercise and nutrition habits are classified by Body Mass Index (BMI), and followed for a period of ten years to see who develops heart problems. The response variable is the incidence rate of heart attacks in each of the groups. The researcher is attempting to figure out whether there is a relationship between BMI and the potential for having a heart attack (Note: The researcher is *not* investigating whether BMI *affects* or *influences* the chance of having a heart attack! This is an observational study, not an experiment.)

- Several children who attended and graduated from elite preschools in New York City are tracked throughout elementary and high school to see if their standardized test scores are higher than students who did not attend elite preschools.

- Employees at a large, multinational organization are now required to attend mandatory sexual harassment training. The company wants to determine if there has been a decrease in the number of sexual harassment reports that are filed per month.

This last example can be used to show the contrast between an observational study and an experiment. If the company wanted to determine whether the new sexual harassment training *caused* a decrease in the number of reports that were filed, they could randomly assign employees to a control group (who received no training), a treatment group where the people received one day of training, and another treatment group where the people received one day of training and follow-up reminders each month.

Here are some examples of *retrospective* observational studies:

- After an outbreak of measles in the US in December 2014 and January 2015, a retrospective study was launched to determine what factors were associated with the spread of the infection. By comparing incidence rates of patients who had recently traveled to California, versus incidence rates of people who had *not* recently traveled to California, the researchers were able to determine that Disneyland played a role in the spread of the disease. (Note: The researchers did not find that Disneyland *caused* the spread of measles... only that it was associated with the spread of measles! This is an observational study, not an experiment.)

- An insurance company wants to determine whether black ice (in the winter) is associated with a higher level of major accidents. They know that more fender benders occur during black ice, but they haven't yet studied whether major accidents are more prevalent during this time, and the company is trying to determine whether they should increase insurance rates in regions where there is a higher incidence of black ice on the roads. To do this, they look back through two decades of archived weather reports and archived accident reports, to determine whether there is a higher incidence of major accidents when black ice has been reported. (Note: The investigator is not able to tell whether black ice *causes* these accidents... this is not an experiment!)

Correlation Does Not Imply Causation!

Beware of observational studies that inadvertently claim causation! News reports often take the results from observational studies and inaccurately present them as causal links. Here are some example headlines you might see that *suggest* a causal relationship when in fact, the actual research that was performed likely indicates that there is *none*:

- Moderate exercise improves sleep
- Playing too many video games makes children more disruptive
- Drinking diet soda leads to depression
- Performing random acts of kindness improves self-esteem
- Reducing time spent on social media decreases stress levels

How do you tell the difference between an observational study and an experiment? **Just ask yourself these questions:** Is there a control group? Is there (at least one) treatment group? Did the researcher randomly assign subjects to one of these groups? Did the researcher manipulate the environment in some way? If you answer NO to any of these questions, then an experiment has <u>not</u> been performed, and you can't claim that one factor *causes*, *effects*, *impacts*, or *influences* changes in another factor.

Just because there is an association between two or more factors does not mean that there is a causal relationship underlying the association! For example: 100% of people who drink water DIE. (That means YOU!! So are you going to stop drinking water? Of course not.) You can find more fantastic examples of spurious correlations that do not imply causation at http://www.tylervigen.com/ (and you can also follow him on Twitter at @TylerVigen). Even though a correlation or a relationship does not *imply* causation, it can *suggest* that there is a causal relationship. But you'll have to do an experiment (and preferably many experiments to ensure reproducibility!) to be able to say this for sure.

Analyzing Data from Experiments

Data from experiments is often analyzed by creating models with multiple factors and sometimes, interaction terms, then applying two-way analysis of variance (ANOVA) or higher. For example, in one experiment that I participated in, we wanted to see whether adding an expensive fertilizer would help us yield more seeds in a particular crop. We examined two independent variables (farm and fertility) and one dependent (or response) variable, the total number of seeds. For each combination of factors, we made measurements of the number of seeds produced within a one-acre plot:

	Farm One	Farm Two
	A-	A+
Control (No Fertilizer) B-	10 observations (one per one-acre plot)	10 observations (one per one-acre plot)
Fertilizer Added B+	10 observations (one per one-acre plot)	10 observations (one per one-acre plot)

Although the complete analysis is beyond the scope of this book, we'll show you what the results looked like. In addition to exploring the potential impact of farm and fertility on the total number of seeds, we also suspected that there might be an interaction effect between the fertilizer and the farm itself – that is, because of soil type or weather conditions or some other influence, that the fertilizer might be more effective on one farm than on the other.

```
> model <- aov(sub2$total.no.seeds ~ sub2$farm * sub2$fertility)
> summary(model)
                        Df   Sum Sq    Mean Sq F value Pr(>F)
sub2$farm                1 210547911 210547911 257.204 <2e-16 ***
sub2$fertility           1     35820     35820   0.044 0.8355
sub2$farm:sub2$fertility 1   3208656   3208656   3.920 0.0554 .
Residuals               36  29469709    818603
---
Signif. codes:  0 `***' 0.001 `**' 0.01 `*' 0.05 `.' 0.1 ` ' 1
```

Tiny p-values under `Pr(>F)` are what we look for to determine the significance of a factor. It looks like farm is a significant factor, and fertility is not – but there is possibly an interaction between the fertilizer and the particular farm on which it is used.

Additional Resources

You should be able to determine, at this point, whether you plan to embark on a full-fledged *experiment*, or just an observational study. If you are collecting survey data from a sample of respondents, you are doing an observational study. If you want to explore a cause and effect relationship, and you plan on having a control group and one or more treatment groups, then you're ready to start thinking about an experiment.

There are many considerations that you need to make while designing an experiment, and none are covered in this book. If you'd like to find out more about what's been covered in this chapter, visit the following links.

- There is a nice tutorial covering the basic concepts in design of experiments at https://www.moresteam.com/toolbox/design-of-experiments.cfm
- We just skimmed the surface of what it means to design an effective experiment in this chapter. If you want to know more of the gory details, there is a great (and long!) chapter on design of experiments by StatSoft, which can be found at http://www.statsoft.com/Textbook/Experimental-Design
- A nice set of alternative definitions for experimental design can be found at http://www.stat.yale.edu/Courses/1997-98/101/expdes.htm
- A/B Testing is a very practical application of experimental design. Find out more at http://en.wikipedia.org/wiki/A/B_testing and Amazon's "The Math Behind A/B Testing" at https://developer.amazon.com/sdk/ab-testing/reference/ab-math.html

3.3 Dr. R's 7 Steps

Objective

In this chapter, you'll learn how to solve every statistical inference problem using the same, simple recipe. Not a statistical chef? No problem! As long as you can read the recipe book, and follow some simple instructions for how to mix and bake your data, you'll do great.

Here's some background. When I was in grad school, I had an excellent professor named Dr. Mike Hayden. He indoctrinated us into his "Hayden's 16 Steps" for doing hypothesis testing, which involved documenting our process and results in a comprehensive way. After I started teaching statistics, I consolidated and streamlined his process into 12 Steps (which felt reminiscent of 12 step addiction recovery programs, adding to the "therapeutic feel" of the approach). When I graduated, I became Dr. Radziwill, which can be hard to pronounce; students tend to shorten it. Several of them pointed out how appropriate it is that "Dr. R is in love with R" so we christened the methodology "Dr. R's 12 Steps."

After teaching the 12 steps for a few years, we found that we relied on seven of the steps for most of our problem-solving, and only used the additional steps when we were writing research reports. Whether we use some steps, or all of the steps, the overall process is the same: 1) **Estimate** the solution, 2) solve **Analytically** using equations, 3) solve the problem **Computationally** using R, and then 4) **Compare** the answers to check your results.

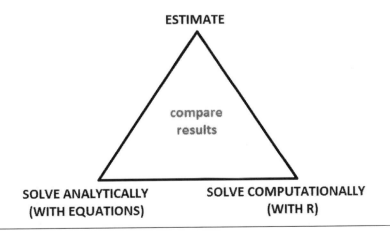

ESTIMATE

compare
results

SOLVE ANALYTICALLY
(WITH EQUATIONS)

SOLVE COMPUTATIONALLY
(WITH R)

The 7 Steps in the Context of a Research Report

The general recipe you will follow starts with **Step 0**, in part because I'm a programmer (we regularly start counting with zero) and in part because if your assumptions don't check out, you can't even more to the first real step of the inference problem. The 7 Steps are performed for *each research question* (RQ), and most research projects have 3-4 RQs.

Abstract – This 200-400 word executive summary briefly describes the problem and why it's important; the methodology, results, and conclusions; and what those conclusions *mean*. A reader should be able to read this part *only* and completely understand everything you did.

I – Introduction: Describe the overall problem and why it's important to solve.

II – Background: Have previous studies been done like this? What did they conclude?

III – Methodology: Describe how you plan to collect your data, what sampling strategy you will use, and what sample size you need to achieve the statistical power you want. List the categorical and quantitative variables you will gather. List your RQs and specify which statistical test you will perform for each one. Briefly state your Null & Alternative Hypotheses so your readers know what's coming next.

IV – Results: Provide some descriptive statistics, with charts, graphs, and tables to give the reader a sense of what the data you collected looks like. Then, for each RQ, execute your problem-solving recipe:

> Step 0: Check Assumptions
> Step 1: Set Null & Alternative Hypotheses
> Step 2: Set α, the Level of Significance
> Step 3: Calculate Test Statistic (T.S.) Analytically
> Step 4: Draw a Picture
> Step 5: Find the P-Value
> Step 6: Draw Conclusion – Is the P-Value < α? If so, Reject the Null
> Step 7: Find the Confidence Interval & Confirm Work in R

V – Discussion and Conclusions: At this point, you have drawn one conclusion for each of your RQs. What did you figure out about your population? How do you explain it to your grandmother? What future research *could* you do now?

References – Include your sources in <u>APA format</u>, which you can get from Google Scholar.

Tips for the Introduction and Background Sections

In the introduction, frame your problem and get the reader interested in it:

- What's this project all about? Why did you decide to do this project, why is it interesting, and *to whom* is it interesting?
- State one or more substantive research question(s) that can be investigated by the technique focused on in the assignment. Remember that a question ends in a question mark. (A problem statement is not a statement of what you plan to do! "I am going to..." is not a problem.)
- The background section usually contains a *literature review*. Most students think this means "find some web pages that give general information about your topic and list them in the reference section" which is unfortunately incorrect. Your job in describing the background is to figure out *all the people who have studied this problem – or problems similar to it – in the past.* This provides the basis for you to justify that you're doing something new and different, and also gives you a rich landscape of knowledge against which you can compare your results.

Tips for the Methodology Section

In the methodology section, describe everything you did to obtain your results, including:

- The survey questions that you ask your subjects are NOT your research questions.
- Describe the population you're attempting to characterize, the sample you are collecting, and justify the sampling *strategy* you selected based on what you know about the population. Did you use simple random sampling, systematic sampling, cluster sampling, or some other technique?
- Describe how you collected the data, that is, the data collection technique and any *instrumentation* used. Did you collect the data directly, or did you use data that you got from some other source (such as an archive)?
- Describe units and sampling frequency (if appropriate). Describe the scope of your data collection (which is important, for example, if you only collected data on weekends, or only at night, or only during a particular week).

- How many respondents did you sample, and were they people, events, or what? **Most importantly, how did you compute the appropriate sample size?** If you did a power analysis, explain and justify the trade-offs you considered in terms of Type I Error, Type II Error, and power.

- Did you use someone else's survey? If so, report its reliability and validity.

- List all of the quantitative and categorical variables you collected, being sure to note which variables are *quantitative* and which are *categorical*. Describe recoding or computing schemes that may have been used, for example to transform quantitative variables into categorical variables. If you are *defining* categories based on some external factor (e.g. "honors students are considered to be those with a cumulative GPA of 3.5 or higher") state those definitions as well as a justification for why you split up the categories in that way. If you had to calculate any data based on the raw data you collected, explain it here as well.

- Set your alpha (Type I Error) and explain why this alpha was selected in terms of cost (especially cost of gathering more data), risk (of incurring a Type I or Type II error), and ethical considerations (envisioning if and how the results of your study might be used by other people).

Tips for the Results Section

In the results section, your job is to present the results of your analytical solution (using equations), your computational solution (in R), and compare to make sure they yield the same conclusions. Check to make sure that the conclusion you draw from the confidence interval MATCHES the conclusion you drew from your statistical inference test. You don't have to interpret any of the results; that happens in the final section.

Tips for the Discussion and Conclusions Section

Finally, which null hypotheses did you reject? Which null hypotheses did you *fail to reject*? Note that these are the only two conclusions you can draw. You cannot accept a null hypothesis; if you reject the null, you cannot say that you accept the alternative. There's always a chance (due to sampling error) that you're not getting an accurate view of the population at all. This is a game of *disproving*, not proving. Additionally:

- Discuss any important assumptions, limitations, threats to validity or other pertinent factors related to the statistical technique selected. Describe how the assumptions were tested, how you *interpreted* the test of the assumption, and what your choices were for moving forward if all of the assumptions were not met.
- At the very end, provide a summary of the story that *all* of your conclusions present when considered together. **You may want to make it exciting, like Elon Musk does:** https://medium.com/firm-narrative/want-a-better-pitch-watch-this-328b95c2fd0b#.si932sh7l.

Acknowledgements

You can find out more about Dr. Mike Hayden, who originally inspired this approach with his 16 Steps, at http://technology.indstate.edu/directory/haydenm.htm

3.4 The Art of Developing Research Questions

Objective

To 1) **construct** well-formed research questions (RQs) that can be explored using various methods for statistical hypothesis testing, and to 2) **deconstruct** research questions to figure out which statistical methodology *should* be used. Note that RQs are much different than survey questions, which you write to obtain each of the variables you collect. An example of a survey question is "What is your age?" An example of an RQ is "Are people who watch TV on a daily basis older than those who do not?"

Background

Fortunately, once you know what variables you plan to collect, putting together research questions is pretty easy - it's just like filling in Mad Libs (which, if you weren't so fortunate to grow up during the days when these were one of the fun things you did at home after school, play with some now before you keep reading at http://www.madlibs.com.) With a properly phrased research question, it's much easier to select the appropriate statistical test to answer it. RQ development is covered for each of these tests:

- One-sample t-test
- Two-sample t-test
- Paired t-test
- One-way Analysis of Variance (ANOVA)
- One proportion z-test
- Two proportion z-test
- Chi-Square Test of Independence
- Linear Regression
- F Test for Equality of Variances

Concepts that are fundamental to this chapter are 1) the difference between *categorical* and *quantitative variables*, and 2) the difference between a *sample* and a *population*. (If you need to, review Chapters 1.3 and 3.1 before proceeding.) Each statistical test requires that you have data: some combination of categorical and quantitative variables. **The types of data you have collected dictate what types of statistical inference tests you can apply.**

Where Do I Begin?

First, pick a <u>topic</u> – any topic you are interested in. I've had students start with all sorts of topics: fishing, skeet shooting, exercising, cooking, cars, plants, animals, knitting, attitudes towards parking, attitudes towards political issues, attitudes towards sex and drugs, computers, computer/app use, food preferences, customer service, cognitive responses, or maybe even improving a particular process.

Next, determine your <u>unit of analysis</u>. In the M&M data referenced earlier in this book, the unit of analysis was one M&M, and we recorded color and defect for each candy. In the weather data used earlier, the unit of analysis was one day. (In other weather data I've analyzed, the unit of analysis was one hour, or one minute.) If you give people a survey, your unit of analysis is a person. If you are improving a process, your unit of analysis might be one run of that process.

Finally, what information could you gather for each of those units of analysis? If you're surveying people, what categorical variables could you collect from them? Similarly, what quantitative variables could you collect from them? <u>Create a list of categorical variables</u> on the left side of your paper, <u>and a list of quantitative variables</u> on the right side of your paper. You don't have to collect them all, but this will help you brainstorm potential RQs.

When you identify an interesting RQ, <u>write down the null hypothesis</u> (which represents what you *think* is happening in the population) and <u>choose one alternative hypothesis</u>.

One-Sample t-test

For this test, you only need <u>ONE quantitative variable</u> measured from your sample. You will compare the measurements you take from your sample with a *standard*, a *target*, or a *recommended value*. For example, the *speed limit of a particular stretch of highway* would be a standard. The typical temperature of the healthy human body is 98.6 degrees F, and the expected value of the boiling point of water is 100 degrees C or 212 degrees F. A recommended value for *how many hours of sleep an adult should get each night* could be 7 hours, but this will depend on who or what is making the recommendation. **Whenever you use a recommended value in your one-sample t-test, be sure to get the recommendation from a valid, reputable source.** (For example, get medical recommendations from journal articles or reputable sources like Centers for Disease Control – references you can cite.)

RQs for the one-sample t-test are phrased like this:

- Is the value of [Quantative Variable] for [Unit of Analysis] [*greater than OR less than OR different than*] [the value of the standard, target, or recommended value for the Quantitative Variable]?
- Do [Unit of Analysis] [meet, exceed, or fall short of the standard, target,or recommended value for the Quantitative Variable], on average?

That means, for this test, there are **three elements** you need to glom together:

Name of a Quantitative Variable	A Sign: >, <. or ≠	Standard, Target, or Recommended Value
Body Temperature	>	98.6 F
Speed	>	25 mph
Length of a Ruler	≠	12.0 in

The three signs *greater than, less than, and different than* represent the three possible alternative hypotheses. Here are some examples with variable names inserted:

- Is the **average body temperature** [Quantitative Variable] of **students on our campus** [Unit of Analysis] greater than **the expected value of 98.6 degrees F for healthy individuals** [Expected Value for the Quantitative Variable]?

- Do **cars on this road** [Unit of Analysis] drive faster than the **posted speed limit** [Standard for the Quantitative Variable]?
- If I work for a company that makes rulers, is the **length of each ruler** equal to the target of exactly **12.0 inches**?
- When I add two tablespoons of salt to my water, does it **boil at a temperature** [Quantitative Variable] greater than **100°C** [Expected Value]?
- Did **students in this class** [Unit of Analysis] do better than **last year's students** [Target for the Quantitative Variable] on **Exam 1**?

		What it means
H₀:	$\mu = 0$	There is no difference between the REAL means of this quantitative variable and the standard, typical/expected value, or recommendation we are comparing it to
Hₐ:	$\mu > 0$ (one-tailed)	The REAL mean of this quantitative variable is bigger than the standard, typical/expected value, or recommendation we are comparing it to
	$\mu < 0$ (one-tailed)	The REAL mean of this quantitative variable is less than the standard, typical/expected value, or recommendation we are comparing it to
	$\mu \neq 0$ (two-tailed)	The REAL mean of this quantitative variable is different than the standard, typical/expected value, or recommendation we are comparing it to (either greater or less than... doesn't matter which)

Because this is a t-test, the Test Statistic (T.S.) that you will calculate will be a **t**.

Two-Sample t-test

This test compares the means of a quantitative variable that is observed in each of two groups. For this test, you need at LEAST one categorical AND one quantitative variable:

- Each category will be represented by *one sample each*
- A *single quantitative variable* is measured across cases in both categories

Research questions are of the form:

- Is the average of [Quantitative Variable] [*greater than, less than, different than*] for [Category 1] than it is for [Category 2]?
- Do [entities in Category 1] have [*greater than, less than, different than*] [Quantitative Variable] than [entities in Category 2]?

That means, for this test, there are **three elements** you need to glom together:

Quantitative Variable in Bag 1	A Sign: >, <. or ≠	Quantitative Variable in Bag 2
Product Ratings from women age 30-40	>	Product Ratings from men age 30-40
Mean Time to Failure (MTTF) for Energizer batteries	>	Mean Time to Failure (MTTF) for Duracell batteries
Exam Scores for Summer Students	<	Exam Scores for Spring Students

The three signs *greater than, less than, and different than* represent the three possible alternative hypotheses. Here are some examples with variable names inserted:

- Do **women between the ages of 30-40** [Category 1] provide higher **ratings for our product** [Quantitative Variable] than **men between the ages of 30-40** [Category 2]?
- Do **Energizer batteries** [Category 1] **last longer** [Quantitative Variable] than **Duracell batteries** [Category 2]?
- Is **job satisfaction** [Quantitative Variable] in our organization greater **after the annual company picnic** [Category 1] than **before it** [Category 2]?
- Are **exam scores in our class** [Quantitative Variable] lower for **students who enrolled this summer** [Category 1] than for **students who enrolled last spring** [Category 2]?

- Is the average **number of nights a person drinks each month** [Quantitative Variable] greater for **male students in the College of Business** [Category 1] than it is for **male students in the College of Technology** [Category 2]?
- Did employees remember a greater **number of initiatives from our strategic plan** [Quantitative Variable] **after the new training** we just developed [Category 1], as compared **to before the training** [Category 1]?

		What it means
H$_0$:	$\mu_1 - \mu_2 = 0$	There is no difference between the REAL means of this quantitative variable in Category 1 and Category 2
H$_a$:	$\mu_1 - \mu_2 > 0$ (one-tailed)	The REAL mean of this quantitative variable is bigger for Category 1 than it is for Category 2
	$\mu_1 - \mu_2 < 0$ (one-tailed)	The REAL mean of this quantitative variable is less for Category 1 than it is for Category 2
	$\mu_1 - \mu_2 \neq 0$ (two-tailed)	The REAL mean of this quantitative variable is different in Category 1 than it is for Category 2, but it could be different in EITHER direction (greater than *or* less than)

Because this is a t-test, the Test Statistic (T.S.) that you will calculate will be a **t**.

Paired t-test

This test is JUST like the two-sample t-test, although there's one critical difference: the two samples have to be UNITED by "who" is observed. For this test, you need <u>one quantitative variable</u> *measured at two different times* or *under two different conditions*. This is the "pre-test/post-test" or "before and after" statistical test that tells you whether an improvement occurred from the first administration of the test until the last. Research questions are of the form:

- Is the mean *difference* of the [Quantitative Variable] from the beginning to the end of the evaluation period [*greater than, less than, different*] than zero?
- Did **performance** [Quantitative Variable] improve **from the beginning** of the period **to the end**?

		What it means
H₀:	$\mu_D = D$	There is no difference between the REAL mean-of-the-differences of this quantitative variable and what we anticipated (D; note that D often equals 0)
Hₐ:	$\mu_D > D$ (one-tailed)	The REAL mean-of-the-differences of this quantitative variable is greater than D
	$\mu_D < D$ (one-tailed)	The REAL mean-of-the-differences of this quantitative variable is less than D
	$\mu_D \neq D$ (two-tailed)	The REAL mean-of-the-difference of this quantitative variable is NOT D but we don't know for sure whether it's on the "greater than" side or the "less than" side

Because this is a t-test, the Test Statistic (T.S.) that you will calculate will be a **t**.

One-way Analysis of Variance (ANOVA)

This is the "one of these things is not like the other" test. For this test, you need <u>one categorical variable and one quantitative variable, and there must be three or more groups that you split your observations into using the categorical variable</u>. The one-way ANOVA is very similar to the two-sample t-test, but instead of comparing the mean of a quantitative variable between only *two* groups, you compare the mean of a quantitative variable between *three or more* groups. So, if you have *n* different groups:

- Each of the *n* categories will be represented by *one sample each*
- A *single quantitative variable* is measured in each of the 3+ categories
- In an experiment, each of the *n* groups can represent different experimental treatments

- Each of the *n* groups can also represent different time periods in which the quantitative variables are measured (e.g. months, or days of the week)

Research questions are of the form:

- Is the average value of [Quantitative Variable] the same [in all *n* Categories]?
- Do [entities in Category 1], [entities in Category 2], or... [entities in Category *n*] report different [Quantitative Variables]?
- Which of the *n* treatments works best to achieve [a particular goal]?
- Was the average [Quantitative Variable] different at any of the *n* time periods when it was measured?

		What it means
H₀:	$\mu_1 = \mu_2 = \mu_3 = ... \mu_n$	All of the n samples (1, 2, 3, etc.) have the same mean
Hₐ:	At least one of the means is different	Not all of the samples have the same mean. However, we can't tell WHICH sample (or samples) are different... we need to do follow-up tests, which are called TESTS OF MULTIPLE COMPARISONS. Or a whole lot of two sample t-tests to compare each of the combinations (which is NOT advised... it will propagate errors *fast*).

Because this is NOT a t-test, the Test Statistic (T.S.) that you will calculate will be an **F**.

One Proportion z-test

This test helps you compare a *proportion* that you have observed in your sample with a *standard or recommended* proportion. Often, the standard or recommended proportion will come from a previous belief or opinion, or a published report or published academic journal article. We test to see whether the observed proportion differs from what we expected.

- Your observed proportion should be the *proportion of successes* you observe within a particular group

- You can define *success* any way you want to!
  - People who *have* a certain characteristic
  - People who *hold* a certain belief or opinion
  - People who have *succeeded* in meeting a certain condition, such as winning a game, or *demonstrating a characteristic* within your study

That means, for this test, there are **three elements** you need to glom together:

Observed Proportion	Sign: >, <. or ≠	Standard, Target, or Recommended Value
% of customers who are satisfied	>	0.75
% of students who pass my class	<	0.90
% of defective product	≠	0.08

Research questions are of the form:

- Is the proportion of [subjects who meet a particular condition or are members of a particular category] [*greater than, less than, different than*] [the standard]?
- Do a majority of subjects [meet this particular condition]? Note: If you're testing for majority opinion or majority participation, you will always set your alternative hypothesis to be H_a: $p > 0.50$.

		What it means
H_0:	$p = p_0$	There is no difference between the REAL population proportion p and what we anticipated (p_0)
H_a:	$p > p_0$ (one-tailed)	The REAL population proportion p is greater than what we anticipated (p_0)
	$p < p_0$ (one-tailed)	The REAL population proportion p is less than what we anticipated (p_0)
	$p \neq p_0$ (two-tailed)	The REAL population proportion p is NOT what we anticipated (p_0) but we don't know for sure whether it's on the "greater than" side or the "less than" side

Because this is a z-test, the Test Statistic (T.S.) that you will calculate will be a <u>z</u>.

Two Proportion z-test

This test helps you compare <u>a *proportion that you have observed in one group*</u> in your sample, with a <u>*proportion that you have observed in another group*</u> within your sample. Your groups will most likely be determined by a categorical variable that you have acquired in your data collection.

- Your observed proportion for each of the two groups should be the *proportion of successes* you observe within each group
- You can define *success* any way you want to! People who *have* a certain characteristic? People who hold a certain belief or opinion? People who have succeeded in meeting a certain condition, such as winning a game, or *demonstrating* a certain characteristic under the constraints of your study?

That means, for this test, there are **three elements** you need to glom together:

Proportion in Bag 1	Sign: >, <. or ≠	Proportion in Bag 2
% of men who favor a political candidate	>	% women who favor a political candidate
% of defective products this month	>	% of defective products last month
% passing certification this year	≠	% passing certification last year

Research questions are of the form:

- Is the proportion of [subjects who meet a particular condition or are members of a particular category] [*greater than, less than, different*] than the proportion of [subjects who meet a particular condition or are members of a particular category]?

- Is there a difference between the proportion of [subjects who meet one condition] and [subjects who meet another condition]?

		What it means
H₀:	$p_1 - p_2 = p_0$	There is no difference between the two population proportions p_1 and p_2 and what we anticipated (p_0)
Hₐ:	$p_1 - p_2 > p_0$ (one-tailed)	The difference between the REAL population proportion p_1 and the REAL population proportion p_2 is greater than what we anticipated (p_0)
	$p_1 - p_2 < p_0$ (one-tailed)	The difference between the REAL population proportion p_1 and the REAL population proportion p_2 is less than what we anticipated (p_0)
	$p_1 - p_2 \neq p_0$ (two-tailed)	The difference between the REAL population proportion p_1 and the REAL population proportion p_2 is *different* than what we anticipated (p_0)

Because this is a z-test, the Test Statistic (T.S.) that you will calculate will be a **z**.

Chi-Square Test of Independence

With this test, you are comparing *counts of observations that have been classified according to two categorical variables* to see if they are distributed evenly between all the combinations of categories. If they are not distributed evenly, that indicates that there must be some *relationship* or some *preference* between the variables. But there's no way to tell exactly what that relationship is -- barring further tests! For Chi-Square:

- You need *exactly two* categorical variables
- You should have them arranged in a *contingency table* (that's the one that looks like a bunch of boxes, with values for one categorical variable across the top spanning the columns, and values for the other categorical variable down the left side, spanning the rows) with *counts of observations* tallied up in each cell:

	Male	Female
In favor of that really critical decision	# of men in favor	# of women in favor
Opposed to that really critical decision	# of men opposed	# of women opposed

Research questions take one of two forms, so it is very easy to brainstorm possible RQs that could be solved using the Chi-square test of independence. Just pick *any* two of the categorical variables that you could collect, and plug them into the following sentences to see if any of them would be interesting to investigate:

- Are [Categorical Variable 1] and [Categorical Variable 2] independent?
- Is there a relationship between [Categorical Variable 1] and [Categorical Variable 2]?

		What it means
H₀:	[Categorical Variable 1] and [Categorical Variable 2] are independent.	The counts of your observations have been uniformly distributed across your cells, given the number of observations you made.
Hₐ:	[Categorical Variable 1] and [Categorical Variable 2] are NOT independent.	The counts of your observations are NOT uniformly distributed across your cells, given the number of observations you made.

Because this is a Chi-square-test, the Test Statistic (T.S.) that you calculate will be a χ^2.

Simple Linear Regression

Linear regression helps you determine whether there is a linear relationship between <u>two quantitative variables.</u> The variables have to be matched based on the unit of analysis so that x is the independent variable, y is the dependent variable, and a scatterplot can be generated from (x, y) points. Research questions are of the form:

- Is there a linear relationship between [Quantitative Variable 1] and [Quantitative Variable 2]?

- Can the [Dependent Variable] be predicted from the [Independent Variable]?
- Does the [Independent Variable] predict the [Dependent Variable]?

		What it means
H₀:	$\beta = 0$	The slope of the regression line is zero (that is, there is no linear relationship between x and y)
Hₐ:	$\beta \neq 0$	The slope of the regression line is nonzero (that is, there *is* a linear relationship between x and y)

Inference tests can also be performed to see if the slope of a best fit line is significant. In addition, this test for the significance of a regression slopes translates very well to multiple regression: if you are testing a linear model with *multiple potential predictors*, looking at the p-value associated with the slope attached to each predictor can tell you whether that predictor is significant. (These p-values appear on R output from the `lm` command.)

The Test Statistic (T.S.) used for this test is a **t**.

F Test for Equality (Homogeneity) of Variances

This test helps you compare <u>a *variance* observed in *one group* in your sample, with a variance that you have observed within *another group* within your sample</u>. Your groups will most likely be determined by a categorical variable that you also sampled. Because the test statistic involves the *ratio* between the two variances, if we always put the larger variance in the numerator, then only the one one-tailed alternative makes sense. This test can be used to check assumptions for other tests that require groups with equal variances.

- This test is *very* sensitive to normality. Make sure the observations are normally distributed, using a QQ plot or a Shapiro-Wilk test.
- There are several variations of this test, including Bartlett's test (which is not as sensitive to whether your data are normal or not) and Levene's test (which is kind of like ANOVA but for comparing many different variances).

Research questions are of the form:

- Is the variance of [a quantitative variable] in [subjects who meet a particular condition or are members of a particular category] [*greater than, less than, different*] than the variance of [a quantitative variable] in [subjects who meet a particular condition or are members of a particular category]?
- Has the variance of a particular physical value *changed* since a process improvement effort was implemented?

		What it means
H₀:	$\sigma_1^2 = \sigma_2^2$	There is no difference between the population variance in the first group and the second group
Hₐ:	$\sigma_1^2 > \sigma_2^2$ (one-tailed)	One of the population variances is larger than the other

Because this is an F-test, the Test Statistic (T.S.) that you will calculate will be a **F**.

3.5 Calculating Sample Sizes with Power Analysis

Objective

You're about to embark on a research project that will involve collecting data and performing tests of statistical inference, and you'd like to start your data collection. But as a savvy practitioner of statistics, you know how important is to estimate your sample size *before* you start collecting data, to ensure that you will be able to generate results that are statistically sound. There is nothing worse than being all ready to compute your results and generate your conclusions and then realizing... *oh no, I don't have enough data for my results to be valid!* (This happened to me when I was preparing my *first* dissertation proposal. Trust me, it can be not only unpleasant, but soul crushing.)

For each of your research questions, you will perform one sample size calculation using R; then, select the *largest number* from this collection. That's the minimum sample size you should collect to ensure that the conclusions you draw from each RQ are valid. You'll have to do some estimating (and make some educated guesses), but this is OK. Just be sure to articulate what assumptions you made when you were computing your appropriate sample size, and what trade-offs factored into your final decision. Feel free to consult the academic literature or do a pilot study to help support your estimates and guesses. Finally, consult **APPENDIX L: PLOTTING POWER CURVES** to supplement your analysis with a graph.

Background

Sample size calculation is an aspect of *power analysis*. If the population really is different than what you thought it was like when you set up your null hypothesis, then you want to be able to collect enough data to detect that difference! Similarly, sometimes you *know* you'll only have a small sample to begin with, so you can use power analysis to make sure you'll still be able to carry out a legitimate statistical study at a reasonable level of significance α.

The **power** of a statistical test, then, answers the question:

What's the probability that I will have enough data to know that what I originally *thought* the population was like (as expressed by my null hypothesis) was **incorrect**?

Clearly, having a zero percent chance of being able to use your sample to detect whether the population is unlike what you originally thought... would be bad. Similarly, having a 100% chance of being able to detect a difference would *also* probably be bad: your sample size would be comparatively large, and collecting more data is usually costlier (in both time and effort). When determining an appropriate sample size for your study, look for a power of *at least* 0.80, although higher is better; higher power is always associated with bigger sample sizes, though. The standard of 0.80 or higher just reflects that the community of researchers are usually comfortable with studies where the power is at least at this level.

The smaller the difference between what you *think* the population is like (as described by the null hypothesis) and what the *data* tells you the population is like... the more data you'll *need* to actually detect that difference. This difference between your hypothesized mean and the sample mean, or the hypothesized proportion and the sample proportion, or the hypothesized distribution of values over a contingency table and the actual distribution of values in that contingency table, is called an **effect size**.

For example, if you were trying to determine whether there was a difference between the average age of freshmen and the average age of seniors at your university, it wouldn't require such a large sample size because the *effect size* is about three years in age. However, if you were trying to determine whether there was a difference between the average age of freshmen and the average age of sophomores at your university, it would require a much larger sample size because the *effect size* is less than one year in age. If there is a difference, you will need more data in your sample to know for sure.

Effect size is represented in R as **how many standard deviations the real estimate is away from the hypothesized estimate**. Closer to zero, the effect size is small; around 0.5, the effect size becomes more significant. An effect size of 0.8 to 1 is considered large, because you're saying that the true difference between the hypothesized value of your population parameter and the sample statistic from your data is approaching one standard deviation. A value of 0.1 or 0.2 is a small effect size. (Cohen, 1988) Your job is to estimate what you think the effect size is before you perform the computation of sample size. If you really have *no way at all* of knowing what the effect size is (and this is actually a pretty common dilemma), just use 0.5 as recommended by Bausell & Li (2002).

To increase or improve your *power to detect an effect*, do one or more of these:

- **Increase your sample size.** The more items you have in your sample, the better you will have captured a snapshot of the variation throughout the population... as long as your random sample is also a representative sample.
- **Increase your level of significance**, α, which will make your test *less stringent*.
- **Increase the effect size.** Of course, this is a characteristic of your data and your a priori knowledge about the population... so this one may be really hard to change.
- **Use covariates or blocking variables**. (I won't explain this in detail; just know that if you're designing an experiment with treatment and control groups, and you need to improve your experimental design to increase the power of your statistical test, you should look into this.)

Now that you understand power and effect size, it will be much easier to get a sense of what **Type I and Type II Errors** are and what they really mean. You may have heard that Type I Error, α, reflects *how likely you are to reject the null hypothesis when you shouldn't have done it.* You know how sampling error means that on any given day, you might get a sample that's representative of the population, or you might get a sample that estimates your mean or proportion too high or too low?

Type I Error asks (and note that all of these questions ask *exactly* the same thing, just in different ways):

- **How willing am I** to reject the null hypothesis when in fact, it actually pretty accurately represents what's going on with the population?
- **How willing am I** to get a false positive, where I *detected* an effect but *no effect actually exists*?
- What's the probability of **incorrectly rejecting** the null hypothesis?

This probability, the Type I Error, is the level of significance α. If you choose an α of 0.05, that means you are willing to be wrong like this 1 out of every 20 times (1/20 = 0.05) you collect a sample and run the test of inference. If you choose an α of 0.01, that means you are willing to be wrong like this 1 out of every 100 times (1/100 = 0.01) you collect a sample and run the test of inference -- making this selection of α a more stringent test. On the other hand, if you choose an α of 0.10, that means you are willing to be wrong like this 1 out of every 10 times (1/10 = 0.10) you collect a sample and run the test of inference -- making this selection of α a much less stringent test. Type I Error and Type II Error have to be *balanced* depending upon what your goals are in designing your study. Here is how they are related:

| | | What's really going on with the population | |
		H$_0$ is True	**H$_0$ is False**
The decision you make as a result of your statistical test:	**Reject H$_0$**	Type I Error α *FALSE POSITIVES*	**Accurate Results!** You rejected H$_0$ and you were supposed to, because your data showed that the population was different than what you originally thought
	Fail to Reject H$_0$	**Accurate Results!** You didn't reject H$_0$ because it was an accurate description of the population	Type II Error β *FALSE NEGATIVES*

Power, 1 - β, is related to the Type II Error... it is:

The probability that you DON'T get a FALSE NEGATIVE

The probability that you DO detect an effect that's REAL

Process

For each of your RQs, you should have already selected the appropriate methodology for inference that you'll use to draw your conclusions. The inferential tests covered here are:

- One sample t-test
- Two sample t-test
- Paired t-test
- One-proportion z-test
- Two proportion z-test
- Chi-Square Test of Independence
- One-way Analysis of Variance (ANOVA)
- Linear Regression

All of these commands are provided by the `pwr` package, except the last one, which is in the base R installation. Be sure to install the `pwr` package first, then load it into active memory using the `library` command, before you move on.

R Command	Statistical Methodology (*=not covered in this chapter)
`pwr.t.test`	One sample, two sample, and paired t-tests; also requires you to specify whether the alternative hypothesis will be one tailed or two
`pwr.t2n.test`	*Two sample t-test where the sizes of the sample from each of the two groups is different
`pwr.p.test`	One proportion z-test
`pwr.2p.test`	Two proportion z-test
`pwr.2p2n.test`	*Two proportion z-test where the sizes of the sample from each of the two groups is different
`pwr.chisq.test`	Chi-square Test of Independence
`pwr.anova.test`	Analysis of Variance (ANOVA)
`pwr.f2.test`	Linear Regression
`power.t.test`	*Another way to perform power analysis for one sample, two sample, and paired t-tests; here, the advantage is there's an easy method to plot Type I & Type II Errors & power vs. effect

Calculating Sample Sizes for Tests Involving Means (T-Tests)

This section covers sample size calculations for the one sample, two sample, and paired t-tests. You are also required to specify whether your alternative hypothesis will be one tailed or two, so be sure you have defined your H_0 and H_a prior to starting your calculations.

The `pwr.t.test` command takes *five* arguments, which means you can use it to compute power and effect size in addition to just the sample size (if you want). So the one sample t-test, we can use `pwr.t.test` like this to compute required sample size:

```
> pwr.t.test(n=NULL,sig.level=0.05,power=0.8,d=0.3,type="one.sample")

        One-sample t test power calculation

              n = 89.14936
              d = 0.3
      sig.level = 0.05
          power = 0.8
    alternative = two.sided

> pwr.t.test(n=NULL,sig.level=0.05,power=0.8,d=0.3,type="one.sample",
alternative="greater")

        One-sample t test power calculation

              n = 70.06793
              d = 0.3
      sig.level = 0.05
          power = 0.8
    alternative = greater
```

To get the sample size, we use the `n=NULL` argument to `pwr.t.test`. As expected, the one-tailed test below requires a smaller sample size than the two-tailed test above. And always round your n's up!! We can't sample an extra 0.14936 person for the first test above... we have to sample the entire person. So our correct sample size should be 90 for that test, and 71 for the test below.

We can use the same command to determine sample sizes for the two sample t-test:

```
> pwr.t.test(n=NULL,sig.level=0.05,power=0.8,d=0.3,type="two.sample",
alternative="greater")

        Two-sample t test power calculation

              n = 138.0715
              d = 0.3
      sig.level = 0.05
          power = 0.8
    alternative = greater

NOTE: n is number in *each* group
```

And the paired t-test:

```
> pwr.t.test(n=NULL,sig.level=0.05,power=0.8,d=0.3,type="paired",
alternative="greater")

        Paired t test power calculation

              n = 70.06793
              d = 0.3
      sig.level = 0.05
          power = 0.8
    alternative = greater

NOTE: n is number of *pairs*
```

Observe that you can calculate any of the values if you know *all* of the other values. For example, if you know you can only get 28 pairs for your paired t-test, you can first see what the power would be if you kept everything else the same, and then you can check and see what would happen if the effect size were just a little bigger (and thus easier to detect with a smaller sample):

```
> pwr.t.test(n=28,power=NULL,sig.level=0.05,d=0.3,type="paired",
alternative="greater")

        Paired t test power calculation
```

```
          n = 28
          d = 0.3
  sig.level = 0.05
      power = 0.4612366
alternative = greater
```

NOTE: n is number of *pairs*


```
> pwr.t.test(n=28,power=0.8,sig.level=0.05,d=NULL,type="paired",
alternative="greater")
```

```
     Paired t test power calculation

          n = 28
          d = 0.4821407
  sig.level = 0.05
      power = 0.8
alternative = greater
```

NOTE: n is number of *pairs*

In the first example, we used power=NULL to tell R that we wanted to compute a power value, given that we knew the number of pairs n, the estimated effect size d, the significance level of 0.05, and that we are using the "greater than" form of the alternative hypothesis. But a power of 0.46 is really not good, so we'll have to change something else about our study. If we force a power of 0.8, and instead use d=NULL to get R to compute the effect size, we find that using the 28 pairs of subjects we have available, we can detect an effect size that's about half a standard deviation from what we hypothesized at a power of 0.8 and a level of significance of 0.05. That's not so bad.

You can also access the sample size n directly, if that's all you're interested in, like this:

```
> pwr.t.test(n=NULL,sig.level=0.05,power=0.8,d=0.3,type="paired",
alternative="greater")$n
[1] 70.06793
```

Here is a summary of all the arguments you can pass to `pwr.t.test` to perform your sample size calculations and power analysis for tests of means:

Argument to `pwr.t.test`	What it means
n	Your sample size! Set to `NULL` if you want to compute it.
power	Sets the desired power level. Best to set it at 0.80 or above! But beware: the higher the desired power, the bigger your required sample size will be.
sig.level	Sets the level of significance α. Typically this will be 0.1, 0.05, or 0.01 depending upon how stringent you want your test to be (the smaller numbers correspond to more stringent tests, like you might use for high-cost or high-risk scenarios).
d	This is the effect size. A reasonable heuristic is to choose 0.1 for a small effect size, 0.3 for a medium effect size, and 0.5 for a large effect size.
type=c(" ")	Specify which t-test you are using: the one sample t-test ("one.sample"), the two-sample t-test ("two.sample"), or the paired t-test ("paired")? Put that word inside the quotes.
alternative=c(" ")	Specify which form of the alternative hypothesis you'll be using... the one with the < sign ("less")? The one with the > sign ("greater")? Or the two-tailed test with the ≠ sign ("two.sided")? Put that word inside the quotes.

Calculating Sample Sizes for Tests Involving Proportions (Z-Tests)

This section covers sample size calculations for the one proportion and two proportion z-tests. You are also required to specify whether your alternative hypothesis will be one tailed or two, so be sure you have defined your H_0 and H_a prior to starting your calculations. The `pwr.p.test` and `pwr.2p.test` commands take *five* arguments, which means you can use it to compute power and effect size in addition to just the sample size (if you want). So for the one proportion z-test, we can use `pwr.p.test` to get sample size like this:

```
> pwr.p.test(h=0.2,n=NULL,power=0.8,sig.level=0.05,alternative="two.sided")
```

proportion power calculation for binomial distribution (arcsine
transformation)

```
             h = 0.2
             n = 196.2215
     sig.level = 0.05
         power = 0.8
   alternative = two.sided
```

You can access the sample size directly here as well:

```
> pwr.p.test(h=0.2,n=NULL,power=0.8,sig.level=0.05,
alternative="two.sided")$n
[1] 196.2215
```

And for the two proportion z-test, we can use pwr.2p.test like this to compute required sample size (or access it directly using the $n variable notation at the end):

```
> pwr.2p.test(h=0.2,n=NULL,power=0.8,sig.level=0.05,
alternative="two.sided")
```

     Difference of proportion power calculation for binomial distribution
(arcsine transformation)

```
             h = 0.2
             n = 392.443
     sig.level = 0.05
         power = 0.8
   alternative = two.sided
```

NOTE: same sample sizes

```
> pwr.2p.test(h=0.2,n=NULL,power=0.8,sig.level=0.05,
alternative="two.sided")$n
[1] 392.443
```

Here are summaries of the arguments you can pass to pwr.p.test and pwr.2p.test:

Argument to `pwr.p.test`	What it means
n	Your sample size! Set to `NULL` if you want to compute it.
power	Sets the desired power level. Best to set it at 0.80 or above! But beware: the higher the desired power, the bigger your required sample size will be.
sig.level	Sets the level of significance α. Typically this will be 0.1, 0.05, or 0.01 depending upon how stringent you want your test to be (the smaller numbers correspond to more stringent tests, like you might use for high-cost or high-risk scenarios).
h	This is the effect size. A reasonable heuristic is to choose 0.2 for a small effect size, 0.5 for a medium effect size, and 0.8 for a large effect size.
alternative=c(" ")	Specify which form of the alternative hypothesis you'll be using... the one with the < sign ("less")? The one with the > sign ("greater")? Or the two-tailed test with the $\neq$ sign ("two.sided")? Put that word inside the quotes.

Argument to `pwr.2p.test`	What it means
n	Your sample size! Set to `NULL` if you want to compute it.
power	Sets the desired power level. Best to set it at 0.80 or above! But beware: the higher the desired power, the bigger your required sample size will be.
sig.level	Sets the level of significance α. Typically this will be 0.1, 0.05, or 0.01 depending upon how stringent you want your test to be (the smaller numbers correspond to more stringent tests, like you might use for high-cost or high-risk scenarios).
h	This is the effect size. A reasonable heuristic is to choose 0.2 for a small effect size, 0.5 for a medium effect size, and 0.8 for a large effect size.
alternative=c(" ")	Specify which form of the alternative hypothesis you'll be using... the one with the < sign ("less")? The one with the > sign ("greater")? Or the two-tailed test with the $\neq$ sign ("two.sided")? Put that word inside the quotes.

Calculating Sample Sizes for the Chi-Square Test of Independence

This section covers sample size calculations for the Chi-Square Test of Independence, which is performed on a contingency table created by tallying up observations that fall in each of two categories. The purpose of this test is to determine whether the two categorical variables are *independent* or *not* (that there is *some* kind of dependency within the data; you won't be able to tell what, specifically, without further experimentation). The `pwr.chisq.test` command takes *five* arguments, and like the other tests, you can find out the value of *any* of them with the remaining values. For a 3x3 contingency table where you expect a moderate effect size and `df=(r-1)(c-1)`, you would do this:

```
> pwr.chisq.test(w=0.3,N=NULL,df=4,sig.level=0.05,power=0.8)

        Chi squared power calculation

              w = 0.3
              N = 132.6143
             df = 4
      sig.level = 0.05
          power = 0.8

NOTE: N is the number of observations
```

Argument to `pwr.chisq.test`	What it means
N	Your sample size! Set to `NULL` if you want to compute it. Note: it's a **CAPITAL N**!
power	Sets the desired power level. Best to set it at 0.80 or above! But beware: the higher the desired power, the bigger your required sample size will be.
sig.level	Sets the level of significance α. Typically, this will be 0.1, 0.05, or 0.01 depending upon how stringent you want your test to be.
w	This is the effect size. A reasonable heuristic is to choose 0.1 for a small effect size, 0.3 for medium, and 0.5 for large.
df	Degrees of freedom; calculate by taking one less than the number of rows in the table, and one less than the number of columns in the table... then multiply them together.

Calculating Sample Sizes for One-Way Analysis of Variance (ANOVA)

This section covers sample size calculations for the one-way ANOVA, which tests for equivalence between several group means, and aims to determine whether *one of these means is not like the others*. The `pwr.anova.test` command takes *five* arguments, and like the other tests, you can find out the value of *any* of them with the remaining values. For an ANOVA test with four groups, you would do this:

```
> pwr.anova.test(k=4,f=0.3,sig.level=0.05,power=0.8)

     Balanced one-way analysis of variance power calculation

              k = 4
              n = 31.27917
              f = 0.3
      sig.level = 0.05
          power = 0.8

NOTE: n is number in each group
```

Here are summaries of all the arguments you can pass to `pwr.chisq.test`:

Argument to `pwr.anova.test`	What it means
n	Your sample size, in terms of *number of observations per group*! Set to NULL if you want to compute it.
power	Sets the desired power level. Best to set it at 0.80 or above! But beware: the higher the desired power, the bigger your required sample size will be.
sig.level	Sets the level of significance α. Typically this will be 0.1, 0.05, or 0.01 depending upon how stringent you want your test to be.
f	This is the effect size. A reasonable heuristic is to choose 0.1 for a small effect size, 0.3 for a medium effect size, and 0.5 for a large effect size.
k	Number of groups (Check the null hypothesis here... how many μ's do you see in it? That's your number of groups.)

Calculating Sample Sizes for Linear Regression

This section covers sample size calculations for regression tests, which examine linear relationships between predictor variables and response variables, and aims to determine *whether the linear relationship exists*. The `pwr.f2.test` command takes *five* arguments, and like the other tests, you can find out the value of *any* of them with the remaining values in place. For linear regression with `k` number of predictors (or independent variables), and `n` pairs of observations, you will set `u=k` and usually let `v=NULL` (although the expression for v is `n-(k+1)`). The last variable, `f2`, is the estimated effect size:

```
> pwr.f2.test(u=1, v=NULL, f2=0.15, sig.level=0.01, power=0.8)

      Multiple regression power calculation

              u = 1
              v = 79.23892
             f2 = 0.15
      sig.level = 0.01
          power = 0.8
```

Here are summaries of all the arguments you can pass to `pwr.2f.test`:

Argument to `pwr.2f.test`	What it means
u	The number of independent variables in the regression you want to do. For simple linear regression, u=1; for multiple regression, choose the number of factors you are using in your model.
v	Your sample size, in terms of *number of pairs of observations* - set to `NULL` if you want to compute it.
sig.level	Sets the level of significance α. Typically, this will be 0.1, 0.05, or 0.01 depending upon how stringent you
f2	This is the effect size. According to Cohen, 0.02, 0.15, and 0.35 represent small, medium, large effect sizes
power	Sets the desired power level. Best to set it at 0.80 or above! But beware: the higher the desired power, the bigger your required sample size will be.

213

Other Resources:

- http://en.wikipedia.org/wiki/Statistical_power
- http://en.wikipedia.org/wiki/Type_I_and_type_II_errors
- http://osc.centerforopenscience.org/2013/11/03/Increasing-statistical-power/
- http://www.r-bloggers.com/power-and-sample-size-analysis-z-test/
- Bausell, R. B. and Li, Y. (2002). Power Analysis for Experimental Research: A Practical Guide for the Biological, Medical and Social Sciences. Cambridge University Press, New York, New York.
- Cohen, J. (1988). Statistical power analysis for the behavioral sciences (2nd ed.). Hillsdale, NJ: Erlbaum.
- Cohen, J. (1992). A Power Primer. *Psychological Bulletin,* 112(1), p. 155-159.
- More guidelines for determining representative effect sizes: http://www.ats.ucla.edu/stat/mult_pkg/faq/general/effect_size_power/effect_size_power.htm

3.6 Sampling Distributions and the Central Limit Theorem

Objective

Why does the normal model play such a prominent role in so many basic statistical procedures? Why do we spend so much time studying and using it? Turns out, it's a mathematical artifact that emerges *often*, thanks to the Central Limit Theorem. This chapter describes several critical concepts that make it possible to do statistical inference using hypothesis tests, including sampling error and sampling distributions. Without sampling distributions, we wouldn't be able to construct confidence intervals (that is, estimate a *range of values* within which we believe the real population parameter lies) in the way most everyone does it. The Central Limit Theorem relates the characteristics of the sampling distribution to the population model and thus is very important in statistical thinking.

Sampling Error

Why do statistics in the first place? One big reason is this: we want to be able to determine the characteristics of a large *population* (the population parameters) by gathering data from just a small *sample* (the sample statistics). But getting information from all members of a population (called a *census*) can be costly, in terms of time, effort, and money. The United States Census (http://www.census.gov), for example, is only performed once every decade because of the challenges and costs associated with obtaining data from over 300 million people, and ensuring that it is accurate. In some cases, there's no way to get information from all the members of the population you're interested in studying (like if you're studying birds; really, you're going to catch *all* of them? Have fun.)

Each time you collect a sample, you're going to get a different sample: an entirely new collection of values from which you'll get a sample mean, a sample variance or standard deviation, and other characteristics. Those *sample statistics* can provide an approximation to what the *true population parameters* will be, but unless you have a super large sample size (that's guaranteed to cover all the possible values you might encounter in that population) you'll never exactly know what those values are for the whole population.

The difference between a sample statistic and its corresponding population parameter is called the sampling error. For example, if large-scale studies show that the average height of American women between 20-29 is 177.6 cm (http://en.wikipedia.org/wiki/Human_height), and I take a sample of 522 women who have a mean height of 175.1 cm, then the *sampling error* I've incurred is the difference between those two values.

A sample statistic is a random variable, and subject to random variation. Any time you collect a sample, there will *always* be a sampling error... unless you are performing a census.

Three Types of Distributions

Recall that a distribution just tells you how frequently different possible outcomes have been observed in a sample or in a population, and so they are often visualized using a histogram or a boxplot.

In the sections that follow, we talk about three different types of distributions:

- The **distribution of a sample** describes how frequently different outcomes have been observed within a small portion of the population (the sample).

- The **distribution of a population** describes how frequently different outcomes *can* be observed in a larger population. Since for many populations we can't actually observe all the possibilities, this is just a theoretical (or imagined, or envisioned) distribution.

- The **sampling distribution** of a sample statistic (often a *mean* or *proportion*) describes what you see after **repeatedly sampling** a population an infinite number of times. It is constructed by taking a statistic from each sample (often the sample mean), and collecting them all together into a distribution. It is a theoretical (or imagined) distribution that contains all of those sample statistics *as if you had collected an **infinite** number of samples*.

It can be difficult to keep all these definitions straight, so don't worry if it takes you a little time to get a good grasp on the differences. There will be a lot of repetition in this chapter to help, and hopefully, the simulation exercises in this chapter will also be useful. After you execute the code in this chapter yourself, you should try other variations like changing the sample size, the target statistic, and the input distributions, and see what happens.

Distribution of the Sample vs. Sampling Distribution

When you collect the data from your sample, you can plot a distribution of all of those values. This is called the ***distribution of the sample***. The mean of this distribution will provide an estimate of the real population mean. But they probably won't ever be *exactly* the same because of sampling error.

However, imagine what would happen if you collected another sample the next day. The histogram would look different, because you have different data! For every new sample you collect, even when the sample comes from the same population, you will have a new data set and a new collection of sample statistics (e.g. mean and variance). Let's say you repeated this process 100 times. What would happen if you created a histogram containing *all the means from all your samples?* Let's say it was possible for you to take *an infinite number of samples* and plot a histogram of their means. What would the distribution of sample means look like then???

That is the ***sampling distribution***: a model of a true population parameter, based on imagining that we can take smaller samples of that population an infinite number of times, and then plot our collection of sample statistics.

As an example, for the sampling distribution model of a mean, this model tells us that:

- The mean of the sampling distribution *is* the mean of the population

- The standard deviation of the sampling distribution is smaller than the standard deviation of the population. (It's calculated by taking the standard deviation of the population, and dividing by the square root of the number of individual samples, n). **The bigger the n, the thinner the sampling distribution will be... meaning the standard error of your estimate will be smaller.**

It doesn't matter what the sample size is... these two points are always true! What *does* change as the sample size gets bigger is that the *sampling distribution starts to look more and more like a normal distribution.*

Let's take a look at this by *approximating* some sampling distributions now.

> **But first, a warning!!** Because the sampling distribution of a sample statistic is the population of *all possible values* that you could get for that statistic when you take your own sample, the simulations that follow aren't going to produce perfect sampling distributions. We can't ever simulate *all possible values*, but we can simulate *a lot of values.* This is why in all the simulations you'll see here, we use *at least 10,000 replications.* The sampling distribution isn't really a sampling distribution unless you use a lot of replications.

This process of obtaining many, many, many random samples pulled from a distribution of our choice can be easily accomplished in R. This code <u>r</u>andomly pulls values from an **exp**onential distribution with a mean of 1/3 (the inverse of whatever number you give to the `rexp` command).

```
> n <- 10 # Number of observations in each sample
> r < 10000  # Number of replications (or total samples)
> my.samples <- matrix(rexp(n*r,3),r)
```

Now that we have 10,000 samples, we can take the mean *of each one* using the `apply` command, and then plot the 10,000 means we've calculated. This code will produce two plots: a **distribution of the sample** on the left, and a **sampling distribution of the means** on the right:

```
> all.sample.means <- apply(my.samples,1,mean)
> par(mfrow=c(1,2))
> hist(my.samples[1,],col="gray",main="Distribution of One Sample")
> text(0.9,4.1,paste("Mean of One\nSample =", round(mean(my.samples[1,]),
      2)), pos=2, cex=0.8)
> hist(all.sample.means,col="gray",main="Sampling Distribution of the
      Mean")
> text(1.0,1510,paste("Mean of Sampling\nDistribution Over\n",r," Samples
      of ", n,"\nObs Each =", round(mean(all.sample.means),2)), pos=2,
      cex=0.8)
```

Distribution of One Sample

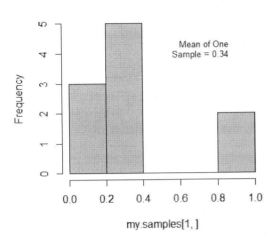

Sampling Distribution of the Mean

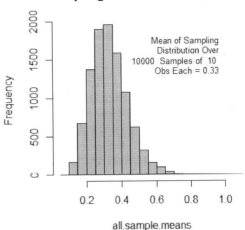

The plot on the LEFT is the distribution of one (only one!) of the 10,000 samples that we generated. It includes only 10 observations. It is the **distribution of the sample**. You can kind of even see that it looks like an exponential distribution (which is what we expect, because we used `rexp` to generate the values) even though the sample size is so tiny. The plot on the RIGHT is the distribution of the means from each of those 10,000 samples. It includes 10,000 observations, because we obtain one mean from each sample. It is **an approximation of the sampling distribution of the mean**, and it is starting to look kind of normal, even though it has a little tail and is somewhat skewed to the right.

Now, let's increase the sample size, n. For the plots above, we only used 10 observations in each sample. Now let's use 200, which is a more realistic large sample size. (I can easily see myself conducting a survey, and my power analysis telling me that I need 200 respondents.) So let's simulate that:

```
> n <- 200 # Number of observations in each sample
> r <- 10000  # Number of replications (or total samples)
> my.samples <- matrix(rexp(n*r,3),r)
> all.sample.means <- apply(my.samples,1,mean)
> par(mfrow=c(1,2))
> hist(my.samples[1,],col="gray",main="Distribution of One Sample")
```

219

```
> text(1.8,80,paste("Mean of One\nSample =", round(mean(my.samples[1,]),
    2)), pos=2, cex=0.8)
> hist(all.sample.means,col="gray",main="Sampling Distribution of the
    Mean")
> text(.43,1400,paste("Mean of Sampling\nDistribution Over\n",r,"
    Samples\nof ", n,"Obs\n Each =", round(mean(all.sample.means),2)),
    pos=2, cex=0.8)
```

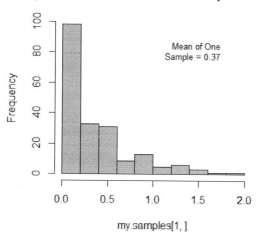

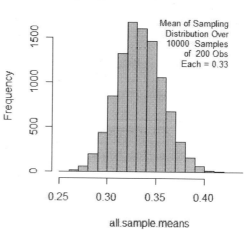

Notice how the histograms have changed? First, the distribution of the sample (on the left) is looking more and more like an exponential distribution. Next, look at the scale of the y axes. The frequencies are different for the distributions of one sample, because we had 10 observations in each sample earlier, and we have 200 observations in each sample now. With 10,000 sample means, each created from a sample containing 200 observations, we should be able to get a good sense of the shape and parameters of the sampling distribution. And we do: the nice, symmetric normal shape of the sampling distribution is now readily apparent.

Here's the cool part about this simulation: we actually *know* what the true population parameters are, so we can compare our *estimate* of the mean (that's just the mean from one of our samples) to the *mean of our simulated, approximated sampling distribution* to the *real population mean* that we know because we decided what it would be in the beginning. Remember the first time we called `rexp`, because we wanted to get a bunch of values that had been randomly sampled from an exponential distribution with a mean of 1/3?

Estimate of the means from two of our samples	0.34 and 0.37
Mean of our approximate sampling distribution (10,000 replications)	0.33
Mean of the exact sampling distribution (∞ replications)	0.33
Real population mean	0.33

Our approximate sampling distribution of the mean did provide a pretty good estimate of the population mean in this case, but sometimes it will be slightly off. But the exact sampling distribution will always have the same mean as the population. As sample size n gets larger, the approximations to the mean won't get better, but the variability about the mean will decrease... providing us with a more constrained estimate. We can be even more sure about it.

(Note: If you do the sampling distribution simulations yourself, you'll get a different collection of random values every time unless you set your random number seed with `set.seed(n)` where `n` is some integer. Also, applying the text to the histograms above is tricky, and requires that you adjust those first two numbers passed to `text` to approximate the `x, y` coordinates of where you want that text to print. Those coordinates depend on the actual dimensions of the x-axis and the y-axis, though, which will depend on exactly what numbers come out when you generate your simulated data with `rexp`.)

How Accurate is My Estimate?

The sampling distribution model provided the basis for determining how accurate your estimate of a population parameter is, given what you know about your sample. So if you want to know "How accurate is my estimate of the mean, $\bar{y}$?" just compute the standard error of the mean, SE($\bar{y}$), which is equal to $\sigma/\sqrt{n}$. If you want to know "How accurate is my estimation of the difference between population means?" just calculate the standard error of the difference, or SE(p-hat$_1$ – p-hat$_2$).

The Central Limit Theorem

<u>If you take many repeated samples from a population, and calculate the *averages* or *sum* of each one, the collection of those averages will be normally distributed</u>. It doesn't matter what distribution they came from (pretty much). **This is the Central Limit Theorem**.

It doesn't matter what the source distribution is: it can be normal, exponential, uniform, triangular, or any other distribution imaginable! According to the Central Limit Theorem, the population of all possible sample means (or sums) will be normal, so we can use our sample and the normal model to get a sense of what the population's characteristics are. There are two lessons here for answering your own research questions:

- Yes, a bigger sample size (n) is usually better, because this will force the variability of the sampling distribution to become tinier.
- In practice, you do NOT have to draw multiple samples to make valid statistical inferences. One sample is OK.

The sampling distributions that we get from repeated sampling can help us hone in on characteristics of the larger population from which the samples were collected.

Other Sampling Distributions

In the description of the Central Limit Theorem above, we mentioned that other sampling distributions of sample statistics also exist, and as the sample size n gets bigger, they will begin to look more and more like normal distributions:

```
> n <- 200 # Number of observations in each sample
> r <- 10000  # Number of replications (or total samples)

> my.samples <- matrix(rexp(n*r,3),r)
```

```
> all.sample.sums <- apply(my.samples,1,sum)
> all.sample.means <- apply(my.samples,1,mean)
> all.sample.vars <- apply(my.samples,1,var)
> par(mfrow=c(2,2), mar=c(5,5,5,3), oma=c(3,3,5,3))
> hist(my.samples[1,],col="gray",main="Distribution of One Sample")
> hist(all.sample.sums,col="gray",main="Sampling Distribution\nof the
        Sum")
> hist(all.sample.means,col="gray",main="Sampling Distribution\nof the
        Mean")
> hist(all.sample.vars,col="gray",main="Sampling Distribution\nof the
        Variance")
> mtext("Approximate SDMs for\nExponential Source Distribution (n=200)",
        outer=TRUE, line=1, cex=1.5)
```

Approximate SDMs for
Exponential Source Distribution (n=200)

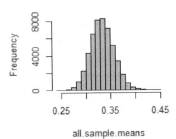

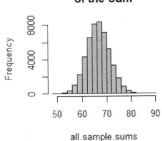

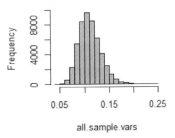

A Custom Function for SDM Simulations in R

Explore how the Central Limit Theorem comes into play for more source distributions here. Load the function with the first line of code... the rest is shown so you can see what it does.

```
source("https://raw.githubusercontent.com/NicoleRadziwill/R-
Functions/master/sdmsim.R")
```

```
sdm.sim <- function(n,src.dist=NULL,param1=NULL,param2=NULL) {
    r <- 10000   # Number of replications/samples - DO NOT ADJUST
    # This produces a matrix of observations with
    # n columns and r rows. Each row is one sample:
    my.samples <- switch(src.dist,
        "E" = matrix(rexp(n*r,param1),r),
        "N" = matrix(rnorm(n*r,param1,param2),r),
        "U" = matrix(runif(n*r,param1,param2),r),
        "P" = matrix(rpois(n*r,param1),r),
        "B" = matrix(rbinom(n*r,param1,param2),r),
        "G" = matrix(rgamma(n*r,param1,param2),r),
        "X" = matrix(rchisq(n*r,param1),r),
        "T" = matrix(rt(n*r,param1),r))
    all.sample.sums <- apply(my.samples,1,sum)
    all.sample.means <- apply(my.samples,1,mean)
    all.sample.vars <- apply(my.samples,1,var)
    par(mfrow=c(2,2))
    hist(my.samples[1,],col="gray",main="Distribution of One
        Sample")
    hist(all.sample.sums,col="gray",main="Sampling Distribution\nof
        the Sum")
    hist(all.sample.means,col="gray",main="Sampling Distribution\nof
        the Mean")
    hist(all.sample.vars,col="gray",main="Sampling Distribution\nof
        the Variance")
}
```

There are 8 population distributions to choose from: exponential (E), normal (N), uniform (U), Poisson (P), binomial (B), gamma (G), Chi-Square (X), and the Student's t distribution (t). Note also that you have to provide either one or two parameters, depending upon what distribution you are selecting. For example, a normal distribution requires that you specify the mean and standard deviation to describe where it's centered, and how fat or thin it is (that's two parameters). A Chi-square distribution requires that you specify the degrees of freedom (that's only one parameter). You can find out what to specify for *all* of them here: http://en.wikibooks.org/wiki/R_Programming/Probability_Distributions. Here are examples of simulations you can construct using `sdm.sim`. Notice that you aren't ever asked to specify the number of replications, because the sampling distribution is (by definition) what you get when you take an *infinite number of samples* from a population. I set that number of replications to 10,000, not because it's ideal, but because it's close enough to infinity to characterize the right shape and center of the sampling distributions, and far enough away from infinity to *not* crash your computer. I think that's a good compromise. Try these to see how the patterns described by the CLT emerge as you increase the number of observations:

```
sdm.sim(10,src.dist="E",1)
sdm.sim(50,src.dist="E",1)
sdm.sim(100,src.dist="E",1)
sdm.sim(10,src.dist="X",14)
sdm.sim(50,src.dist="X",14)
sdm.sim(100,src.dist="X",14)
sdm.sim(10,src.dist="N",param1=20,param2=3)
sdm.sim(50,src.dist="N",param1=20,param2=3)
sdm.sim(100,src.dist="N",param1=20,param2=3)
sdm.sim(10,src.dist="G",param1=5,param2=5)
sdm.sim(50,src.dist="G",param1=5,param2=5)
sdm.sim(100,src.dist="G",param1=5,param2=5)
```

Other Resources:

- If you're a statistics instructor, you'll definitely be interested in this article, which raises awareness of how (and how not!) to use simulation to demonstrate the concepts of sampling distribution and the Central Limit Theorem. Sampling distributions, by definition, model what you would see only if an infinite number of samples were selected from a population. Watkins, A. E., Bargagliotti, A., & Franklin, C. (2014). Simulation of the Sampling Distribution of the Mean Can Mislead. *Journal of Statistics Education,* 22(3). http://www.amstat.org/publications/jse/v22n3/watkins.pdf
- Although we typically refer to the Central Limit Theorem for means when we say "Central Limit Theorem," it is actually a family of theorems which includes the Central Limit Theorem for sums. You can find out more about that one here: http://www.saylor.org/site/wp-content/uploads/2011/06/MA121-4.1.2.pdf

3.7 P-Values, Confidence Intervals, and Controversy

Objective

Answering a research question using statistical inference involves setting up a *null hypothesis*, that describes what you *think or believe* about a characteristic of a population, and an *alternative hypothesis* that represents some other possibility. The **P-Value** answers this question: assuming the null hypothesis is indeed true, what is the probability that the sample you collected *actually* came from the population that the null hypothesis describes?

Although many research studies *just* report their P-Values, it can be useful to provide a range of values that (based on your sample statistics) could potentially represent the values of population parameters. Those are called **confidence intervals**.

However, there are pitfalls both with P-Values and confidence intervals that many people don't ever hear about. For one, the concept of "statistical significance" is sensitive to both sampling error and *how* you set up your research questions. Also, there are many different ways to calculate confidence intervals, and some approaches are much better than others. In this chapter, we don't aim to cover all of the subtleties, just to help you become aware that they exist.

Background

The P-Value is a portion of the area underlying a probability distribution function. It's located either to the *right* of the test statistic that you've calculated from your sample (for the one-tailed test where your alternative hypothesis has a "*greater than*" sign in it) or to the *left* of that calculated test statistic (for the one-tailed test where your alternative hypothesis has a "*less than*" sign in it). For a two-tailed test, in which your alternative hypothesis contains the "*not equal to*" sign ($\neq$), you multiply your calculated P-Value by 2 to reflect that you want the areas *both to the right and left* of the positive and negative signs on your computed test statistic.

Since the total area under a probability distribution is always 100%, the smallest P-Value that you can observe would be 0 (meaning that there's no way your sample came from the population that you've envisioned in your null hypothesis). The largest P-Value you could observe would be 1 (suggesting that it's pretty likely that your sample came from the population you described by your null hypothesis. The higher the P-Value, the more likely it is that your null hypothesis actually describes the overall population from which you took your sample. The tinier the P-Value, the more likely it is that your sample didn't come from the population you thought it did, and so with tiny P-Values you reject your null hypothesis in favor of the alternative.

Lots of people think there is something magical about $\alpha=0.05$, that level of significance that says you're willing to accept the risk that 1 out of every 20 samples you collect (1/20=0.05), you will reject the null hypothesis - when in fact it's an accurate representation of the population. But this is kind of a scary thing to accept, and here's why. Most of my classes have about 25 students in them, so sometimes I will have each student go collect a sample of the same quantitative variable from the student population (say, for example, cumulative Grade Point Average or GPA). They each come back with a sample collected from 30 other students (because, according to the Central Limit Theorem, a sample size of 30 is considered "large enough" for it to be in effect). Based on the mean cumulative GPA from their samples, each student performs a hypothesis test, comparing their own sample's mean to the University's published average GPA of 3.2 (a one sample t-test). As their alternative hypothesis, they choose that the real population's cumulative GPA is less than 3.2.

Every time we do this, at least one or two students rejects the null hypothesis (detecting an effect that wasn't really there, and incurring a false positive!) And that's expected, with an α of 0.05! If those same students who rejected the null hypothesis went to collect a second sample of student GPAs, it's likely that their P-Value would not indicate that they should reject the null. It's so easy to draw an incorrect conclusion just due to sampling error... and as a researcher, we are selectively drawn to our "statistically significant" findings and thus are more apt to publish them and share them with the world. Replication, particularly by multiple researchers, can help. So can making sure that you've done a power analysis prior to your research, and having an understanding of what *effect size* you're trying to detect. With GPAs, it's much easier to detect a real 0.5 difference from what the University believes the average GPA is as compared to a real 0.02 difference.

Confidence Intervals

> *"Statistical significance is often a crutch, a catchier-sounding but less informative substitute for a good confidence interval."*

> *--Alex Reinhart in* **Statistics Done Wrong**

Conveniently, you don't even *need* to develop a null hypothesis or decide upon an alternative hypothesis if you have a sample of data collected, and you just want to figure out *the range of likely values* for a population parameter based on statistics from your sample. Confidence intervals are powerful because they will give you some sense of the effect size, that is, *how big (really!) is the difference between these groups I'm observing*?

Unfortunately, not all formulas to construct confidence intervals are created equal. The most commonly used expression to compute the confidence interval of a proportion (the Wald confidence interval), for example, has been shown to be wildly inaccurate for proportions less than 0.2 and greater than 0.8, and not even accurate as advertised for the confidence level you think you should be getting. That is, if you construct a 95% confidence interval even when you're well inside the bounds of 0.2 to 0.8, you'll only be getting a 90-92% confidence interval for real. That's called *coverage probability*, and in this case, it's not too nice.

The entirety of **Section 4: Confidence Intervals and Standard Error** provides recipes for producing confidence intervals with good coverage probabilities, and for calculating standard error to answer the question "How accurate is the estimate I obtained from my sample?"

Controversy

Much of what follows comes from a post that I wrote in March of 2015, entitled "Why the Ban on P-Values? And What Now?" You can find it on my Quality and Innovation blog at http://qualityandinnovation.com/2015/03/07/why-the-ban-on-P-Values-and-what-now/. It was motivated by an early 2015 decision made by the editors of *Basic and Applied Social Psychology*, an academic journal, to ban P-Values from any research results submitted to their journal. Their editorial stated that "the p < 0.05 bar is too easy to pass and sometimes serves as an excuse for lower quality research." I can't disagree, based on the fact that an inference test at this level just within one of my 25-student classes will usually result in at least one student rejecting the null hypothesis when they shouldn't have, thus incurring Type I Error (a false positive). That seems like a lot to me. Almost immediately after those editors published their announcement, a few academics chimed in on the debate (which is at http://www.statslife.org.uk/opinion/2114-journal-s-ban-on-null-hypothesis-significance-testing-reactions-from-the-statistical-arena):

Peter Diggle – RSS president and professor of biostatistics, epidemiology and population health at Lancaster University	"I share the editors' concerns that inferential statistical methods are open to mis-use and mis-interpretation, but do not feel that a blanket ban on any particular inferential method is the most constructive response.
Stephen Senn - Head of Competence Center for Methodology and Statistics at the Luxembourg Institute of Health	"Attempting to eliminate false positives in inference is to attempt scientific sterility and banning formal inferential methods won't even help to achieve this foolish aim."
Andrew Gelman - Professor of statistics and political science and director of the Applied Statistics Center at Columbia University	" I think standard errors, P-Values, and confidence intervals can be very helpful in research when considered as convenient parts of a data analysis. Standard errors etc. are helpful in giving a lower bound on uncertainty. The problem comes when they're considered as the culmination of the analysis, as if 'p less than 0.05' represents some kind of proof of something. I do like the idea of requiring that research claims stand on their own without requiring the (often spurious) support of P-Values."
Geoff Cumming - Emeritus professor at the School of Psychological Science at La Trobe University	"One big problem is that p is a single value, which suggests certainty, whereas the extent of a confidence interval makes uncertainty salient. On replication, P-Values bounce around amazingly - the 'dance of the P-Values'. Confidence intervals also bounce, but the extent of any interval gives a reasonable idea of the amount of bouncing. In stark contrast, a single P-Value gives almost no idea how much p is likely to bounce on replication."
Robert Grant - Senior lecturer in health and social care statistics at St George's, University of London	"If we trained researchers to consider all subjectivities and personal biases, and to be open about them, in the

and Kingston University	way that good qualitative researchers are, far fewer errors would be made. A little dose of philosophy of science early on in training could help avoid common pitfalls later. A crude response like banning P-Values serves as a fig leaf, because the problem is in how researchers think."

"Dance of the P-Values"

As indicated by Geoff Cumming, P-Values are very sensitive to sampling error. Here's a simulation I wrote to illustrate it, based on the example I gave earlier about students going out to collect samples of cumulative GPAs.

"You're a student at a university in a class full of other students. I tell you to go out and randomly sample 100 students, asking them what their cumulative GPA is. You come back to me with 100 different values, and some mean value that represents

the average of all the GPAs you went out and collected. You can also find the standard deviation of all the values in your sample of 100. Everyone has their own unique sample.

It's pretty intuitive that everyone will come back with a different sample... and thus everyone will have a different point estimate of the average GPA that students have at your university. But, according to the central limit theorem, we also know that if we take the collection of all the average GPAs and plot a histogram, it will be normally distributed with a peak around the real average GPA. Some students' estimates will be really close to the real average GPA. Some students' estimates will be much lower (for example, if you collected the data at a meeting for students who are on academic probation). Some students' estimates will be much higher (for example, if you collected the data at a meeting for honors students). This is sampling error, which can lead to incorrect inferences during significance testing.

Inferential statistics is good because it lets us make decisions about a whole population just based on one sample. It would require a lot of time, or a lot of effort, to go out and collect a whole bunch of samples. Inferential statistics is bad if your sample size is too small (and thus you haven't captured the variability in the population within your sample) or have one of these unfortunate too-high or too-low samples, because you can make incorrect inferences. Like this."

The Input Distribution

I wanted to make this example as realistic as possible:

"Since we want to randomly sample the cumulative GPAs of students, let's choose a distribution that reasonably reflects the distribution of all GPAs at a university. To do this, I searched the web to see if I could find data that might help me get this distribution. I found some data from the University of Colorado Boulder that describes GPAs and their corresponding percentile ranks. From this data, I could put together an empirical CDF, and then since the CDF is the integral of the PDF, I approximated the PDF by taking the derivatives of the CDF. (I know this isn't the most efficient way to do it, but I wanted to see both plots):

```
score <- c(.06,2.17,2.46,2.67,2.86,3.01,3.17,3.34,3.43,3.45,
        3.46,3.48,3.5,3.52,3.54,3.56,3.58,3.6,3.62,3.65,3.67,3.69,
        3.71,3.74,3.77,3.79,3.82,3.85,3.88,3.91,3.94,3.96,4.0,4.0)
perc.ranks <- c(0,10,20,30,40,50,60,70,75,76,77,78,79,80,81,
        82,83,84,85,86,87,88,89,90,91,92,93,94,95,96,97,98,99,100)
fn <- ecdf(perc.ranks)
xs <- score
ys <- fn(perc.ranks)
slope <- rep(NA,length(xs))
for (i in 2:length(xs)) {
        slope[i] <- (ys[i]-ys[i-1])/(xs[i]-xs[i-1])
}
slope[1] <- 0
slope[length(xs)] <- slope[length(xs)-1]
```

I plotted them together so that I might be able to choose a probability distribution that looked like it would model these real GPAs:

```
> par(mfrow=c(1,2))
> plot(xs,slope,type="l",main="Estimated PDF")
```

231

```
> plot(xs,ys,type="l",main="Estimated CDF")
> dev.off()
```

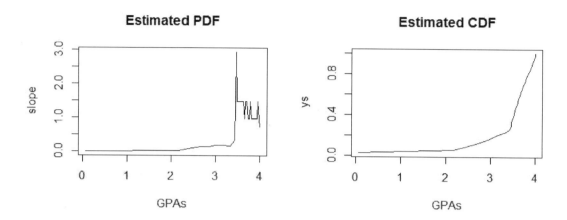

Estimated PDF

Estimated CDF

GPAs

GPAs

"I looked around for a distribution that might approximate what I saw… I found the ***Stable Distribution***, *and played around with the parameters until I plotted something that looked like the empirical PDF from the Boulder data:"*

```
> x <- seq(0,4,length=100)
> hx <- dstable(x, alpha=0.5, beta=0.75, gamma=1, delta=3.2)
> plot(x,hx,type="l",lty=2,lwd=2)
```

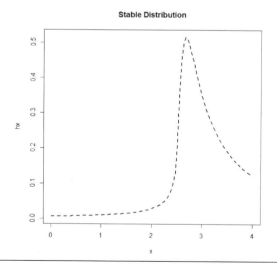

Stable Distribution

The Simulation

Using the stable distribution with the parameters above, here's how I used R to pretend like I had 10,000 students who were all collecting samples from this population and performing inference tests where they would make decisions with their P-Values:

"First, I used `pwr.t.test` to do a power analysis to see what sample size I needed to obtain a power of 0.8, assuming a small but not tiny effect size, at a level of significance of 0.05. It told me I needed at least 89. So I'll tell my students to each collect a sample of 100 other students.

Now that I have a distribution to sample from, I can pretend like I'm sending 10,000 students out to collect a sample of 100 students' cumulative GPAs. I want each of my 10,000 students to run a one-sample t-test to evaluate the null hypothesis that the real cumulative GPA is 3.0 against the alternative hypothesis that the actual cumulative GPA is greater than 3.0. (Fortunately, R makes it easy for me to pretend I have all these students.)"

```
sample.size <- 100
numtrials <- 10000
p.vals <- rep(NA,numtrials)
gpa.means <- rep(NA,numtrials)
compare.to <- 3.00
for (j in 1:numtrials) {
    r <- rstable(n=1000,alpha=0.5,beta=0.75,gamma=1,delta=3.2)
    meets.conds <- r[r>0 & r<4.001]
    my.sample <- round(meets.conds[1:sample.size],3)
    gpa.means[j] <- round(mean(my.sample),3)
    p.vals[j] <- >t.test(my.sample, mu=compare.to,
            alternative="greater")$p.value
    if (p.vals[j] < 0.02) {
    # capture the last one of these data sets to look at later
    capture <- my.sample
    }
}
```

Next, I wanted to summarize the outcomes for all these different P-Values, and count just how many of the 10,000 samples were associated with "significant" P-Values:

```
> summary(p.vals)
 Min. 1st Qu. Median Mean 3rd Qu. Max.
0.005457 0.681300 0.870900 0.786200 0.959300 1.000000
> p.vals.under.pointohfive <- p.vals[p.vals<0.05]
> length(p.vals.under.pointohfive)
[1] 46
> par(mfrow=c(1,2))
> hist(capture,main="One Rogue Sample",col="purple")
> boxplot(p.vals,main="All P-Values")
```

The plot on the left represents *just one of the samples*, specifically chosen to be one of those samples that was particularly impacted by sampling error. That means the histogram below is the *distribution of the sample*. The boxplot on the right displays all of the different P-Values that were obtained by each of my 10,000 students:

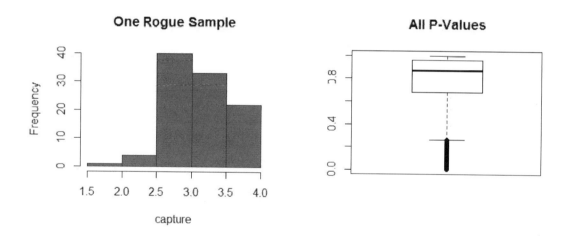

Although many P-Values are well above 0.05, there are 46 that are not - even though the population of GPAs is clearly well below the 3.0 we compared these students to! Even for a study where we *know* we shouldn't have rejected the null, 46 times out of 10,000 we will incur a false positive and possibly make incorrect decisions that impact peoples' lives. But 46 out of 10,000 isn't that much, you might say! That's true, unless you were the one who performed the research where you got one of those 46 P-Values under 0.05, and you ended up making harmful decisions that embarrassed you later.

> *"It is misleading to emphasize the statistically significant findings of any single team. What matters is the totality of the evidence."* – John P. A. Ioannidis in **Why Most Published Research Findings Are False**

What Do We Do? How Can We Be Good Researchers?

As you can see, P-Values are very sensitive to sampling error. Is there a solution for the inadequacies of using P-Values to make decisions? What can we do to become better researchers? There are a few things to keep in mind. First, we shouldn't give up on P-Values entirely. They play an important role in helping us determine whether there are differences between values measured from multiple groups. However, we need to remember that conducting and communicating research is complex: rather than telling a story using just one piece of evidence (the P-Value) we should be telling our story using multiple methods. What pieces of evidence should be presented, in addition to our P-Values and conclusions?

- Construct **confidence intervals** around your estimates
- Perform **power analysis** to ensure that your sample sizes are large enough to detect an effect (see more details in Chapter 3-5)
- Pay more attention to methods that focus on determining **effect sizes**
- Start exploring the new techniques of **accuracy in parameter estimation (AIPE)** and see how you can apply them to your work (caveat: I don't know how to do this yet, but I'll definitely be learning)
- Supplement your study with **meta-analysis** (that is, specifically look for the results other researchers have come up with and see how your results fit)
- Share results that you get that are **not** statistically significant
- Make your **data open and accessible**, and provide enough information to other researchers to ensure *replicability:* make it feasible for them to re-run your study using the same methods or slightly different methods.

This last element makes it possible for other researchers to replicate our studies, or to combine new data with the data we have collected (called "Open Science"). Collecting more data, and replicating our studies, can be costly (in terms of time, money, and effort). As a result, we don't typically do it ourselves, and we don't make it easy for other investigators to do it. This is one thing that the community of researchers needs to collectively change.

"Null Hypothesis" - an XKCD cartoon by Randal Munroe
(https://xkcd.com/892/)

Other Resources:

- Everyone who's interested in being a careful researcher should read Alex Reinhart's 2015 book entitled *Statistics Done Wrong*. Everyone.
- To find out more about the various incarnations of expressions for the confidence interval on a single proportion, check out Newcombe's 1998 article from *Statistics in Medicine*: http://www.stats.org.uk/statistical-inference/Newcombe1998.pdf
- Large portions of this chapter (in quotes) were drawn from a March 7, 2015 blog post that I wrote at http://qualityandinnovation.com/2015/03/07/why-the-ban-on-P-Values-and-what-now/.
- The University of Colorado - Boulder GPA data was obtained from this site: http://www.colorado.edu/pba/records/cumgpa/147/pctl.htm

3.8 A Sample Project Proposal: Tattoos

Objective

The previous sections in Chapter 3 have presented the difference between experiments and observational studies, the 12-step process for conducting your study and presenting your results, a system for developing sound research questions, and methods for determining the appropriate sample size based on how much cost and risk you are willing to accept. But before my students start their research projects, it's important for me to know that they have scoped their projects effectively, and will be able to complete the work during the course of the semester. Here is the basic information that I ask them to compile prior to beginning the data collection activities. This can serve as a basis for *you* to plan your research study. If you can't answer all of these questions, you're not ready to start! **Fortunately, everything in the proposal can be duplicated in the Methodology section.**

Sample Project Proposal

Statistics Semester Project:
Are Tattoos Only for Degenerates?

Team Members: Mary, Tim S., Tim C., Nasima Q.

Description: We plan to see if some of the stereotypes regarding tattoos are supported by data. We want to find out whether people with tattoos are more likely to have smoked marijuana, been arrested for crimes, or have lower GPAs. It is important because tattoos are met with disapproval in certain areas of society, such as business and politics.

This data can show whether or not there is a relationship between tattoos and the negative things our research questions ask about. This data could be useful to young people who have or are interested in getting tattoos, and want additional data before making such a permanent decision.

Data Collection: This is an observational study. We will use cluster sampling, obtaining survey data from 189 students we randomly sample at the Quad, D Hall/E Hall, inside the ISAT building, and in front of the Carrier Library. We will exclude all the responses where students have gotten their tattoos for religious reasons. This will allow us to draw conclusions at the $\alpha=0.05$ level with a power of 0.80.

Categorical Variables:
1. Do you have tattoos (yes or no)
2. Have you tried marijuana or not (yes or no)
3. Have you been arrested for a crime or not (yes or no)
4. Are your tattoos religious or not (yes or no)
5. Gender (male or female)

Quantitative Variables:
1. Cumulative GPA
2. Number of tattoos

Research Questions:

	Research Question	Statistical Test Selected to Answer Question
1	Is there a relationship between whether a student has tattoos and whether they have tried marijuana?	Chi-Square Test of Independence
2A & 2B	Do students without tattoos have higher GPAs than students with tattoos? Do students with more than 2 tattoos have higher GPAs than students who have less than 2 tattoos?	Two 2-sample t-tests
3	Is there a relationship between whether a student has tattoos and whether they have been arrested for a crime?	Chi-Square Test of Independence
4	Is the proportion of JMU males that have tattoos different than the proportion of JMU females that have tattoos?	2-proportion z-test

SECTION 4: CONFIDENCE INTERVALS AND STANDARD ERROR

- How to Compute Standard Error for Many Different Kinds of Samples
- How to Construct Confidence Intervals - Good Ones!!
- Understand the Concept of Coverage Probability and that Not All Confidence Intervals Are Created Equal

4.1 One Mean

Objective

How well does a *sample* mean (x-bar or y-bar) provide an estimate of the *population* mean μ? By constructing a confidence interval around the estimate from our sample, we determine a *range of values* that we believe contains the true population mean. We choose a *confidence level* (e.g. 90%, 95%, 99%) that tells us how likely it is that the true population mean lies within that interval. As a result, an interval estimate provides much more information than a point estimate. Here's one way to imagine it:

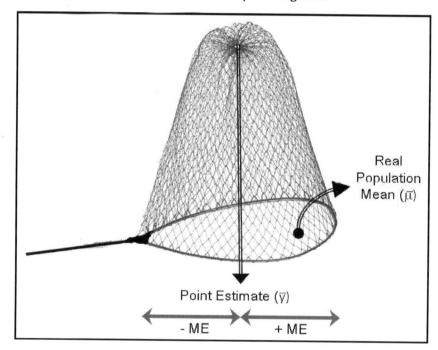

- You're standing on the number line where your point estimate (y-bar) is. On a boat.
- The real mean, μ, is a fish floating somewhere out there, either ahead of you or behind you, compared to that estimate.
- You want to catch that fish, so you cast a net (that's the confidence interval).

- How confident do you want to be that you *actually* catch that fish? That's your confidence level (90%, 95%, 99%). So you cast a symmetric net that extends behind you a certain distance (the margin of error), as well as *ahead* of you that same distance.
- If you want to be more confident that you actually catch that μ fish, you're going to need a bigger net. That's why 99% confidence intervals are bigger than 95% confidence intervals, and 95% confidence intervals are bigger than 90% confidence intervals.

Since the margin of error is half the size of the confidence interval net, the margin of error will also increase as the confidence level increases.

Sampling Distribution and Standard Error of the Mean

To compute the confidence interval, we need to know the **sampling distribution** for the mean: that is, the entire collection of possible samples that *I could have acquired* even though I only went out to collect one sample. (We can think of the sampling distribution as the *distribution of all possible random samples of a particular size*.)

Each one of your random samples will have its own mean (x-bar). All of those potential means are drawn from a normal model with its center at the real population mean μ, and a standard deviation calculated by dividing the population's standard deviation σ by the square root of the number of observations:

$$\overline{X} \sim N\left(\mu, \frac{\sigma}{\sqrt{n}}\right)$$

The standard deviation of the sampling distribution is all that stuff to the right of the comma. It's referred to as the "standard error of the mean", because the bigger our random sample *n* is, the better we can use our sample mean to approximate the real population mean.

In contrast to the standard deviation, which tells us the spread or dispersion of *all the values* within a population, standard error tells us how much the *means* of those values will be spread around (depending on how big a sample size we choose). <u>Consequently, standard error is a characteristic of a random sampling *process*, NOT of the population.</u>

Form of the Confidence Interval for One Mean

The general form of a confidence interval is:

$$CI \, : \, Estimate \, \pm \, Margin \, of \, Error$$

The specific form of the confidence interval for one mean is:

$$\overline{y} \pm C^* SE(\overline{y})$$

Our *estimate* for the mean is the average value computed from our sample (y-bar). C is a critical value (either a t* or a z*) that describes how **fat** we want our confidence interval to be, based on how much we want to catch the fish that is the real population mean. The standard error calculation depends on whether we know the variance of the population.

If You DON'T Know the Variance or Standard Deviation of the Population

Typically, you won't have any idea what the scatter or dispersion is of all your values across the entire population. In that case, this expression will provide the best estimate of the population standard deviation:

$$\overline{y} \pm t^*_{df} \frac{s}{\sqrt{n}}$$

Critical values of t (t^*_{df}) will depend on how big the sample size is. The confidence interval net needs to be *bigger* if we have a smaller sample size, and thus are not certain we've captured the variability in the population within our sample.

| | 4.1 CI for One Mean | | |
Confidence Interval	R Code to Find Critical t (t*) for n=30 (df=29)	Critical t (t*) for n=30 (df=29)	Critical t (t*) for df = 1000 (same as z*)
90% CI	qt(0.95,df=29)	1.699	1.645
95% CI	qt(0.975,df=29)	2.045	1.962
99% CI	qt(0.995,df=29)	2.756	2.576

If You DO Know the Variance or Standard Deviation of the Population

Sometimes, you do know the variance in the overall population. If your sample size is big enough (that is, $n \geq 30$), you've probably captured the variability of the entire population in your sample, and can use the sample standard deviation *s* as an approximation for the population standard deviation σ.

You might also have *other* ways to know the variance across the population. For example, if you manage a dairy farm, you might know from observations over many years or from scientific studies *exactly* what the variance in daily milk production is for a dairy cow. IF YOU KNOW IT, USE IT! You'll get a much better estimate for the confidence interval:

$$\bar{y} \pm z^* \frac{\sigma}{\sqrt{n}}$$

You can take the critical z's (z*) from the rightmost column on the table for the previous page. They are the equivalent of the critical t values for a really, really large sample. As *n* gets bigger and bigger, the standard error is going to get tinier and tinier (because there's a bigger number in the denominator that we are dividing by). As a result, the margin of error (everything on the right-hand side of the confidence interval expression) will get smaller and smaller. This makes sense: the more observations we have, the more accurately our sample mean will approximate our population mean.

Computing the Confidence Interval from Raw Data

If you have *every single one* of the individual elements of your dataset, go to Chapter 5.2 (One Sample t-test). The current chapter is just intended to give you a *quick* way to get the confidence interval when you only have the mean and standard deviation of the data you collected, and know your number of observations *n*.

A Custom R Function to Compute the Confidence Interval from Summary Data

If you only have your sample mean (y-bar), your sample standard deviation s, OR your population standard deviation σ and your number of observations *n*, you can compute the confidence interval at any confidence level with this function:

```
ci.mean <- function(n,ybar,s=NULL,sigma=NULL,
    vname="[value of the quantitative variable]",conf.level=0.95) {
        z.star <- NULL
        t.star <- NULL
        ME <- NULL
        cint <- NULL
            if(!is.null(s)) {
                # We only know the sample SD so look up t* instead
                t.star <- qt(conf.level+((1-conf.level)/2),df=(n-1))
                ME <- t.star*(s/sqrt(n))
            }
            if(!is.null(sigma)) {
                # we know the population SD so look up z*
                z.star <- qnorm(conf.level+((1-conf.level)/2))
                ME <- z.star*(sigma/sqrt(n))
            }
        cint <- ybar + c(-ME,ME)
        short <- sprintf("%s%% CI: %.3f+/-%.3f or (%.3f, %.3f)",
                (conf.level*100), ybar, ME, cint[1], cint[2])
        verbose <- sprintf("We are %s%% confident that the true %s is
                between %.3f and %.3f.",(conf.level*100),
                vname, cint[1], cint[2])
    return(list(short=short,verbose=verbose,cint=cint))
}
```

Just cut and paste the function above into your R session, or source it directly from GitHub:

```
source("https://raw.githubusercontent.com/NicoleRadziwill/R-
Functions/master/cimean.R")
```

Here are the arguments you can provide to the `ci.mean` function:

Arguments to `ci.mean`	What each one specifies
n	The number of observations in your sample
ybar	The mean of the values in your sample
s	The standard deviation of your SAMPLE, if you have it; you can leave it blank
sigma	The standard deviation of your POPULATION, if you have it; you can leave it blank
vname (optional)	Words that describe the quantitative variable you are building a confidence interval around
conf.level	Size of the CI (e.g. 0.90, 0.95, 0.99)

Example: Planning a Drug Bust

The `ci.mean` function provides three kinds of output: a short interpretation of the confidence interval (`short`), a sentence that provides the full interpretation of the confidence interval (`verbose`), and the lower and upper bounds of the confidence interval (`cint`). Here's how it works.

Imagine that you are an agent of the Drug Enforcement Agency (DEA) working in a location where the cultivation of opium is illegal. You suspect that a local farmer is using his 3,000-acre farm to grow poppies. Before you plan the big bust, you want to make sure it's worth your while. You randomly sample 30 1-acre segments and find an average of 16 plants on each one, with a sample standard deviation from those 30 segments of 11.7 plants. You won't go in unless you think there are more than 50,000 plants on the property.

```
> ci.mean(30,16,s=11.7,vname="number of opium poppies per acre")
$short
[1] "95% CI: 16.000+/-4.369 or (11.631, 20.369)"

$verbose
```

[1] "We are 95% confident that the true number of opium poppies per acre is between 11.631 and 20.369."

```
$cint
[1] 11.63115 20.36885
```

We can predict that there are between (11.63*3,000=34,890) and (20.37*3,000=61,110) plants on the whole farm, so it looks like this field might be a candidate for a bust. You can also store the results in a variable, and call each of the returned values independently:

```
> my.ci <- ci.mean(30,16,s=11.7)
> my.ci$verbose
[1] "We are 95% confident that the true [value of the quantitative variable]
is between 11.631 and 20.369."
> my.ci$cint[1] # lower limit
[1] 11.63115
> my.ci$cint[2] # upper limit
[1] 20.36885
```

4.2 Two Means

Objective

How well does the difference between two *sample* means (y-bar$_1$ − y-bar$_2$) provide an estimate of the difference between *population* means μ_1 - μ_2? By constructing a confidence interval around the estimate from our samples, we determine a *range of values* that we believe contains the true population mean. We choose a *confidence level* (e.g. 90%, 95%, 99%) that tells us how likely it is that the true difference between population means lies within that interval. As a result, an interval estimate provides much more information than a point estimate. Here's one way to imagine it:

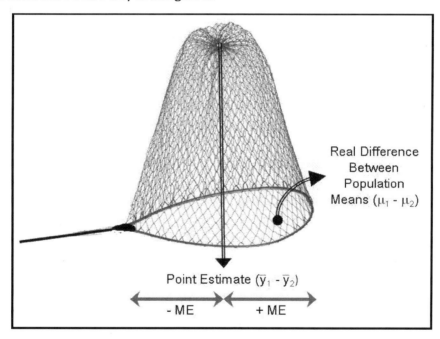

- You're standing on the number line where your point estimate (y-bar$_1$ − y-bar$_2$) is located. You are on a boat.
- The real difference between means, μ_1 - μ_2, is a fish floating somewhere out there, either ahead of you or behind you, compared to that estimate.
- You want to catch that fish, so you cast a net (that's the confidence interval).

- How confident do you want to be that you *actually* catch that fish? That's your confidence level (90%, 95%, 99%). You cast a symmetric net that extends *behind* you a certain distance (the margin of error), as well as *ahead* of you that same distance.
- If you want to be more confident that you actually catch that μ fish, you're going to need a bigger net. That's why 99% confidence intervals are wider than 95% confidence intervals, and 95% confidence intervals are wider than 90% confidence intervals.

Since the margin of error is half the size of the confidence interval net, the margin of error will also increase as the confidence level increases.

Sampling Distribution and Standard Error of the Difference Between Means

To compute the confidence interval, we need to know the **sampling distribution** for the difference between means: that is, the entire collection of differences that *could have been observed* even though we only went out to collect one sample. (We can think of the sampling distribution as the *distribution of all possible random samples of a particular size*.) Each of your random samples will have a difference between their means, (x-bar$_1$ – x-bar$_2$). All of those potential means are drawn from a normal model with its center at the real population mean μ_1 - μ_2, and a standard deviation approximated by the standard error of the difference, which you can find an expression to compute:

$$\overline{X_1} - \overline{X_2} \sim N\left(\mu_1 - \mu_2, \frac{\sigma_1^2}{n_1} + \frac{\sigma_2^2}{n_2}\right)$$

The standard deviation of the sampling distribution is all that stuff to the right of the comma: it's called the "standard error of the difference between means." The bigger our random sample n becomes, the better we can use our sample means to approximate the real difference between population means. In contrast to the standard deviation, which tells us the spread or dispersion of *all the differences* within a population, standard error tells us how much the *mean difference* of those values will be spread around (depending on how big a sample size we choose). <u>Standard error is a characteristic of a random sampling process, NOT of the population.</u>

Form of the Confidence Interval for Two Means

The general form of a confidence interval is:

$$CI \ : \ Estimate \ \pm \ Margin \ of \ Error$$

The specific form of the confidence interval for the difference between two means is:

$$(\overline{y_1} - \overline{y_2}) \pm C^* SE(\overline{y_1} - \overline{y_2})$$

Our *estimate* for the difference between means is the difference between the average values from our samples, (y-bar$_1$ − y-bar$_2$). C is a critical value (either t* or z*) that describes how **fat** we want our confidence interval to be, and depends on *just how likely we want to be to catch that fish* (90% likely? 95% likely? 99% likely?).

Standard error calculation (the rightmost part of this expression) depends on two things: whether we know the variances of the populations, and whether they have equal variances (or not).

Choose the Right Expression for Standard Error

Before we can compute actual values for the standard error of the difference between means, we need to pick which of these four SE(y-bar$_1$ − y-bar$_2$) expressions to use. Note that if your sample sizes are small (< 30), you may want to *assume* unequal variances. It's not easy to get a sense for the true variability within a population when you don't have lots of items in your sample with which you can make that decision.

Here's a table you can use to choose which expression is the right one to use to determine standard error. One of these expressions requires the *pooled standard deviation* which requires another formula to figure it out. Your job is just to figure out which equations are appropriate, and then plug in the value from *your* data.

	If you **DON'T Know** the Population Variance	If you **DO Know** the Population Variance
The Two Groups Have an **Equal Variance**	$(\overline{y_1} - \overline{y_2}) \pm t^*_{df} S_{pooled} \sqrt{\dfrac{1}{n_1} + \dfrac{1}{n_2}}$	$(\overline{y_1} - \overline{y_2}) \pm z^* \sigma \sqrt{\dfrac{1}{n_1} + \dfrac{1}{n_2}}$
The Two Groups Have **Unequal Variances**	$(\overline{y_1} - \overline{y_2}) \pm t^*_{df} \sqrt{\dfrac{s_1^2}{n_1} + \dfrac{s_2^2}{n_2}}$	$(\overline{y_1} - \overline{y_2}) \pm z^* \sqrt{\dfrac{\sigma^2}{n_1} + \dfrac{\sigma^2}{n_2}}$

Calculate Pooled Standard Deviation (If You Need It)

If you DON'T know the variance or standard deviation of the population, but the two groups DO have an equal variance (the top left case in the table above), you will have to compute the *pooled* standard deviation, s_{pooled}. Use this equation:

$$S_{pooled} = \frac{(n_1 - 1)s_1^2 + (n_2 - 1)s_2^2}{n_1 + n_2 - 2}$$

Choose the Right Expression for Degrees of Freedom

You will also need to determine degrees of freedom if yours is one of the two cases where the variance of the population is not known. You will need this value when you are looking up your critical t value, t^*_{df}.

	If you **DON'T Know** the Population Variance
The Two Groups Have an **Equal** Variance	$$df = n_1 + n_2 - 2$$
The Two Groups Have **Unequal** Variances	$$df = \frac{\left(\frac{s_1^2}{n_1} + \frac{s_2^2}{n_2}\right)^2}{\frac{1}{n_1-1}\left(\frac{s_1^2}{n_1}\right)^2 + \frac{1}{n_2-1}\left(\frac{s_2^2}{n_2}\right)^2}$$ **Note**: Round this result *down* before using.

Critical values of t (t*$_{df}$) depend on how you calculate the degrees of freedom using the expressions above. If we are not certain we've captured the variability in the population within our sample (which is what happens when our sample size is small), the confidence interval net needs to be *bigger* to capture the true difference between means in the population. As the degrees of freedom increase, the values for critical t get smaller, and approach the values you would compute for critical z.

Confidence Interval	R Code to Find Critical t (t*) (use the df number you calculated using the appropriate expression above)	Critical t (t*) for n=30 (df=29)	Critical t (t*) for df = 1000 *(same as z*)*
90% CI	qt(0.95,df=29)	1.699	1.645
95% CI	qt(0.975,df=29)	2.045	1.962
99% CI	qt(0.995,df=29)	2.756	2.576

Computing the Confidence Interval from Raw Data

If you have *every single one* of the individual elements of your dataset from both of the two groups, go to Chapter 5.3 (Two Sample t-test for Equal Variances) or 5.4 (Two Sample t-test for Unequal Variances). The current chapter is just intended to give you a *quick* way to get the confidence interval when you only have the means and standard deviations of the data you collected, and know your number of observations *n* from each group.

A Custom R Function to Compute the Confidence Interval from Summary Data

If you only have your sample means (y-bar$_1$ and y-bar$_2$), your sample standard deviations (s$_1$ and s$_2$) OR your population standard deviations (σ_1 and σ_2), and your number of observations from both groups (*n$_1$* and *n$_2$*), you can compute the confidence interval at any confidence level with this function:

```
ci.twomeans <- function(ybar1,ybar2,n1,n2,sd1=NULL,sd2=NULL,
    sigma1=NULL,sigma2=NULL,eq.var=FALSE,conf.level=0.95,
    vname="[difference between the quantitative variables]") {
        # We assume a conf.level of 0.95 and eq.var=FALSE just so
        # you have to change it to TRUE if you REALLY mean it
        z.star <- NULL
        t.star <- NULL
        ME <- NULL
        cint <- NULL
        my.df <- NULL # we need this if we DO know the population variance
        diff.ybars <- ybar1-ybar2
            if(!is.null(sigma1)) {
                # we've been given two population SD's so we
                # DO know the population variance
                z.star <- qnorm(conf.level+((1-conf.level)/2))
                ME <- z.star*sigma1*(sqrt((1/n1)+(1/n2)))
            }
            if(!is.null(sd1)) {
                # we've been given two sample SD's so we
                # DON'T know the population variance
                if(eq.var==FALSE) {
                    my.df <- ((sd1^2/n1)+(sd2^2/n2))^2)/((((sd1^2/n1)^2)/(n1-
1))+(((sd2^2/n2)^2)/(n2-1)))
```

```
            t.star <- qt(conf.level+((1-conf.level)/2),df=my.df)
            ME <- t.star*sqrt((sd1^2/n1)+(sd2^2/n2))
        } else {
            my.df <- n1+n2-1
            s.pooled <- (((n1-1)*(sd1^2))+((n2-1)*(sd2^2)))/my.df
            t.star <- qt(conf.level+((1-conf.level)/2),df=my.df)
            ME <- t.star*s.pooled*sqrt((1/n1)+(1/n2))
        }
    }
    cint <- diff.ybars + c(-ME,ME)
    short <- sprintf("%s%% CI: %.3f+/-%.3f or (%.3f, %.3f)",
            (conf.level*100), diff.ybars, ME, cint[1], cint[2])
    verbose <- sprintf("We are %s%% confident that the true %s is
            between %.3f and %.3f.",(conf.level*100),
            vname, cint[1], cint[2])
  return(list(short=short,verbose=verbose,cint=cint))
}
```

Just cut and paste the function into your R session, or source it directly from GitHub:

```
source("https://raw.githubusercontent.com/NicoleRadziwill/R-
Functions/master/citwomeans.R")
```

It allows you to specify either the sample standard deviations (sd1 and sd2) OR the population standard deviations (sigma1 and sigma2). Even if you specify two different standard deviations, you can still use the eq.var=TRUE option which will force the function to choose the first one. You can also specify an optional string, vname, that describes the variable name that you want to put a confidence interval around. This name will be reported in the $verbose variable that comes when you save your ci.twomeans output to a variable.

Here are the arguments you can provide to the ci.twomeans function:

Arguments to ci.twomeans	What each one specifies
ybar1	The mean of the values in your first group
ybar2	The mean of the values in your second group
n1	The number of observations in your sample
n2	The number of observations in your sample
sd1	The standard deviation of your FIRST SAMPLE, if

sd2	you have it; if not you can leave it blank
	The standard deviation of your SECOND SAMPLE, if you have it; if not, you can leave it blank
sigma1	The standard deviation of your FIRST POPULATION, if you have it; if not, you can leave it blank
sigma2	The standard deviation of your SECOND POPULATION, if you have it; if not, you can leave it blank
vname (optional)	Words that describe the difference of the quantitative variables you are building a confidence interval around
conf.level	Size of the CI (e.g. 0.90, 0.95, 0.99)

The `ci.twomeans` function provides three kinds of output: a short interpretation of the confidence interval (`short`), a sentence that provides the full interpretation of the confidence interval (`verbose`), and the lower and upper bounds of the confidence interval (`cint`). Here's how it works. Imagine that you are a quality improvement specialist, tasked with identifying interventions that can help improve the effectiveness of a training program at your company. You decide to look at the difference in certification exam scores between two classes. Each one had the same facilitator, but one of the classes used a new, updated training manual. How do you put a 99% confidence interval around the difference between the means of certification exam scores? Using `ci.twomeans`, you can do it like this:

```
> ci.twomeans(86.71,78.57,7,7,sd1=6.45,sd2=7.85,conf.level=.99,
vname="difference between test scores")
$short
[1] "99% CI: 8.140+/-11.811 or (-3.671, 19.951)"

$verbose
[1] "We are 99% confident that the true difference between test scores is
between -3.671 and 19.951."

$cint
[1] -3.670545 19.950545
```

You can also just load your data into R, and then *pass all the arguments as calculations* to ci.twomeans. **Note that we do a test of variance first with** var.test **to see if we should use the** eq.var=TRUE **or** eq.var=FALSE **argument. With a P-Value that's not even close to being tiny, we can definitely assume** eq.var=TRUE **(which is the default option):**

```
> x <- c(84,89,77,81,95,93,88)
> y <- c(79,82,90,65,83,74,77)
> var.test(x,y)$p.value
[1] 0.6447913
> ci.twomeans(mean(x),mean(y),length(x),length(y),sd1=sd(x),
sd2=sd(y),conf.level=.99)
$short
[1] "99% CI: 8.143+/-11.809 or (-3.666, 19.952)"

$verbose
[1] "We are 99% confident that the true [difference between the quantitative
variables] is between -3.666 and 19.952."

$cint
[1] -3.665992 19.951706
```

4.3 Paired Means

Objective

Sometimes, an observation of a quantitative variable in one group is *paired* with an observation of a quantitative variable in a second group - meaning they are **dependent observations**. How well does the average difference between observations in two *sample* groups that are paired (d-bar) provide an estimate of the average difference in a *population*? By constructing a confidence interval around the estimate from our samples, we determine a *range of values* that we believe contains the true population mean. We choose a *confidence level* (e.g. 90%, 95%, 99%) that tells us how likely it is that the true difference between population means lies within that interval. As a result, an interval estimate provides much more information than a point estimate. Here's one way to imagine it for the paired means case:

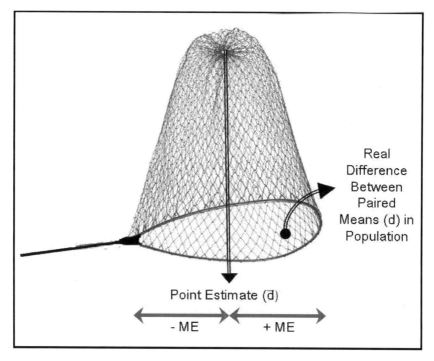

- You're standing on the number line where your point estimate (d-bar) is located. You are on a boat.
- The real difference between means, d, is a fish floating somewhere out there, either ahead of you or behind you, compared to that estimate.
- You want to catch that fish, so you cast a net (that's the confidence interval).
- How confident do you want to be that you *actually* catch that fish? That's your confidence level (90%, 95%, 99%). So you cast a symmetric net that extends *behind* you a certain distance (the margin of error), as well as *ahead* of you that same distance.
- If you want to be more confident that you actually catch that d fish, you're going to need a bigger net. That's why 99% confidence intervals are bigger than 95% confidence intervals, and 95% confidence intervals are bigger than 90% confidence intervals.

Since the margin of error is half the size of the confidence interval net, the margin of error will also increase as the confidence level increases.

Sampling Distribution and Standard Error of the Difference Between Means

To compute the confidence interval, we need to know the **sampling distribution** for the mean difference: that is, the entire collection of differences that *could have been observed* even though we only collected one sample. (We can think of the sampling distribution as the *distribution of all possible random samples of a particular batch size*.)

Each pair of observations will have a difference between them (d_i). As a result, your random sample will have a mean difference (d-bar) that you get by averaging all of the individual d_i's in your data set. All of those potential means can be represented as a normal model with its center at the real population mean d, and a standard deviation approximated by the *standard error of the difference*. By treating the paired differences as if they came from a single sample, the sampling distribution ends up looking almost identical to the sampling distribution for one mean:

$$\overline{X} \sim N\left(d, \frac{\sigma_d}{\sqrt{n}}\right)$$

The standard deviation of the sampling distribution is all that stuff to the right of the comma: the "standard error of the differences between the paired observations." The bigger our random sample n becomes, the better we can use the mean difference from the sample to approximate the real mean difference in the population. In contrast to the standard deviation, which tells us the spread or dispersion of all the differences that could be observed in the population, standard error tells us how much the *mean difference* of of our samples will be spread around (depending on how big a sample size we choose). *So standard error is a characteristic of a random sampling process, NOT of the population.*

Form of the Confidence Interval for Paired Means

The general form of a confidence interval is:

$$CI : Estimate \pm Margin\ of\ Error$$

The specific form of the confidence interval for the difference between two means is:

$$\overline{d} \pm t_{df}{}^{*} SE(\overline{d})$$

$$\overline{d} \pm t_{df}{}^{*} \frac{s_d}{\sqrt{n}}$$

Our *estimate* for the difference is determined by taking each one of the matched pairs in our sample, computing the difference between the two observations that make up that matched pair, and then taking an average over the collection of differences. The critical t (t*) depends on the degrees of freedom, which is one less than the number of pairs (n-1). The standard error is computed by taking the standard deviation of the collection of differences, s_d, and diving by the square root of the number of pairs.

Critical values of t (t*$_{df}$) establish how big our confidence interval net needs to be, and depend on the sample size. The smaller the sample size, the bigger the net needs to be, so that we're sure we've estimated the variability of differences across the whole population of possibilities. As the degrees of freedom increase, the values for critical t get smaller, and approach the values you would compute for critical z.

Confidence Interval	R Code to Find Critical t (t*) (use the df number you calculated using the appropriate expression above)	Critical t (t*) for n=30 (df=29)	Critical t (t*) for df = 1000 (same as z*)
90% CI	qt(0.95,df=29)	1.699	1.645
95% CI	qt(0.975,df=29)	2.045	1.962
99% CI	qt(0.995,df=29)	2.756	2.576

Computing the Confidence Interval from Raw Data

If you have *every single one* of the individual observations and differences in your dataset, go to Chapter 5.5 (Paired T-test). The current chapter is just intended to give you a *quick* way to get the confidence interval when you only have summary data.

A Custom R Function to Compute the Confidence Interval from Summary Data

If you only have your mean difference $\bar{d}$, the standard deviation of those differences s_d, and the number of observations *n*, you can compute the confidence interval at any confidence level with this function:

```
ci.paired <- function(n,dbar,s.d,conf.level=0.95,
    vname="[difference between the quantitative variables]") {
        t.star <- NULL
        ME <- NULL
        cint <- NULL
        if(!is.null(s.d)) {
            t.star <- qt(conf.level+((1-conf.level)/2),df=(n-1))
            ME <- t.star*(s.d/sqrt(n))
        }
        cint <- dbar + c(-ME,ME)
```

```
   short <- sprintf("%s%% CI: %.3f+/-%.3f or (%.3f, %.3f)",
          (conf.level*100), dbar, ME, cint[1], cint[2])
   verbose <- sprintf("We are %s%% confident that the true %s is between
%.3f and %.3f.",(conf.level*100),vname,cint[1],cint[2])
   return(list(short=short,verbose=verbose,cint=cint))
}
```

Just cut and paste the function into your R session, or source it directly from GitHub:

```
source("https://raw.githubusercontent.com/NicoleRadziwill/R-
Functions/master/cipaired.R")
```

Here are the arguments you can provide to the `ci.paired` function. You can also specify an optional string, `vname`, that describes the variable name of the difference you want to put a confidence interval around. This name will be reported in the `$verbose` variable that comes when you save your `ci.paired` output to a variable.

Arguments to `ci.paired`	What each one specifies
n	The number of pairs in your sample
dbar	The mean of all the differences between observations in a pair
s.d	The standard deviation of the differences from your sample
vname (optional)	Words that describe the difference of the quantitative variables you are building a confidence interval around
conf.level	Size of the CI (e.g. 0.90, 0.95, 0.99)

Example: Weight Loss

The `ci.paired` function provides three kinds of output: a short interpretation of the confidence interval (`short`), a sentence that provides the full interpretation of the confidence interval (`verbose`), and the lower and upper bounds of the confidence interval (`cint`). Here's how it works.

Imagine that you've started drinking one cup of lemon and pomegranate juice in the morning every day before work. After six weeks, you find that you've lost 15 pounds. Several of your friends are intrigued, so they decide to start doing the same thing. Because you appreciate data-driven decision making, you ask each of them to record their starting weight, and their weight after six weeks of drinking lemon-pomegranate every morning. After several weeks, you collect all their starting weights and ending weights, and compute the *differences* between the two *for each person*. Most people lost weight, but a couple people actually gained weight. The *mean difference* in pounds lost, based on your sample of 12 people, was 8.6. You also found that the standard deviation of those 12 differences was 6.5 pounds, and you'd like to put a 95% confidence interval around the estimate:

```
> ci.paired(12,8.6,6.5,vname="number of pounds lost")
$short
[1] "95% CI: 8.600+/-4.130 or (4.470, 12.730)"

$verbose
[1] "We are 95% confident that the true number of pounds lost is between
4.470 and 12.730."

$cint
[1]   4.470097 12.729903
```

Based on your data, you can be 95% confident that the true number of pounds people will lose by adding lemon-pomegranate to their morning routine is between 4.47 and 12.73 - definitely a result that might make you want to do a followup study with a controlled experiment that could reveal a causal relationship between your discovery and weight loss.

4.4 One Proportion

Objective

How well does a *sample* proportion, p̂, provide an estimate of that proportion in a *population* (p)? By constructing a confidence interval around the estimate from our sample, we determine a *range of values* that we believe contains the true population proportion. We choose a *confidence level* (e.g. 90%, 95%, 99%) that tells us how likely it is that the true population proportion lies within that interval. As a result, an interval estimate provides much more information than a point estimate.

Unlike other confidence intervals, the "net" that you cast around each side of your estimate in this case (the *sample* proportion p̂) isn't necessarily symmetric. That makes sense, because proportions only range from 0% to 100%. It wouldn't make sense if your net extended beyond the bounds of what proportions can be. However, like other confidence intervals, the more confident that you want to be that you've captured the *true* population proportion, the bigger your confidence interval net will have to be.

There are **many** variations on equations for the confidence interval for one proportion, and some are *definitely* better than others. The most commonly used expression for the confidence interval on a proportion (called the *Wald confidence interval*) is covered in Chapter 5.6 along with the hypothesis test to compare one proportion to a standard or recommended value. Unfortunately, the Wald interval is consistently and extremely inaccurate, unless you have large sample sizes *and* your proportions aren't too close to the edges... and still, it's taught to everyone in introductory statistics classes, as the be all and end all of single proportion confidence intervals!

The purpose of *this* chapter is to help you learn about two forms of the confidence interval that are much more accurate and reliable: the Agresti-Coull method, which is just a simple adjustment of Wald's expression and very easy to calculate by hand, and the Wilson Score Interval (which is used in `prop.test` in R). We will not cover the Clopper-Pearson (Exact) method analytically. Even though it's the most conservative of all the methods, and provides fantastic coverage that's always *above* your stated confidence level, it requires using the *inverse transform of the beta distribution* which is not as easy to work out by hand.

Which Methods Are Discussed Here?

In this chapter, we will discuss:

- the traditional (Wald) confidence interval for a proportion,
- the Agresti-Coull correction to the Wald confidence interval,
- the Clopper-Pearson (Exact) binomial confidence interval,
- and the Wilson score interval.

Although the exact method is the most accurate, it also generates the widest confidence intervals. You might want one that's a little tighter, so you have a better idea of where the true population proportion can be found. **The Wilson score interval is the one you should use** if you are OK with relying on the R software to compute your intervals for you. It's very accurate, but working with the formula always feels like choking or suffocating, and I don't want to scare off my students by making them work with it.

The Agresti-Coull correction is the one you should use if you want a reasonably accurate confidence interval that you would *also* like an easy way to compute analytically.

Coverage Probabilities

The reason why this is so important is because of *coverage probability*. Did you know that if you use the Wald expression to generate a 95% confidence interval for a proportion that you measured in your sample, it will actually contain the true population proportion much less than 95% of the *time*? And that in many cases, you could actually only be capturing the true value 70 to 85% of the time... even when you think you're computing a 95% confidence interval (which sounds like it should be a lot more accurate).

As you can imagine, this is just really bad. As a result, there have been several instances where statisticians have developed alternative expressions for the confidence interval, and the relative strength of each method can be assessed in terms of the *coverage probability*. Coverage probability is defined as the proportion of *time* that the confidence interval actually contains the true population parameter. Here are what some coverage probability maps look like for the Wald, the Agresti-Coull adjusted Wald, and the Clopper-Pearson exact binomial confidence intervals for sample sizes of n=5 and n=10.

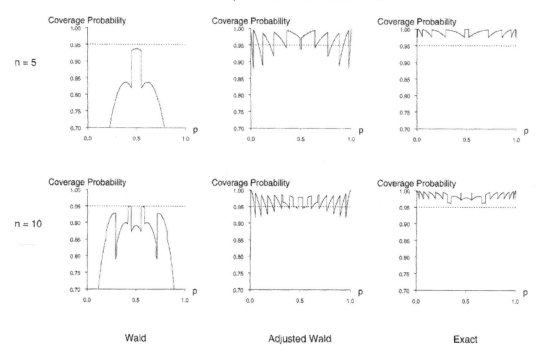

Wald   Adjusted Wald   Exact

The plot above is from Agresti & Coull's 1988 paper in *The American Statistician,* titled
Approximate Is Better than "Exact" for Interval Estimation of Binomial Proportions

What does this all mean? The horizontal axis shows the p̂ values from your sample. If you observed a small proportion, those are at the left (near 0.0), and if you observed a larger proportion, those will be towards the right (near 1.0).

Now, take a look at the horizontal lines crossing each plot. This is where the plots *should be* if you were actually getting a 95% confidence interval. In the case of the Agresti-Coull adjusted Wald interval in the middle, you're bouncing around 95% but generally above it. That's pretty good. For the Clopper-Pearson (Exact) binomial confidence interval, you're *always* above 95%. That's great. But for the Wald confidence interval that's usually taught as THE confidence interval for a proportion? You're lucky if you even GET to 95%! If your sample size is low (top left plot), you only have a chance of that if your proportions are near 0.50. If your sample size is a little larger (bottom left plot), you might get near 95% if your observed proportion is between 0.3 and 0.7, but maybe not even then! (See the jagged ups and downs?)

The Wilson Score Interval, which is also covered in this chapter, has a pretty good coverage probability - as good as the Agresti-Coull adjusted Wald, but not quite as conservative and wide as the Clopper-Pearson (Exact). Here's it's coverage probability plot:

Wilson Interval

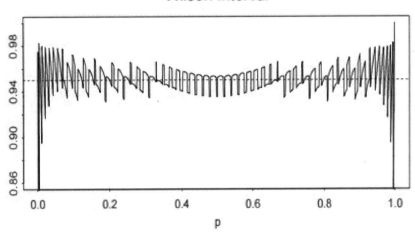

The plot above is from Brown, Cai, & DasGupta's 1988 paper in *arXiv.org*, titled *Interval Estimation for a Binomial Proportion*

The bottom line is that **THE WALD CONFIDENCE INTERVAL IS PAINFULLY AND FATALLY FLAWED** and even if you see it in another introductory statistics textbook, please don't use it!! Tell your instructors and certification boards. Show them this chapter. Be part of the noble movement to rid intro stats classes of the Wald interval.

The Wald Confidence Interval and the Agresti-Coull Correction

The general form of a confidence interval is:

$$CI \; : \; Estimate \; \pm \; Margin \; of \; Error$$

The specific form of the confidence interval for one proportion that's *traditionally* used in introductory textbooks is the *Wald confidence interval*:

$$\hat{p} \pm z^* SE(\hat{p})$$

$$\hat{p} \pm z^* \sqrt{\frac{pq}{n}}$$

This is based on a sampling distribution for one proportion that is normal, with a mean at the estimate $\hat{p}$, and a standard deviation of the square root of pq over n. It requires that you estimate the proportion ($\hat{p}$) from the data you collect in your sample, know your sample size n, and know the critical value of z that corresponds to the size of the confidence interval net that you want to cast onto the sea of all possible values (shown in the following table). Without having a null hypothesis to compare your sample to, this expression also requires that you estimate p using $\hat{p}$, and estimate q using the value of (1 - $\hat{p}$).

Unfortunately, this confidence interval performs really badly. Fortunately, statisticians Alan Agresti and Brent Coull developed a quick adjustment that can be done to the values in this expression - which magically improves the coverage probability even when you have a small sample size OR your proportions are closer to the edges (below 0.20 or above 0.80). To perform the adjustment, you just need to recalculate $\hat{p}$ based on **adding 2 "successes" to your observations** and **adding 4 total observations.** Then, you can use the expression above - and voila, you have a confidence interval with vastly improved coverage probability.

Confidence Interval	Critical z (z*)
90% CI	1.645
95% CI	1.96
99% CI	2.58

In R, you can construct a confidence interval that uses the Agresti-Coull correction using the add4ci function in the `PropCIs` package. After you install the `PropCIs` package from CRAN, all you need to know are your **original** number of successes and **original** number of observations and the confidence level you're looking for. For example, if you do an ESP test with Zener cards and you correctly guess 39 cards out of 120, you can construct a confidence interval around your success rate like this:

```
> library(PropCIs)
Warning message:
package 'PropCIs' was built under R version 3.1.3
> add4ci(39,120,conf.level=0.95)

data:

95 percent confidence interval:
 0.2478421 0.4134483
sample estimates:
[1] 0.3306452
```

The Wilson Score Interval

Even though the expression looks unwieldy, Agresti and Coull both recommend that the Wilson Score Interval be taught in introductory classes. It's a great confidence interval. Its coverage probability is fantastic, and it's not quite as wide as the Clopper-Pearson, meaning you can hone in on the true population proportion just a little better.

$$\frac{(2n\hat{p} + z^{*2}) \pm z^{*2}\sqrt{z^{*2} + 4n\hat{p}\hat{q}}}{2(n + z^{*2}}$$

All you need to know is your sample size n, the observed proportion of successes $\hat{p}$, the observed proportion of failures $\hat{q}$, and the critical z (z^*) for the confidence level you desire. So, from the Zener cards example earlier, where you correctly guessed 39 cards out of 120, a 95% confidence interval would be computed like this:

$$\frac{(2 \; x \; 120 \; x \; 0.325 + 1.96) \pm 1.96\sqrt{1.96 + 4 \; x \; 120 \; x \; 0.325 \; x \; 0.675}}{2(120 \; + \; 1.96)}$$

This means the 95% confidence interval has 0.243 as a lower bound, and 0.409 as an upper bound. We are 95% confident that the *true* proportion of successes will be between 24.3% and 40.9%. In addition to `prop.test`, which uses the Wilson score interval, there is also a function in the `PropCIs` package that you can use. Be sure to install and wake up `PropCIs` before trying this line of code:

```
> scoreci(39,120,conf.level=0.95)

data:

95 percent confidence interval:
 0.2478 0.4131
```

A slight shift to the right can be expected, because `scoreci` also applies a continuity correction to make the confidence interval even more accurate.

Clopper-Pearson (Exact) Method

The exact method is really complicated: it uses a relationship between the F distribution and the cdf of a binomial distribution to work its magic. I won't go into any of the analytic details here, but I will show you the expression for the confidence interval:

$$\left[\frac{r}{r + (n - r + 1)F_{1-\alpha/2;2(n-r+1),2r}} , \frac{(r+1)F_{1-\alpha/2;2(r+1),2(n-r)}}{(n-r) + (r+1)F_{1-\alpha/2;2(r+1),2(n-r)}} \right]$$

However, it's very easy to run this test in R, using the `exactci` function which is also in the `PropCIs` package:

```
> exactci(39,120,conf.level=0.95)

data:

95 percent confidence interval:
 0.2423451 0.4165272
```

Notice that the Clopper-Pearson estimate for the 95% confidence interval on the ESP data is *wider* (that is, more conservative) than the other alternatives. If you want to be absolutely sure to capture the true population proportion, this method is great... but if you need a tighter confidence interval so you have a better sense of where the true population proportion *actually is*... then use the Wilson score interval (or the Agresti-Coull correction, if you don't have a statistical software package handy).

Other Resources

- Here's a discussion that provides more background for how binomial confidence intervals (that is, confidence intervals around proportions) work: http://www.sigmazone.com/binomial_confidence_interval.htm
- Agresti & Coull's (1998) paper in The American Statistician is here: http://www.stat.ufl.edu/~aa/articles/agresti_coull_1998.pdf
- Brown et al.'s paper can be downloaded here: http://citeseerx.ist.psu.edu/viewdoc/download?doi=10.1.1.50.3025&rep=rep1&type=pdf
- This paper contains a great summary of many of the different ways to determine confidence intervals for one proportion: http://ncss.wpengine.netdna-cdn.com/wp-content/themes/ncss/pdf/Procedures/PASS/Confidence_Intervals_for_One_Proportion.pdf
- The documentation for the `PropCIs` package is here: http://cran.r-project.org/web/packages/PropCIs/PropCIs.pdf

4.5 Two Proportions

Objective

How well does the difference between two *sample* proportions ($\hat{p}_1 - \hat{p}_2$), provide an estimate of the difference between those proportions in a *population* ($p_1 - p_2$)? By constructing a confidence interval around the estimate from our sample, we determine a *range of values* that we believe contains the true population proportion. We choose a *confidence level* (e.g. 90%, 95%, 99%) that tells us how likely it is that the true difference between population proportions lies within that interval. As a result, an interval estimate can provide much more information than a point estimate.

Unlike other confidence intervals, the "net" that you cast around each side of your estimate (the *sample* proportion $\hat{p}$) isn't necessarily symmetric. That makes sense, because proportions only range from 0% to 100%. It wouldn't make sense if your net extended beyond the bounds of what proportions can be, even though using some recipes to compute the confidence interval for two proportions, you do end up overshooting those endpoints. (Typically, you just chop off whatever part of your net didn't fall between 0% and 100%, but that always feels rather kludgey.) However, exactly like other confidence intervals, the more confident that you want to be that you've captured the *true* population proportion, the bigger your confidence interval net will have to be.

There are **many** variations on equations for the confidence interval for two proportions, and some are *definitely* better than others. The most commonly used expression for the confidence interval on a proportion (called the *Wald interval with no continuity correction*) is covered in Chapter 5.7 along with the hypothesis test to compare two proportions to each other. Unfortunately, the Wald interval is consistently and extremely inaccurate, unless you have large sample sizes *and* your proportions aren't too close to the edges... and still, it's taught to everyone in introductory statistics classes, as the be all and end all of two proportion confidence intervals!

The purpose of *this* chapter is to help you learn about alternative forms of the confidence interval for the difference between proportions that are much more accurate and reliable.

Which Methods Are Discussed Here?

In this chapter, we review:

- The traditional (Wald) confidence interval for the difference between two proportions, both with and without a continuity correction,
- The Agresti-Caffo adjusted Wald confidence interval, and
- The Newcombe Hybrid Score.

There is also a class of confidence interval expressions that use the binomial distribution, called "Exact" methods. Although the Exact methods are the most accurate, they also generate the *widest* confidence intervals. For practical purposes, you might want one that's a little tighter, so that you get a better idea of where the true population proportion can be found. But if you have very small samples (<10 items each), you should use the methods in the `ExactCIdiff` package anyway.

The Wald confidence interval can be constructed using the `prop.test` function in R, or alternatively, the `pairwiseCI` function in the `pairwiseCI` package. (You can also do a two proportion z test with `prop.test`, which is covered in Chapter 5.7.)

The Agresti-Caffo ("Adjusted Wald") confidence interval is the one you should use if you want a reasonably accurate confidence interval that you would *also* like an easy way to compute analytically. It is available in the `pairwiseCI` package in R.

The Newcombe Hybrid Score is the one you should use if you are OK with relying on the R software to compute your intervals for you. It's very accurate, and it's been recommended by several researchers as a method that provides a nice balance between coverage and accuracy. It is part of the `pairwiseCI` package in R.

Coverage Probabilities

The reason why choosing the right confidence interval is so important is because of *coverage probability*. Similar to the case of constructing a confidence interval for one proportion, when you construct a confidence interval for *two* proportions, even when you think you're getting a 95% confidence interval, you might only be getting one that includes the true difference between proportions 80-90% of the time. Here are some coverage probabilities for 11 different ways to calculate this confidence interval:

Table III. Estimated coverage probabilities for 95, 90 and 99 per cent confidence intervals calculated by 11 methods. Based on 9200 points in parameter space with $5 \leqslant m \leqslant 50$, $5 \leqslant n \leqslant 50$, $0 < \psi < 1$ and $0 < \theta < 1 - |2\psi - 1|$

| Method | 95% intervals | | | | | | 90% intervals | | 99% intervals | |
| | Coverage | | Mesial non-coverage | | Distal non-coverage | | Coverage | | Coverage | |
	Mean	Minimum	Mean	Maximum	Mean	Maximum	Mean	Minimum	Mean	Minimum
1. Asympt, no CC	0·8807	0·0004	0·0417	0·7845	0·0775	0·9996	0·8322	0·0004	0·9253	0·0004
2. Asympt, CC	0·9623	0·5137	0·0183	0·4216	0·0194	0·4844	0·9401	0·5137	0·9811	0·5156
3. Haldane	0·9183	0·0035	0·0153	0·0656	0·0664	0·9965	0·8696	0·0035	0·9574	0·0035
4. Jeffreys Perks	0·9561	0·8505	0·0140	0·0606	0·0299	0·1418	0·9123	0·7655	0·9896	0·9083
5. Mee	0·9562	0·8516	0·0207	0·1484	0·0231	0·1064	0·9076	0·8057	0·9919	0·9470
6. Miettinen–Nurminen	0·9584	0·8516	0·0196	0·1484	0·0220	0·1064	0·9114	0·8057	0·9925	0·9478
7. True profile	0·9454	0·8299	0·0268	0·1440	0·0278	0·1384	0·8912	0·6895	0·9893	0·9613
8. 'Exact'	0·9680	0·9424	0·0149	0·0308	0·0170	0·0317	0·9305	0·8862	0·9948	0·9881
9. 'Mid-p'	0·9591	0·9131	0·0197	0·04996	0·0212	0·0470	0·9116	0·8374	0·9933	0·9847
10. Score, no CC	0·9602	0·8673	0·0134	0·0660	0·0264	0·1327	0·9162	0·8226	0·9916	0·9173
11. Score, CC	0·9793	0·9339	0·0061	0·0271	0·0147	0·0661	0·9553	0·9012	0·9957	0·9399

CC: continuity correction

The table above is from Newcombe's 1988 paper In *Statistics in Medicine,* titled *Interval Estimation for the Difference Between Independent Proportions: Comparison of Eleven Methods*

The Wald ("Asymptotic") Confidence Interval

The general form of a confidence interval is:

$$CI \ : \ Estimate \ \pm \ Margin \ of \ Error$$

The specific form of the confidence interval for the difference between two proportions that's *traditionally* used in introductory textbooks is the *Wald confidence interval*, based on a sampling distribution that is normal, centered around the difference between the observed proportions, and with a standard deviation that is based on the observed proportions from the two groups as well as the sizes of each group:

$$(\hat{p_1} - \hat{p_2}) \pm z^* SE(\hat{p_1} - \hat{p_2})$$

$$(\hat{p_1} - \hat{p_2}) \pm z^* \sqrt{\left(\frac{\hat{p_1}\hat{q_1}}{n_1} + \frac{\hat{p_2}\hat{q_2}}{n_2} \right)}$$

It requires that you estimate the proportions of success ($\hat{p}_1$ and $\hat{p}_2$) from the two groups in your sample, know your sample sizes for each of the groups (n_1 and n_2), and know the critical value of z that corresponds to the size of the confidence interval net that you want to cast onto the sea of all possible values (shown in the following table). Without having a null hypothesis to compare your sample to, this expression also requires that you estimate your p's using your $\hat{p}$'s, and estimate your q's using the values of (1 - the $\hat{p}$'s).

Confidence Interval	Critical z (z*)
90% CI	1.645
95% CI	1.96
99% CI	2.58

Let's construct a 95% confidence interval around some results from A/B testing as an example. A/B testing is used often by user interface designers to determine whether people prefer one design ("Design A") over another ("Design B"). By constructing a confidence interval around the difference between proportions from a sample, where you actually ask people which design they preferred, you can figure out where the true difference between proportions lies. If zero does *not* appear in the confidence interval, you have some evidence to show that people have a particular preference. Furthermore, you can assess *just how overwhelmingly* they prefer one design over another.

So let's assume we take two samples, each containing 200 people, and 92 people out of 200 prefer Design A (that's $\hat{p}_1$ = 92/200 = 0.46) while 64 people out of 200 prefer Design B (that's $\hat{p}_2$ = 64/200 = 0.32). That means $\hat{q}_1$ = 1-0.46 = 0.54 and $\hat{q}_2$ = 1-0.32 = 0. Now plug all those values into the expression for the confidence interval:

$$(0.46 - 0.32) \pm 1.96 \sqrt{\left(\frac{0.46 \; x \; 0.32}{200} + \frac{0.46 \; x \; 0.32}{200} \right)}$$

When each of the terms is calculated, we find that the 95% confidence interval for the difference between two proportions is (0.045,0.235). As a result, we are 95% confident that between 4.5% and 23.5% *more* people prefer Design A.

In R, you can find the Wald confidence interval a couple different ways. First, you can use `prop.test` in the base R package as long as you insert your data into a data frame using this general structure:

```
my.props <- cbind(c(successes1,successes2),c(failures1,failures2))
```

(For this to work, you have to replace your *actual number of successes in group 1 and group 2* and your *actual number of failures in group 1 and group 2*.) Next, give your data to the `prop.test` function, and find the confidence interval:

```
> prop.test(my.props,200,correct=FALSE)

        2-sample test for equality of proportions without continuity
        correction

data:  my.props
X-squared = 8.2388, df = 1, P-Value = 0.004101
alternative hypothesis: two.sided
95 percent confidence interval:
 -0.23460761 -0.04539239
sample estimates:
prop 1 prop 2
  0.32   0.46
```

If you want to be just a little more accurate, you can include a *continuity correction* that accounts for using a normal model to get information about data that's actually binomial (that is, expressed as a percentage of successes). Just remove correct=FALSE to include the continuity correction:

```
> prop.test(my.props,200)

        2-sample test for equality of proportions with continuity
        correction
```

```
data:  my.props
X-squared = 7.6608, df = 1, P-Value = 0.005643
alternative hypothesis: two.sided
95 percent confidence interval:
 -0.23960761 -0.04039239
sample estimates:
prop 1 prop 2
  0.32   0.46
```

You can also generate the confidence interval this way by using an option from `pairwiseCI` in the `pairwiseCI` package. It requires that you load your data in like this:

```
> successes <- c(92,64)
> failures <- c(108,136)
> group <- c(1,2)
> my.props <- data.frame(cbind(successes,failures,group))
```

Then you can generate the confidence interval:

```
> pairwiseCI(cbind(successes,failures)~group, data=my.props,
method="Prop.diff", CImethod="CC")

95  %-confidence intervals
 Method:  Continuity corrected interval for the difference of proportions

    estimate    lower    upper
2-1     -0.14  -0.2396  -0.0404
```

Notice that all of these methods give us exactly what we computed analytically, even though we might see rounding error or truncation error at times.

The Agresti-Caffo ("Adjusted Wald") Interval

Unfortunately, the Wald confidence interval is not that good in terms of coverage probability. Fortunately, statisticians Alan Agresti and Brian Caffo developed a quick adjustment that can be done to the values in this expression - which magically improves the coverage probability even when you have a small sample size OR your proportions are closer to the edges (below 0.20 or above 0.80). To perform the adjustment, you just need to recalculate p̂ based on **adding 1 "success" to the observations in each group** (for a total of 4 additional "dummy" successes) and **adding 2 total observations to each group** (for a total of 4 additional "dummy" observations). Then, you can use the expression for the Wald confidence interval - and voila, you have a confidence interval with improved coverage probability. In R, you can find the Agresti-Caffo confidence interval a couple different ways, either with `wald2ci` in the `PropCIs` package, or `pairwiseCI` in the `pairwiseCI` package. With `wald2ci`, you have the option of using a continuity correction by specifying `adjust=TRUE`, or you can turn it off using `adjust=FALSE`. (But I like to use the continuity corrections always.)

```
> wald2ci(92,200,64,200,conf.level=0.95,adjust=TRUE)

data:

95 percent confidence interval:
 0.04440813 0.23281959
sample estimates:
[1] 0.1386139
```

Here is the output from `pairwiseCI`. Notice that to get the Agresti-Caffo correction, we have to specify `CImethod="AC"` at the end:

```
> pairwiseCI(cbind(success,failure)~group, data=my.props,
method="Prop.diff", CImethod="AC")

95  %-confidence intervals
 Method:  Agresti-Caffo interval for the difference of proportions

    estimate   lower   upper
2-1    -0.14  -0.2328  -0.0444
```

The Newcombe Hybrid Score

From all of the academic articles I've read, everyone seems to recommend this method, so it must be pretty good - except for very small sample sizes, where the Exact methods seem to be more widely recommended. You can construct this confidence interval using the `pairwiseCI` package as well:

```
> pairwiseCI(cbind(successes,failures)~group, data=my.props,
method="Prop.diff", CImethod="NHS")

95 %-confidence intervals
 Method:  Newcombes Hybrid Score interval for the difference of proportions

     estimate   lower   upper
2-1     -0.14  -0.2321 -0.0444
```

Comparing the Various Confidence Intervals

Using our sample problem for A/B design, you can see how the size and position of the confidence interval changes based on which approach you choose. The Wald intervals are the widest and have the lowest coverage probabilities, meaning that you can't hone in very accurate on where the true difference in population proportions lies. The Newcombe Hybrid approach, however, generates the thinnest confidence interval and also has a high coverage probability: it's a good one to choose, in general.

Method	R Command for this Example	Lower CI	Upper CI
Wald (no correction) using `prop.test`	`prop.test(my.props,200,correct=FALSE)`	0.04539	0.23461
Wald (with correction) using `prop.test`	`prop.test(my.props,200)`	0.04039	0.23961
Wald (with correction) using `pairwiseCI` in `pairwiseCI` package	`pairwiseCI(cbind(successes,failures)~ group, data=my.props, method="Prop.diff", CImethod="CC")`	0.0404	0.2396
Agresti-Caffo using `wald2ci` in `PropCIs`	`wald2ci(92,200,64,200,conf.level=0.95, adjust=TRUE)`	0.04441	0.23282

Agresti-Caffo using `pairwiseCI` in `pairwiseCI`	`pairwiseCI(cbind(successes,failures)~group, data=my.props, method="Prop.diff", CImethod="AC")`	0.0444	0.2328
Newcombe Hybrid using `pairwiseCI` in `pairwiseCI` package	`pairwiseCI(cbind(successes,failures)~group, data=my.props, method="Prop.diff", CImethod="NHS")`	0.0444	0.2321

Other Resources

- Newcombe's (1998) paper that performs a comparative study on all the different confidence interval approaches for proportion can be found here: http://site.uottawa.ca/~nat/Courses/csi5388/Newcombe.1998.pdf

- Fagerland et al.'s (2011) article on recommended confidence intervals, called *Recommended Tests and Confidence Intervals for Paired Binomial Proportions*, can be downloaded from Researchgate (http://www.researchgate.net)

- Agresti & Caffo's (2000) paper in *The American Statistician* can be downloaded here: http://drsmorey.org/bibtex/upload/Agresti:Caffo:2000.pdf

- The R documentation for `PropCIs` and `pairwiseCI` can be found at http://cran.r-project.org/web/packages/PropCIs/PropCIs.pdf and http://cran.r-project.org/web/packages/pairwiseCI/pairwiseCI.pdf

- Shan and Wang prepared an academic article on Exact methods with the `ExactCIdiff` package, which is on page 62 of the R Journal located here: http://rjournal.github.io/archive/2013-2/RJ-2013-2.pdf

- Sean Wallis has fantastic articles discussing these issues extensively at https://corplingstats.wordpress.com/2012/03/31/binomial-distributions/ and https://corplingstats.wordpress.com/2014/04/10/imperfect-data/

4.6 One Variance

Objective

How well does a *sample* variance, s^2, provide an estimate of the *population* variance σ^2? By constructing a confidence interval around the estimate from our sample, we determine a *range of values* that we believe contains the true population variance. We choose a *confidence level* (e.g. 90%, 95%, 99%) that tells us how likely it is that the true population variance lies within that interval. As a result, an interval estimate provides much more information than a point estimate.

The confidence interval for the variance is used often in Six Sigma quality improvement projects, where you're trying to make sure that you're keeping the variance for a product, process, or service within acceptable bounds.

Sampling Distribution and Standard Error of the Variance

To compute the confidence interval, we need to know the **sampling distribution** for the variance: that is, the entire collection of possibilities that *could have happened* even though I only went out to collect one sample. (We can think of the sampling distribution as the *distribution of all possible random samples of a particular size.*)

Unlike other confidence intervals, the confidence interval for the variance is *not symmetric* around the estimate of the variance. Additionally, it's very sensitive to whether or not the sample is normal or nearly normal. As a result, the sampling distribution for the variance is a $\chi 2$ distribution with degrees of freedom equal to one less than the sample size (n-1). When you assume normality (and only under this assumption!) the standard error of the variance can be computed like this:

$$SE(\sigma^2) = s^2 \sqrt{\frac{2}{n-1}}$$

In contrast to the standard deviation, which tells us the spread or dispersion of *all the variances* within a population, standard error tells us how much the *means* of those variances will be spread around (depending on how big a sample size we choose). <u>Standard error is a characteristic of a random sampling process, NOT of the population.</u>

Form of the Confidence Interval for One Variance

The form of the confidence interval for the variance does not follow the "estimate $\pm$ margin of error" pattern seen in other confidence intervals, because according to the $\chi 2$ sampling distribution, the confidence interval is not symmetric around the estimate of the variance that you get from your sample.

The specific form of the confidence interval for one variance is:

$$\frac{(n-1)s^2}{\chi^2_{upper}} \leq \sigma^2 \leq \frac{(n-1)s^2}{\chi^2_{lower}}$$

Constructing this confidence interval only requires that we know the standard deviation of the observations in our sample (s2), the number of items in our sample (n), and the values of $\chi 2$ that demarcate the lower tail and the upper tail that *won't* be a part of our confidence interval.

Example: Thickness of Smartphones

Imagine that you manufacture smartphones. You take a sample of 32 phones, and measure the thickness of each of them. The average thickness is 0.82 cm, and the standard deviation of thickness in your sample is 0.008 cm. You want to build a 99% confidence interval around the variance of thicknesses in your sample. First, you need to find the critical values of $\chi 2$, which will depend on how big the sample size is. To begin, calculate *how much of the net will NOT be included in your confidence interval.* For a 99% CI, 1% of the area under the $\chi 2$ distribution will *not* be part of your net. For a 95% CI, 5% of the area under the $\chi 2$ distribution will not be part of your net.

Once you have this value, **chop it in half**. For the 99% CI, half of the area in the tails is 0.5%, and for a 95% CI, half of the area in the tails is 2.75%. Take that tiny little value that represents the area of half the tails. *Use that to find the critical value of χ2 from the lower tail.* Now, add the size of the confidence interval to that tiny value. In a 95% CI, the tiny area representing one of the two tails is 2.75%. Add them together and you get 97.5%. *Use that number to find the critical value of χ2 from the upper tail.*

The first argument to qchisq is either the confidence level plus half of the tails, or just half of the tails. The numbers look funny because these functions only look up the area to the *left* of whatever value you specify.

Confidence Interval	R Code to Find $\chi2_{upper}$ for n=32 (df=31)	R Code to Find $\chi2_{lower}$ for n=32 (df=31)
90% CI	qchisq(0.95,df=31)	qchisq(0.05,df=31)
95% CI	qchisq(0.975,df=31)	qchisq(0.025,df=31)
99% CI	qchisq(0.995,df=31)	qchisq(0.005,df=31)

(**Note**: In the expression for the confidence interval for the variance, you'll notice that the upper tail value appears on the *left*, and the lower tail value appears on the *right*. This might seem counterintuitive, but yes, that's the way it's supposed to be.)

For the smartphone example, the confidence interval works out like this:

```
> qchisq(0.995,df=31)  # Find Chi-Square UPPER
[1] 55.0027
> qchisq(0.005,df=31)  # Find Chi-Square LOWER
[1] 14.45777
```

Then we just replace all the values into the expression for the confidence interval:

$$\frac{(31)(0.08^2)}{55.003} \leq \sigma^2 \leq \frac{(31)(0.08^2)}{14.458}$$

$$0.0036 \leq \sigma^2 \leq 0.0137$$

We are 99% confident that the true variance of thickness of our smartphones is between 0.0036 and 0.0137 cm.

4.7 Two Variances

Objective

How well does the ratio of two *sample* variances, s_1^2/s_2^2, provide an estimate of the true ratio between *population* variances σ_1^2/σ_2^2? By constructing a confidence interval around the estimate from our sample, we determine a *range of values* that we believe contains the true ratio of population variances. We choose a *confidence level* (e.g. 90%, 95%, 99%) that tells us how likely it is that the true ratio of variances in the population lies within that interval. As a result, an interval estimate provides more information than a point estimate.

The confidence interval for the ratio of two variances is used often in Six Sigma quality improvement projects, where you're trying to reduce the variability of a process to make it more robust or more reliable. If the confidence interval *does not contain 1,* meaning that the ratios would be equal to each other, then there is evidence that the variance is different between the groups. If the groups represent measurements taken before and after a process improvement is made, then the confidence interval can suggest whether the goal of reducing variation was achieved.

Sampling Distribution and Standard Error of the Variance

To compute the confidence interval, we need to know the **sampling distribution** for the ratio of variances: that is, the entire collection of possibilities that *could have happened* even though I only went out to collect one sample. (We can think of the sampling distribution as the *distribution of all possible random samples of a particular size.*)

Unlike other confidence intervals, the confidence interval for the ratio of variances is *not symmetric* around the estimate of the ratio. Additionally, it's *extremely* sensitive to whether or not the samples are normal or nearly normal! So please do a test of normality (e.g. Shapiro-Wilk) before producing this kind of confidence interval. The sampling distribution for the variance is an F distribution with *numerator* degrees of freedom equal to one less than the sample size (n-1), and *denominator* degrees of freedom also equal to one less than the sample size (n-1). Yes, you have to know two different degrees of freedom to generate this confidence interval!

Form of the Confidence Interval for the Ratio of Two Variances

The form of the confidence interval for the ratio of variances does not follow the "estimate ± margin of error" pattern seen in other confidence intervals, because the F distribution is skewed with a long tail to the right: the confidence interval is not symmetric around the estimate of the ratio between variances that you get from your sample.

The specific form of the confidence interval for the ratio between variances is:

$$\frac{s_1^2}{s_2^2} F_{lower} \leq \frac{\sigma_1^2}{\sigma_2^2} \leq \frac{s_1^2}{s_2^2} F_{upper}$$

Constructing this confidence interval only requires that we know the variances of the observations in each of our sample groups (s_1^2 and s_2^2), the number of items in each group in our sample (n_1 and n_2), and the values of F that demarcate the lower tail and the upper tail that *won't* be a part of our confidence interval.

Example: Temperature Between Cities

Imagine that you live in one town and you're thinking about moving to another town about an hour away, that's not in the mountains where you are now. You are really sensitive to changes in weather, and you'd prefer that the low temperatures are less variable than where you live now. You take a random sample of low temperatures over 20 winter days for each of the cities. Where you live now, the average low is 29°F, and the variance of temperature is 2.6°F. In the new town you are considering, 24 reports indicate that the average low is 25°F, and the variance of temperature is 3.2°F. You want to build a 99% confidence interval around the ratio of variances from your sample.

First, you need to find the critical values of F, which will depend on how big the sample size is. To begin, calculate *how much of the net will NOT be included in your confidence interval.* For a 99% CI, 1% of the area under the F distribution will *not* be part of your net. For a 95% CI, 5% of the area under the F distribution will not be part of your net.

Once you have this value, chop it in half. For the 99% CI, half of the area in the tails is 0.5%, and for a 95% CI, half of the area in the tails is 2.75%. Take that tiny little value that represents the area of half the tails. *Use that to find the critical value of* F *from the lower tail.* Now, add the size of the confidence interval to that tiny value. In a 95% CI, the tiny area representing one of the two tails is 2.75%. Add them together and you get 97.5%. *Use that number to find the critical value of* F *from the upper tail.*

Confidence Interval	R Code to Find F_{upper} for $n_1=20$ ($df_1=19$) and $n_2=24$ ($df_2=23$)	R Code to Find F_{lower} for $n_1=20$ ($df_1=19$) and $n_2=24$ ($df_2=23$)
90% CI	`qf(0.95,df1=19,df2=23)`	`qf(0.05,df1=19,df2=23)`
95% CI	`qf(0.975,df1=19,df2=23)`	`qf(0.025, df1=19,df2=23)`
99% CI	`qf(0.995,df1=19,df2=23)`	`qf(0.005,df1=19,df2=23)`

For the temperature example, the confidence interval works out like this:

```
> qf(0.995,df1=19,df2=23) # Find F - UPPER
[1] 3.146105
> qf(0.005,df1=19,df2=23) # Find F - LOWER
[1] 0.3005517
```

Then we just replace all the values into the expression for the confidence interval:

$$\left(\frac{2.6}{3.2}\right) 0.301 \leq \frac{\sigma_1^2}{\sigma_2^2} \leq \left(\frac{2.6}{3.2}\right) 3.146$$

$$0.245 \leq \frac{\sigma_1^2}{\sigma_2^2} \leq 2.556$$

We are 99% confident that the true ratio of variances is between 0.245 and 2.556. Since the value 1 *does* appear in this interval, there is no evidence that the variability in temperatures between the two locations is different.

4.8 Regression Slope & Intercept

Objective

How well do those slope and intercept for a linear model based on your *sample*, $\hat{\beta}$ and $\hat{\alpha}$, provide an estimate slope and intercept for a linear model based on your *population,* β and α? By constructing a confidence interval around the estimates from our linear model, we determine *ranges of values* that we believe contain the true values were we considering the full population. We choose a *confidence level* (e.g. 90%, 95%, 99%) that tells us how likely it is that the true slope or intercept lies within that interval. As a result, an interval estimate provides much more information than a point estimate.

Remember that your regression line is a model for the relationship between two quantitative variables *from your sample*. There's a whole big population out there, and if you collected additional response (y) values using the exact same predictors (x), you would expect that your new values for y would be close to (but not exactly equal to) those original values for y. That means the y's are values of some random variable.

(For multiple regression models, we have more than one slope: each one corresponds to an independent variable, and represents the change in the response variable that occurs given a change in the predictor. Those cases will be covered here. However, there are also ways to find confidence intervals for a predicted mean and a predicted value, but these will not be covered in this book.)

Sampling Distribution and Standard Error of the Slope

To compute the confidence interval, we need to know the **sampling distribution** for the slope: that is, the entire collection of possibilities that *could have happened* even though we only collected one sample. (We can think of the sampling distribution as the *distribution of all possible random samples of y's, given a selection of x's that we have to find out those y's*.)

From each one of your random samples, you will have an estimated slope, β. All of those potential slopes are drawn from a normal model with its center at the real slope, and a standard deviation calculated by dividing the standard deviation of the population of all slopes σ by the sum of the deviations in the x-values. You can approximate the numerator by taking the sum of squares of all the residuals (SSE) and dividing by (n-2):

$$\beta \sim N\left(\beta_1, \frac{\sigma^2}{\sum(x_1 - \bar{x})^2}\right)$$

The standard deviation of the regression slope is all that stuff to the right of the comma. It's referred to as the "standard error of the slope", because the bigger our random sample *n* is, the better we can use our sample mean to approximate the real population mean.

In contrast to the standard deviation, which tells us the spread or dispersion of *all the values* within a population, standard error tells us how much the *means* of those values will be spread around (depending on how big a sample size we choose). **So standard error is a characteristic of a random sampling process, NOT of the population.**

Form of the Confidence Interval for a Regression Coefficient (Slope)

The general form of a confidence interval is:

$$CI \ : \ Estimate \ \pm Margin \ of \ Error$$

The specific form of the confidence interval for one regression coefficient (slope) is:

$$\hat{\beta} \pm t^*_{df} SE(\hat{\beta})$$

Our *estimate* for the regression coefficient is just the value computed by fitting the linear model to our sample data (beta-hat). The standard error calculation depends on the standard deviation of the residuals (also called the "standard error of the estimate"), the standard deviation of the predictor values, and the number of points in the sample.

Let's break it down, and find out how to compute the standard error of our beta-hat:

$$SE(\hat{\beta}) = \frac{s_e}{s_x \sqrt{n - 1}}$$

288

This says that the standard error of the slope we've estimated can be found by dividing the standard error of the estimate, s_e, by the standard deviation of the x coordinates of our points (s_x) and the square root of one less than the sample size (n-1). But how do we find the s_e? Just use this expression:

$$s_e = \sqrt{\frac{\Sigma\,(Residuals)^2}{n-2}}$$

The critical value of t, $t_{df}*$, depends on the number of degrees of freedom in your sample, which for the regression case is n-2 (two less than the number of points in your sample).

Finding a Confidence Interval for a Regression Coefficient (Slope)

We can use data to compute the confidence interval for the regression coefficient analytically, and there is also an option in R to compute them automatically. First, let's use the equations to form a confidence interval around a regression model that uses average daily temperature (TEMP) from 2013 to predict dewpoint temperature (DEWP) at the Shenandoah Regional Airport near Staunton, Virginia.

Before we begin, let's load the data in from my repository on GitHub:

```
> shd.wx <-
read.table("https://raw.githubusercontent.com/NicoleRadziwill/Data-for-R-
Examples/master/kshd-2013.txt",header=TRUE)
```

First, let's find out how many observations are in this dataset, and compute the standard error of the estimate, s_e. Notice that in order for us to *do* this in the first place, because s_e *requires* us to know the residuals, we need to have a linear least squares model in place!

```
> length(shd.wx$TEMP)
[1] 365
```

We will create a variable called `simple.fit` to store the linear model. We're calling it `simple.fit` to remind us that we have performed a simple linear regression, with only one independent variable `wx$TEMP` , and one dependent variable `wx$DEWP`:

```
> simple.fit <- lm(shd.wx$DEWP ~ shd.wx$TEMP)
> summary(simple.fit)

Call:
lm(formula = shd.wx$DEWP ~ shd.wx$TEMP)

Residuals:
     Min       1Q    Median       3Q      Max
-21.7451   -2.9158   0.5821    3.7044   12.2540

Coefficients:
              Estimate Std. Error t value Pr(>|t|)
(Intercept)  -18.05264    1.05973   -17.04   <2e-16 ***
shd.wx$TEMP    1.10742    0.01886    58.70   <2e-16 ***
---
Signif. codes:  0 '***' 0.001 '**' 0.01 '*' 0.05 '.' 0.1 ' ' 1

Residual standard error: 5.603 on 363 degrees of freedom
Multiple R-squared:  0.9047,    Adjusted R-squared:  0.9044
F-statistic:  3446 on 1 and 363 DF,  p-value: < 2.2e-16
```

What this means is that we now have a linear equation to model the relationship between our predictor (temperature) and our response variable (dewpoint), which is:

dewpoint = (1.107 * TEMP) - 18.053

To put a 99% confidence interval around 1.107 (our estimate for the slope), we now have enough information to compute the standard error of the estimate s_e:

```
> se <- sqrt((sum((simple.fit$residuals^2))/(length(shd.wx$TEMP)-2)))
> se
[1] 5.603435
```

We can use this value to calculate the standard error of the slope, or SE(beta-hat):

```
> se.slope <- se/ (sd(wx$TEMP)*sqrt(length(wx$TEMP)-1))
> se.slope
[1] 0.0188643
```

The last thing we need to find to have all the ingredients together for our confidence interval is to find the critical t, $t_{df}*$, for (n-2) or 363 degrees of freedom. Remember that to find a 99% confidence interval, we have to give qt an area of 0.995, which is the 99% plus half of the remaining tail area:

```
> t.star <- qt(0.995,df=363)
> t.star
[1] 2.589441
```

Finally, we can replace all the values for these variables into our expression for the confidence interval to determine the bounds on the slope. Note that our estimate of the slope is contained in the coefficients part of the simple.fit object, we can access its value directly by asking for the value in position 2 of that list (since the value in position 1 is the y intercept for the model):

```
> simple.fit$coefficients[2] + c(-1*t.star*se.slope,+1*t.star*se.slope)
[1] 1.058575 1.156271
```

We are 99% confident that the true slope of the regression line is between 1.059 and 1.156.

Using confint to Find Confidence Intervals

Of course, there's an easier way to do this in R. Just give the confint function the entire object containing the linear model, and *voila*:

```
> confint(simple.fit,level=0.99)
                 0.5 %      99.5 %
(Intercept) -20.796751 -15.308525
wx$TEMP       1.058575   1.156271
```

These calculations match what we determined analytically, and it's also easy to adjust the size of the confidence interval by specifying a different value for level. Notice that confint also provides a confidence interval for the intercept of the regression model. But how is this computed analytically?

Form of the Confidence Interval for the Intercept

As indicated in the output from `confint`, we can also find a confidence interval for the *intercept* of the linear model. The general form of a confidence interval is:

$$CI \; : \; Estimate \pm Margin \; of \; Error$$

The specific form of the confidence interval for the y intercept is:

$$\hat{\alpha} \pm t_{df}^{*} SE(\hat{\alpha})$$

The alpha with the hat on it is our *estimate* of what we think the intercept is, based on the results from the linear fit that we performed on our sample. The critical t, t_{df}*, depends on the degrees of freedom, which is calculated by taking the number of points in our dataset (n) and subtracting 2. The standard error of the slope estimate is calculated like this:

$$SE(\hat{\alpha}) = s_{y.x} \sqrt{\frac{1}{n} + \frac{\overline{x}^2}{SS_{xx}}}$$

To calculate this standard error, we will need to know the standard deviation of y, which is a measure of random error of y-values ($s_{x.y}$) and the sum of squares of the deviations between each individual x and the mean of all the x's (SS_{xx}):

$$s_{y.x} = \frac{Sum \; of \; Squares \; of \; Errors}{n-2}$$

$$SS_{xx} = \sum (x_i - \overline{x})^2$$

Now, let's compute a 99% confidence interval around the estimated intercept for our regression line. We'll start with SS_{xx} and then gradually move up until we have all the ingredients that we'll need to include in our expression for the confidence interval. Before we can do this, we need to store the results of an analysis of variance on our model, which we will save into the variable `a.fit`:

```
a.fit <- anova(simple.fit)
ss.xx <- sum( (wx$TEMP-mean(wx$TEMP))^2 )
sy.x <- sqrt( a.fit$"Sum Sq"[2] / (length(wx$TEMP)-2) )
se.alpha <- sy.x * sqrt( (1/length(wx$TEMP)) + (
        (mean(wx$TEMP)^2)/ss.xx)     )
t.star <- qt(0.995,df=(length(wx$TEMP)-2))
```

Since all the ingredients are in place, we can now compute the confidence interval:

```
> ME <- t.star * se.alpha
> CI <- fit$coefficients[1] + c(-ME,ME)
> CI
[1] -20.79675 -15.30853
```

Notice that these are exactly the same results as we got from confint:

```
> confint(simple.fit,level=0.99)
                  0.5 %      99.5 %
(Intercept) -20.796751 -15.308525
wx$TEMP       1.058575   1.156271
```

We are 99% confident that the true intercept is between -20.797 and -15.309.

Plotting the Confidence Interval and Prediction Interval for a Regression Line

Sometimes, it's nice to plot interval estimates along with your original data (represented as a scatterplot) and the line of best fit that you determined from your data. (This works better for simple linear regression, since you don't have to imagine a multidimensional regression line.) Note that there are two completely different kinds of intervals that you tend to encounter with linear models:

- The **confidence interval** says "we are X% confident that the mean response for a particular x value will be between the lower and upper bounds."

- The **prediction interval** says that "we are X% confident *any* observation of the response, given a particular x, will fall within these bounds." As a result, the prediction interval is much *broader* than the confidence interval, which only cares about the mean (at the center of the band).

- The **tolerance interval** establishes what proportion of the observations can be expected to fall within a certain band.

To plot the intervals, I use the wonderful function `plot.add.ci`, which was written by John Gosink, bioinformatics specialist. His code at http://gosink.org/?page_id=120, features a fancier, ggplot-based function for doing the same thing. I like the least fancy version, and will show you how it works on the Shenandoah weather data. Source it to use in your R session with this `source` line (code below provided for your review):

```
source("https://raw.githubusercontent.com/NicoleRadziwill/R-
Functions/master/plotaddci.R")
```

```
plot.add.ci <- function(x, y, interval='prediction', level=0.9,
regressionColor='red', ...) {
        xOrder   <- order(x)
        x        <- x[xOrder]
        y        <- y[xOrder]
        fit      <- lm(y ~ x, data=data.frame(x=x, y=y))
        newX     <- data.frame(x=jitter(x))
        fitPred <- predict.lm(fit, newdata=newX, interval=interval,
                        level=level, ...)
        abline(lm(y ~ x), col=regressionColor)
        lines(newX$x, fitPred[,2], lty=2, ...)
        lines(newX$x, fitPred[,3], lty=2, ...)
}
```

Now we can use it to plot our 99% confidence interval and 99% prediction interval on the scatterplot. Notice that the code *defaults* to displaying a prediction interval, and you have to specifically tell it to add in the confidence interval. To change the level of confidence, just adjust the `level` argument.

```
plot(shd.wx$TEMP,shd.wx$DEWP,pch=19,main="Confidence and Prediction
Intervals")
plot.add.ci(shd.wx$TEMP, shd.wx$DEWP, col="red", level=0.99, lwd="3")
plot.add.ci(shd.wx$TEMP, shd.wx$DEWP, col="blue", level=0.99,
interval="confidence", lwd=3)
```

Confidence and Prediction Intervals

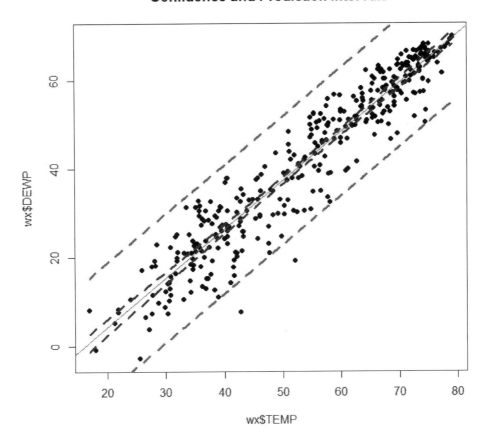

Other Resources

- The best explanation I've found about where the equations for the standard errors of the slope, intercept, predicted mean, and predicted values come from originates

at my high school, the North Carolina School of Science and Math (NCSSM) in Durham, NC. I graduated from S&M in 1992. Go Unis!
http://www.ncssm.edu/courses/math/Talks/PDFS/Standard%20Errors%20for%20Regression%20Equations.pdf

- There is a great reference discussing the not-so-subtle differences between confidence intervals, prediction intervals, and tolerance intervals at http://blog.minitab.com/blog/adventures-in-statistics/when-should-i-use-confidence-intervals-prediction-intervals-and-tolerance-intervals

SECTION 5: STATISTICAL INFERENCE

- A "Choose Your Own Adventure" Process for Finding the Right Test
- One and Two Sample t-tests for Means
- One and Two Sample z-tests for Proportions
- Chi-Square Test of Independence for Categorical Data
- One-Way Analysis of Variance (ANOVA) for Means
- F Test for Equality of Variances

5.1 Which Statistical Test Should I Use?

Objective

The bulk of this section contains details on how to execute *parametric* statistical inference tests. But how do you how *which one* to use? The following decision tree and table should help you make a reasonable decision. (Also, refer to Chapter 3.3 on developing research questions and matching them to a methodology, and Appendix K which provides a quick reference table.) This shouldn't be construed as a one-size-fits-all approach, and note that there are often times when your data can legitimately be analyzed in more than one way.

Questions to Find an Appropriate Statistical Approach

1. Does your research question involve tests on *categorical* or *quantitative* variables?
   - If CATEGORICAL, go to Question 2.
   - If QUANTITATIVE, or if you are interested in your categorical variables expressed as PROPORTIONS (even though technically, that's a way to represent categorical variables), go to Question 7.

2. Is your categorical data *ordinal* (that is, the ordering of the categories is important)?
   - If NO, go to Question 3.
   - If YES, it's time to proceed with caution. Why? Because if you do the Chi-square goodness of fit test OR the Chi-square test of independence when one or both variables are ordinal, your results *may* lack precision. Go to question 6.

3. How many categorical variables (groups) do you have to compare?
   - If you have 1 GROUP, you are probably trying to see whether your observations are randomly distributed, or if they come from a particular distribution. Perform a ***Chi-square goodness of fit test***. (This is just like the Chi-square test of independence, only you'll calculate your expected values based on the distribution you're trying to compare your data to.)

- If you have 2 GROUPS, you are probably trying to see if your two categorical variables are independent. Go to Question 4.

4. Do each of your groups have *exactly* two levels in them (a 2x2 contingency table), and are your two categorical variables *paired* (that is, you are testing for a before and after condition)?
   - If NO, go to Question 5.
   - If YES, then do **McNemar's test** (not covered in this book).

5. Do you have any cells with fewer than 5 observations?
   - If NO, then perform a **(Pearson) Chi-square test of independence**.
   - If YES, then do **Fisher's exact test** (not covered in this book).

6. How many categorical variables (groups) do you have to compare?
   - If you have 1 GROUP, you are probably trying to see whether your observations are randomly distributed, or if they come from a particular distribution. Perform a **Kolmogorov-Smirnov test** (not covered in this book).
   - If you have 2 GROUPS, you are probably trying to see if your two categorical variables are independent. If both categorical variables are *ordinal*, try the **Kendall's rank correlation tau** or **Mantel-Haenszel (MH) linear-by-linear association test** (not covered in this book). This means that an increase is the value of one variable is associated with an increase (or decrease) in the other. If only one is ordinal, a **(Pearson) Chi-square test of independence** may be OK.

7. Are you primarily interested in *means* or *proportions* from your sample, and how they compare to expected values (or to each other), or *relationships* between variables?
   - If MEANS, go to Question 8.
   - If PROPORTIONS, go to Question 13.
   - If RELATIONSHIPS, go to Question 16.

8. Do you want to see whether there is a difference between your sample mean and a *standard, recommended, or target value* for that mean?

- If NO, go to Question 9.
- If YES, use the **One sample t-test**.

9. Do you want to see whether there is a difference between your sample mean from *one* group, and a sample mean that you also collected for *another* group?
- If NO, go to Question 12.
- If YES, go to Question 10.

10. Are the observations in your first group and your second group linked by *who* the data was collected on? (For example, does one of your groups contain a "before" measurement, while the other has an "after" measurement, and you have measurements for each experimental subject in each group?)
- If NO, go to Question 11.
- If YES, use the **Paired t-test**.

11. Is the *variance* of the values from your first group approximately equal to the variance of the values from your second group?
- If YOU DON'T KNOW, go to Question 20.
- If YES, use the **Two sample t-test (equal variances)**.
- If NO, use the **Two sample t-test (unequal variances)**.

12. Do you want to see whether there is a difference between sample means you collected from *several groups*?
- If NO, I'm not sure what you're trying to do and can't provide a recommendation for what test to do. Sorry :(
- If YES, do a **One-way Analysis of Variance (ANOVA)**. If this test shows that indeed, at least one of your sample means is different than the others, you may want to follow up with a *test of multiple comparisons* (like Bonferroni's test or Tukey's test), or if you like doing things the long and hard way, several two sample t-tests. Beware, though, because in addition to being longer and harder you also increase your chance of incurring Type I Error (false positives).

13. Do you want to see whether there is a difference between your sample proportion and a *standard, recommended, or target value* for that proportion?
    - If NO, go to Question 14.
    - If YES, use the ***One proportion z-test***.

14. Do you want to see whether there is a difference between your sample proportion from *one* group, and a sample proportion that you also collected for *another* group?
    - If NO, go to Question 15.
    - If YES, use the ***Two proportion z-test***.

15. Are the observations in your first group and your second group linked by *who* the data was collected on? (For example, does one of your groups contain a "before" measurement, the other has an "after" measurement, and you have measurements for *each* experimental subject in each group?)
    - If NO, have you considered whether you can use one of the tests for categorical variables? If you have enough observations to create a contingency table, you might be able to perform a Chi-square test of independence. Consider starting over at Question 1 with this in mind.
    - If YES, use ***McNemar's test*** (not covered in this book).

16. Do you want to see whether there is a *relationship* between variables, possibly one that you can use to predict one variable based on the values of another?
    - If NO, go to Question 20.
    - If YES, go to Question 17.

17. Is your dependent variable (the one you'd like to be able to predict) *binary or categorical*?
    - If NO, go to Question 18.
    - If YES, and your response variable is *binary* (meaning you'd like to predict a 0 or 1, or membership in one of two groups), then use ***Logistic Regression*** (not covered in this book). If your response variable is categorical, you may want to consider ***Neural Networks for Classification*** (also not covered in this book).

18. Is your dependent variable (the one you'd like to be able to predict) *quantitative*?
    - If NO, I'm not sure what you're trying to do and can't provide a recommendation for what test to do. Sorry :(
    - If YES, go to Question 19.

19. How many independent (predictor) variables do you have?
    - If ONE, consider using **Simple Linear Regression**. In addition to building a model, you can also perform a statistical inference test (and create confidence intervals) around the regression coefficients.
    - If TWO OR MORE, consider using **Multiple Linear Regression.**

20. Are you trying to determine whether the *variance* of two populations is equal?
    - If NO, then consult Appendix K to see if you can choose an appropriate methodology to answer your research questions.
    - If YES, use the **F Test for Equality of Variances** or **Bartlett's test**. (Note that it is also important to run this test before attempting a **Two sample t-test**.)

What if the Assumptions Aren't Met?

If you've selected an approach using the questions above, the next step you should take is to *check to make sure you can meet the assumptions for the statistical test you want to do.* In each of the sections in this book that cover statistical tests, there is a list of the assumptions that you need to check.

- **Are your observations independent?** Usually, you're trying to assure that your observations are independent *of one another* - that there wasn't some pattern or bias you encountered in collecting your data. (For example, could one person's response have affected what another person answered? If so, your observations are not independent.) If you know the order in which you collected the data, you can test for *autocorrelation* or do *runs tests* (both not covered in this book) which may detect when your observations are not independent. As an example of autocorrelated data, think about what would happen if you collected data about the wait times people experience at your favorite coffee shop. The amount of time *you* wait is dependent on the amount of time that the people in front of you wait... because they're in your way! The solution is to get observations that *are* independent. And yes, this may require going back to the drawing board and collecting a new sample.

- **Are your data normal or nearly normal?** This is easy to test: just do a QQ plot or perform the Shapiro-Wilk test or Anderson-Darling test described in Chapter 1.8.

- **Is the variance within each of your groups equal?** This is also easy to test: just perform an F test for equality of variances, which is covered in Chapter 5.10.

Nonparametric tests can sometimes be used when your data is not at the interval or ratio level (that is, when it's categorical/nominal or ordinal), when the populations are not normal or nearly normal, or when the variances in the groups is not equal. Nonparametric tests do not rely on the data being from a particular distribution - they are "distribution free."

Other Resources

- This is another great resource that can help you figure out which statistical test is the most appropriate to use to analyze your data.
  http://www.ats.ucla.edu/stat/stata/whatstat/whatstat.htm
- This site provides one or two examples of pretty much every statistical test. You can use this to compare your data and your problem to worked examples:
  http://www.statext.com/howtouse.php
- This resource can help you determine the appopriate nonparametric test to use:
  http://www.isixsigma.com/tools-templates/hypothesis-testing/nonparametric-distribution-free-not-assumption-free/

5.2 One Sample t-test

Objective

The one sample t-test checks to see if there is a *difference* between one quantitative variable that you collect from your sample, and a *standard or recommended value*. Sometimes, we're comparing our data against a *goal or target*. Some examples of research questions where you might use the one sample t-test include:

- You're growing tomatoes from seeds. On the back of the seed packet, it says that from the time you plant each seed, it should take 62 days until your first tomato is ready. Out of the 12 seeds you planted, the average time-to-tomato was 65 days. Did it take your plants longer to mature?

- On average, everyone at the restaurant you work at makes $180 in tips on a typical weekend evening. Do you earn more than $180 in tips on weekends?

- Process output (which is defined as accounts receivable as a percentage of sales) has averaged 24% in your company over the past year. Benchmarking across similar businesses indicates that excellent performance is indicated by process output of no more than 18%. One of the managers claims that 24% isn't that much greater than 24%, so you shouldn't worry about improving the process. Is your process output significantly above 18%?

- You want to make sure you're not overeating, so you looked up the number of calories you should be ingesting a day to maintain your weight. You found out that you should be eating 1800 calories a day, and you've been keeping track of your calories now for the past two months. On average, are you meeting your target of 1800 calories a day?

- Is the average speed of cars that drive down Reservoir Rd. in Harrisonburg, Virginia more than 5 miles per hour (mph) above the speed limit?

The last question will be our example for the one sample t-test. After observing drivers on this road for a few years, I'm *pretty sure* they go much faster than the speed limit, but *statistics can help me know for sure.*

Our Process for Inference Testing

We'll use Dr. R's 7 Steps in this chapter:

Step 0: Check Your Assumptions

Step 1: Set Null and Alternative Hypotheses

Step 2: Choose α, the Level of Significance

Step 3: Calculate Test Statistic (T.S.)

Step 4: Draw a Picture

Step 5: Find the P-Value

Step 6: Draw Conclusion - Is the P-Value $< \alpha$? If So, Reject the Null

Step 7: Compute Confidence Interval & Double Check with R

We will solve the one sample t-test problem *analytically* (meaning, using the equations and doing the calculations by hand) and *also by using R* to do our calculations. If you are doing research, it's always good to solve the problem both ways to check your work! That way, you have a better chance of being correct. If you are writing a research paper to document your study, be sure to include *all* of Dr. R's 7 Steps in your report or journal article.

Before we begin with our one sample t-test about the speeding cars, we need to make sure we have data and that it is in the right format. I got the data from a friend who knew someone at the police department. They had gone out to Reservoir Rd. one day with a radar gun, and measured the speeds of 32 cars. The average speed was 33 miles per hour, with a sample standard deviation of 5.6 miles per hour. I asked if I could have their complete set of raw data, but apparently, they had lost it. All they had for me was the summary data. That's OK, I told them... we can still do some statistical inference without knowing the complete contents of the data set.

Step 0: Check Your Assumptions

Before beginning an inference test, it's important to check and see if your data meets the assumptions and conditions for the test. If it doesn't, you either need to 1) explain why you're still doing the test in the limitations portion of your study, 2) abandon the test entirely, 3) choose a *nonparametric alternative* if your problem is just that your sample differences aren't normally distributed, or you have rank-ordered data instead of continuous quantitative data. (The nonparametric alternative for the one sample t-test is the Wilcoxon One Sample Signed Rank test, which is not covered in this book.)

1. **Random sample**: Was each of the items in your data set randomly selected from the population of all values? In the speeding cars example, we don't know for sure. Ideally, we would have a random sample that covered multiple times of day, multiple days during the week. But we just don't have the information, so we will assume for the purposes of this test that the sample is random.

2. **Observations are independent**: Do the values from one measurement influence the values in another measurement? If the speeds of our cars were measured on the same day at around the same time, we might have a problem here. Ever wanted to go faster, but the car in front of you is going really slow? Ever wanted to slow down, but you have a speed demon on your tail? Car speeds are often, but not always, dependent upon the speeds of the cars around them. However, for the purposes of this test, we will assume that the observations of speed are indepedent.

3. **Sample is small enough**: Is the size of your sample, n, less than 10% of the entire population size? Our sample size is 32, and this is definitely less than 10% of the population of all potential cars driving down Reservoir Rd. that we could have sampled from.

4. **Values are nearly normal, OR the sample size is large**: For the one sample t-test to be valid, you should examine a histogram or QQ plot of the values you collected. A "large" sample size is considered to be anything over n=30 or n=40 (it's different in various statistics textbooks). But we don't have the complete data set, so we'll never

know! We have to assume that our data set is normal *enough* and large *enough* to move forward.

Later in the chapter, we'll perform a similar speed test, only with the *complete* data available so you can get a feel for how to check assumptions when you actually have enough data to do it properly.

Step 1: Set Null and Alternative Hypotheses

The forms of the null and alternative hypotheses for the one sample t-test are:

H_0: $\mu = \mu_0$

H_a: $\mu > \mu_0$ (one-tailed test)

           $\mu < \mu_0$ (one-tailed test)

           $\mu \neq \mu_0$ (two-tailed test)

The value you choose for μ_0 is your *standard, recommended value, goal,* or *target*. For our speeds example, we will set these null and alternative hypotheses with μ_0 at 5 miles per hour above the speed limit, or 30 mph. We want to test against the alternative hypothesis that the mean speed is actually *greater* than 35 mph, because we are pretty sure (based on past experience driving on this road) that it's full of speeders. We pick ONE alternative hypothesis to describe this, and our null and alternative hypotheses become:

H_0: $\mu = 30$ mph   (the mean speed is 5 mph above the speed limit)

H_a: $\mu > 30$ mph   (the cars are, on average, going even faster than that)

Step 2: Choose α, the Level of Significance

The level of significance α is often set to 0.05, indicating that we're willing to *incorrectly reject the null hypothesis* one out of every 20 times we collect a sample and run this test. This is acceptable for our current example because 1) the **cost** of collecting new observations is comparatively low, in terms of time, effort, and money, 2) the **risk** associated with drawing incorrect conclusions is also low (after all, I'm performing this test just for my own personal edification) and 3) there are no significant **ethical considerations** that I have to keep in mind based on how the results from my study may be applied by other people who read about or make decisions based on my study. All I want to know is whether people are consistently speeding down one of the roads I drive on every day. There are no policy decisions riding on my conclusion.

In contrast, if I were performing this study on behalf of the police department, and they were trying to figure out whether to impose harsher penalties on the speeders (or maybe even just invest money in constructing speed bumps) I might want to make my test more stringent, and set my level of significance α to 0.01, meaning I am only willing to reject my null hypothesis and assert that *people are driving pretty darn fast on this road* if I will be incorrect 1 out of every 100 times I collect data and perform the test, due to sampling error.

Step 3: Calculate Test Statistic (T.S.)

Because this is a t-test, our test statistic will be a t. It's calculated by subtracting the value that's on the right-hand side of the null and alternative hypotheses (μ_0) from the *average of the quantitative values* you've calculated from your sample. The formula is:

$$ t = \frac{\overline{y} - \mu_0}{SE(\overline{y})} = \frac{\overline{y} - \mu_0}{s/\sqrt{n}} $$

The summary statistics that I found from my sample of n=32 cars are a sample mean (y) of 33 mph, and a sample standard deviation of 5.6 mph. [That's *all we know*... we don't have access to the full data set, but that's OK.] We can calculate the test statistic like this:

$$ t = \frac{33 - 30}{5.6/\sqrt{32}} = 3.03 $$

Step 4: Draw a Picture

T-distributions look an awful lot like normal distributions, even though they have *peakier peaks* and *longer tails*. As a result, I'll draw this picture using the `shadenorm` function, which draws normal curves, because they are so similar. Because our alternative hypothesis is "greater than," I want to shade the area that's to the RIGHT (greater than) our computed test statistic t of 3.03, so I enter the following code into R:

```
source("https://raw.githubuscrcontent.com/NicoleRadziwill/R-
Functions/master/shadenorm.R")

shadenorm(between=c(3.03,Inf),color="black")
```

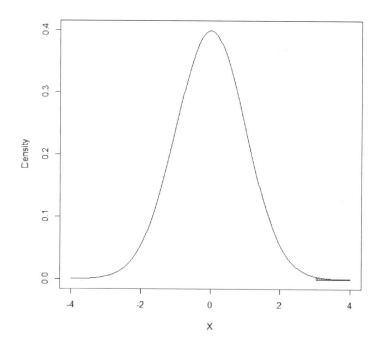

Wow, there's just a *tiny* little area shaded to the right of t=3.03. But this makes sense, because according to the 68-95-99.7 rule for the normal distribution, we know that only 0.3% of the total area is going to be in the tails beyond ±3 standard deviations from the

310

mean (thus only 0.15% of the area is in the right tail). Even though we use a t-distribution for this problem, we can be pretty sure that the P-Value we need to calculate is very close to zero. But we'll calculate it anyway.

Step 5: Find the P-Value

The command to calculate areas under the t distribution in R is `pt`. Using the `pt` command, we can only find areas to the *left* of a particular t value. Since we want to find the area in the right tail, we have to ask R to compute "100% of the total area under the t distribution, minus the area to the left of t=3.03" like this:

```
> 1-pt(3.03,df=31)
[1] 0.002450379
```

Our P-Value is approximately 0.002 or 0.2% of the total area.

Step 6: Is the P-Value < α? If So, Reject the Null

Now we have to ask ourselves the question: Is the P-Value we just calculated (0.002) less than our α of 0.05? Yes, it is. So we should REJECT our null hypothesis that the average speed of cars driving along Reservoir Rd. is 30 mph. But what does this *mean*? It means that we have evidence to indicate that the cars drive, on average, more than 30 mph. Definitely above the posted speed limit of 25 mph. But there are some limitations to our study: first, we only worked with summary data, so we don't know if our data actually met the assumptions and conditions of the one sample t-test. We don't know if we actually got a representative sample of car speeds on different days, at different times of day, and the values might not be independent.

Step 7: Compute Confidence Interval & Double Check with R

We can also construct a confidence interval to double-check our work. Let's do that, and build a 95% CI. The general form of the confidence interval is:

$$CI \; : \; Estimate \; \pm \, Margin \; of \; Error$$

The specific form of the confidence interval for one mean is:

$$\bar{y} \pm t^{*}_{df} SE(\bar{y})$$

$$\bar{y} \pm t^{*}_{df} \frac{s}{\sqrt{n}}$$

Our *estimate* for the mean is just the average value that we have for our dataset: 33 mph. The standard deviation of our sample, s, is 5.6 mph. Our sample size n=32. We can compute the value of critical t, t*, by using the `qt` command in R based on the size of the confidence interval net we want to cast, and the degrees of freedom for this particular data set (df = n - 1 = 31). We choose a critical t of 2.045 (shaded). Then, plug the values in:

Confidence Interval	R Code to Find Critical t (t*)	Critical t (t*) for df = 31
90% CI	`qt(0.95,df=29)`	1.699
95% CI	`qt(0.975,df=29)`	2.045
99% CI	`qt(0.995,df=29)`	2.756

$$33 \pm \left(2.045 \; x \; \frac{5.6}{\sqrt{32}} \right) = (30.98, 35.02)$$

Our confidence interval ranges from a lower bound of 30.98 to an upper bound of 35.02. This is interpreted in the following way:

> *"We are 95% confident that the true average speed of cars on Reservoir Rd. is between 30.98 mph and 35.02 mph."*

Notice how the value on the right-hand side of our null hypothesis, 30 mph, is *not* inside this confidence interval? We are 95% confident that the real average speed is between

30.98 mph and 35.02 mph, but 30 mph is *not even a possible value* here. Even more significantly, the 95% confidence interval is *far away* from including the speed limit of 25 mph! This affirms the decision that we made to *reject the null hypothesis*.

If we had the full data set, we could double check with `t.test` in R. Unfortunately, we don't, so let's do an entire example end-to-end so you can see the verification process.

One sample t-test Example in R

To execute a hypothesis test in R, we actually need all the data. But as you recall, if we *had* the raw data, we would actually be able to check our assumptions and conditions more effectively. We decided to collect our own sample data, and this time, we randomly sampled 17 cars *just during rush hour* (between 5pm and 6pm) on three different days during the week. We made sure that we picked cars who weren't boxed in, or being tailed by fast drivers, to ensure that our observations would be independent this time. Here is our data, and some of the descriptive statistics about our sample:

```
> speeds <- c(29,25,22,34,38,40,27,29,30,30,23,34,42,36,35,27,37)
> length(speeds)
[1] 17
> summary(speeds)
   Min. 1st Qu.  Median    Mean 3rd Qu.    Max.
  22.00   27.00   30.00   31.65   36.00   42.00
> sd(speeds)
[1] 5.926014
```

We will use the same null hypothesis and alternative hypothesis as the previous example. Since we want to test against the alternative that the mean speed is *greater* than 30 mph, we can do it like this:

```
> t.test(speeds,mu=30,alternative="greater")

        One Sample t-test

data:  speeds
t = 1.146, df = 16, P-Value = 0.1343
alternative hypothesis: true mean is greater than 30
```

95 percent confidence interval:
 29.13775   Inf
sample estimates:
mean of x
 31.64706

Let's double check the computations that R did. First, we want to check the calculation of the test statistic (T.S.):

$$t = \frac{\bar{y} - \mu_0}{SE(\bar{y})} = \frac{31.65 - 30}{5.93/\sqrt{17}} = 1.147$$

And now, we ask R for the P-Value that corresponds to t=1.147. R only looks up areas to the *left* of a test statistic, but we selected the alternative hypothesis with the *greater than* option. That means we need the area to the *right* of the test statistic we calculated. To find this, we start with 1 and then subtract off the area to the left of t=1.147:

```
>   1-pt(1.147,df=16)
[1] 0.1341225
```

Now we have additional confirmation of our computations. But there's only one problem: see (in the t.test output on the previous page) how R calculated the 95% confidence interval to be between 29.13775 and infinity? This looks kind of suspect, so let's calculate the confidence interval ourselves. We have to look up the critical value of t, t*, for df = 17 - 1 = 16 first, which we do using the R command qt(0.975,df=16) which gives us 2.12. Then we can plug all the values into our expression for the confidence interval:

$$\bar{y} \pm t^*_{df} \frac{s}{\sqrt{n}}$$

$$31.65 \pm \left(2.12 \; x \; \frac{5.926}{\sqrt{17}} \right) = (28.6, 34.7)$$

This is definitely different than what R just told us. But there's a solution. If we want to find the confidence interval in R, we just have to drop the alternative hypothesis from t.test.

314

You know how it's possible to compute a confidence interval even if you *don't* go ahead with the full inference test? All you need to do is use the estimates from your sample in place of the values you were supposed to take from the right-hand side of your null hypothesis. Well, R doesn't need to do the inference test to report a confidence interval. We can solve this problem by just eliminating the `alternative` argument from our `t.test` command:

```
> t.test(speeds,mu=30)

        One Sample t-test

data:  speeds
t = 1.146, df = 16, P-Value = 0.2687
alternative hypothesis: true mean is not equal to 30
95 percent confidence interval:
 28.60018 34.69393
sample estimates:
mean of x
 31.64706
```

This looks much better, and supports the computation of the confidence interval that we got by doing the problem analytically. What conclusion should we draw? <u>First of all, we ask ourselves that important question that everyone should memorize: "Is the P-Value < α? If so, reject the null."</u> Our P-Value of 0.1343 is NOT less than an α of 0.05, so we FAIL TO REJECT the null hypothesis. This means – using the data we collected ourselves, we *cannot* conclude that the cars driving down Reservoir Rd. are going any faster, on average, than 30 mph. Our confidence interval is interpreted like this:

> *"We are 95% confident that the true average speed of cars driving down Reservoir Rd. at rush hour is between 28.6 mph and 34.7 mph."*

Notice how 30 mph is right in the middle of this confidence interval? That supports our decision *not* to reject the null hypothesis, because the average speed of those cars could indeed be the 30 mph that we hypothesized. However, notice that the speed limit of 25 mph is not contained within our confidence interval, giving us some evidence that the cars, on average, are indeed still driving over the speed limit of 25 mph.

Other Resources:

- Here's an example problem that takes a look at whether the average IQ for people who take a certain medication is different than 100. Although there's lots of problems with this example (including the fact that IQ becomes a much less reliable measurement the older you get), the process is sound:
  http://www.statisticslectures.com/topics/onesamplet/
- Even though it uses Excel, here is a great example of the one sample t-test that even integrates calculation of effect size and power analysis into the problem:
  http://www.real-statistics.com/students-t-distribution/one-sample-t-test/
- Here's a nice online calculator for the one sample t-test:
  http://vassarstats.net/t_single.html
- Here's another online calculator for the one sample t-test:
  http://www.danielsoper.com/statcalc3/calc.aspx?id=98

5.3 Two Sample t-test with Equal Variances

Objective

The two-sample t-test checks to see if there is a *difference* between one quantitative variable that you collect from *each of two groups*, or samples. This is one of the most common hypothesis tests performed during Six Sigma quality improvement activities. Some examples of research questions where you might use this two-sample t-test include:

- There are two pizza places that deliver to your house. You want to know if the one that has the pizza you don't like quite as much delivers *faster* than the pizza place with the pizza you prefer. Because if there's a difference, and you know if one of them gets the pizza to your house faster... that might change your buying habits.

- The time to convert sales leads into customers used to be 98 days with a standard deviation of 18 days. But you changed your process for engaging new customers, and now it's an average of 83 days with a standard deviation of 14 days. You have lots of data to examine. Is the difference significant?

- Do business students have a higher cumulative GPA than technology students at your school right now?

- Do females have a higher cumulative GPA than males at your school right now?

- The stability of beer foam is one characteristic that influences the overall perceived quality of beer. This can be measured by a variable called tau (τ) which characterizes the half-life of the *foam stand* on top of the poured beer. For his capstone project, one of my students asked: Is there a difference between the foam stand of a particular beer if it's poured at room temperature, versus poured cold?

The last question will be our example for the two-sample t-test. This is an interesting question because we can guess that pouring beer cold has an influence on the perceived quality of the beer, possibly due to enhanced foam stability, but *statistics can help us know for sure*.

Our Process for Inference Testing

We'll use Dr. R's 7 Steps in this chapter:

Step 0: Check Your Assumptions

Step 1: Set Null and Alternative Hypotheses

Step 2: Choose α, the Level of Significance

Step 3: Calculate Test Statistic (T.S.)

Step 4: Draw a Picture

Step 5: Find the P-Value

Step 6: Draw Conclusion - Is the P-Value < α? If So, Reject the Null

Step 7: Compute Confidence Interval & Double Check with R

We will solve the two-sample t-test problem *analytically* (meaning, using the equations and doing the calculations by hand) and *also by using R* to do our calculations. If you are doing research, it's always good to solve the problem both ways to check your work! That way, you have a better chance of being correct. If you are writing a research paper to document your study, be sure to include *all* of Dr. R's 7 Steps in your results section.

Before we begin with our two-sample t-test about the beer foam, we need to get data. You can load in my beer foam data directly from GitHub:

```
> foam <- read.csv("https://raw.githubusercontent.com/NicoleRadziwill/Data-
for-R-Examples/master/beer-foam.csv",header=TRUE)
> names(foam)
 [1] "pour"           "time"           "test.case"      "brewery"
 [5] "temp"           "wet.foam.ht"    "beer.ht"        "dry.foam.ht"
 [9] "tau"            "dry.foam.ratio"
```

This is a CSV file with 10 independent variables: pour number, time (in seconds after initial pour), test case number, brewery, temperature of beer, height of beer from bottom of glass (beer.ht), and wet and dry foam heights (in cm). I have one variable that I've calculated from the earlier variables: tau (τ), the half-life of the beer foam.

Here is the header from that data:

```
> head(foam)
  pour time test.case brewery temp wet.foam.ht beer.ht dry.foam.ht
1    1   30   SH-COLD      SH COLD       18.60    4.10       13.15
2    1   60   SH-COLD      SH COLD       15.85    6.40       12.70
3    1   90   SH-COLD      SH COLD       14.25    7.45       12.15
4    1  120   SH-COLD      SH COLD       13.00    8.05       11.50
5    1  150   SH-COLD      SH COLD       12.00    8.50       10.95
6    1  180   SH-COLD      SH COLD       11.40    8.80       10.65
        tau dry.foam.ratio
1 235.2300          0.707
2 208.6780          0.801
3 228.4630          0.853
4 247.0435          0.885
5 265.1174          0.913
6 291.6962          0.934
```

There are four test cases: SH-COLD, SH-RT, 3B-COLD, and 3B-RT. SH and 3B are two coded craft breweries, and COLD and RT indicate whether the measurements were taken at 39 degrees Fahrenheit (COLD) or 68 degrees Fahrenheit (marked RT, for room temperature). We want to compare whether there is a difference between the half-life of the foam at any given time for the SH product poured cold versus poured at room temperature. We also want to compare whether there is a difference between the half-lives of the foam at any given time for the 3B product poured cold versus poured at room temperature. There are two different two sample t-tests that we plan to execute.

Step 0: Check Your Assumptions

Before beginning any inference test, it's important to check and see if your data meets the assumptions and conditions for the test. If it doesn't, you either need to 1) explain why you're still doing the test in the limitations portion of your study, 2) abandon the test entirely, 3) if your problem is just that your sample differences aren't normally distributed, or you have rank-ordered data instead of continuous quantitative data, then you should choose a *nonparametric alternative* to use for your test. (The nonparametric alternative for the two-sample t-test with equal variances is the Mann-Whitney U test, which is not covered in this book.) Here are the assumptions for the two-sample t-test with equal variances:

1. **Random sample**: Was each of the items in your data set randomly selected from the population of all values? (For the beer data, we can't be totally sure, but we can assume that each tau measurement was randomly sampled from the population of all possible values that any beer could have.)

2. **Observations are independent**: Do the values from one collection of data influence the values in another? For our beer data, we measure tau at regular intervals, so one value will certainly depend on the value that comes *before* it. However, we're combining data from multiple pours into our sample, and each of the pours are independent by design. We will assume that the elements of our sample are independent enough to meet the requirements of this assumption, and we'll move forward with the test.

3. **Sample is small enough**: Is the size of your sample, n, less than 10% of the entire population size? Our sample size is 80 for each test, and this is definitely less than 10% of the population of all potential beer foam decay observations (every time someone pours a beer, they *could* observe the foam). There are many more beers poured in a single day than what's in our sample.

4. **Values are nearly normal, OR the sample size is large**: For the two-sample t-test to be valid, you should examine a histogram or QQ plot of the values you collected. A "large" sample size is considered to be anything over n=30 or n=40 (it's different in various statistics textbooks).

In both cases, we have a large sample, and all but one of the four distributions (pictured below with the code that produced them) are nearly normal.

Here are two distributions of half-life, representing two temperatures and one brewery:

Tau for Cold and Room Temperature Cases (SH)

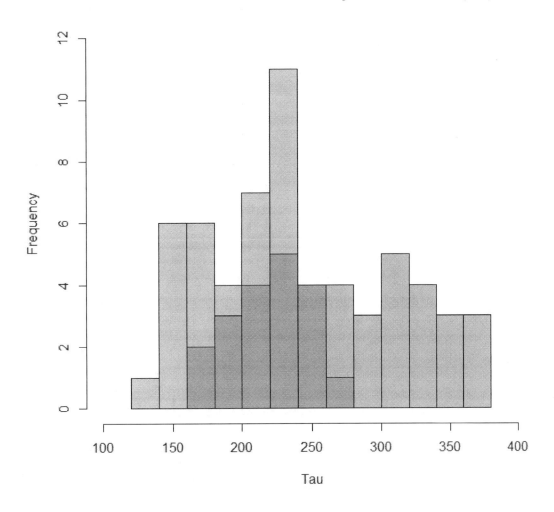

```
cold <- hist(foam[foam$test.case=="SH-COLD",]$tau, breaks=12)
rt <- hist(foam[foam$test.case=="SH-RT",]$tau, breaks=6)
plot(cold, col=rgb(0,0,1,1/4), xlim=c(100,400), ylim=c(0,12),
     main="Tau for Cold and Room Temperature Cases (SH)",
     xlab="Tau", ylab="Frequency")
plot(rt, col=rgb(1,0,0,1/4), xlim=c(100,400), add=T)
```

And here are two distributions of half-life, for two temperatures at another brewery:

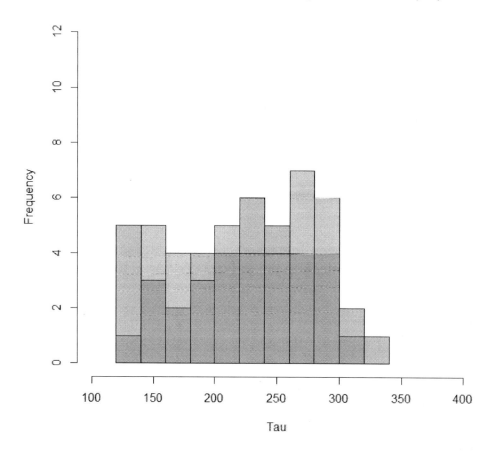

Tau for Cold and Room Temperature Cases (3B)

```
cold2 <- hist(foam[foam$test.case=="3B-COLD",]$tau, breaks=12)
rt2 <- hist(foam[foam$test.case=="3B-RT",]$tau, breaks=12)
plot(cold2, col=rgb(0,0,1,1/4), xlim=c(100,400), ylim=c(0,12),
     main="Tau for Cold and Room Temperature Cases (3B)",
     xlab="Tau", ylab="Frequency")
plot(rt2, col=rgb(1,0,0,1/4), xlim=c(100,400), add=T)
```

But we're not finished checking out the assumptions. One more to go.

5. **Equal variances**: For this version of the two-sample t-test to be valid, each of the two samples must have distributions with similar variability. To check this out:

1) Use this heuristic: **if the larger standard deviation is no more than twice the smaller standard deviation, then we consider the two population variances to be equal.**

2) **Take a look at the histograms,** and see if they both have approximately the same width. (In both of our histograms above, the variances are comparable). This is an informal approach and not that rigorous.

3) Perform **an F test for equality of variances** using the `var.test` command in R (see Chapter 5.10). This is a rigorous and formal approach.

Let's quickly run a test of variances for the SH product data, then for 3B:

```
> var.test(foam[foam$test.case=="SH-COLD",]$tau,foam[foam$test.case=="SH-RT",]$tau)

        F test to compare two variances

data:  foam[foam$test.case == "SH-COLD", ]$tau and foam[foam$test.case == "SH-RT", ]$tau
F = 2.646, num df = 39, denom df = 39, P-Value = 0.003049
alternative hypothesis: true ratio of variances is not equal to 1
95 percent confidence interval:
 1.399459 5.002811
sample estimates:
ratio of variances
        2.645983

> var.test(foam[foam$test.case=="3B-COLD",]$tau,foam[foam$test.case=="3B-RT",]$tau)

        F test to compare two variances
```

```
data:   foam[foam$test.case == "3B-COLD", ]$tau and foam[foam$test.case ==
"3B-RT", ]$tau
F = 1.1919, num df = 39, denom df = 39, P-Value = 0.5862
alternative hypothesis: true ratio of variances is not equal to 1
95 percent confidence interval:
 0.6303963 2.2535523
sample estimates:
ratio of variances
          1.191902
```

We focus on the P-Values for these two tests. If the P-Value is less than α (nominally 0.05), then we reject the null hypothesis that the variances are equal. To meet the assumptions of the two-sample t-test with equal variances, we *want* to see large P-Values... at least larger than α! As a result, our tau distributions for 3B are OK, but the tau distributions for the SH product are not OK. **We can move forward with the two-sample t-test with equal variances *only* for the 3B product.**

Not to worry, though... we'll do the two-sample t-test with *unequal* variances on our SH data in the next chapter.

Step 1: Set Null and Alternative Hypotheses

The forms of the null and alternative hypotheses for the two-sample t-test are:

H_0: $\mu_1 - \mu_2 = D_0$

H_a: $\mu_1 - \mu_2 > D_0$ (one-tailed test)

$\mu_1 - \mu_2 < D_0$ (one-tailed test)

$\mu_1 - \mu_2 \neq D_0$ (two-tailed test)

The value you choose for D_0 is the difference you *believe* exists between the two samples (and is very frequently zero in these tests, indicating that the means of the two groups are the same). For our beer foam example for the 3B product, we will set D_0 to zero:

H_0: $\mu_{COLD} - \mu_{RT} = 0$ (there is no difference between mean tau)

H_a: $\mu_{COLD} - \mu_{RT} > 0$ (cold beer has higher tau than room temperature)

This test is significant because if we can show that the cold pours have a consistently higher tau, and we know that higher tau corresponds to higher perceived product quality, we may advise the brewery that they recommend this particular beer to only be served cold.

Step 2: Choose α, the Level of Significance

The level of significance α is often set to 0.05, indicating that we're willing to *incorrectly reject the null hypothesis* 1 out of every 20 times we collect a sample and run this test. We're going to select a more stringent level of significance α of 0.01, indicating that we're only willing to be wrong 1 in every 100 times. This is because 1) the **cost** of collecting new observations is substantial, in terms of time and effort (but not money), 2) the **risk** associated with drawing incorrect conclusions is moderate, particularly if the brewery will be making recommendations to their distributors based on our conclusions, and 3) the **ethical considerations** that I should keep in mind include the possibility that my research results may be used to make significant business decisions that could impact the brewery's reputation (and in fact, the product's reputation).

Step 3: Calculate Test Statistic (T.S.)

Because this is a t-test, our test statistic will be a t. It's calculated by taking the difference between the sample means and subtracting off whatever value is on the right-hand side of the null hypothesis (D_0) in the numerator, and then dividing by the *pooled standard error of the differences*. This denominator, SE_{pooled}, breaks down into a complex expression involving the sample sizes n_1 and n_2, and the sample standard deviations s_1 and s_2. The variable s_p refers to the *pooled standard deviation*. Because the two distributions have nearly the same scatter, we can mash them together (or "pool" them) and just use one standard deviation.

The formulas are:

$$t = \frac{\overline{y}_1 - \overline{y}_2 - D_0}{SE_{pooled}(\overline{y}_1 - \overline{y}_2)} = \frac{\overline{y}_1 - \overline{y}_2 - D_0}{s_p\sqrt{\frac{1}{n_1} + \frac{1}{n_2}}}$$

$$s_p = \sqrt{\frac{(n_1 - 1)s_1^2 + (n_2 - 1)s_2^2}{n_1 + n_2 - 2}}$$

To calculate my test statistic, I like to start from the inside out and find s_p first. Before I do that, it's useful to know all the means and standard deviations of my variable of interest, tau, inside my data set. So I can ask R for this information first to plug into my equations:

```
> aggregate(foam$tau, by=list(foam$test.case), FUN=sd)
   Group.1        x
1 3B-COLD 55.53293
2   3B-RT 50.86631
3 SH-COLD 57.66225
4   SH-RT 35.44852

> aggregate(foam$tau, by=list(foam$test.case), FUN=mean)
   Group.1        x
1 3B-COLD 221.1892
2   3B-RT 226.8597
3 SH-COLD 271.6084
4   SH-RT 202.0040
```

Remembering that our first group is the COLD group, and our second group is the RT group, and we're doing the test for the 3B product (the only one that checked out on all of the assumptions of this test), we plug in the equation for s_p like this:

$$s_p = \sqrt{\frac{(39)(55.53^2) + (39)(50.87^2)}{40 + 40 - 2}} = 53.25$$

And then we can plug it into the equation for the test statistic (T.S.) t:

$$t = \frac{221.19 - 226.86}{53.25\sqrt{\frac{1}{40} + \frac{1}{40}}} = -0.476$$

Step 4: Draw a Picture

Because t-distributions have the normal bell-curve shape, I'll draw the picture using shadenorm, which draws normal curves. Because our alternative hypothesis is "greater than," I want to shade the area that's to the RIGHT (greater than) our computed test statistic t of -0.476, so I enter the following code into R and notice that more than 50% of the area under the curve is shaded:

```
source("https://raw.githubusercontent.com/NicoleRadziwill/R-
Functions/master/shadenorm.R")

shadenorm(between=c(-0.476,Inf),color="black")
```

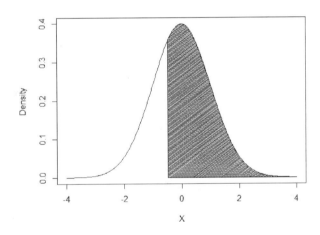

Step 5: Find the P-Value

The P-Value is large... greater than 0.5, because more than half the area is shaded. We don't even need to calculate the exact P-Value.

Step 6: Is the P-Value < α? If So, Reject the Null

With a P-Value that large, the answer to our question "Is the P-Value less than α?" is bound to be NO, so we *fail to reject* the null hypothesis. We have no evidence to suggest that the mean tau for the cold pours is greater than the mean tau for the room temperature pours.

Step 7: Compute Confidence Interval & Double Check with R

We can also construct a confidence interval to double-check our work. Let's do that, and build a 95% CI. The general form of the confidence interval is:

$$CI \;:\; Estimate \;\pm\; Margin\ of\ Error$$

The specific form of the confidence interval for the difference between two means is:

$$(\overline{y_1} - \overline{y_2}) \pm t^*_{df} SE(\overline{y_1} - \overline{y_2})$$

$$(\overline{y_1} - \overline{y_2}) \pm t^*_{df} S_{pooled}\sqrt{\frac{1}{n_1} + \frac{1}{n_2}}$$

Our *estimate* for the difference between means is just the numerator for our test statistic: -5.67. The standard error is the denominator, 11.91. Our sample size n=40. We compute the value of critical t, t*, by using the `qt` command in R based on the size of the confidence interval net we want to cast, and the degrees of freedom for this particular data set (df = n - 1 = 39).

Once we select the appropriate critical t value (2.023; shaded in the table on the next page), we plug all of these numbers into the expression for the confidence interval:

$$(-5.67) \pm (2.023\ x\ 11.91) = (-29.76, 18.42)$$

Confidence Interval	R Code to Find Critical t (t*)	Critical t (t*) for df = 39
90% CI	qt(0.95,df=39)	1.685
95% CI	qt(0.975,df=39)	2.023
99% CI	qt(0.995,df=39)	2.708

Our confidence interval ranges from a lower bound of -29.76 to an upper bound of 18.42. Tau is *dimensionless*; the confidence interval has no units. The CI is interpreted like this:

> *"We are 95% confident that the true difference between tau from a cold pour of the 3B brand beer and tau from a room temperature pour of the same beer is between -29.76 and 18.42."*

Notice how the value zero is inside this confidence interval? We are 95% confident that the true difference between tau values is *somewhere in a range that includes zero*. The difference could very possibly be zero! This affirms the decision that we made to *fail to reject the null hypothesis*.

Step 7 Continued: Two Sample t-test with Equal Variances: Example in R

Executing the two-sample t-test in R is straightforward. To make the code easier to read, I first created the variables cold and rt to store the tau values from the cold pour of the 3B product, and the tau values from the room temperature pour of the 3B product. Finally, run the t.test:

```
> cold <- foam[foam$test.case=="3B-COLD",]$tau
> rt <- foam[foam$test.case=="3B-RT",]$tau
> t.test(cold,rt,alternative="greater",var.equal=TRUE)

        Two Sample t-test

data:  cold and rt
```

```
t = -0.4762, df = 78, P-Value = 0.6824
alternative hypothesis: true difference in means is greater than 0
95 percent confidence interval:
 -25.49157        Inf
sample estimates:
mean of x mean of y
 221.1892   226.8597
```

Notice that the test statistic (T.S.) t is the same as what we calculated analytically. The P-Value is well over 50%, like we suspected, at 0.6824. We can also easily test to see if the room temperature values are *higher* than the cold pour values by flipping the alternative argument:

```
> t.test(cold,rt,alternative="less",var.equal=TRUE)

        Two Sample t-test

data:  cold and rt
t = -0.4762, df = 78, P-Value = 0.3176
alternative hypothesis: true difference in means is less than 0
95 percent confidence interval:
     -Inf 14.15057
sample estimates:
mean of x mean of y
 221.1892   226.8597
```

Once again, when we ask ourselves the question "Is the P-Value < α?" we find that no, it is not, and so we FAIL TO REJECT the null hypothesis. There does not appear to be a difference between the tau values from the cold pours, and the tau values from the room temperature pours. We can obtain the confidence interval if we leave out the alternative argument to t.test like this:

```
> t.test(cold,rt,var.equal=TRUE)

        Two Sample t-test

data:  cold and rt
t = -0.4762, df = 78, P-Value = 0.6352
```

```
alternative hypothesis: true difference in means is not equal to 0
95 percent confidence interval:
 -29.37598  18.03498
sample estimates:
mean of x mean of y
 221.1892  226.8597
```

Notice that the confidence interval has been calculated, and it's very close to what we obtained analytically. Don't be concerned if the values are different between your calculations and R in the second or third decimal places. R may use more exact formulas for computing the pooled standard deviation and pooled standard error, and sometimes it does odd things with formatting (where it stores a value with many decimal places, but it rounds up or down – or truncates – values it displays on the screen). But your analytical solutions should be close enough to give you the sense that you're on target.

Other Resources:

- Here's an example from a school of health that uses blood pressure data: http://sphweb.bumc.bu.edu/otlt/MPH-Modules/BS/BS704_Confidence_Intervals/BS704_Confidence_Intervals5.html
- This example uses other statistical software, but you should be able to follow along with the output: http://rt.uits.iu.edu/visualization/analytics/docs/ttest-docs/ttest4.php
- Here is an example in Excel: http://www.real-statistics.com/students-t-distribution/two-sample-t-test-equal-variances/

5.4 Two Sample t-test with Unequal Variances

Objective

The two-sample t-test checks to see if there is a *difference* between one quantitative variable that you collect from *each of two groups*, or samples. In this chapter, we will perform essentially the same test as in the last chapter, only for the case the distributions from each of the two groups have different widths: one is fatter, and one is thinner. Some examples of research questions where you might use this two-sample t-test include:

- There are two pizza places that deliver to your house. You want to know who delivers faster, but whereas one place consistently delivers within about 45 minutes, the other place ranges anywhere from 15 minutes to an hour and a half. Knowing which place delivers faster might change your buying habits.

- The time to convert sales leads into customers used to be 98 days with a standard deviation of 4 days. But you changed your process for engaging new customers, and now it's an average of 83 days with a standard deviation of 20 days. You have lots of data to examine. Is the difference significant?

- Do business students have a higher cumulative GPA than technology students at your school right now? Or, do females have a higher cumulative GPA than males at your school right now? Our sample average is a 3.4 with a standard deviation of 0.3, but for the second group, it is 3.5 with a standard deviation of 0.7.

- The stability of beer foam is one characteristic that influences the overall perceived quality of a beer. This can be measured by a variable called tau (τ) which characterizes the half-life of the *foam stand* on top of the poured beer. For his capstone project, one of my students asked: Is there a difference between the foam stand of a particular beer if it's poured at room temperature, versus poured cold? For one case, we found that the distributions had unequal variances, so we have to perform this variety of the two-sample t-test.

The last question will be our example for the two-sample t-test. This is an interesting question because we can guess that pouring beer cold has an influence on the perceived quality of the beer, possibly due to enhanced foam stability, but *statistics can help us know for sure.*

Our Process for Inference Testing

We'll use Dr. R's 7 Steps in this chapter:

> **Step 0**: Check Your Assumptions
> **Step 1**: Set Null and Alternative Hypotheses
> **Step 2**: Choose α, the Level of Significance
> **Step 3**: Calculate Test Statistic (T.S.)
> **Step 4**: Draw a Picture
> **Step 5**: Find the P-Value
> **Step 6**: Draw Conclusion - Is the P-Value < α? If So, Reject the Null
> **Step 7**: Compute Confidence Interval & Double Check with R

We will solve the two-sample t-test problem *analytically* (meaning, using the equations and doing the calculations by hand) and *also by using R* to do our calculations. If you are doing research, it's always good to solve the problem both ways to check your work! That way, you have a better chance of being correct. If you are writing a research paper to document your study, be sure to include *all* of Dr. R's 7 Steps and supporting material in the results section of your report or journal article.

Before we begin with our two-sample t-test about the beer foam, we need to get data. You can load in my beer foam data directly from GitHub:

```
> foam <- read.csv("https://raw.githubusercontent.com/NicoleRadziwill/Data-
for-R-Examples/master/beer-foam.csv",header=TRUE)
> names(foam)
 [1] "pour"           "time"            "test.case"      "brewery"
 [5] "temp"           "wet.foam.ht"     "beer.ht"        "dry.foam.ht"
 [9] "tau"            "dry.foam.ratio"
```

This is a CSV file with 10 independent variables: pour number, time (in seconds after initial pour), test case number, brewery, temperature of beer, height of beer from bottom of glass (beer.ht), and wet and dry foam heights (in cm). I have one variable that I've calculated from the earlier variables: tau (τ), the half-life of the beer foam.

```
> head(foam)
  pour time test.case brewery temp wet.foam.ht beer.ht dry.foam.ht
1    1   30   SH-COLD      SH COLD       18.60    4.10       13.15
2    1   60   SH-COLD      SH COLD       15.85    6.40       12.70
3    1   90   SH-COLD      SH COLD       14.25    7.45       12.15
4    1  120   SH-COLD      SH COLD       13.00    8.05       11.50
5    1  150   SH-COLD      SH COLD       12.00    8.50       10.95
6    1  180   SII-COLD     SH COLD       11.40    8.80       10.65
       tau dry.foam.ratio
1 235.2300           0.707
2 208.6780           0.801
3 228.4630           0.853
4 247.0435           0.885
5 265.1174           0.913
6 291.6962           0.934
```

There are four test cases: SH-COLD, SH-RT, 3B-COLD, and 3B-RT. SH and 3B are two local craft breweries, and COLD and RT indicate whether the measurements were taken at 39 degrees Fahrenheit (COLD) or 68 degrees Fahrenheit (RT, for room temperature). We want to compare whether there is a difference between the half-life of the foam at any given time for the SH product poured cold versus poured at room temperature. We also want to compare whether there is a difference between the half-life of the foam at any given time for the 3B product poured cold versus poured at room temperature. As a result, there are two different two sample t-tests that we plan to execute.

Step 0: Check Your Assumptions

Before beginning any inference test, it's important to check and see if your data meets the assumptions and conditions for the test. If it doesn't, you either need to 1) explain why you're still doing the test as part of outlining the assumptions and limitations of your study),

2) abandon the test entirely, 3) if your problem is just that your sample differences aren't normally distributed one of the things you can choose to do is *transform* your data (see, e.g., http://www.basic.northwestern.edu/statguidefiles/ttest_unpaired_alts.html) or you can choose a *nonparametric alternative* to use for your test. (The nonparametric alternative for the two-sample t-test with unequal variances is the Mann-Whitney U test or Satterthwaite's approximate t-test, which are not covered in this book.) Here are the assumptions for the two-sample t-test with equal variances:

1. **Random sample**: Was each of the items in your data set randomly selected from the population of all values? (For the beer data, we can't be totally sure, but we can assume that each tau measurement was randomly sampled from the population of all possible values that any beer could have.)

2. **Observations are independent**: Do the values from one measurement influence the values in another measurement? For our beer data, we measure tau at regular intervals, so one value will certainly depend on the value that comes before it. However, we're combining data from multiple pours into our sample, and each of the pours are independent by design. We will assume that the elements of our sample are independent enough to meet the requirements of this assumption, and we'll move forward with the test.

3. **Sample is small enough**: Is the size of your sample, n, less than 10% of the entire population size? Our sample size is 80 for each test, and this is definitely less than 10% of the population of all potential beer foam decay observations. There are many more beers poured in a single day than what's in our sample.

4. **Values are nearly normal, OR the sample size is large**: For the two-sample t-test to be valid, you should examine a histogram or QQ plot of the values you collected. A "large" sample size is considered to be anything over n=30 or n=40 (it's different in various statistics textbooks). We are *just* working with the beer from the SH brewery, because we *know* the tau profiles have unequal variances after running our `var.test` in the last chapter:

Tau for Cold and Room Temperature Cases (SH)

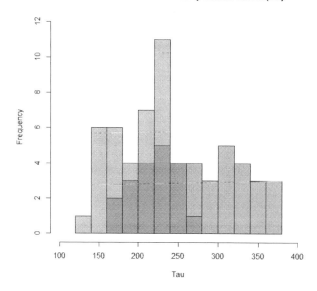

```
cold <- hist(foam[foam$test.case=="SH-COLD",]$tau, breaks=12)
rt <- hist(foam[foam$test.case=="SH-RT",]$tau, breaks=6)
plot(cold, col=rgb(0,0,1,1/4), xlim=c(100,400), ylim=c(0,12),
     main="Tau for Cold and Room Temperature Cases (SH)",
     xlab="Tau", ylab="Frequency")
plot(rt, col=rgb(1,0,0,1/4), xlim=c(100,400), add=T)
```

Here is the F test we performed in the last chapter which confirmed that our cold pour and room temperature pour tau distributions have *different variances and standard deviations*.

```
> var.test(foam[foam$test.case=="SH-COLD",]$tau,
foam[foam$test.case=="SH-RT",]$tau)

        F test to compare two variances

data:  foam[foam$test.case == "SH-COLD", ]$tau and foam[foam$test.case ==
"SH-RT", ]$tau
F = 2.646, num df = 39, denom df = 39, P-Value = 0.003049
alternative hypothesis: true ratio of variances is not equal to 1
95 percent confidence interval:
```

```
   1.399459 5.002811
sample estimates:
ratio of variances
          2.645983
```

That P-Value of 0.003049 says "Reject the null hypothesis that the variances in these two distributions are the same, and perform the *unequal variances* t-test."

Step 1: Set Null and Alternative Hypotheses

The forms of the null and alternative hypotheses for the two-sample t-test with unequal variances are identical to those for the two-sample t-test with equal variances. Remember that one of your jobs is to pick which form of the alternative hypothesis matches the research question you want to answer.

H_0:	$\mu_1 - \mu_2 = D_0$	
H_a:	$\mu_1 - \mu_2 > D_0$	(one-tailed test)
	$\mu_1 - \mu_2 < D_0$	(one-tailed test)
	$\mu_1 - \mu_2 \neq D_0$	(two-tailed test)

The value you choose for D_0 is the difference you *believe* exists between the two samples (and it's very frequently zero in tests like this, indicating that we think the means of the two groups are the same). For our beer foam example for the SH product, D_0 will be zero:

H_0:	$\mu_{COLD} - \mu_{RT} = 0$	(there is no difference between mean tau)
H_a:	$\mu_{COLD} - \mu_{RT} > 0$	(cold beer has higher tau than room temperature)

This test is significant because if we show that cold pours have a consistently higher tau, and we know that higher tau corresponds to higher perceived product quality, we may advise the brewery to recommend that this particular beer only be served cold – enhancing the perceived quality of the beer by its consumers.

Step 2: Choose α, the Level of Significance

The level of significance α is often set to 0.05, indicating that we're willing to *incorrectly reject the null hypothesis* 1 out of every 20 times we collect a sample and run this test. This time, we're going to select a more stringent level of significance α of 0.01, indicating that we're only willing to be wrong 1 in every 100 times. This is because 1) the **cost** of collecting new observations is substantial, in terms of time and effort (but not money), 2) the **risk** associated with drawing incorrect conclusions is moderate, particularly if the brewery will be making recommendations to their distributors based on our conclusions, and 3) the **ethical considerations** that I should keep in mind include the possibility that my research results may be used to make significant business decisions that could impact the brewery's reputation (and in fact, the product's reputation).

Step 3: Calculate Test Statistic (T.S.)

Because this is a t-test, our test statistic will be a t. It's calculated by taking the difference between the sample means and subtracting off whatever value is on the right-hand side of the null hypothesis (D_0) in the numerator, and then dividing by the *pooled standard error of the differences.* This denominator, SE_{pooled}, breaks down into a complex expression involving the sample sizes n_1 and n_2, and the sample standard deviations s_1 and s_2. The variable s_p refers to the *pooled standard deviation.* Because the two distributions have nearly the same scatter, we can mash them together (or "pool" them) and just use one standard deviation.

The formulas are:

$$t = \frac{\overline{y}_1 - \overline{y}_2 - D_0}{SE(\overline{y}_1 - \overline{y}_2)} = \frac{\overline{y}_1 - \overline{y}_2 - D_0}{\sqrt{\frac{s_1^2}{n_1} + \frac{s_2^2}{n_2}}}$$

The calculation itself is not so onerous... the hard part is figuring out the exact degrees of freedom. You can approximate the degrees of freedom df by adding ($n_1 - 1$) and ($n_2 - 1$), but this estimate will be large. The formal calculation is done with this formula:

$$df = \frac{(\frac{s_1^2}{n_1} + \frac{s_2^2}{n_2})^2}{\frac{1}{n_1-1}(\frac{s_1^2}{n_1})^2 + \frac{1}{n_2-1}(\frac{s_2^2}{n_2})^2}$$

To calculate the degrees of freedom, we need to know the sample sizes (n_1 and n_2 are each 40), and the standard deviations of each group (so s_1 is 57.66 and s_2 is 35.45):

```
> aggregate(foam$tau, by=list(foam$test.case), FUN=sd)
  Group.1        x
1 SH-COLD 57.66225
2   SH-RT 35.44852
> aggregate(foam$tau, by=list(foam$test.case), FUN=mean)
  Group.1        x
1 SH-COLD 271.6084
2   SH-RT 202.0040
```

Our approximation to the degrees of freedom is to add 39 and 39, which yields 78. But we know that estimate is too large, so we refine it with this calculation:

$$df = \frac{(\frac{57.66^2}{40} + \frac{35.45^2}{40})^2}{\frac{1}{40-1}(\frac{57.66^2}{40})^2 + \frac{1}{40-1}(\frac{35.45^2}{40})^2} = 64.79$$

Now that we know the degrees of freedom, let's calculate our test statistic (T.S.) t:

$$t = \frac{271.61 - 202.0}{\sqrt{\frac{57.66^2}{40} + \frac{35.45^2}{40}}} = 6.5$$

Step 4: Draw a Picture

We don't even need to draw a picture. With a computed test statistic (T.S.) t of 6.5, our P-Value is determined by the tiny, tiny, tiny area out in the right tail beyond t = 6.5.

Step 5: Find the P-Value

With the picture from Step 4 in mind, we already know that the P-Value is basically zero. We don't even need to calculate it. We can write "p < 0.001" in our report because that computed t is very, very far out onto the right tail of the t distribution.

How much area *exactly* is in the tail to the right of t=6.5? We know we are looking to the right of our test statistic because when we make an arrow out of the sign in the alternative hypothesis, that's where it points. Here's the result:

```
> 1-pt(6.5,df=64.79)
[1] 6.645458e-09
```

Just as we suspected, the P-Value is very nearly zero.

Step 6: Is the P-Value < α? If So, Reject the Null

With a P-Value that is nearly zero, the answer to our question "Is the P-Value less than α?" is bound to be YES, so we reject the null hypothesis. The mean tau for the cold beer pours is certainly greater than the mean tau for the room temperature pours for this product.

Step 7: Compute Confidence Interval & Double Check with R

We can also construct a confidence interval to double-check our work. Lett's do that *and* build a 95% CI. The general form of the confidence interval is:

$$CI : Estimate \pm Margin\ of\ Error$$

The specific form of the confidence interval for the difference between two means is:

$$(\overline{y_1} - \overline{y_2}) \pm t^*_{df} SE(\overline{y_1} - \overline{y_2})$$

$$(\overline{y_1} - \overline{y_2}) \pm t^*_{df} \sqrt{\frac{s_1^2}{n_1} + \frac{s_2^2}{n_2}}$$

Our *estimate* for the difference between means is just the numerator for our test statistic: 69.61. The standard error is the denominator, 10.7. Our sample size n is 40. We compute the value of critical t (t*) by using the `qt` command in R based on the size of the confidence interval net we want to cast to catch the *real* difference between means, and the degrees of freedom for this particular data set (df = n - 1 = 39). Once we select the appropriate critical t value, we plug all of these numbers into the expression for the confidence interval:

Confidence Interval	R Code to Find Critical t (t*)	Critical t (t*) for df = 39
90% CI	`qt(0.95,df=39)`	1.685
95% CI	`qt(0.975,df=39)`	2.023
99% CI	`qt(0.995,df=39)`	2.708

$$69.61 \pm (2.023 \ x \ 10.7) = (47.96, 91.26)$$

Our confidence interval ranges from a lower bound of 47.96 to an upper bound of 91.26. Tau is dimensionless so the confidence interval has no units. The interpretation is:

> *"We are 95% confident that the true difference between tau from a cold pour of the SH brand and tau from a room temperature pour is between 47.96 and 91.26."*

Notice how the value zero is *nowhere near* this confidence interval? We are 95% confident that the true difference between tau values is huge. This affirms our decision to *reject the null hypothesis* that there is no difference. There **is** a difference between the taus!

Step 7 Continued: Double Check in R

Executing the two-sample t-test in R with unequal variances is also straightforward. To make the code easier to read, I first created the variables `cold` and `rt` to store the tau values from the cold pour of the SH product, and the tau values from the room temperature pour, respectively. Then I ran the t-test using those variable names:

```
> cold <- foam[foam$test.case=="SH-COLD",]$tau
> rt <- foam[foam$test.case=="SH-RT",]$tau
> t.test(cold,rt,alternative="greater",var.equal=FALSE)

        Welch Two Sample t-test
data:  cold and rt
t = 6.5037, df = 64.794, P-Value = 6.545e-09
alternative hypothesis: true difference in means is greater than 0
95 percent confidence interval:
 51.74542       Inf
sample estimates:
mean of x mean of y
 271.6084   202.0040
```

Notice that the test statistic (T.S.) t, the degrees of freedom df, and the P-Value are very nearly what we calculated analytically. We can also check the confidence interval if we leave out the `alternative` argument to `t.test`, and it's thinner but nearly the same:

```
> t.test(cold,rt,var.equal=FALSE)

        Welch Two Sample t test
data:  cold and rt
t = 6.5037, df = 64.794, P-Value = 1.309e-08
alternative hypothesis: true difference in means is not equal to 0
95 percent confidence interval:
 48.22924 90.97958
sample estimates:
mean of x mean of y
 271.6084   202.0040
```

Each of our approaches corroborates the conclusion that there's a difference in beer foam stability between the cold and room temperature pours. The answers may slightly differ, but your analytical solutions should be *close enough* to give you the sense that you're on target.

Other Resources:

- Here's some more background on this test: http://www.real-statistics.com/students-t-distribution/two-sample-t-test-uequal-variances/

5.5 Paired t-test

Objective

The paired t-test checks to see if there is a *difference* between two quantitative variables measured at different times, or under different circumstances, but *linked by the same subject* (called "matched pairs"). Throughout this chapter, I'll refer to the first values collected as `pre` and the later quantitative values as `post`, since this test is often applied to determine whether there is a change in a quantitative variable in a pretest/posttest or before/after scenario. Some examples of research questions where you might use the paired t-test include:

- Is there a difference in water quality from measurements taken at the *same location* at a lake between summer 2014 and summer 2015? (*The subject that links the matched pairs is the location at the lake.*)

- Does a new diet plan really help people lose 10 pounds, on average, over a 6-week period? (*The subject that links the matched pairs is the person who is embarking on the diet plan, whose weight can be measured at the beginning and the end of the 6-week period.*)

- Do students who take my class show an improvement, on average, in a standardized assessment test from the beginning to the end of the semester? (*The subject that links the matched pairs is the individual student, for whom I will have a pre-test score and a post-test score to evaluate.*)

- Are average daily high temperatures in the summer for Harrisonburg, Virginia (where I live now) lower than the average daily high temperatures in summer for Charlottesville, Virginia (where I used to live)? I'm pretty sure that it's colder in Harrisonburg, even though it's only about 50 miles away from Charlottesville as the crow flies. (*The subject that links the matched pairs is the day, because we will have a daily high temperature for each location.*)

The last question will be example for the paired t-test. After four years of commuting, I'm *pretty sure* it's colder in Harrisonburg, but *statistics can help me know for sure*.

Our Process for Inference Testing

We'll use Dr. R's 7 Steps in this chapter:

> **Step 0**: Check Your Assumptions
>
> **Step 1**: Set Null and Alternative Hypotheses
>
> **Step 2**: Choose α, the Level of Significance
>
> **Step 3**: Calculate Test Statistic (T.S.)
>
> **Step 4**: Draw a Picture
>
> **Step 5**: Find the P-Value
>
> **Step 6**: Draw Conclusion - Is the P-Value < α? If So, Reject the Null
>
> **Step 7:** Compute Confidence Interval & Double Check with R

We will solve the paired t-test problem *analytically* (meaning, using the equations and doing the calculations by hand) and *also by using R* to do our calculations. If you are doing research, it's always good to solve the problem both ways to check your work! That way, you have a better chance of being correct. If you are writing a research paper to document your study, be sure to include *all* of Dr. R's 7 Steps in your results section.

Before we begin, we need to make sure we have data and that it is in the right format. I used the web interface to the archive at the National Climactic Data Center (NCDC) in Asheville, NC, at http://cdo.ncdc.noaa.gov/qclcd/QCLCD?prior=N, to acquire the data. I had to do a lot of data cleaning because the data at Charlottesville (where the airport code is CHO) is summarized on a daily basis, whereas the data at the Shenandoah Valley Airport (SHD) near where I live now in Harrisonburg is collected on an hourly basis. I had to aggregate the temperature data for each day at SHD, and then pick the maximum from all of the hourly measurements. You can access the data frame through its GitHub location to play along:

```
> comp.temps <-
read.csv("https://raw.githubusercontent.com/NicoleRadziwill/Data-for-R-
Examples/master/comp-temps.csv",header=TRUE)
> head(comp.temps)
  id      date cho shd diff
1  1 20140601  75  73    2
2  2 20140602  81  80    1
3  3 20140603  83  81    2
4  4 20140604  88  84    4
5  5 20140605  81  78    3
6  6 20140606  81  77    4
```

Step 0: Check Your Assumptions

Before beginning an inference test, check and see if your data meets the assumptions and conditions for the test. If it doesn't, you need to 1) explain why you're still doing the test in the limitations section of your study 2) opt to abandon the test entirely, 3) or choose a *nonparametric alternative* to use for your test. (A nonparametric alternative is the Wilcoxon Paired Signed Rank test, which is not covered in this book.) This third option works well when your problem is that your sample differences aren't normally distributed, or when you have rank-ordered data instead of continuous quantitative data.

1. **Matched pairs**: Each observation in the two groups must be *linked together via a common unit of analysis*. In our example, each temperature is part of a matched pair because they were measured in different places *on the same day*.

2. **Random sample**: Was each of the items in your data set randomly selected from the population of all values? In the temperatures example, we should randomly select summer days from the population of all summer days where data is available. (Since we only have data from the summer of 2014, we randomly select 30 values from that sampling frame to do our paired t-test using the `sample` command.)

```
r.s <- comp.temps[sample(nrow(comp.temps), 30),]
```

3. **Observations are independent**: Do the values from one pair (or group) influence the values in another pair (or group)? We will assume for our temperature data that each of the pairs of values are independent from the others.

4. **Sample is small enough**: Is the size of your sample, n, less than 10% of the entire population size? Our sample size is 30, and this is definitely less than 10% of the population of all potential summer days we could have sampled from.

5. **Differences are nearly normal, OR the sample size is large**: For the paired t-test to be valid, you should examine a histogram or QQ plot of the *differences* between your two sets of values. A "large" sample size is considered to be anything over n=30 or n=40 (it's different in various statistics textbooks). Let's take a look at our histogram and QQ plot to make sure we can move forward:

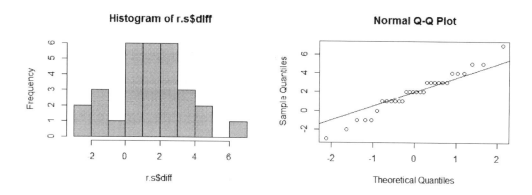

The histogram has that unimodal, symmetric shape (in general), and the dots on the QQ plot line up almost along the line of equality, so we can say our data meets the assumption of being nearly normal. The code that produced the chart above is:

```
par(mfrow=c(1,2))
hist(r.s$diff,breaks=12,col="gray")
qqnorm(r.s$diff)
qqline(r.s$diff)
```

Step 1: Set Null and Alternative Hypotheses

The forms of the null and alternative hypotheses for the paired t-test are:

H_0: $d = d_0$

H_a: $d > d_0$ (one-tailed test)

         $d < d_0$ (one-tailed test)

         $d \neq d_0$ (two-tailed test)

The value you choose for d_0 is often (but not always) zero. For our temperature example, we will set these null and alternative hypotheses with d_0 at zero, indicating the baseline condition that there's no difference in the average daily high temperature between the CHO and SHD sites:

H_0: $d = 0$ (the difference between temps at CHO and SHD is zero)

H_a: $d > 0$ (the CHO temps are higher than the SHD temps)

In contrast, the value of d_0 that you would have selected for the diet plan example at the beginning of the chapter would be 10. In that case, you were trying to figure out whether the people on the test diet lost *at least* 10 pounds on your diet. You don't care if there's *any* difference... you want to know only if the difference is greater than 10 pounds.

Step 2: Choose α, the Level of Significance

The level of significance α is often set to 0.05, indicating that we're willing to *incorrectly reject the null hypothesis* one out of every 20 times we collect a sample and run this test. This is acceptable for our current example because 1) the **cost** of collecting new observations is extremely low, in terms of time, effort, and money, 2) the **risk** associated with drawing incorrect conclusions is also low (I'll just be disappointed that indeed, my new town *is* colder on a daily basis, on average, than my new town) and 3) there are no significant **ethical considerations** that I have to keep in mind based on how the results from my study may be applied by other people who read about my study. After all, it's just temperature data. All I want to know is whether it's really colder in Harrisonburg than I think it was in Charlottesville. There are no policy decisions riding on my conclusion.

Step 3: Calculate Test Statistic (T.S.)

Because this is a t-test, our test statistic will be a t. It's calculated by subtracting the value that's on the right-hand side of the null and alternative hypotheses (d_0) from the *mean difference* you've calculated from your sample. The formula is:

$$t = \frac{\bar{d} - d_0}{SE(\bar{d})} = \frac{\bar{d} - d_0}{s_d/\sqrt{n}}$$

The summary statistics that I found from my randomly selected sample of n=30 measurements from CHO temperatures and SHD temperatures during the summer of 2014 (which I named `r.s` for "randomly sampled") are:

```
> summary(r.s)
      date               cho              shd             diff
 Min.   :20140601   Min.   :73.00   Min.   :72.0   Min.   :-3.0
 1st Qu.:20140621   1st Qu.:81.00   1st Qu.:79.0   1st Qu.: 1.0
 Median :20140724   Median :83.00   Median :81.0   Median : 2.0
 Mean   :20140722   Mean   :83.60   Mean   :81.7   Mean   : 1.9
 3rd Qu.:20140808   3rd Qu.:86.75   3rd Qu.:84.0   3rd Qu.: 3.0
 Max.   :20140831   Max.   :93.00   Max.   :91.0   Max.   : 7.0
> sd(r.s$diff)
[1] 2.186952
```

With this data, I can calculate my test statistic (T.S.) this way:

$$t = \frac{1.9 - 0}{2.187/\sqrt{30}} = 4.758$$

Step 4: Draw a Picture

T-distributions look an awful lot like normal distributions, even though they have *peakier peaks and longer tails*. As a result, I'll draw the picture using the `shadenorm` function (which draws normal curves) because they look the same. Because our alternative hypothesis is "greater than," I want to shade the area that's to the RIGHT (greater than) our computed test statistic t of 4.758, so I enter the following code into R:

```
source("https://raw.githubusercontent.com/NicoleRadziwill/R-
Functions/master/shadenorm.R")

shadenorm(between=c(4.758,Inf),color="black")
```

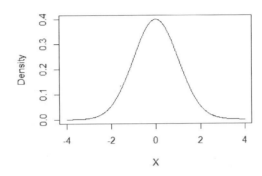

But hold on! There's NO area shaded in that graph, even though I asked R to shade the whole area between our computed test statistic t of 4.758 and infinity (all the way to the right)!! What's the problem??!?!!

Fortunately, there's no problem. If a z-score of 4.758 indicates the point at which you're 4.758 standard deviations above the mean (that's a LOT!) then a t-score with that value means something similar. We're talking about a value that's really, really, *really* far to the right on that bell curve... off the screen. And what do we think the area (that is, the P-Value) under the curve to the right of about 4.758 standard deviations above the mean is? Pretty much zero. It's so far in the tail, we can't even *see* the shaded region. Thus, our P-Value is (basically) zero, and we can report it as "p < 0.001".

Step 5: Find the P-Value

But what if we want to find the P-Value the old-fashioned way? Just to make sure it's *really* zero? Yeah, let's do that, with the `pt` function in R, which determines the area under the t-distribution to the left of a calculated value we give it. We will use 29 for the degrees of freedom, since we had n=30 observations, and the degrees of freedom is calculated by subtracting 1 from n:

```
> 1-pt(4.758,df=29)
[1] 2.484283e-05
```

Indeed, our P-Value is basically zero.

Step 6: Is the P-Value < α? If So, Reject the Null

Now we have to ask ourselves the question: Is the P-Value we just calculated (zero) less than our α of 0.05? Yes, zero is less than pretty much everything that's positively valued. We should REJECT our null hypothesis that there is no difference in average daily high temperature in summer between Charlottesville and Harrisonburg (as measured at the Shenandoah Valley Airport, SHD). What does this mean? It means that there is some difference between the temperatures. It seems like Charlottesville is indeed warmer than Harrisonburg in the summer. But there are some limitations to our study: first, we only looked at data from 2014. So we can't conclude that Charlottesville is warmer than Harrisonburg for all years... we would need a random sample spanning many more years to be able to make this claim. And we can't say that Charlottesville is warmer than Harrisonburg in all seasons... just for this particular summer. If we wanted to know whether Charlottesville is warmer than Harrisonburg all the time, we'd have to take a random sample that spanned all seasons.

You can also construct a confidence interval to double-check your work. So let's do that, and build a 95% CI. The general form of the confidence interval is:

$$CI : Estimate \pm Margin\ of\ Error$$

The specific form of the confidence interval for the difference between paired means is:

$$\bar{d} \pm t^*_{df} SE(\bar{d})$$

$$\bar{d} \pm t_{df}^* \frac{s_d}{\sqrt{n}}$$

Our *estimate* for the mean difference is just the average value of the differences that we computed for our dataset: 1.9. The standard deviation of our sample, s_d, is 2.187. Our sample size n is 30. We can compute the value of critical t, t*, by using the `qt` command in R based on the size of the confidence interval net we want to cast and the degrees of freedom for this particular dataset (df = n - 1 = 29). Then, plug the values in:

Confidence Interval	R Code to Find Critical t (t*)	Critical t (t*) for df = 29
90% CI	`qt(0.95,df=29)`	1.699
95% CI	`qt(0.975,df=29)`	2.045
99% CI	`qt(0.995,df=29)`	2.756

$$1.9 \pm \left(2.045 \ x \ \frac{2.187}{\sqrt{30}} \right) = (1.08, 2.72)$$

Our confidence interval ranges from a lower bound of 1.08 to an upper bound of 2.72. This is interpreted in the following way:

"We are 95% confident that the true difference between average daily high temperatures at CHO versus SHD is between 1.08 degrees and 2.72 degrees."

Notice how the value zero is *not* inside this confidence interval? We are 95% confident that there is actually a *nonzero difference* between the temperatures. On average, Charlottesville is between 1.08 and 2.72 degrees warmer in the summer than Harrisonburg. This affirms the decision that we made to *reject the null hypothesis*.

Step 7: Compute Confidence Interval & Double Check with R

Here is the R output from the paired t-test that we executed on our data:

```
> t.test(r.s$cho,r.s$shd,paired=TRUE,alternative="greater")

        Paired t-test

data:   r.s$cho and r.s$shd
t - 4.7586, df = 29, P-Value = 2.48e-05
alternative hypothesis: true difference in means is greater than 0
95 percent confidence interval:
 1.221571       Inf
sample estimates:
mean of the differences
                 1.9
```

Note that the value of the test statistic (T.S.) t is exactly what we computed analytically (about 4.758) and the P-Value is basically zero (telling us to reject our null hypothesis).

However, if we want to get the confidence interval, we have to eliminate the `alternative` hypothesis option from the `t.test` command. Let's do that:

```
> t.test(r.s$cho,r.s$shd,paired=TRUE)

        Paired t-test

data:   r.s$cho and r.s$shd
t = 4.7586, df = 29, P-Value = 4.961e-05
alternative hypothesis: true difference in means is not equal to 0
95 percent confidence interval:
 1.083379 2.716621
sample estimates:
mean of the differences
                 1.9
```

Note that the test statistic (T.S.) t has also been computed as 4.758 (the same value we got analytically), and the lower and upper bounds of the confidence interval are approximately 1.08 and 2.72 (the same as the answers we got analytically). Mission accomplished!

Other Resources:

- http://www.r-tutor.com/elementary-statistics/inference-about-two-populations/population-mean-between-two-matched-samples
- https://heuristically.wordpress.com/2011/09/28/paired-sample-t-test-in-r/
- http://www.statstutor.ac.uk/resources/uploaded/paired-t-test.pdf

5.6 One Proportion z-test/Exact Binomial Test

Objective

The one proportion z-test checks to see if there is a *difference* between counts of observations that from your sample expressed as a *proportion* of the total observations, and a *standard or recommended proportion.* Sometimes, we're comparing our data against a *goal or target.* (It is related to the more exact *binomial test* because it uses the normal approximation to the binomial distribution.) Some examples of research questions where you might use the one proportion z-test include:

- You know that given a certain combination of two cards initially dealt to you in a hand of Texas Hold 'Em, there is a 30% you will win that hand due to chance. Does bluffing improve your chances of winning the hand?

- Environmental activists have noticed that there seems to be a higher incidence of a particular type of allergy around one city. Knowing that approximately 16% of the population in the whole country has this allergy, is the incidence of the allergy higher in this city?

- Zener cards (pictured below) were used in the 1930's by parapsychology researcher J. B. Rhine to test for extrasensory perception (ESP). A card would be held up out of the sight of the subject, who would guess which symbol was shown. Since there are 5 cards, you have a 20% chance of guessing correctly due only to chance. Are you more successful with your guesses than the 20% that can be expected?

- On a national scale, it has been estimated that 90% of home buyers are well educated about energy efficiency and would pay a premium for energy efficient features. A new engineering consulting firm wants to know if the sentiment is similar in their local area. If less than 90% of people feel this way, they will launch an educational campaign prior to their planned marketing campaign.

The last question will be our example for the one proportion z-test. After living in this local area for a few years, I'm pretty sure that we're going to need that education program to ensure our success, but *statistics can help me be more confident*.

Our Process for Inference Testing

We'll use Dr. R's 7 Steps in this chapter:

> **Step 0**: Check Your Assumptions
> **Step 1**: Set Null and Alternative Hypotheses
> **Step 2**: Choose α, the Level of Significance
> **Step 3**: Calculate Test Statistic (T.S.)
> **Step 4**: Draw a Picture
> **Step 5**: Find the P-Value
> **Step 6**: Draw Conclusion - Is the P-Value < α? If So, Reject the Null
> **Step 7:** Compute Confidence Interval & Double Check with R

We will solve the one proportion z-test problem *analytically* (meaning, using the equations and doing the calculations by hand) and *also by using R* to do our calculations. If you are doing research, it's always good to solve the problem both ways to check your work! That way, you have a better chance of being correct. If you are writing a research paper, be sure to include *all* of Dr. R's 7 Steps in your report or journal article in the results section.

Before we begin with our one proportion z-test regarding how home buyers feel about energy efficiency, we need to make sure we have data and that it is in the right format. Our consultants used cluster sampling to survey 360 home buyers in the 8 areas used by real estate agents. They asked the prospective buyers whether they would invest at last 2-3% of the home's value in an energy efficient home to permanently reduce their utility bills. 312 of the respondents said yes. Is the proportion of *all* members of the population who would make this investment less than 90%?

Step 0: Check Your Assumptions

Before beginning an inference test, it's important to check and see if your data meets the assumptions and conditions for the test. If it doesn't, you either need to 1) explain why you're still doing the test in your limitations section, 2) abandon the test entirely, 3) choose an *exact test* to use. (The Exact Binomial test, which you can use if this happens, is briefly introduced at the end of this chapter.)

> 1. **Random sample**: Was each of the items in your data set randomly selected from the population of all values? In the energy survey example, I bet we can trust that the engineers at the firm have effectively planned their sampling strategy so that the sample is both random and representative.
>
> 2. **Observations are independent**: Do the values from one measurement influence the values in another measurement? We can assume that the homeowners are not attempting to influence one another, or otherwise conspiring to alter the observed proportions.
>
> 3. **Sample is small enough**: Is the size of your sample, n, less than 10% of the entire population size? Our sample size is 360, so the city should have more than 3600 residents for this to work. It does, so the assumption checks out.
>
> 4. **Sample is big enough to observe a proportion that's not too close to 0% or 100%**: If $\hat{p}$ represents the proportion of observed successes, and $\hat{q}$ represents the proportion of observed failures (thus, the sum of these proportions must equal 1), then $n\hat{p}$ and $n\hat{q}$ must be greater than 10. <u>Be sure to calculate $n\hat{p}$ and $n\hat{q}$ to make sure this assumption checks out.</u>

In my opinion, the last assumption is the most interesting. Why do we need to check it?

We need to check it because <u>the one proportion z-test uses the *normal approximation to the binomial distribution*,</u> and those distributions don't match each other quite as well out at the extreme values. We're superimposing a nice, smooth bell curve over the distinct, spiky binomial distribution and saying "*yeah, that looks like it's about the same, sort of.*" For this example, our values are well over 10. If the values aren't over 10, we should use the Exact Binomial test instead (at the end of this chapter).

Step 1: Set Null and Alternative Hypotheses

The forms of the null and alternative hypotheses for the one sample t-test are:

H_0: $p = p_0$

H_a: $p > p_0$ (one-tailed test)

        $p < p_0$ (one-tailed test)

        $p \neq p_0$ (two-tailed test)

The value you choose for p_0 is your *standard, recommended value, goal,* or *target*. For our homeowners' investment example, we set these null and alternative hypotheses with p_0 at the national estimate of 0.9, or 90%. We want to test against the alternative hypothesis that the observed proportion of the population that's already educated about energy efficiency is *less than* 90%, because if this is indeed the case, we are going to invest quite a bit of money in an education and outreach program. Our null and alternative hypotheses are:

H_0: $p = 0.9$ (90% of the homeowners would invest)

H_a: $p < 0.9$ (less than 90% of the homeowners would invest)

Step 2: Choose α, the Level of Significance

The level of significance α is often set to 0.05, indicating that we're willing to *incorrectly reject the null hypothesis* one out of every 20 times we collect a sample and run this test. This is acceptable because 1) the **cost** of collecting new observations is comparatively low, in terms of time, effort, and money, 2) the **risk** associated with drawing incorrect conclusions is also low (after all, we're only going to invest $2000 in our education program) and 3) there are no significant **ethical considerations** that I have to keep in mind based on how the results from my study may be applied by other people who read about or make decisions based on my study. All I want to know is whether home buyers in my local area are in favor of energy efficient investments. There are no policy decisions riding on my conclusion.

Step 3: Calculate Test Statistic (T.S.)

Because this is a z-test, our test statistic will be a z. It's calculated by subtracting the value that's on the right-hand side of the null and alternative hypotheses (p_0) from the *observed proportion* you've determined from your sample. The formula is:

$$z = \frac{\hat{p} - p_0}{SE(\hat{p})} = \frac{\hat{p} - p_0}{\sqrt{\frac{pq}{n}}}$$

Unfortunately, most of the time you won't know the true proportion of successes in the population (p) or the true proportion of failures (q), so you have to approximate those values by the *assumed proportion* p_0 that shows up on the right-hand side of your null hypothesis (along with its corresponding q_0):

$$z = \frac{\hat{p} - p_0}{\sqrt{\frac{p_0 q_0}{n}}}$$

For our example, the proportion observed in our sample is 312/360 (or 0.867), which makes the test statistic z=-2.108:

$$z = \frac{0.867 - 0.9}{\sqrt{\frac{0.9 \, x \, 0.1}{360}}} = -2.09$$

Step 4: Draw a Picture

Because we're using the normal approximation to the binomial for this test, I can draw the picture using the `shadenorm` function, which draws normal curves. Because our alternative hypothesis is "less than," I want to shade the area that's to the LEFT (less than) our computed test statistic z of -2.09, so I enter the following code into R:

```
source("https://raw.githubusercontent.com/NicoleRadziwill/R-
Functions/master/shadenorm.R")

shadenorm(between=c(-Inf,-2.09),color="black")
```

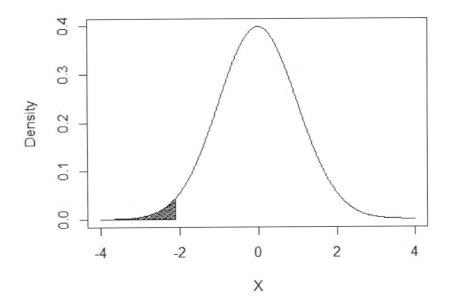

There's just a small area shaded to the left of t=-2.9. According to the 68-95-99.7 rule for the normal distribution, we can estimate that a little less than 2.5% of the total area is going to be in the left tail beyond -2.09 standard deviations from the mean.

Step 5: Find the P-Value

The command to calculate areas under the normal distribution in R is `pnorm`. Using the `pnorm` command, we can *only* find areas to the left of a particular z value, which is fortunate in this case because that's exactly what we need. We ask R to compute the area to the left of z=-2.09 like this:

```
> pnorm(-2.09)
[1] 0.0183089
```

So our P-Value is approximately 0.018 - 1.8% of the area under the curve is in the left tail.

Step 6: Draw Conclusion - Is the P-Value < α? If So, Reject the Null

Now we have to ask ourselves the question: Is the P-Value we just calculated (0.0175) less than our α of 0.05? Yes, it is. We should REJECT our null hypothesis that the proportion of homeowners that would invest in energy efficient solutions is 90%, and we do so *in favor of the alternative* that less than 90% agree.

Step 7: Compute Confidence Interval & Double Check with R

We can also construct a confidence interval to double-check our work. Let's do that, and build a 95% CI. The general form of any confidence interval is:

$$CI \; : \; Estimate \; \pm Margin \; of \; Error$$

The specific form of the confidence interval for one proportion that's usually covered in introductory statistics textbooks is the *Wald confidence interval*:

$$\hat{p} \pm z^* SE(\hat{p})$$

$$\hat{p} \pm z^* \sqrt{\frac{pq}{n}}$$

But there's a Catch. Two, in fact. Catch #1: Since the true population proportion p is unknown, we usually use $\hat{p}$ and $\hat{q}$ as estimates in the standard error of the estimate, $\hat{p}$. However, when we are doing a hypothesis test (which means we assume we *know* the true population proportion p, which we specify on the right-hand side of our alternative hypothesis as p_0), we use p_0 to estimate p. Once we have hypothesized what the population proportion p is, we have to use it – but before that hypothesis is established, we use $\hat{p}$.

Our *estimate* for the population proportion is just the value that we observed from our data: 312/360=0.867. If we call these our "successes", then the observed proportion of "failures" is 1-0.867=0.133. Our sample size n is 360. We find the value of critical z, z*, by using the table below (or by remembering that 1.96 is the critical value of z for a 95% confidence interval... this is one number I think everyone should memorize. Then, plug the values in:

$$0.867 \pm 1.96\sqrt{\frac{0.9 \, x \, 0.1}{360}} = (0.836, 0.898)$$

Confidence Interval	Critical z (z*)
90% CI	1.645
95% CI	1.96
99% CI	2.58

Our confidence interval ranges from a lower bound of 83.6% to an upper bound of 89.8%. This is interpreted in the following way:

> *"We are 95% confident that the true proportion of homeowners in our city who would make a significant investment in energy efficiency to permanently reduce their utility bills is between 83.6% and 89.8%."*

Notice how our target value of 0.90 from the null hypothsis *is not* contained inside this confidence interval? It's *close* to the edge, but not within our boundary. However, a 98% or

99% confidence interval would *definitely* capture 0.90 as a possibility for the true population proportion. This means that our decision to *reject the null hypothesis* is right on the edge. If the cost and risk associated with running a new study is low, we may want to collect a new sample and start over... just to make sure we're making the right decision.

Catch #2: <u>The Wald confidence interval is notoriously bad</u>; it's tragic that this is presented as the only solution in so many introductory statistics courses and textbooks. It is significantly improved by applying a correction advocated by Agresti and Coull (1998), which asks that you <u>compute a new p̂ by adding 2 to the number of successes, and adding 4 to the total number of observations</u> before proceeding with the confidence interval calculation. (Also consider your total number of observations as n+4.)

If we make this correction, our n becomes 360+4=364, and our modified p̂ becomes (312+4=316)÷364=0.863. Plugging this back into the Wald formula, we get:

$$0.863 \pm 1.96 \sqrt{\frac{0.9 \, x \, 0.1}{364}} = (0.832, 0.894)$$

This is a ***more accurate*** confidence interval around our proportion. It's a little thinner than the one we calculated earlier because we're honing in on the true population proportion.

One proportion z-test Example using a Custom Function in R

Many of the proportions tests in R (including `prop.test` and `binom.test`) use sophisticated adjustments and corrections to make assessment of the P-Value and estimating the bounds of the confidence interval more accurate and precise. As a result, don't be confused if you use these other tests and get a P-Value or confidence interval bounds that are *different* than what you calculate by hand. Here is a function I wrote (`z.test`) that will let you do a one proportion z-test the same way we did it analytically. It lets you specify the number of successes x, the total number of observations n, the proportion p that you'd like to compare your sample to, the confidence level `conf.level` that you want for your confidence interval, and the form of the `alternative` hypothesis (which can be `"less"`, `"greater"`, or "two.sided" but defaults to "less"). No corrections are used to make the estimates more accurate or more precise. As a result, you may be able to get a better P-Value or confidence interval using prop.test. If you only want a confidence interval, just specify the number of successes x and the total number of observations n. To begin, source the ztest function:

```
source("https://raw.githubusercontent.com/NicoleRadziwill/R-
Functions/master/ztest.R")
```

Here is the code that that line activates:

```
z.test <- function(x,n,p=NULL,conf.level=0.95,alternative="less") {
    ts.z <- NULL
    cint <- NULL
    p.val <- NULL
        phat <- x/n
        qhat <- 1 - phat
        # If you have p0 from the population or H0, use it.
        # Otherwise, use phat and qhat to find SE.phat:
        if(length(p) > 0) {
            q <- 1-p
            SE.phat <- sqrt((p*q)/n)
            ts.z <- (phat - p)/SE.phat
            p.val <- pnorm(ts.z)
            if(alternative=="two.sided") {
                p.val <- p.val * 2
            }
            if(alternative=="greater") {
              p.val <- 1 - p.val
            }
        } else {
        # If all you have is your sample, use phat to find
        # SE.phat, and don't run the hypothesis test:
            SE.phat <- sqrt((phat*qhat)/n)
        }
        cint <- phat + c(
            -1*((qnorm(((1 - conf.level)/2) + conf.level))*SE.phat),
            ((qnorm(((1 - conf.level)/2) + conf.level))*SE.phat) )
    return(list(estimate=phat,ts.z=ts.z,p.val=p.val,cint=cint))
}
```

If all we had was our sample (that is, we hadn't *yet* hypothesized that the true population proportion was 0.90), we find the 95% confidence interval like this. It does not match the values we calculated, but instead, presents a *wider* confidence interval:

```
> z.test(312,360)
$estimate
[1] 0.867

$ts.z
NULL

$p.val
NULL

$cint
[1] 0.832 0.902
```

By specifying that we have hypothesized a true population proportion of 0.90, the 95% confidence interval is now tightened a little bit around our estimate of the population proportion, $\hat{p}$. The test statistic z (`ts.z`) is presented, along with the P-Value associated with that value. The function defaults to an alternative hypothesis where the true population proportion is less than what was hypothesized.

```
> z.test(312,360,p=0.9)
$estimate
[1] 0.867

$ts.z
[1] -2.11

$p.val
[1] 0.0175

$cint
[1] 0.836 0.898
```

You can also access the confidence interval directly, which is *different* given p=0.9:

```
> z.test(312,360,p=0.9)$cint
[1] 0.836 0.898
```

Step 7 Continued: One Proportion z-test Example Using `prop.test` **in R**

To execute this test in R, all we need is the number of successes and total number of observations, just like in the custom function above. However, `prop.test` automatically applies the Yates continuity correction, which accounts for the fact that we're using a normal (continuous) distribution to approximate a binomial (discrete) distribution. We can turn this off by specifying `correct=FALSE`. It doesn't mean that we don't want the answer to be correct... it means we want the Yates correction turned off (`FALSE`). The first example below has the Yates correction ON, while the second has the Yates correction OFF:

```
> prop.test(312,360)

        1-sample proportions test with continuity correction

data:  312 out of 360, null probability 0.5
X-squared = 192, df = 1, P-Value < 0.00000000000000022
alternative hypothesis: true p is not equal to 0.5
95 percent confidence interval:
 0.826 0.899
sample estimates:
    p
0.867


> prop.test(312,360,correct=FALSE)

        1-sample proportions test without continuity correction

data:  312 out of 360, null probability 0.5
X-squared = 194, df = 1, P-Value < 0.00000000000000022
alternative hypothesis: true p is not equal to 0.5
95 percent confidence interval:
 0.828 0.898
sample estimates:
    p
0.867
```

With the Yates continuity correction ON, the confidence interval is a little wider. Notice that with both tests, the null hypothesis would still be rejected (the P-Value is very tiny, almost zero) even though the value of the $\chi 2$ test statistic differs by a small amount.

The hypothesis test that `prop.test` is displaying does NOT use the z statistic, like we did when we solved the problem analytically (and using the custom function)! It uses an entirely different test: a Chi-square test on a contingency table with only one categorical variable. (However, there is a relationship between the Chi-square distribution with 1 degree of freedom and the normal distribution, so they're not *completely* different.)

However, there's an odd issue with the confidence intervals here! If you take the midpoint between the lower limit and the upper limit of the first computed confidence interval, you get 0.862. If you take the midpoint between the lower limit and the upper limit of the second computed confidence interval, you get 0.863. Neither of these values is the point estimate of our population proportion of 0.867! **This is not an error**: `prop.test` uses the *Wilson score interval* concept to construct the confidence interval. It gives **more accurate** confidence intervals when the estimate of the population proportion is closer to 0 and 1.0, but unlike the analytically computed confidence interval, the "net" isn't symmetric! Instead, it appears skewed because the estimate is shifted. Just be aware that if you decide to use the confidence interval that R reports via `prop.test`, it does not have the same properties as other confidence intervals, even though it might be more accurate with respect to the real population of proportions.

Let's perform exactly the same hypothesis test that we did earlier, assuming that the true population proportion is 0.90, with the alternative hypothesis that the true population proportion is *less than* 0.90:

```
> prop.test(312,360,p=0.9,alt="less",correct=FALSE)

        1-sample proportions test without continuity correction

data:  312 out of 360, null probability 0.9
X-squared = 4.44, df = 1, P-Value = 0.01751
alternative hypothesis: true p is less than 0.9
95 percent confidence interval:
 0.000 0.893
sample estimates:
    p
0.867
```

Even though a different inference test is used, we get a P-Value that's nearly identical to the one we originally computed analytically.

Step 7 Continued: One proportion z-test Example using `binom.test` in R

If you don't meet all the assumptions to perform the one proportion z-test, you can use the Exact Binomial Test, which is very similar. Instead of using the normal approximation to the binomial distribution, you use the actual binomial distribution (hence, the name of the test). By default, `binom.test` executes a two-sided test, where H_a: $p \neq p_0$:

```
> binom.test(312,360,p=0.9)

        Exact binomial test

data:   312 and 360
number of successes = 312, number of trials = 360, P-Value = 0.04268
alternative hypothesis: true probability of success is not equal to 0.9
95 percent confidence interval:
 0.827 0.900
sample estimates:
probability of success
             0.867
```

Dividing the P-Value by 2 gives 0.0213, which is close to what we computed analytically using the normal approximation to the binomial.

A Final Warning on Wald Confidence Intervals!

The Wald confidence interval is really not that accurate... in fact, it's notoriously bad. Simulation studies show that the *coverage probability* of the confidence interval using that formula is really bad... if you compute a 95% confidence interval, even in the best of cases with a sample size that's not tiny, you'll only *actually* get an 85-90% confidence interval. It gets even worse when your sample proportion is smaller than 0.20 or larger than 0.80! If you have to use a Wald confidence interval, you might want to compute a more stringent confidence interval (say, 98% or 99%) knowing that you'll only get about 95% coverage. Alternatively, you can use the **Agresti-Coull** formula (which is pretty simple), or the **Wilson**

score interval (which is pretty complex, but still feasible). The Agresti-Coull confidence interval is covered in Chapter 4.4 under confidence intervals for one proportion. If you want to use the Wilson approach, use the instructions in the current chapter under `prop.test`.

Other Resources:

- Find out more about the Agresti-Coull correction to the confidence interval at http://graphpad.com/support/faq/the-modified-wald-method-for-computing-the-confidence-interval-of-a-proportion/
- In practice, the Wilson interval that's provided by `prop.test` seems to the most reliable for computing the confidence interval: http://www-stat.wharton.upenn.edu/~tcai/paper/Binomial-StatSci.pdf
- This article by Sean Wallis of University College London explains everything you might want to know about continuity corrections, Wilson's score interval, and why your confidence interval as estimated by R might not be symmetric around the point estimate. It is comprehensive and, quite frankly, beautiful. http://www.ucl.ac.uk/english-usage/staff/sean/resources/binomialpoisson.pdf
- A great source for more information about `prop.test` is here: http://wiener.math.csi.cuny.edu/Statistics/R/simpleR/stat010.html
- Find out more about the Wilson score interval on Wikipedia at http://en.wikipedia.org/wiki/Binomial_proportion_confidence_interval#Wilson_score_interval

5.7 Two Proportion z-test

Objective

The two-proportion z-test checks for a difference between counts of observations that you collect from your sample *expressed as a proportion of the total* observations in one group, and compares it to the same thing, but measured in ANOTHER group. (This test is related to the more exact *binomial test* because it uses the normal approximation to the binomial distribution.) Some examples of research questions include:

- You play Texas Hold 'Em in person, with your friends, as well as online. You've kept track of your wins, so you know what percentage of the time you've won in person, and you know what percentage of the time you've won online. However, your sample size is much bigger online. Which forum presents you with a higher percentage of wins?

- Environmental activists have noticed that there seems to be a higher incidence of complications from a particular type of allergy around one city. Is the proportion of allergy sufferers who experienced respiratory complications higher this year than it was last year?

- Zener cards (pictured below) were used in the 1930's by parapsychology researcher J. B. Rhine to test for extrasensory perception (ESP). A card would be held up out of the sight of the subject, who would guess which symbol was shown. Since there are 5 cards, you have a 20% chance of guessing correctly due only to chance. Are you more successful with your guesses than your best friend, partner, or spouse is?

- Based on observing each other at parties, students in the college of technology are convinced that they don't drink nearly as heavily as the students in the college of business. Is there a greater proportion of heavy drinkers in the college of business than in the college of technology? (Note: this is based on a real observational study performed by some of my students in the college of technology a few years ago.)

The last question will be our example for the two-proportion z-test. After observing each other for a couple of years, they were *pretty sure* there weren't as many heavy drinkers in their classes, but *statistics can help them be more confident about their conclusion.*

Our Process for Inference Testing

We'll use Dr. R's 7 Steps in this chapter:

Step 0: Check Your Assumptions
Step 1: Set Null and Alternative Hypotheses
Step 2: Choose α, the Level of Significance
Step 3: Calculate Test Statistic (T.S.)
Step 4: Draw a Picture
Step 5: Find the P-Value
Step 6: Draw Conclusion - Is the P-Value < α? If So, Reject the Null
Step 7: Compute Confidence Interval & Double Check with R

We will solve the two-proportion z-test problem *analytically* (meaning, using the equations and doing the calculations by hand) and *also by using R* to do our calculations. If you are doing research, it's always good to solve the problem both ways to check your work! That way, you have a better chance of being correct. If you are writing a research paper, be sure to include *all* of Dr. R's 7 Steps in your report or journal article in the results section.

Before we begin with our two-proportion z-test on heavy drinking, we need to make sure we have data and that it is in the right format. Our students used stratified sampling to survey 206 students in the college of business and 170 students in the college of technology. They found that 71 business students drank more than six beers or the equivalent four nights or more a week, whereas 46 technology students reported the same pattern. (They considered that one mixed drink or shot would equal two beers for the sake of their study.) Is the proportion of heavy drinkers in the college of business greater than the proportion of heavy drinkers in the college of technology?

Step 0: Check Your Assumptions

Before beginning an inference test, it's important to check and see if your data meets the assumptions and conditions for the test. If it doesn't, you either need to 1) explain why you're still doing the test as part of outlining the assumptions and limitations of your study, 2) abandon the test entirely, 3) if your problem is that you violate the assumptions of the test, choose an *exact test* to use. (The Exact Binomial test, which is briefly covered at the end of this chapter.) The assumptions are the *same* as for the one proportion z-test, PLUS one more:

1. **Random sample**: Was each of the items in your data set randomly selected from the population of all values? In the drinking example, we're going to have to assume that the students have effectively planned their sampling strategy so that the sample is both random and representative.

2. **Observations are independent**: Do the values from one measurement influence the values in another measurement? If the survey is confidential, and we aren't asking our respondents questions in front of their friends, we should be able to assume that one student's answers are independent of the others.

3. **Sample is small enough**: Is the size of your sample, n, less than 10% of the entire population size? Our sample size is 360, which means this city should have more than 3600 residents. It does, so the assumption checks out.

4. **Sample is big enough to observe a proportion that's not too close to 0% or 100%**: If $\hat{p}$ represents the proportion of observed successes, and $\hat{q}$ represents the proportion of observed failures (thus, the sum of these proportions must equal 1), then $n\hat{p}$ and $n\hat{q}$ must be greater than 10.

5. **Independent Groups:** The two samples need to be *independently collected*, indicating that the groups are independent of one another. The responses from one group do not influence the responses from the other group.

Just like for the one proportion z-test, the "is the sample big enough" assumption is the most interesting. We need to check because the two-proportion z-test uses the *normal approximation to the binomial distribution*, and the distributions don't match each other quite as well at the extreme values. In this example, our values are well over 10. If the values aren't over 10, we use the Exact Binomial test instead (at the end of this chapter).

Step 1: Set Null and Alternative Hypotheses

The forms of the null and alternative hypotheses for the one sample t-test are:

H_0: $p_1 - p_2 = p_0$

H_a: $p_1 - p_2 > p_0$ (one-tailed test)

           $p_1 - p_2 < p_0$ (one-tailed test)

           $p_1 - p_2 \neq p_0$ (two-tailed test)

The value you choose for p_0 is the difference you *believe* exists between the proportions in the two groups. For our drinking example, we will set these null and alternative hypotheses with p_0 at 0, indicating that there is no difference between the proportions in each group.

We want to test against the alternative hypothesis that the observed proportion of the population that's already educated about energy efficiency is *less than* 90%, because if this is indeed the case, we are going to invest quite a bit of money in an education and outreach program. Our null and alternative hypotheses are:

H_0: $p_{BUSINESS} - p_{TECHNOLOGY} = 0$ (no difference between proportions)

H_a: $p_{BUSINESS} - p_{TECHNOLOGY} > 0$ (a greater proportion of business
           students are heavy drinkers)

Step 2: Choose α, the Level of Significance

The level of significance α is often set to 0.05, indicating that we're willing to *incorrectly reject the null hypothesis* one out of every 20 times we collect a sample and run this test. This is acceptable for our current example because 1) the **cost** of collecting new observations is comparatively low, in terms of time, effort, and money, 2) the **risk** associated with drawing incorrect conclusions is also low (after all, we're not going to inflict penalties on the business students if indeed they are heavier drinkers) and 3) there are minimal **ethical considerations** that we have to keep in mind based on how the results may be applied by other people who read about or make decisions based on my study. We're not going to publish the results, we're just curious. All we want to know is whether those business students really are heavier drinkers, in general. There are no policy decisions riding on our conclusion. There may, however, be a whole host of new jokes and new opportunities to deepen the rivalry between the colleges.

Step 3: Calculate Test Statistic (T.S.)

Because this is a z-test, our test statistic will be a z. It's calculated by subtracting the value that's on the right-hand side of the null and alternative hypotheses (p_0) from the *observed difference in proportions* you've determined from your sample. The formula is:

$$z = \frac{\hat{p_1} - \hat{p_2} - p_0}{SE(\hat{p_1} - \hat{p_2})} = \frac{\hat{p_1} - \hat{p_2} - p_0}{\sqrt{pq\left(\frac{1}{n_1} + \frac{1}{n_2}\right)}}$$

The p and q in the standard error in the denominator are *pooled* proportions. We pool them because under the null hypothesis, **we assume the two proportions come from a shared population** and there is no difference between them. This gives us a better estimate for z. To compute p, we add up all successes and divide by all observations:

$$p = \frac{x_1 + x_2}{n_1 + n_2}$$

All we need to do to get q is to take 1, and subtract p... because p + q always has to equal 1. To get p, we just add up all successes and divide by all opportunities: 117/376=0.31. As a result, q must be 1-0.31 or 0.69. Now let's calculate our test statistic z:

$$z = \frac{0.345 - 0.270}{\sqrt{0.31 \, x \, 0.69 \left(\frac{1}{206} + \frac{1}{170}\right)}} = 1.56$$

Step 4: Draw a Picture

Because we're using the normal approximation to the binomial for this test, I can draw the picture using the `shadenorm` function, which draws normal curves. Because our alternative hypothesis is "greater than," I want to shade the area that's to the RIGHT (less than) our computed test statistic z of 1.56, so I enter the following code into R:

```
source("https://raw.githubusercontent.com/NicoleRadziwill/R-
Functions/master/shadenorm.R")

shadenorm(between=c(1.56,Inf),color="black")
```

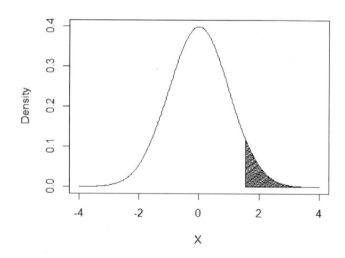

There's just a small area shaded to the right of z=1.56. According to the 68-95-99.7 rule for the normal distribution, we can estimate that around 15% of the total area is going to be in the area to the right beyond 1.56 standard deviations from the center.

Step 5: Find the P-Value

The command to calculate areas under the normal distribution in R is `pnorm`. Using the `pnorm` command, we can *only* find areas to the left of a particular z value, which is fortunate in this case because that's exactly what we need. We ask R to compute the area to the right of z=+1.56 like this:

```
> 1-pnorm(1.56)
[1] 0.05937994
```

Our P-Value is approximately 0.059, or 5.9% of the total area in the right tail.

Step 6: Draw Conclusion – Is the P-Value < α? If So, Reject the Null

Now we have to ask ourselves the question: Is the P-Value we just calculated (0.0059) less than our α of 0.05? No, it's NOT! But just barely. We should FAIL TO REJECT our null hypothesis that the difference between the proportion of heavy drinkers in the college of business and the proportion of heavy drinkers in the college of technology is the same. We just don't have evidence that agrees with their reputation of being heavy drinkers.

Step 7: Compute Confidence Interval & Double Check with R

We can also construct a confidence interval to double-check our work. Let's do that, and build a 95% CI. The general form of any confidence interval is:

$$CI \; : \; Estimate \; \pm \; Margin \; of \; Error$$

The specific form of the confidence interval for the difference between proportions is:

$$(\hat{p}_1 - \hat{p}_2) \pm z^* SE(\hat{p}_1 - \hat{p}_2)$$

$$(\hat{p}_1 - \hat{p}_2) \pm z^* \sqrt{\left(\frac{\hat{p}_1 \hat{q}_1}{n_1} + \frac{\hat{p}_2 \hat{q}_2}{n_2} \right)}$$

Our *estimate* for the difference between proportions is just the difference between the values we observed from our sample: 0.345-0.27=0.075. Because we know each p plus each q must equal 1, we can find out every p and q that has a hat on it. Our sample size n_1 is 206 and our sample size n_2 is 170. We find the value of critical z, z*, by using the table below (or by remembering that 1.96 is the critical value of z for a 95% confidence interval... one of the numbers I think everyone should memorize.) Then, just plug the values in:

$$(0.345 - 0.270) \pm 1.96 \sqrt{\left(\frac{(0.345)(0.655)}{206} + \frac{(0.270)(0.730)}{170} \right)} = (-0.019, 16.9)$$

Confidence Interval	Critical z (z*)
90% CI	1.645
95% CI	1.96
99% CI	2.58

Performing these calculations, we find that our confidence interval ranges from a lower bound of -1.9% to an upper bound of 16.9%. There might be at -1.9% difference between proportions (meaning that the proportion of business students who drink heavily is *slightly less* than the proportion of technology students who drink heavily), or there might be a 16.9% difference (meaning that the proportion of business students who drink heavily is *more* than the proportion of technology students who drink heavily.) This is interpreted in the following way:

"We are 95% confident that the true difference in the proportion of business students who are heavy drinkers and the proportion of technology students who are heavy drinkers is between -1.9% and 16.9%."

Notice how a ZERO PERCENT DIFFERENCE is contained *inside* this confidence interval? That means there's a possibility that there's no difference at all between the proportion of heavy drinkers in the two groups. As a result, our decision *not to reject the null hypothesis* is supported. The technology students will have to find some other way to find differences between them and their rivals, the business students.

Step 7 Continued: One Proportion z-test Example Using a Custom Function in R

Many of the proportions tests that are available in R (including prop.test and binom.test) use sophisticated adjustments and corrections to make assessment of the P-Value and estimating the bounds of the confidence interval more accurate and precise. As a result, don't be confused if you use these other tests and get a P-Value or confidence interval bounds that are *different* than what you calculate by hand.

Here is a function I wrote (z2.test) that will let you do a two-proportion z-test the same way we did it analytically. It lets you specify the number of successes in group 1 (x1), the total number of observations in group 1 (n1), the number of successes in group 2 (x2), the total number of observations in group 2 (n2), the confidence level conf.level that you want for your confidence interval, and the form of the alternative hypothesis (which can be "less", "greater", or "two.sided" but defaults to "two.sided" since it can be difficult to remember who's in group 1 and who's in group 2). No corrections are used to make the estimates more accurate or more precise. As a result, you may be able to get a better P-Value or confidence interval using the other tests that we'll cover later in this chapter.

To use z2.test, source this function:

```
source("https://raw.githubusercontent.com/NicoleRadziwill/R-
Functions/master/z2test.R")
```

Here is the code that that line activates:

```
z2.test <- function(x1,n1,x2,n2,conf.level=0.95,
        alternative="two.sided") {
  ts.z <- NULL
  cint <- NULL
  p.val <- NULL
    phat1 <- x1/n1
    qhat1 <- 1 - phat1
    phat2 <- x2/n2
    qhat2 <- 1 - phat1
    diff.phats <- phat1 - phat2
    pooled.p <- (x1 + x2)/(n1 + n2)
    pooled.q <- 1 - pooled.p
    SE.diffs <- sqrt( ((phat1*qhat1)/n1) + ((phat2*qhat2)/n2) )
    SE.pooled <- sqrt(pooled.p*pooled.q*((1/n1)+(1/n2)))
        # Why two SE's? SE.pooled is used in the calculation of
        # the test statistic z. We can pool because we are making
        # the assumption in the null hypothesis that there is no
        # difference between the two proportions.
    ts.z <- diff.phats/SE.pooled
    p.val <- pnorm(ts.z) # defaults to alternative="less"
        if(alternative=="two.sided") {
            p.val <- p.val * 2
            if(p.val > 1) { p.val - 1 }
        }
        if(alternative=="greater") {
            p.val <- 1 - p.val
        }
    cint <- diff.phats + c(
        -1*((qnorm(((1 - conf.level)/2) + conf.level))*SE.diffs),
        ((qnorm(((1 - conf.level)/2) + conf.level))*SE.diffs) )
  return(list(estimate=diff.phats,ts.z=ts.z,p.val=p.val,cint=cint))
}
```

If we run this on our drinking example, the values are very similar to what we computed analytically. Differences from what you calculate by hand here are often due to rounding or truncation errors in multiple terms.

```
> z2.test(x1=71,x2=46,n1=206,n2=170,alternative="greater")
$estimate
[1] 0.07407196
```

```
$ts.z
[1] 1.544056

$p.val
[1] 0.0612874

$cint
[1] -0.01658682  0.16473074
```

You can also access the confidence interval directly:

```
> z2.test(x1=71,x2=46,n1=206,n2=170)$cint
[1] -0.01658682  0.16473074
```

Step 7 Continued: One Proportion z-test Example Using `prop.test` in R

To execute this test in R, we need the number of successes and number of observations in both groups, just like in the custom function above. The order you send your data to `prop.test` is important. There were 71 successes out of 206 total observations in group 1:

```
> prop.test(x=c(71,46),n=c(206,170),alternative="greater")
```

And there were 46 successes reported out of 170 total observations in group 2:

```
> prop.test(x=c(71,46),n=c(206,170),alternative="greater")
```

The `prop.test` command defaults to applying the Yates continuity correction, which accounts for the fact that we're using a normal (continuous) distribution to approximate a binomial (discrete) distribution. We can turn this off by specifying `correct=FALSE`. It doesn't mean that we don't want the answer to be correct... it means we want the Yates correction turned off (`FALSE`). The first example below has the Yates correction ON, while the second has the Yates correction OFF:

```
> prop.test(x=c(71,46),n=c(206,170),alternative="greater")

        2-sample test for equality of proportions with continuity
        correction
```

```
data:   c(71, 46) out of c(206, 170)
X-squared = 2.0511, df = 1, P-Value = 0.07605
alternative hypothesis: greater
95 percent confidence interval:
 -0.009447819  1.000000000
sample estimates:
   prop 1    prop 2
0.3446602 0.2705882


> prop.test(x=c(71,46),n=c(206,170),alternative="greater",correct=FALSE)

        2-sample test for equality of proportions without continuity
        correction

data:   c(71, 46) out of c(206, 170)
X-squared = 2.3841, df = 1, P-Value = 0.06129
alternative hypothesis: greater
95 percent confidence interval:
 -0.004079458  1.000000000
sample estimates:
   prop 1    prop 2
0.3446602 0.2705882
```

Notice that with both tests, the null hypothesis would still be rejected (the P-Value is very tiny, almost zero) even though the value of the χ^2 test statistic differs by a small amount. Like the one proportion case, prop.test uses the *Wilson score interval* concept to construct the confidence interval. It gives more accurate confidence intervals when the estimate of the population proportion is closer to 0 and 1.0, but unlike the analytically computed confidence interval, the "net" isn't symmetric! Instead, it is somewhat skewed. Just be aware that if you decide to use the confidence interval that R reports via prop.test, it does not have the same properties as other confidence intervals, even though it might be more accurate with respect to the real population of differences between proportions.

The confidence interval can be computed by removing information about the alternative hypothesis:

```
> prop.test(x=c(71,46),n=c(206,170))
```

2-sample test for equality of proportions with continuity correction

```
data:  c(71, 46) out of c(206, 170)
X-squared = 2.0511, df = 1, P-Value = 0.1521
alternative hypothesis: two.sided
95 percent confidence interval:
 -0.02441956  0.17256348
sample estimates:
   prop 1    prop 2
0.3446602 0.2705882
```

Note that both the P-Value and the confidence interval are similar to what we calculated analytically, but they are not exactly the same: `prop.test` applies adjustments and corrections that should make the confidence interval more accurate.

Step 7 Continued

The hypothesis test that `prop.test` conducts is NOT the two-proportion z-test, so don't be surprised when the test statistic is different than what you calculated analytically! It uses an entirely different test – a Chi-square test of independence on a contingency table with two categorical variables. If we create a contingency table and add up the observations in the margins, we can see what's happening in the background. First, find the *expected values* by multiplying (row total) x (column total) and dividing that product by the total total (376). They are in italics:

	Business	**Tech**	
Drinking	71 *(64.1)*	46 *(52.9)*	117
Not Drinking	135 *(141.9)*	124 *(117.1)*	259
	206	170	376

Using these values, we can compute a Chi-square test statistic, and use that to look up a P-Value:

$$\chi^2 = \sum \left(\frac{(Observed - Expected)^2}{Expected} \right)$$

$$\chi^2 = \frac{(71 - 64.1)^2}{64.1} + \frac{(46 - 52.9)^2}{52.9} + \frac{(135 - 141.9)^2}{141.9} + \frac{(124 - 117.1)^2}{117.1} = 2.386$$

We can use `1-pchisq(2.386,df=1)` to find the P-Value for the two-tailed alternative, which gives us an area of 0.1226. These are the same values that we get from `prop.test`:

```
> prop.test(x=c(71,46),n=c(206,170),correct=FALSE)

        2-sample test for equality of proportions without correction

data:   c(71, 46) out of c(206, 170)
X-squared = 2.3841, df = 1, p-value = 0.1226
alternative hypothesis: two.sided
95 percent confidence interval:
 -0.0190512  0.1671951
sample estimates:
   prop 1    prop 2
0.3446602 0.2705882
```

Other Resources:

- This article by Sean Wallis of University College London explains everything you might want to know about continuity corrections, Wilson's score interval, and why your confidence interval as estimated by R might not be symmetric around the point estimate. It is comprehensive and, quite frankly, beautiful.
  http://www.ucl.ac.uk/english-usage/staff/sean/resources/binomialpoisson.pdf
- A great source for more information about `prop.test` is here:
  http://wiener.math.csi.cuny.edu/Statistics/R/simpleR/stat010.html
- An R-Bloggers article discussing the difference between the z test and the Chi square version of the two proportion test: http://www.r-bloggers.com/comparison-of-two-proportions-parametric-z-test-and-non-parametric-chi-squared-methods/
- Find out more about the Wilson score interval on Wikipedia at
  http://en.wikipedia.org/wiki/Binomial_proportion_confidence_interval#Wilson_score_interval

5.8 Chi-Square Test of Independence/Goodness-of-Fit

Objective

The Chi-Square Test of Independence explores whether two *categorical* random variables are independent, or alternatively, whether some dependency between them appears to exist. Note that if a dependency is detected, this does not imply that a *causal* relationship is present: it just suggests that the distribution of observed frequencies is not likely to have come about by pure chance. (This test is also sometimes called the Pearson Chi-Square Test. Don't be confused... they are the same thing.) Potential research questions include:

- Is there a dependence between our viewers' political affiliation and whether or not they agree with our message?
- Are passing grades in this class dependent on regular attendance?
- Is the satisfaction status for our customers' most recent interactions with us independent of their age group?

This chapter explains `chisq.test` in R, and how to assess the *degree* of association between the two categorical variables using Contingency Coefficient and Cramer's V.

Our Process for Inference Testing

We'll use Dr. R's 7 Steps in this chapter:

Step 0: Check Your Assumptions
Step 1: Set Null and Alternative Hypotheses
Step 2: Choose α, the Level of Significance
Step 3: Calculate Test Statistic (T.S.)
Step 4: Draw a Picture
Step 5: Find the P-Value
Step 6: Draw Conclusion - Is the P-Value < α? If So, Reject the Null
Step 7: Compute Confidence Interval & Double Check with R

Step 0: Check Your Assumptions

Before beginning an inference test, it's important to check and see if your data meets the assumptions and conditions for the test. If it doesn't, you need to 1) explain why you're still doing the test in your limitations section, 2) abandon the test entirely, 3) select a nonparametric alternative to the current test, like Fisher's Exact test (not covered in this book). The Chi-Square Test of Independence has the following assumptions:

1. **Random Sample**: Each case should be randomly sampled from the larger population. Every member of the population who was chosen should have had an equal probability of selection.

2. **Independence**: The observations themselves must be independent of one another. This may not be the case, for example, when one of the categorical variables has values like "before" and "after" - if an observation falls in the "before" category, then conditions have not been met for that observation to fall in the "after" category, and there is a possible dependence. If the independence assumption is not met, you can consider doing McNemar's Test as an alternative.

3. **Sample is Small Enough (n < 10%)**: The number of observations (that is, when you add up *all* the frequencies in *all* the cells) should be less than 10% of the total number of possible observations in the population.

4. **Enough Expected and Observed Values**: Do you have enough observations in each cell? If any of your cells have fewer than 5 observed (or expected!) values, you may have a problem. Although attributed to an academic named Cochran in the 1950's, I wasn't able to find any academic references explaining why the number 5 is recommended, or if this is a hard and fast rule. If it was *my* data, I'd want at least 10 observations per cell, with expected frequencies all greater than 10 as well – just to be safe. If more than 20% of your cells have very few observations (< 5), and you still want to run the inference test, you may want to consider Fisher's Exact Test. ("Expected" values represent how many observations would be in a particular cell if all of the observations in the contingency table were distributed randomly – we'll calculate them shortly.)

Step 1: Set Null and Alternative Hypotheses

The null and alternative hypotheses for the Chi-Square Test of Independence are:

> H_0: The two categorical variables are independent.
>
> H_a: The two categorical variables are not independent.

To be more specific, you can explicitly state the names of your categorical variables in the null and alternative. For example, your null hypothesis might be "customer satisfaction and age are independent" or "stress level and political affiliation are independent."

Step 2: Choose α, the Level of Significance

The level of significance α is often set to 0.05, indicating that we're willing to *incorrectly reject the null hypothesis* one out of every 20 times we collect a sample and run this test. This is acceptable for our example using customer satisfaction and age group because 1) the **cost** of collecting new observations is extremely low, in terms of time, effort, and money, 2) the **risk** associated with drawing incorrect conclusions is also low (I'll just be disappointed that indeed, my new town *is* colder on a daily basis, on average, than my new town) and 3) there are no significant **ethical considerations** that I have to keep in mind based on how the results from my study may be applied by other people who read about my study.

Step 3: Calculate Test Statistic (T.S.)

Because this is a Chi-Square test, our test statistic will be a χ^2. It's calculated by computing the difference between the observed and expected value in a cell, squaring it, then dividing by the expected value... and adding it up over all the cells. The formula is:

$$\chi^2 = \Sigma \left(\frac{(Observed - Expected)^2}{Expected} \right)$$

The tricky thing is, you need to know what the *expected values* are. And if you just collected your own data, and you have a contingency table sitting in front of you, how can you possibly figure out what frequencies you were supposed to *expect* to see?

Fortunately, there is a simple pattern to follow to compute expected frequencies. First, you'll need to make sure that you have the *marginal distributions* available (that is, the totals you get when you add up frequencies across each row, or down each column). Then, you'll need to compute an expected value for *each and every cell* that you have observations for! (This does not include the margins... just the cells that contain your observations).

The formula is:

$$Expected\ Value = \frac{Row\ Total \times Column\ Total}{Total\ Total}$$

For example, I'll create a contingency table called `ct` to store customer satisfaction data that I've scrawled down in my notebook:

```
> satisfied <- c(36,39,11)
> unsatisfied <- c(8,7,14)
> ct <- rbind(satisfied, unsatisfied)
> colnames(ct) <- c("18-34","35-49","50+")
> ct
            18-34 35-49 50+
satisfied      36    39  11
unsatisfied     8     7  14
```

First, I need to compute the totals across each row, then the totals down each column, and finally add up all my observations to get a total of all the totals (which I'll put in the bottom right corner). For each cell, I compute the expected value by multiplying the row total by the column total, and dividing by the total observations in the whole table (which is 115). Here is how I work out the calculation of the χ^2 test statistic analytically:

```
> satisfied <- c(36,39,11)
> unsatisfied <- c(8,7,14)
> col.totals <- satisfied+unsatisfied
```

386

```
> row.totals <- c(sum(satisfied),sum(unsatisfied),
sum(satisfied)+sum(unsatisfied))
> ct <- rbind(satisfied,unsatisfied,col.totals)
> ct <- cbind(ct,row.totals)
> ct
                      row.totals
satisfied   36 39 11          86
unsatisfied  8  7 14          29
col.totals  44 46 25         115

> expected.values.row.1 <- c( ((86*44)/115), ((86*46)/115), ((86*25)/115))
> expected.values.row.2 <- c( ((29*44)/115), ((29*46)/115), ((29*25)/115))
> expected.values <- rbind(expected.values.row.1,expected.values.row.2)
>
> expected.values
                        [,1] [,2]      [,3]
expected.values.row.1 32.90435 34.4 18.695652
expected.values.row.2 11.09565 11.6  6.304348

> chisq.1 <- ((satisfied[1]-
expected.values.row.1[1])^2)/expected.values.row.1[1]
> chisq.2 <- ((satisfied[2]-
expected.values.row.1[2])^2)/expected.values.row.1[2]
> chisq.3 <- ((satisfied[3]-
expected.values.row.1[3])^2)/expected.values.row.1[3]
> chisq.4 <- ((unsatisfied[1]-
expected.values.row.2[1])^2)/expected.values.row.2[1]
> chisq.5 <- ((unsatisfied[2]-
expected.values.row.2[2])^2)/expected.values.row.2[2]
> chisq.6 <- ((unsatisfied[3]-
expected.values.row.2[3])^2)/expected.values.row.2[3]
> ts.chisq <- chisq.1 + chisq.2 + chisq.3 + chisq.4 + chisq.5 + chisq.6
> ts.chisq
[1] 16.15592
```

"There's got to be an easier way to calculate that χ^2 test statistic," you might say. And you're right, because we have R. But since *as soon as we calculate the χ^2, our test will be over*, let's take a quick diversion and draw a picture.

Step 4: Draw a Picture

Chi-Square distributions look like normal distributions that have one tail stretched out pretty far towards the right on the horizontal axis. We can generate a Chi-Square probability density by asking R to randomly sample a collection of values (in this case, 100 of them), and plotting them using the `curve` function. We will also plot a vertical line using `abline` somewhere down on the tail of the Chi-Square distribution:

```
> x <- rchisq(100,5)
> curve(dchisq(x, df=5), xlim=c(0,20), main="Chi-Square Distribution")
> abline(v=12,lwd=3)
```

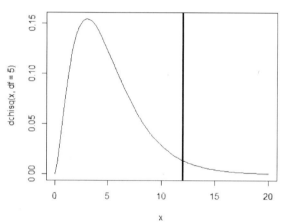

When we do a Chi-Square test, the value of the computed test statistic corresponds to that vertical line. **The P-Value is the area in the tail**. Clearly, the bigger the χ^2 is, the smaller the area in the tail, and the tinier the P-Value.

Step 5: Find the P-Value

If you computed χ^2 by hand, you can use R as a lookup table for the P-Value as long as you know your degrees of freedom, which you find by multiplying `(rows-1)` and `(columns-1)` together (which in this case, is 2 x 1 = 2):

388

```
> 1-pchisq(16.1559,df=2)
[1] 0.0003103065
```

This P-Value matches, almost exactly, the one that R displayed in the output from the `chisq.test` command.

Step 6: Draw Conclusion – Is the P-Value < α? If So, Reject the Null

Now we have to ask ourselves the question: Is the P-Value we just calculated (zero) less than our α of 0.05? Yes, 0.00031 is very, very small and definitely less than our alpha. We REJECT our null hypothesis that our two categorical values are independent... there does seem to be some relationship between customer satisfaction and their age category. Looking at the data, it seems like the older folks are more disgruntled. We may want to follow up on this Chi-Square test with a Root Cause Analysis to explore the reasons why... and then maybe do something about it.

Step 7: Compute Confidence Interval & Double Check with R

Regarding confidence intervals... **there is no specific confidence interval for this test.** You can place confidence intervals on the individual proportions within your contingency table, or on differences between proportions from your contingency table. But we can still make R doing all the heavy lifting required to complete a Chi-Square test of independence.

First, we create the variables `row1` and `row2` to store the values in the first and second rows of our contingency table, respectively. Then, we can use the `rbind` (or "**row** **bind**") command to join the rows together, creating one larger data structure, and the `dimnames` command to give the variables in the contingency table names:

```
row1 <- c(36,39,11)
row2 <- c(8,7,14)
my.ctable <- rbind(row1,row2)
dimnames(my.ctable) <- list(state = c("Satisfied","Unsatisfied"),
        agegroup = c("18 to 34","35 to 49","Over 50"))
```

We can now display the contents of our newly created contingency table:

```
> my.ctable
            agegroup
state        18 to 34 35 to 49 Over 50
  Satisfied        36       39       11
  Unsatisfied       8        7       14
```

Computing the test statistic and finding the P-Value is now an easy one-line task:

```
> chisq.test(my.ctable)

        Pearson's Chi-squared test

data:  my.ctable
X-squared = 16.1559, df = 2, P-Value = 0.0003103
```

The Juicy Innards of `chisq.test`

There is a wealth of information we can access when we store the results of `chisq.test` to a variable, instead of just running the command and examining the output. Let's try it with the contingency table we used earlier by storing the results to a new variable called `Xsq.results` like this:

```
Xsq.results <- chisq.test(my.ctable)
```

What's in there? The easiest way to find out is to use the structure command, `str`:

```
> str(Xsq.results)
List of 9
 $ statistic: Named num 16.2
  ..- attr(*, "names")= chr "X-squared"
 $ parameter: Named int 2
  ..- attr(*, "names")= chr "df"
 $ p.value  : num 0.00031
 $ method   : chr "Pearson's Chi-squared test"
 $ data.name: chr "my.ctable"
 $ observed : num [1:2, 1:3] 36 8 39 7 11 14
```

```
  ..- attr(*, "dimnames")=List of 2
  .. ..$ state   : chr [1:2] "Satisfied" "Unsatisfied"
  .. ..$ agegroup: chr [1:3] "18 to 34" "35 to 49" "Over 50"
 $ expected : num [1:2, 1:3] 32.9 11.1 34.4 11.6 18.7 ...
  ..- attr(*, "dimnames")=List of 2
  .. ..$ state   : chr [1:2] "Satisfied" "Unsatisfied"
  .. ..$ agegroup: chr [1:3] "18 to 34" "35 to 49" "Over 50"
 $ residuals: num [1:2, 1:3] 0.54 -0.929 0.784 -1.351 -1.78 ...
  ..- attr(*, "dimnames")=List of 2
  .. ..$ state   : chr [1:2] "Satisfied" "Unsatisfied"
  .. ..$ agegroup: chr [1:3] "18 to 34" "35 to 49" "Over 50"
 $ stdres   : num [1:2, 1:3] 1.37 -1.37 2.02 -2.02 -4.01 ...
  ..- attr(*, "dimnames")=List of 2
  .. ..$ state   : chr [1:2] "Satisfied" "Unsatisfied"
  .. ..$ agegroup: chr [1:3] "18 to 34" "35 to 49" "Over 50"
 - attr(*, "class")= chr "htest"
```

In addition to being able to do things like access the value of the test statistic directly (via `Xsq.results$statistic`), which can be useful if you're writing more complex programs in R, the part I like best is being able to access the *expected* values from my contingency table so I don't have to compute them directly. Notice that these are the same numbers that I computed analytically and wrote in my notebook:

```
> Xsq.results$expected
           agegroup
state         18 to 34 35 to 49   Over 50
  Satisfied   32.90435     34.4 18.695652
  Unsatisfied 11.09565     11.6  6.304348
```

You can also access the *observed* values via `Xsq.results$observed`. <u>As a result, it is easy to compute the contribution of each cell to the value of the test statistic χ^2:</u>

```
> ((Xsq.results$observed - Xsq.results$expected)^2)/Xsq.results$expected
           agegroup
state        18 to 34  35 to 49   Over 50
  Satisfied  0.2912400 0.6151163 3.167745
  Unsatisfied 0.8636773 1.8241379 9.394003
```

If you want to add them to double check the computed value of χ^2, that's easy to do too:

```
> sum(((Xsq.results$observed -
Xsq.results$expected)^2)/Xsq.results$expected)
[1] 16.15592
```

Measures of Association: Contingency Coefficient & Cramer's V

Let's say you've conducted the test, rejected the null hypothesis, and you're now *aware* that there is some kind of association between your two categorical variables - they are *not* independent. What degree of association do your categorical variables have? This can be assessed using Pearson's Contingency Coefficient, or alternatively, a measure called Cramer's V.

The contingency coefficient scales the value of the χ^2 test statistic so that it ranges from 0 (indicating no association) to 1 (indicating the maximum association). It is useful because it lets you directly compare the degree of association between two Chi-Square tests, *even when the sample sizes are different.* The formula for the contingency coefficient is:

$$C = \sqrt{\frac{\chi^2}{n + \chi^2}}$$

In addition to the test statistic, this calculation also requires you to know the total number of observations in your contingency table (the "total total" from earlier in the chapter). Here is an R function that performs this computation:

```
contin.coeff <- function(xsq) {
    sqrt(xsq$statistic/(sum(xsq$observed)+xsq$statistic))
}
```

Once you cut and paste the above code into your R console, you can pass it the variable that contains your Chi-Square test results, and it will display the contingency coefficient:

```
> contin.coeff(Xsq.results)
X-squared
0.3509715
```

An alternative to the contingency coefficient is Cramer's V. Like the contingency coefficient, it scales the value of the χ^2 test statistic so that it ranges from 0 (indicating no association) to 1 (indicating the maximum association). However, as an added bonus, Cramer's V also takes into account the dimensions of the contingency table (that is, the number of rows and the number of columns). As a result, you can use Cramer's V to compare the strength of association *between two completely different contingency tables*, even if they have a different number of rows and columns! The formula for Cramer's V is:

$$V = \sqrt{\frac{\chi^2}{nt}}$$

In addition to the test statistic, this calculation also requires you to know the total number of observations n, and one less than the *smaller of the number of rows, or number of columns*. (The mathematical way to express this is $t = min(r-1, c-1)$ where r is the number of rows, and c is the number of columns.)

```
cramers.v <- function(xsq) {
        a <- dim(xsq$observed)[1]   # number of rows
        b <- dim(xsq $observed)[2]  # number of columns
        t <- min(a,b)-1
        sqrt(xsq$statistic/(sum(xsq$observed)*t))
}
```

Once you load this function with `source`, you can pass this new function the variable that contains your Chi-Square test results to find Cramer's V measure of association:

```
> source("https://raw.githubusercontent.com/NicoleRadziwill/R-
Functions/master/cramersv.R")
> cramers.v(Xsq.results)
X-squared
 0.374815
```

Chi-Square Goodness-of-Fit Test

You can also conduct a Chi-square test if your contingency table only has *one* categorical variable, and this provides a way to test and see if a set of observations comes from a particular distribution. Take, for example, the case of *rolling dice*. With a fair die, we can be certain that each outcome, from 1 through 6, will come up about 12.5% (1/6) of the time. With an unfair die, we can expect to see a distribution that does not conform with the *expected values* that we would get if indeed each outcome happened 1/6 of the time. Apply the Chi-Square goodness of fit test to see if your dice roll data comes from a uniform distribution or not:

```
> fair.rolls <- c(12,8,11,9,10,10)
> chisq.test(fair.rolls, p=c(1/6,1/6,1/6,1/6,1/6,1/6))

        Chi-squared test for given probabilities

data:  fair.rolls
X-squared = 1, df = 5, p-value = 0.9626

> unfair.rolls <- c(17,3,13,7,5,15)
> chisq.test(unfair.rolls, p=c(1/6,1/6,1/6,1/6,1/6,1/6))

        Chi-squared test for given probabilities

data:  unfair.rolls
X-squared = 16.6, df = 5, p-value = 0.005324
```

In the second case (an unfair die), the tiny p-value means we reject the null hypothesis that our data came from the distribution we specified using the p argument.

Selecting an Appropriate Chi-Square Approach in R

If you are working with a large data frame where each row represents one case, then you should use CrossTable (which is included in the gmodels package) to do your Chi-Square test, rather than chisq.test in the base R installation. Why? Because CrossTable will *tally up all of your values for you* before performing the inference test! It will also draw pretty contingency tables. That makes life a lot easier if your observations haven't already been counted up and displayed within a contingency table. The chapter on contingency tables earlier in the book shows how to draw a contingency table - and conduct a Chi-Square Test of Independence while you're at it - using `CrossTable`.

Postscript: Troubleshooting

If you see this error, it just means that your cell counts may not be big enough for your data to satisfy all of the assumptions of the Chi-square test:

```
Warning message:
In chisq.test(a) : Chi-squared approximation may be incorrect
```

If this happens, try an alternative approach like Fisher's Exact Test (`fisher.test` in R).

Other Resources:

- The original academic paper describing the Chi-square test of independence is Cochran, W. G. (1952). The χ^2 test of goodness of fit. Annals of Mathematical Statistics, 25, p. 315–345. It is at http://projecteuclid.org/euclid.aoms/1177729380
- Here's a site that talks about the Chi-Square test, Fisher's Exact test, and McNemar's test relative to each other: http://yatani.jp/teaching/doku.php?id=hcistats:chisquare

5.9 Chi-Square Test for One Variance

Objective

The Chi-Square test for one variance checks to see if there is a *difference* between the dispersion of values in a population, and how scattered you think that data *should be*: that is, is the distribution of values in the population I'm examining significantly fatter or thinner than I expect? This kind of test is useful if you're responsible for making sure that the output of a process is consistent, since variation (at least the kind that's due to some assignable cause, rather than just random variation) can be an enemy of quality. Some examples of research questions where you might use tests for equality of variances include:

- Imagine that you manufacture smartphones. You take a sample of 32 phones, and measure the thickness of each of them. The average thickness is 0.82 cm, and the standard deviation of thickness in your sample is 0.08 cm. Have you achieved the manufacturer's goal of a 0.075 cm standard deviation?

- The CEO of a prominent five-star restaurant is concerned that one of his chefs is preparing dishes that are too salty. Using a salt refractometer, he collects salinity data from several dishes prepared by each of his two chefs. He wants to see if the variance in saltiness over all of the dishes matches his standard or baseline value before he decides to invest in additional training.

- A Six Sigma Black Belt was recently engaged by her employer, a local craft brewery, to reduce the variance of an industrial process for filling beer bottles from 0.23 oz. After randomly sampling 24 beers, she determines that the mean volume of beer is 12.09 oz with a variance of 0.16 oz. Has she achieved the brewer's goal of a 0.12 oz variance?

The last question will be used as our example for the Chi-Square test for one variance. Notice that in this test, it's *really, really important that you keep variance and standard deviation straight.* Sometimes, dispersion is reported as a variance, and other times, it's reported as a standard deviation - so be careful with this test!

It's always been hard for me to distinguish variance and standard deviation, so here's the trick I use to remember: Put SD and Variance on opposite sides of the equals sign, in alphabetical order (so SD comes first). Then, put the square root sign on the right-hand side, since I'm right handed. Then, square both sides to get the other relationship:

$$SD = \sqrt{Variance}$$

$$SD^2 = Variance$$

Since this is a test for variance, I like to keep my data in terms of variance. If my data contains standard deviations, I'll convert these to variances *before proceeding*. It makes keeping track of who needs to be squared (and who doesn't need to be squared) much easier. To make it easier to remember, I also write "standard deviation" and "variance" in my equations instead of s or s^2 so I don't get confused by notation and variable names.

Our Process for Inference Testing

We'll use Dr. R's 7 Steps in this chapter:

> **Step 0**: Check Your Assumptions
> **Step 1**: Set Null and Alternative Hypotheses
> **Step 2**: Choose α, the Level of Significance
> **Step 3**: Calculate Test Statistic (T.S.)
> **Step 4**: Draw a Picture
> **Step 5**: Find the P-Value
> **Step 6**: Draw Conclusion - Is the P-Value < α? If So, Reject the Null
> **Step 7**: Compute Confidence Interval & Double Check with R

We will solve the Chi-Square test for one variance *analytically* (meaning, using the equations and doing the calculations by hand) and *also by using R* to do our calculations. If you are doing research, it's always good to solve the problem both ways to check your work! That way, you have a better chance of being correct. If you are writing a research paper, be sure to include *all* of Dr. R's 7 Steps in your results section.

Step 0: Check Your Assumptions

Before beginning an inference test, it's important to check and see if your data meets the assumptions and conditions for the test. If it doesn't, you need to 1) explain why you're still doing the test in your limitations section, 2) abandon the test entirely, 3) consider a *nonparametric alternative* to your test if you fail some assumptions, e.g. your sample differences aren't normally distributed, or you have rank-ordered data instead of continuous quantitative data. (The nonparametric alternative for the Chi-Square test of variance is Levene's test, which is not covered in this book.)

1. **Random sample**: Were each of the items in your data set randomly selected from the population of all values? In the beer example, we need to make sure that the 24 bottles were randomly selected. One way to do this is to select the bottles directly from the manufacturing line, rather than pulling a few six-packs off a pallet before they are prepared for shipping.

2. **Observations are independent**: Does the fill volume for one beer influence the fill volume for another beer? Probably not, but we won't know for sure unless we ask one of the engineers at the brewery.

3. **Observations are normal or nearly normal**: For this to be valid, you should examine a histogram or QQ plot of the *actual fill volumes*. Since we don't have this data available, we have to assume that the distribution of observations is normal.

For the beer example we'll cover in this chapter, we don't have any reason to think that our assumptions won't check out, so we proceed – cautiously – with the test. But there are serious consequences associated with a Type I Error that we should also think about. Based on the conclusions we draw from this test, if we find we're not meeting our variance target, we may need to repair the bottling machine. That's really expensive. Since we're not *completely* sure that all our assumptions check out, we might want to run a second round of tests if we reject the null hypothesis from our first round. On the second go, we need to make sure we capture the fill volumes so we can test for normality. If there's no way to get this information, perhaps we should consider an alternate test.

Step 1: Set Null and Alternative Hypotheses

The forms of the null and alternative hypotheses for the Chi-Square test of one variance are:

H_0: $\sigma^2 = \sigma^2_0$

H_a: $\sigma^2 > \sigma^2_0$ (one-tailed test)

         $\sigma^2 < \sigma^2_0$ (one-tailed test)

         $\sigma^2 \neq \sigma^2_0$ (two-tailed test)

The value you choose for σ^2_0 can be zero, but is often a standard, target, or baseline for a process. For our beer example, we will set these null and alternative hypotheses with σ^2 at 0.12 oz indicating that we start out with the brewery's target:

H_0: $\sigma^2 = 0.12$ oz   (the variance in the fill volume is what we want)

H_a: $\sigma^2 > 0.12$ oz   (the variance is *too high... **not** what we want)

We choose the "greater than" alternative for this example because we care if the variance is *smaller* than our target... that's actually rather good. We only need to take action with our bottling process if we're not meeting our variance targets.

Step 2: Choose α, the Level of Significance

The level of significance α is often set to 0.05, indicating that we're willing to *incorrectly reject the null hypothesis* one out of every 20 times we collect a sample and run this test. This is acceptable for our current example because 1) the **cost** of collecting new observations is extremely low, in terms of time, effort, and money, 2) the **risk** associated with drawing incorrect conclusions is also low (if I reject the null, I'll do a more complete test, making sure I have the data to check for the normality assumption) and 3) there are no significant **ethical considerations** that I have to keep in mind based on how the results from my study may be applied by other people. All I want to know is whether we have a variance problem in the fill volume for our beers. There are no policy decisions riding on our conclusion... yet.

Step 3: Calculate Test Statistic (T.S.)

Because this is a Chi-Square test, our test statistic will be a χ^2. The formula is:

$$\chi^2_{df} = \frac{(n-1)s^2}{\sigma^2_0} = \frac{(n-1) \times Sample\ Variance}{Reference\ or\ Target\ Variance}$$

With a sample size of 24, a reference variance of 0.12, and a sample variance of 0.16, I can calculate the test statistic (T.S.) from my data:

$$\chi^2_{df} = \frac{23 \times 0.16}{0.12} = 30.67$$

Step 4: Draw a Picture

To find our P-Value, we shade the area under the Chi-square distribution with `df=23` to the right of χ^2 = 30.67. Here is some R code to draw that (not very elegant, but it works; plot is on the next page).

```
> x.grid = seq(0,100,length=100)
> dens.all = dchisq(x.grid,df=23)
> x.above <- x.grid[x.grid>30.67]
> dens.above <- dens.all[x.grid>30.67]
> plot(dens.all,type="l",lwd=4)
> polygon(c(x.above,rev(x.above)),c(rep(0,length(x.above)),
      rev(dens.above)),col="black",density=40)
```

Step 5: Find the P-Value

Now we look up the P-Value. We subtract from one since we want the upper tail area:

```
> 1-pchisq(30.67,df=23)
[1] 0.1311184
```

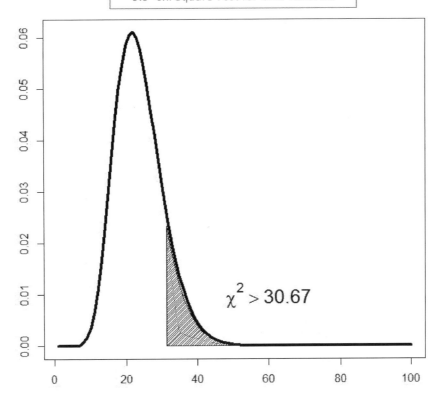

$$\chi^2 > 30.67$$

Step 6: Is the P-Value < α? If So, Reject the Null

Now we have to ask ourselves the question: Is the P-Value we just calculated (0.131) less than our α of 0.05? No, it is not. We FAIL TO REJECT our null hypothesis that the observed variance is at our target of 0.12 oz.

You can also construct a confidence interval to double-check your work. Let's do that, and build a 95% CI. Remember that the confidence interval is not symmetric, and can be computed using this expression:

$$\frac{(n-1)s^2}{\chi^2_{upper}} \leq \sigma^2 \leq \frac{(n-1)s^2}{\chi^2_{lower}}$$

We calculate our upper and lower χ^2 values to plug in first:

```
> qchisq(0.975,df=23)
[1] 38.07563
> qchisq(0.025,df=23)
[1] 11.68855
```

And finally, we plug all the values in:

$$\frac{23 \ x \ 0.16}{38.08} \leq \sigma^2 \leq \frac{23 \ x \ 0.16}{11.69}$$

$$0.097 \leq \sigma^2 \leq 0.315$$

Our confidence interval ranges from a lower bound of 0.097 to an upper bound of 0.315. This is interpreted in the following way:

> *"We are 95% confident that the true variance in fill volumes is between 0.097 and 0.315 ounces."*

Notice how the value from the right-hand side of our null hypothesis is contained within this confidence interval? Based on our sample, 0.12 oz could *certainly* be the true population variance, affirming the decision that we made *not to reject the null hypothesis*.

Chi-Square Test of Variance Example in R

Here is an R function that executes the Chi-Square test of one variance in the same way that we did analytically, using the equations above. Source the first line into your R session; the remaining code is there so you can see what this function does:

```
source("https://raw.githubusercontent.com/NicoleRadziwill/R-
Functions/master/chisqvar.R")

chisq.var <- function(n,sample.var,target.var,alternative="greater",
    vname="[population variance]",conf.level=0.95) {
    cint <- NULL
    df <- n-1
```

```
ci.tails <- 1-conf.level
    ts.chisq <- (df*sample.var)/target.var
    chisq.upper <- qchisq((conf.level+(ci.tails/2)),df=df)
    chisq.lower <- qchisq((ci.tails/2),df=df)
    area.upper <- 1-pchisq(ts.chisq,df=df)
    area.lower <- pchisq(ts.chisq,df=df)
    if ((ts.chisq < chisq.lower) || (ts.chisq > chisq.upper)) {
        area.both <- paste("Less Than",ci.tails)
    } else {
        area.both <- paste("Greater Than",ci.tails)
    }
    cint <- c((df*sample.var)/chisq.upper,(df*sample.var)/chisq.lower)
    verbose <- sprintf("We are %s%% confident that the true %s is
            between %.5f and %.5f.", (conf.level*100), vname,
            cint[1], cint[2])
    p.value <- switch(alternative,
            "greater" = area.upper,
            "less" = area.lower,
            "two.sided" = area.both)
return(list(chisq.upper=chisq.upper,
        chisq.lower=chisq.lower,ts=ts.chisq,cint=cint,
        p.value=p.value,verbose=verbose))
}
```

Specify your `n`, your target and sample variances, and your alternative hypothesis at a minimum. Optionally, you can name your variance so that the interpretation of the confidence interval that the function provides will be complete.

Arguments to `chisq.var`	What each one specifies
`n`	The number of observations in your sample
`sample.var`	The variance of the values in your sample
`target.var`	The variance you are comparing your sample to; the value on the right-hand side of the null hypothesis
`alternative`	The alternative hypothesis you have selected. Can be `"less"`, `"greater"`, or `"two.sided"`; defaults to `greater`.
`vname` (optional)	Words that describe the quantitative variable you are building a confidence interval around
`conf.level`	Confidence level (e.g. 0.90, 0.95, 0.99); defaults to 0.95

We can apply this function to our example above:

```
> chisq.var(24,0.16,0.12,alternative="greater")
$chisq.upper
[1] 38.07563

$chisq.lower
[1] 11.68855

$ts
[1] 30.66667

$cint
[1] 0.09664975 0.31483797

$p.value
[1] 0.1312047

$verbose
[1] "We are 95% confident that the true [population variance] is between
0.09665 and 0.31484."
```

If you only had standard deviations, you could also very easily provide those to this function. This statement would provide almost exactly the same output as above (with small differences possibly due to rounding and truncation error):

```
> chisq.var(24,(0.4^2),(0.3464^2),alternative="greater")
$chisq.upper
[1] 38.07563

$chisq.lower
[1] 11.68855

$ts
[1] 30.66847

$cint
[1] 0.09664975 0.31483797

$p.value
[1] 0.1311581
```

```
$verbose
[1] "We are 95% confident that the true [population variance] is between
0.097 and 0.315."
```

You can also call any of these variables in the returned object directly:

```
> chisq.var(24,(0.4^2),(0.3464^2),alternative="greater")$ts
[1] 30.66847
```

Other Resources:

- This is the best resource that I've found that describes all about this test:
  http://www.saylor.org/site/wp-content/uploads/2011/06/MA121-5.3.4-1st.pdf
- Here is a web-based resource (not using R) that lets you input up to 80
  measurements, and automatically compare the variance of those measurements to
  a standard or target using the Chi-Square test for one variance. I think it's pretty
  cool: http://home.ubalt.edu/ntsbarsh/Business-stat/otherapplets/variationtest.htm

5.10 F Test for Homogeneity of Two Variances

Objective

Tests for homogeneity (or equality) of variances check to see if there is a *difference* between the scattered-ness of values in two samples: that is, whether one distribution is significantly fatter or thinner than the other. Since the two-sample t-test and two proportion z-test assume that the variance is similar between your two groups, you need to do an equality of variances test *prior to* one of those tests to make sure that you meet their assumptions. Additionally, tests for equality of variances can also be used to satisfy research questions. Some examples of research questions where you might use tests for equality of variances include:

- The CEO of a prominent five-star restaurant is concerned that one of his chefs is preparing dishes that are too salty. Using a salt refractometer, he collects salinity data from several dishes prepared by each of his two chefs. He wants to compare the variance in saltiness over all of the dishes between each of his chefs before he decides to invest in additional training.

- A Six Sigma Black Belt was recently engaged by her employer, a local craft brewery, to reduce the variance of an industrial process for filling beer bottles from 0.23 oz. After randomly sampling 24 beers (4 different six-packs), she determines that the mean volume of beer is 12.09 oz with a variance of 0.16 oz. Has the goal of reducing the variance for this process been achieved?

- Imagine that you manufacture smartphones. You take a sample of 32 phones, and measure the thickness of each of them. The average thickness is 0.82 cm, and the standard deviation of thickness in your sample is 0.08 cm. You change out two critical parts in the machine, and then collect another sample of 20 phones. The average thickness is 0.818 cm, and the standard deviation is 0.075 cm. Has the variance been reduced as a result of the maintenance on the machine?

- You are an instructor who helps people prepare for certification exams. Over the past year, you've randomly assigned one of three textbooks to each of your students, and you've recorded their final scores from their practice exams. You've already eliminated Book 2 as a possibility. You'd like to two a two-sample t-test to see if the test scores are different for students who used each of the textbooks, but you're aware that there are two versions of that test: one that assumes equal variances, and one that does not. You need to do a test to see if the variances are indeed different before moving to the two-sample t-test.

The last question will be used as our example for the equality of variance tests.

Our Process for Inference Testing

We'll use Dr. R's 7 Steps in this chapter:

Step 0: Check Your Assumptions
Step 1: Set Null and Alternative Hypotheses
Step 2: Choose α, the Level of Significance
Step 3: Calculate Test Statistic (T.S.)
Step 4: Draw a Picture
Step 5: Find the P-Value
Step 6: Draw Conclusion - Is the P-Value < α? If So, Reject the Null
Step 7: Compute Confidence Interval & Double Check with R

We will solve the F test problem *analytically* (meaning, using the equations and doing the calculations by hand) and *also by using R* to do our calculations. If you are doing research, it's always good to solve the problem both ways to check your work! That way, you have a better chance of being correct. If you are writing a research paper to document your study, be sure to include *all* of Dr. R's 7 Steps in your results section.

Let's load in our test data from GitHub. The data frame has two columns: the first column contains an exam `score`, and the second column contains the `textbook` that the person was using (1, 2, or 3) when they got that exam score.

```
> scores <-
read.table("https://raw.githubusercontent.com/NicoleRadziwill/Data-for-R-
Examples/master/anova-textbooks.txt",header=TRUE)
> head(scores)
  score textbook
1    78         1
2    82         1
3    99         1
4    82         1
5    74         1
6    91         1
> nrow(scores)
[1] 48
```

Just so you can get a sense of what the 48 items in our sample look like, here's a comparative boxplot of the test scores:

```
> boxplot(scores$score~scores$textbook, xlab="Textbooks", ylab=Scores")
```

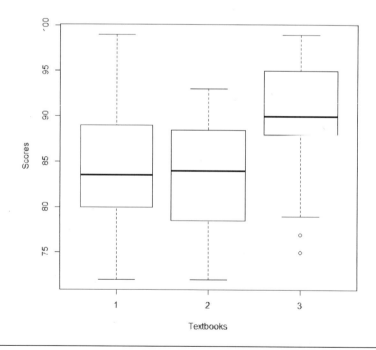

Step 0: Check Your Assumptions

Before beginning an inference test, it's important to check and see if your data meets the assumptions and conditions for the test. If it doesn't, you need to 1) explain why you're still doing the test in your limitations section, 2) abandon the test entirely, 3) choose a *nonparametric alternative* to use for your test, e.g. if your problem is just that the sample differences aren't normally distributed, or you have rank-ordered data instead of continuous quantitative data. (The nonparametric alternative for this test is the squared ranks test, which is not covered in this book. Other alternatives include Levene's Test, Bartlett's Test, and the Brown-Forsythe Test.)

    1. **Random sample**: Was each of the items in your data set randomly selected from the population of all values? In the textbook example, we should randomly select students from the population of all possible students enrolling in the certification prep class. However, we can only control which textbook is selected for our class, so technically we have a *convenience sample* which isn't exactly random. But it's the best we can do, so for the purpose of this test we will assume that it is random enough.

    2. **Observations are independent**: Do the values from one measurement influence the values in another measurement? For our example, we can assume that the students aren't cheating (after all, they are paying lots of money for this training program, and they all want to do well on the certification exam so they can get a better job). As a result, it's unlikely that any student's score will be affected by another student's score. Our observations are independent.

    3. **Observations are normal or nearly normal**: For the F test to be valid, you should examine a histogram or QQ plot of the values whose variances you will be examining, and maybe even follow up with an Anderson-Darling or Shapiro-Wilk test of normality. F tests are very sensitive to the assumption of normality, so try not to rely on "eyeballing" a histogram here.

Our assumptions check out, so we can move to the next stage of the process and set up our F test for homogeneity of variances.

Step 1: Set Null and Alternative Hypotheses

The forms of the null and alternative hypotheses for the F test are:

H_0: $\sigma_1^2 = \sigma_2^2$

H_a: $\sigma_1^2 > \sigma_2^2$ (one-tailed test)

        $\sigma_1^2 \neq \sigma_2^2$ (two-tailed test)

The only important rule of thumb to remember for this test is that you should make group 1 the one with the bigger variance. **But notice**: There are only TWO options for the alternative hypothesis here!! If you put the bigger variance on top *by convention*, you will never have a case where the alternative hypothesis has a "less than" sign in it.

For the textbook selection case, we will choose the two-tailed test. We don't care if one variance is bigger than the other, we just want to know if they are different.

Step 2: Choose α, the Level of Significance

The level of significance α is often set to 0.05, indicating that we're willing to *incorrectly reject the null hypothesis* one out of every 20 times we collect a sample and run this test. This is acceptable for our current example because 1) the **cost** of collecting new observations is low in terms of effort and money, and moderate in terms of time, but 2) the **risk** associated with drawing incorrect conclusions is low (the instructor will just be adopting a textbook that perhaps isn't clearly the best). Also, 3) there are no significant **ethical considerations** that we have to keep in mind based on how the results may be used or applied. After all, it's just textbook data, and it's not for thousands or millions of people. People's lives and safety are not at stake, and there are no policy decisions riding on the conclusion.

Step 3: Calculate Test Statistic (T.S.)

This test uses the F distribution, and has a really simple formula:

$$F = \frac{Larger\ Variance}{Smaller\ Variance}$$

Let's calculate the test statistic for our textbook data:

```
> var(scores[scores$textbook == 1,]$score)
[1] 52.5625
> var(scores[scores$textbook == 3,]$score)
[1] 52.78333
> 52.78333/52.5625
[1] 1.004201
```

Step 4: Draw a Picture

This is the one test I usually don't draw a picture for. I find it counterintuitive to see a picture of the areas we're trying to find to represent our P-Value when it's demarcated by the upper and lower boundaries for F. As a result, it's OK with me if you skip Step 4 this time!

Step 5: Find the P-Value

Since we have computed a test statistic F, we can look up the P-Value as long as we know the *degrees of freedom of the numerator* (that's n_1-1, or one less than the sample size of the first group) and the *degrees of freedom of the denominator* (that's n_2-1, or one less than the sample size of the second group). Since I have 16 test scores in each group, that means my degrees of freedom for both numerator and denominator are 15.

I use the "Rejection Region" approach for this particular inference test. That means that I try and figure out the F values that lie outside the bounds of my confidence level. For example, if I want to determine where the P-Value would be less than 0.05 for a two-tailed test, I look up the F value for a confidence level of 0.025 (representing half the total tail area), and 15 degrees of freedom in both numerator and denominator like this:

```
> qf(0.975,15,15)
[1] 2.862093
```

Alternatively, if I wanted to determine where the P-Value would be less than 0.05 for a one-tailed test, I look up the F value for a confidence level of 0.05 (the entire tail area), and 15 degrees of freedom in both numerator and denominator like this:

```
> qf(0.95,15,15)
[1] 2.403447
```

Step 6: Is the P-Value < α? If So, Reject the Null

If the value that I calculated for F is *bigger* than these critical values, then my P-Value is definitely less than 0.05, so I reject the null hypothesis. As you can see, my calculated F of 1.004 is definitely smaller, and we can't reject the null. There is no evidence that the two variances are different.

Step 7: Compute Confidence Interval & Double Check with R

We can compute a confidence interval to double check our work. Remember that the confidence interval for two proportions is not symmetric like other confidence intervals, and has this form:

$$\frac{s_1^2}{s_2^2} F_{lower} \leq \frac{\sigma_1^2}{\sigma_2^2} \leq \frac{s_1^2}{s_2^2} F_{upper}$$

We already know that the ratio between variances is 1.004, so all we need to know are the upper and lower boundaries on the F distribution that swipe out the size of our confidence interval. Let's look up the F values for a 95% CI and plug them into the expression above:

```
> qf(0.975,df1=15,df2=15)  # UPPER
[1] 2.862093
> qf(0.025,df1=15,df2=15)  # LOWER
[1] 0.3493947
```

$$0.3504 \leq \frac{\sigma_1^2}{\sigma_2^2} \leq 2.873$$

Our confidence interval ranges from a lower bound of 0.3504 to an upper bound of 2.873. This is interpreted in the following way:

"We are 95% confident that the true ratio of variances between the groups is between 0.3504 and 2.873."

Notice how the value 1 is *indeed* inside this confidence interval? Since the value 1 appears in the confidence interval, this suggests that there's a possibility the variances are equal (because that would result in the ratio of the two variances being 1). This corroborates the result from our hypothesis test earlier.

As you may have imagined, it is very easy to perform this test in R with the built-in `var.test` function. Here's how you do it:

```
> group.1 <- scores[scores$textbook == "1",]$score
> group.3 <- scores[scores$textbook == "3",]$score
```

Here comes the *only tricky part:* you have to remember to <u>put the bigger variance on top</u>. After looking at the variances, we see that Group 3's is bigger, so that group gets the numerator position as we conduct the F test for two variances in R:

```
> var.test(group.3,group.1)

        F test to compare two variances

data:  group.3 and group.1
F = 1.0042, num df = 15, denom df = 15, P-Value = 0.9936
alternative hypothesis: true ratio of variances is not equal to 1
95 percent confidence interval:
 0.3508626 2.8741172
sample estimates:
ratio of variances
         1.004201
```

Notice that all of the numbers match up pretty well to what we had computed analytically. There may be some differences in the bounds of your confidence interval, primarily due to rounding and truncation errors.

Other Resources:

- Does your data violate the assumptions for the F test? Does it violate the assumptions, but *really not that much*, and you're wondering if you can run the test anyway? This resource provides advice for all circumstances: http://www.basic.northwestern.edu/statguidefiles/ftest_alts.html
- If you have more than two variances to compare, two common techniques are Bartlett's (http://www.itl.nist.gov/div898/handbook/eda/section3/eda357.htm) and Levene's Tests (http://www.itl.nist.gov/div898/handbook/eda/section3/eda35a.htm)
- If you have more than two variances to compare, here is a fantastic resource that describes the differences between all the options available to you: http://www.lexjansen.com/wuss/1997/WUSS97036.pdf

5.11 One Way Analysis of Variance (ANOVA)

Objective

The one-way analysis of variance (ANOVA) test checks to see if there is a difference between the values of one quantitative variable that you collect from *more than two groups*. It's like a three-or-more-sample t-test, and **it's particularly useful for analyzing data from experiments where you're evaluating changes in a response variable related to a particular treatment**. (An analysis of variance that explores the effects of *two treatments at the same time* is called a two-way ANOVA. We won't cover that in this chapter, other than to help you recognize the difference between the types of research questions that you can explore using each approach.)

The ANOVA test is very similar to the F test that compares two variances to one another, however, in ANOVA there is a special mechanism for boiling down all the variances in your dataset so that you have one to put in the numerator of the test statistic F, and another to put in the denominator of the test statistic.

Some examples of research questions where you might use ANOVA include:

- You need to select the best temperature for a manufacturing process to run. One of your concerns is that the temperature might influence the density of the finished product, so you want to evaluate the density of products that are produced when the process is set at five different temperatures. Does at least one of the processes yield a density that's different than the others? (A two-way ANOVA may explore the effects of five different temperatures *and* three different processing times.)

- A clinical trial is run to assess the impact of a new dietary supplement that aids stress and improves relaxation. Participants are randomly assigned to one of the treatment programs, where they receive a low, medium, or high dose of the supplement (or a placebo). Participants follow the assigned program for 12 weeks. The outcome of interest is stress reduction, defined as the difference in stress (on a scale of 1 to 100, with 100 being most stressed) measured at the start of the study (the baseline) and at the end of the study. (A two-way ANOVA might explore the effects of three different doses plus control, *and* gender.)

- You are a trainer or instructor for a certification program and you want to compare three different textbooks to see which one you should use. You randomly assign each of your students to a textbook, and you keep track of the scores they get on the last practice certification exam they take before they try the real thing. Is one of the textbooks more effective than the others? (A two-way ANOVA could explore the impact of each of the three textbooks *and* two different instructors.)

The last question will be our example for the ANOVA test. This is an interesting question because it's very practical: the instructor could just guess, or go by his or her gut feel. But with statistics, the textbook recommendation can be supported by data.

Our Process for Inference Testing

We'll use Dr. R's 7 Steps in this chapter:

Step 0: Check Your Assumptions

Step 1: Set Null and Alternative Hypotheses

Step 2: Choose α, the Level of Significance

Step 3: Calculate Test Statistic (T.S.)

Step 4: Draw a Picture

Step 5: Find the P-Value

Step 6: Draw Conclusion - Is the P-Value < α? If So, Reject the Null

Step 7: Compute Confidence Interval & Double Check with R

We will solve the ANOVA problem *analytically* (meaning, using the equations and doing the calculations by hand) and *also by using R* to do our calculations. If you are doing research, it's always good to solve the problem both ways to check your work! That way, you have a better chance of being correct. If you are writing a research paper to document your study, be sure to include *all* of Dr. R's 7 Steps in your results section.

Step 0: Check Your Assumptions

Before beginning any inference test, it's important to check and see if your data meets the assumptions and conditions for the test. If it doesn't, you either need to 1) explain why you're still doing the test in the limitations section of your study, 2) abandon the test entirely, or 3) choose a nonparametric alternative like the Kruskal-Wallis test. Here are the assumptions for one-way ANOVA:

1. **Random sample**: Was each of the items in your data set randomly selected from the population of all values? (For the textbooks vs. exam scores data, we're actually using a *convenience sample* because we're choosing the students and the data that were available. But we'll assume that this is sufficient for our purposes, and we'll continue with the test.)

2. **Observations are independent**: Do the values from one measurement influence the values in another measurement? For our example, we can assume that the students aren't cheating (after all, they are paying lots of money for this training program, and they all want to do well on the certification exam so they can get a better job). As a result, it's unlikely that any student's score will be affected by another student's score. Our observations are independent.

3. **Homogeneity of variances**: The variance *within* each of your treatment groups must be the same. That is, if you plot a histogram of your response variable for each of the treatment groups, you won't see heteroscedasticity (that megaphone-shaped pattern). Since ANOVA depends on sorting out where the different contributions to the variance come from (called "partitioning the variances"), and doing this across your entire dataset, it won't work if you *know* those variances are different. You can also perform Levene's test to double check.

4. **Response variable is normal or nearly normal**: If you plot all of your y-values on a histogram, do a QQ plot with them, or perform an Anderson-Darling or Shapiro-Wilk test, you should find that those values are normal or close to it.

5. **The sample size for each treatment group is the same**. (There are ways to do one-way ANOVA when this isn't the case, but the equations are slightly different, so we'll focus on the "equal group size" case here. When you're conducting an experiment, you probably have more control over your sample sizes anyway... so see if you can get them to be the same size.)

Our assumptions are met, so we can move forward with the ANOVA. If the assumptions are not met, you can choose to conduct a *nonparametric alternative* test. In the case of one-way ANOVA, the nonparametric alternative is the Kruskal-Wallis test which can be performed using the `kruskal.wallis` function in the base R package.

Step 1: Set Null and Alternative Hypotheses

The forms of the null and alternative hypotheses for the one-way ANOVA are:

H_0: $\mu_1 = \mu_2 = \mu_3 = \mu_4 = ...$

H_a: At least one of the group/treatment means is *different*

One-way ANOVA won't show you *which* one of those groups has a different mean... if will just tell you whether there is or is not a difference in there somewhere. To drill down on the results of a one-way ANOVA, you need to do a *post hoc* test like Fisher's LSD (not to be confused with the psychoactive substance) or Tukey's HSD. We'll show you how to do those later in the chapter.

(Why, you might ask, can't you just do a whole bunch of two sample t-tests? It's because of the out-of-control manner in which you start stacking up the potential to incur an error with each additional *related* two sample t-test that's part of your discovery process. If your alpha error, for false positives, is 0.05 for your first test - then your total alpha error for the first two tests will be *about* 0.10. Although it doesn't work exactly additively, you still end up incurring more potential for a false positive with each additional t-test. By choosing ANOVA as your methodology, you avoid this really unfortunate outcome.)

Step 2: Choose α, the Level of Significance

The level of significance α is often set to 0.05, indicating that we're willing to *incorrectly reject the null hypothesis* 1 out of every 20 times we collect a sample and run this test. Since we usually have about 100 students in our program each year, we're going to select a more stringent level of significance α of 0.01, indicating that we're only willing to generate a false positive - and say *yeah, one of these books is better than the others* - 1 in every 100 times. This is because 1) the **cost** of collecting new observations is substantial, in terms of time and effort (and recruitment and enrollment investments), and 2) the **risk** associated with drawing incorrect conclusions is moderate, particularly if the textbook is expensive and will result in a hardship for some students. There really are no significant **ethical considerations** for this problem, but the cost and risk definitely justify the more stringent alpha.

Step 3: Calculate Test Statistic (T.S.)

For ANOVA, because we are slicing and dicing *variances* within and between our groups, our test statistic will be a F. It's calculated by taking the *mean square error between the groups* and dividing by the *mean square error within the groups*. This can get kind of confusing, so we'll break it down piece by piece, in excruciating detail. A good way to do this is to introduce the ANOVA table for N (total) observations and k treatments (or groups). We're basically on a mission to **fill in all the blanks in this table**:

Source	SS	df	MS	F	Pr(F>F$_{critical}$)
Between	SSB	k-1	MSB = SSB/(k-1)	MSB/MSW	P-Value
Within	SSW	N-k	MSW = SSW/(N-k)		associated
Total	SST = SSB + SSW	N-1			with calc'd F(df1,df2)

(Note: The N is capital because we need to count up *all of the observations in all of our treatment groups*. Every single one. It's not just the sample size from one of our groups, it's the sample size of everybody all together.)

To understand the ANOVA table, it's important to recognize that there are two different kinds of comparisons you need to make:

- **"Between"** refers to the variances *comparing* Group 1 to Group 2, comparing Group 2 to Group 3, comparing Group 1 to Group 3, and so forth. Sometimes, this will be called "treatments".
- **"Within"** refers to the variances *inside* the groups. What's the variance of Group 1? What's the variance of Group 2? What's the variance of Group 3? Sometimes, you will see this called "Errors" or "Residuals" in the ANOVA table.

Once you compute SSB (sum of squares between the groups), SSW (sum of squares within the groups), and the SST (the sum of SSB and SSW), the remainder of the calculations are straightforward. (If you're looking in different textbooks or on the web, sometimes SSB is called SST, for "sum of squares between treatments". Sometimes SSW is called SSE, for "sum of squares of the errors" or SSR for "sum of squares of residuals".)

Let's load in our test data first, so we can practice on a real example. I have data about the three different textbooks, and the certification exam scores that people got after they used each of the textbooks, on GitHub. The data frame has two columns: the first contains the `score`, and the second column contains the `textbook` that the person used when they got that score (1, 2, or 3):

```
> scores <-
read.table("https://raw.githubusercontent.com/NicoleRadziwill/Data-for-R-
Examples/master/anova-textbooks.txt",header=TRUE)
```

I like to start with SST because to me, it's the easiest to calculate. Follow this recipe:

1. Take the difference between each data point and the grand mean (the mean of all the points in your dataset), and square it.

2. Add all those up. Now you have SST.

Here's how you do it in R, with your data already loaded. (If you `attach(scores)` first, you can drop the leading "`scores$`" from the variable names:)

```
> mean(scores$score)
[1] 85.64583
> dev.from.grand.mean <- (scores$score - mean(scores$score))^2
> dev.from.grand.mean
 [1]  58.4587674  13.2921007 178.3337674  13.2921007 135.6254340
 [6]  28.6671007  40.3754340  18.9587674   5.5421007   2.7087674
[11] 186.2087674   7.0004340   5.5421007   1.8337674 113.3337674
[16]  13.2921007   0.1254340 186.2087674   0.4171007  18.9587674
[21]  28.6671007  13.2921007   7.0004340  21.5837674  93.0421007
[26] 113.3337674  21.5837674  54.0837674   0.1254340 186.2087674
[31]   1.8337674  18.9587674  11.2504340  74.7504340   5.5421007
[36] 152.6254340  54.0837674 107.2087674   5.5421007  28.6671007
[41] 113.3337674   5.5421007  11.2504340  54.0837674  44.1671007
[46] 128.9171007 178.3337674  69.7921007
> sst <- sum(dev.from.grand.mean) # This is your SST!!!
> sst
[1] 2632.979
```

To calculate the SSB, follow this recipe:

1. Each one of the groups has a mean. That is, the group that used textbook 1 has a mean score, the group that used textbook 2 has a mean score, and the group that used textbook 3 *also* has a mean score. Find these group means.

2. Take the difference between the first group mean and the grand mean. Now square it. (You will end up with one of these values for each group.)

3. Now take that square and multiply it by the number of items in the group.

4. Now repeat Steps 2 and 3 for the rest of the groups.

5. Add all those up. Now you have SSB.

Here's how you do it in R, with your data already loaded. First, you find the group means, which you can access one by one using the [1], [2], or [3] notation tacked onto the end of group.means$x (the variable that contains those means):

```
> group.means <- aggregate(scores$score, by=list(scores$textbook), FUN=mean)
```

```
> group.means
  Group.1        x
1        1 84.1875
2        2 83.1250
3        3 89.6250
> group.means$x[1]
[1] 84.1875
```

Once you know the group means, you can calculate all the deviations between the group means and the grand means, and go through the squaring and summation process:

```
> group.dev.from.grand.mean <- ((group.means$x -
      mean(scores$score))^2)*16
> ssb <- sum(group.dev.from.grand.mean)
> ssb
[1] 389.0417  # This is our SSB!
```

Now we have SST and SSB, so it's easy to calculate SSW using (SST - SSB) = (2632.98 - 389.04) = 2243.94. However, we still don't have our test statistic, F. Remember... that's what sent us down this path in the first place! The next step on our path is for us to use SSB, SSW, and SST to calculate the **mean squares**: MSB and MSW. Fortunately, this is easy — using the formulas provided in the ANOVA table, and knowing that the total number of observations N is 48, and the total number of groups is 3, we can do this:

```
> msb <- ssb / 2 # The denominator is (# of groups - 1)
> ssw <- sst - ssb
> msw <- ssw / (48-3)
> msb
[1] 194.5208
> msw
[1] 49.8653
```

Finally, we can compute F! That's what we get when we take MSB and divide by MSW:

```
> msb/msw
[1] 3.900926
```

422

Congratulations! You have now computed your test statistic, F. F is for FINALLY.

Step 4: Draw a Picture

We need to find the area in the tail of the F-distribution to the *right* of that test statistic we just calculated. As you can see, it's *very, very small*... you almost can't see it! (Note: I used a hacked version of the `shadenorm` function called `shadef` to create the graph below. The code is dirty, so I'm just sharing my results with you:)

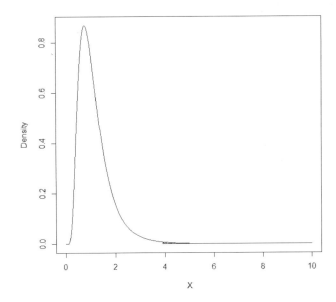

Step 5: Find the P-Value

The P-Value is determined by looking up the area under the F distribution in the tail to the right of our computed test statistic, $F = 3.9$. We can do this lookup in R. All we need to know is the *numerator degrees of freedom* (which is just the number of groups minus one) and the *denominator degrees of freedom* (which is the total number of observations N, minus the number of groups k). Here's how we look up the upper tail area for our example:

```
> 1-pf(3.9,2,45)
[1] 0.0274169
```

Step 6: Draw Conclusion - Is the P-Value < α? If So, Reject the Null

With a P-Value that tiny, the answer to our question "Is the P-Value less than α?" is bound to be YES, so we *reject* the null hypothesis. We have evidence to suggest that at least one of the group means is different than the others. ***But which one is different? We can't stop now... we need to know which one is different!***

Step 7: Compute Confidence Interval & Double Check with R

Fortunately, this problem can be resolved by running the ANOVA in R and doing a post hoc test of multiple comparisons – the post hoc test also generate and plot confidence intervals between each pair of factors, making it easy to spot significant differences.

First, let's run the ANOVA in R (which you'll see is *much* simpler than doing it by hand). Note that we have to convert the `textbook` column in the data frame to a factor. (The ANOVA will still work if `textbook` is not a factor data type, but the multiple comparisons test won't work without it.)

```
> boxplot(score~textbook, data=scores, main="Scores By Textbook Choice")
> model <- aov(score~textbook,data=scores)
> summary(model)
            Df Sum Sq Mean Sq F value Pr(>F)
textbook     2    389  194.52   3.901 0.0274 *
Residuals   45   2244   49.87
---
Signif. codes:  0 `***' 0.001 `**' 0.01 `*' 0.05 `.' 0.1 ` ' 1
```

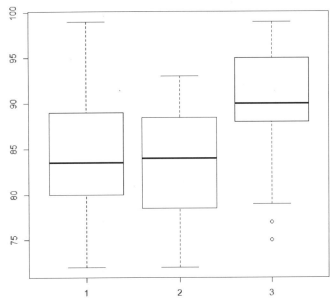

Scores By Textbook Choice

Notice that all of the values for SSB, SSW, SST, MSB, and MSW are exactly the same as the ones we calculated. Even the resultant P-Values are the same, confirming that we applied the equations in exactly the right ways. Now we can use this output to figure out *which one (or more) of the groups are different than the others.*

Tukey's HSD Post Hoc Test

Once you have the ANOVA model stored in the `model` variable, it's very easy to perform a post hoc test of multiple comparisons. Here's how you do it using Tukey's Honestly Significant Differences (HSD) test:

```
> TukeyHSD(model)
  Tukey multiple comparisons of means
    95% family-wise confidence level
```

```
Fit: aov(formula = score ~ textbook, data = a.data)
```

```
$textbook
        diff        lwr        upr      p adj
2-1 -1.0625  -7.1133656   4.988366  0.9052063
3-1  5.4375  -0.6133656  11.488366  0.0860076
3-2  6.5000   0.4491344  12.550866  0.0327321
```

The output is really straightforward: there's a significant difference between textbooks 3 and 2, a less significant difference between books 3 and 1, and a completely insignificant difference between books 2 and 1. If this was my class, I'd adopt book 3, but I'd take a good look at what the differences were between books 3 and 1 before I committed completely. You can also plot the confidence intervals using a confidence level of your choice. In this example, we can see that there's a significant difference between ratings for textbooks 3 and 2, but only at the 95% level, not the 99% level.

```
par(mfrow=c(1,2))
plot(TukeyHSD(model,conf.level=0.95))
plot(TukeyHSD(model,conf.level=0.99))
```

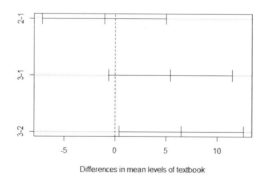

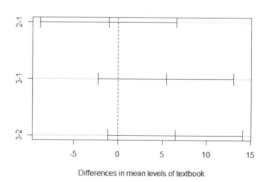

Other Resources:

- Want to see another ANOVA problem that's completely worked out, analytically, from the raw data? There is a great example here:
  http://web.missouri.edu/~dls6w4/Word/Stat%20Chapter%2012.pdf
- Here is a beautiful printout with computational formulas for ANOVA:
  http://www.ucs.louisiana.edu/~rmm2440/CompFormulasANOVA.pdf

SECTION 6: REGRESSION AND INFERENCES ON REGRESSION

- Creating and Using Simple Linear Models with Least Squares
- Multiple Regression for Many Independent Variables
- Inference Tests for Regression Coefficients
- ...and How to Interpret all those F's and t's

6.1 Simple Linear Regression

Objective

To develop a *linear model* to describe and assess the relationship between *two* continuous quantitative variables (where one is the independent variable, or predictor, and the other is the dependent variable, or response) using *simple linear least squares regression*. We can also develop a linear model to describe and assess the relationship between *multiple* continuous quantitative independent variables, and one quantitative response variable, using *multiple regression* which is explained in the next chapter.

Background

Simple linear regression helps us fit a linear model (that is, a *line*) to represent the relatiionship between two continuous quantitative variables. The general form of the linear equation is:

$$y = mx + b + \epsilon$$

where y is the dependent variable (the one you're trying to predict), m is the slope of the line, b is the intercept (or the point along the y-axis where the line crosses), and ϵ (epsilon) is the error term (or residual). Oftentimes, different variables are chosen to represent the slope, intercept, and other coefficients, and the model for simple linear regression sometimes looks like this:

$$y = \beta_0 + \beta_1 x + \epsilon$$

The basic idea is to find the equation of a line that lies somewhere within the field of the scatterplot to *minimize the sum of squares of the residuals*. What does that mean? Let's break it down:

- The **residuals** are the differences between the *actual* value of the dependent variable (or the y coordinate) and the *predicted* value of the dependent variable (the y value that you would get if you plugged a value for x into the equation). Data points above your line of best fit will have positive residuals. Data points below your line of best fit will have negative residuals. (The size of the residual will be the length of the line segment that you get if you start with your data point, and draw a *vertical line* between that point and the line of best fit.)

- We want to place the line so that we have a balance between the magnitudes of the positive residuals, and the magnitudes of the negative residuals. So we take the **squares of the residuals** to eliminate the problem caused by some being negative, and some being positive. Squaring any value, positive or negative, will result in a positive number. Coincidentally, this squared value also represents the *area* of the square that forms when you make one out of the residual (see p. 430 for a picture).

- If we had a perfect linear fit, all of the data points would lie on the line. This means that all of our residuals would be zero, the squares of our residuals would be zero, and when we add them all up, the sum of squares of residuals would also be zero. But real data rarely conforms to a model so perfectly.

- As a result, our goal using the least squares method to find a best fit line is to *minimize the area of all those squares that we can form* (or the **sum of squares of residuals**) from the little vertical lines that represent the residuals.

There are also some relationships between the variables in the simple linear regression model that we can use to *analytically* compute the equation of the best fit least squares line. First, we find a value for the slope (we'll put a hat on it since we're specifically referring to the slope generated by fitting a line to our sample data):

$$\hat{\beta}_1 = r_{xy} \frac{s_y}{s_x}$$

The slope is calculated by multiplying the correlation coefficient (r_{xy}) by the standard deviation of all the x-values (s_x), and then dividing by the standard deviation of all the y-values (s_y) in the dataset. Then, knowing that the regression line will *always* pass through the average of all the x's and average of all the y's, we can find the intercept:

$$\hat{\beta}_0 = \overline{y} - \hat{\beta}_1\overline{x}$$

The picture below illustrates the principle of least squares. The data set (round dots) is identical between the chart on the left, and the chart on the right. However, the line that has been fitted to the data on the left (even though it goes through two of the round dots almost exactly) leaves huge negative residuals on the other three points. The line that has been fitted to the data on right is a better fit. Why? Because there are some positive residuals and some negative residuals, but more importantly, the sum of squares of residuals (that is, the total area in the squares) is smaller.

The goal of least squares regression is to place a line <u>so that the total area of all these squares is as small as possible:</u> to minimize the "sum of squares" of the residuals.

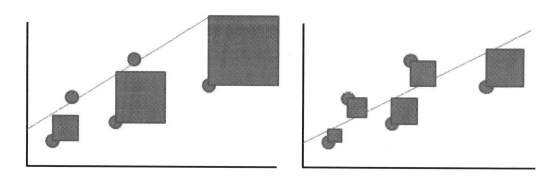

Simple Linear Regression

For the rest of the examples in this chapter, I'm using the data frame of daily weather data reported throughout 2013 from the Shenandoah Valley Airport (SHD) near where I live in Harrisonburg, Virginia. Let's load the data directly from my repository on GitHub:

```
shd.wx <- read.csv("https://raw.githubusercontent.com/NicoleRadziwill/Data-for-R-Examples/master/kshd-2013.txt",header=TRUE)
```

Each column contains one of my variables, and there are 365 rows, one for each day of the year in 2013. They are arranged in order, with January 1st (20130101) on the 1st row, and December 31st (20131231) on the last row.

```
> head(shd.wx)
  YEARMODA TEMP DEWP   STP VISIB WDSP MXSPD  MAX  MIN PRCP
1 20130101 43.3 25.8 971.2  10.0  5.4   8.9 47.8 37.8    0
2 20130102 38.5 29.4 973.3  10.0  1.5   5.1 42.3 32.0    0
3 20130103 32.0 19.2 978.0  10.0  1.4   7.0 42.6 21.9    0
4 20130104 34.6 17.4 978.5  10.0  3.6   8.9 45.9 26.2    0
5 20130105 36.0 17.9 981.0  10.0  3.4   8.0 48.2 25.9    0
6 20130106 40.6 26.9 976.8   9.9  3.8   9.9 47.1 31.1   NA
7 20130106 38.6 17.5 976.8   9.9  3.1   5.9 47.1 40.1   NA
```

I want to 1) create a scatterplot of dewpoint versus temperature, 2) find a line of best fit and also plot it on the scatterplot, 3) plot the residuals so I can examine them to make sure a linear fit is appropriate, and finally 4) determine the equation for that best fit line. Furthermore, 5) I want to calculate the **coefficient of determination**, R^2, which will tell me **what proportion of the variability in the data is explained by the model**. Before we ask R to find the linear least squares regression line, let's first compute it analytically using the expressions above. We will still use R to do the calculations:

```
> slope <- cor(wx$DEWP,wx$TEMP) * ( sd(wx$DEWP)/sd(wx$TEMP) )
> slope
[1] 1.107423
> intercept <- mean(wx$DEWP) - (slope * mean(wx$TEMP))
> intercept
[1] -18.05264
```

By plugging these values back into the linear model, we find that the line of best fit *should* be **y = 1.107x - 18.05**. Let's check in R, starting with Steps 1 and 2:

```
> fit <- lm(shd.wx$DEWP ~ shd.wx$TEMP)
> residuals <- resid(fit)
> par(mfrow=c(1,2))
> plot(shd.wx$TEMP,shd.wx$DEWP,main="Dewpoint vs. Temperature",
```

```
+ xlab="Temperature (deg F)",ylab="Dewpoint (deg F)")
> abline(fit)
> plot(shd.wx$TEMP,residuals,main="Residuals")
> abline(h=0)
```

The first line actually performs the linear regression. Using the `lm` command, which stands for "linear model," we create a new variable called `fit`, and fit `shd.wx$DEWP` (our y values) by `shd.wx$TEMP` (our x values). That squiggly line in between the variables is read as "*by*" - so when you read that line of code aloud, you would say "create a variable `fit` that contains *all of the information R has computed about the equation of the best fit line, and how it relates to all of the data points*, constructing a linear model of dewpoint *by* temperature."

The first argument to `lm` is the dependent variable (whatever is on your y axis); the second argument to `lm` is the independent variable (on your x axis). The third line of code sets the plot area so that it has one row and two columns. The fourth and fifth lines of code describe what will be contained in the first column of our plot area: first, a scatterplot, and then, an "A-B line" (which is R parlance for "straight line") that contains the equation of your best fit. You don't even need to know the equation of your line of best fit for R to plot it from your `fit` object. The sixth line plots the residuals on the y-axis, using the original values you had for your independent variables (the x's) on the x-axis.

Finally, the seventh line plots another "A-B line" (a straight line) that is horizontal and at zero (`h=0`). The final results are:

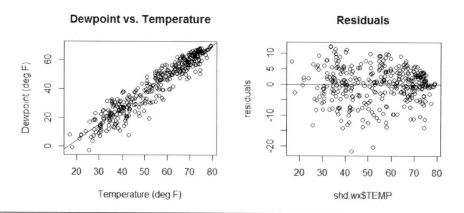

Analyzing the Residuals

Now we can move to Step 3, which is to **examine the plot of residuals** to make sure a linear model is appropriate. There are a couple things we should check for:

- There should be about as many residuals *above* the zero line as there are *below* the zero line. This tells us that there's a balance between the data points that lie above the line of best fit, and the data points that lie below the line. In other words, our best fit line is *about in the middle of all our data points.*

- There should be no pattern in our residuals... they should appear to be randomly scattered above and below the line of best fit for all values of x. If the pattern of residuals looks like a smiley face or a frowny face, *this is bad.* (Even if the residuals appear to be smiling.) A smiley face indicates that we have consistently positive residuals for the highest and lowest values of x, whereas a frowny face indicates that we have consistently negative residuals for the highest and lowest values of x.

- If the residuals plot looks like a scatterplot with strong positive correlation or strong negative correlation, then our linear fit has a *bias*. We are consistently underpredicting or overpredicting at the lowest and highest x's in our dataset. A linear model may not be appropriate.

- If the residuals are close together on the left side of the plot, and farther apart on the right (so it looks like a megaphone with the mouthpiece on the left), OR reversed (so that the plot looks like a megaphone with the mouthpiece on the right), OR if the residuals plot looks like a bow tie, then the variance of the error is not constant across all x's in the data set. This is called *heteroscedasticity*, and it indicates that you've used an inappropriate linear model. Instead of using your x's to predict y, you can *transform* your data and try to predict the logarithm of y from your x values, for example.

A residuals plot that has a pattern in it suggests a *lack of independence* or, even more significantly, *inappropriateness of the linear model.*

It's not the end of the world, though. There are plenty of nonlinear models (including spline fits) that may be much better, or you can *transform* the data and try the linear model again. You just shouldn't use your linear model to explain the variability within your data set.

Finally, we move to Step 4, which is to **determine the equation for the line of best fit**. This information is all contained within the `fit` object, so the first thing we do is ask for a summary by calling `summary(fit)`:

```
> summary(fit)

Call:
lm(formula = shd.wx$DEWP ~ shd.wx$TEMP)

Residuals:
     Min       1Q   Median       3Q      Max
-21.7451  -2.9158   0.5821   3.7044  12.2540

Coefficients:
             Estimate Std. Error t value Pr(>|t|)
(Intercept) -18.05264    1.05973  -17.04   <2e-16 ***
shd.wx$TEMP   1.10742    0.01886   58.70   <2e-16 ***
---
Signif. codes:  0 '***' 0.001 '**' 0.01 '*' 0.05 '.' 0.1 ' ' 1

Residual standard error: 5.603 on 363 degrees of freedom
Multiple R-squared:  0.9047,    Adjusted R-squared:  0.9044
F-statistic:  3446 on 1 and 363 DF,  P-Value: < 2.2e-16
```

To determine our linear model, all we need to do is replace the appropriate values of slope and intercept from the `lm` output above into our equation for the line. We find the slope by looking in the "Coefficients" section, in the row containing the independent variable on our x-axis, under the "Estimate" column. Because I tend to round to two or three decimal places, I'll read the slope as 1.107. Similarly, to find the y-intercept, look in the "Coefficients" section, in the row containing the word "Intercept", under the "Estimate" column. The intercept is -18.053. This means the equation for our line of best fit is **y = 1.107x - 18.053**. (This matches the equation we came up with analytically.)

Also, the point whose coordinates are the average value of all your x's and the average value of all your y's **will always be a point on the line of best fit.** Sometimes this can be a useful trick to double check that you have generated an accurate equation.

Coefficient of Determination, R^2

From the `summary` command, we can also find out *how good our linear fit is* by examining the coefficient of determination, which is the value reported next to "`Multiple R-squared`" at the bottom of the output. This value tells us **the proportion of the variability in our data that is explained by the model.** For the linear model that we generated to predict our dependent variable (dewpoint) from the independent variable (temperature), 0.9047 means that 90.47% of the variability is explained by our model! This is very good. It also tells us that 9.53% of the variability is contained within the residuals (or 100% - 90.47%).

R^2 = the proportion of variability in our data that is explained by the linear fit

$1 - R^2$ = the proportion of variability that is expressed by the residuals

The coefficient of determination is also related to the correlation coefficient, r. Recall that the correlation coefficient gives us a sense of the *scatteredness* of our data. When we square the correlation coefficient, we get the coefficient of determination. Because r can vary from -1 (perfect negative correlation) to +1 (perfect positive correlation), our R^2 will always be positive, and will always be somewhere from zero to 1 (thus enabling us to explain what proportion of the variability in our data, from 0% to 100%, is explained by the model).

We can double check this relationship using our temperature and dewpoint data in R:

```
> cor(shd.wx$DEWP,shd.wx$TEMP)
[1] 0.9511601
> .95116*.95116
[1] 0.9047053
```

The correlation coefficient, r, is computed using the `cor` function which gives us 0.9512. The coefficient of determination R^2 is computed by multiplying r by r, which gives us 0.9047 - the same value reported by the R software as the proportion of variability that is explained by the model. We can also access R^2 directly like this:

```
> summary(fit)$r.squared
[1] 0.9047055
```

You may also have noticed that there is another value in the R `summary` of our `fit` called "Adjusted R-squared." This value should be nearly identical to the "Multiple R-squared" value whenever you are using only one independent variable to predict one dependent variable. If you are doing multiple linear regression, which means you are using more than one independent variable to predict a dependent variable, the adjusted R^2 takes into account that some of the model's ability to explain the variability in the data may just be due to chance... because the more independent variables you have, the more likely you are to predict more accurately just because you have a lot of variables to work with (called "overfitting").

When we have many independent variables, R^2 will be overestimated. In those cases, we should choose the adjusted R^2 to explain what proportion of the variability in our data is explained by the model we have generated.

Plots that Tell Us More About Our Regression Model

You can also pass your linear model to the plot command, which will provide four diagnostic plots that help you evaluate the goodness of your linear model. If you just execute plot(fit), R will prompt you to hit the enter key to see each of the four plots in turn. I like to reconfigure my plot area first so that they all show up on the same graphic screen:

```
> par(mfrow=c(2,2))
> plot(fit)
```

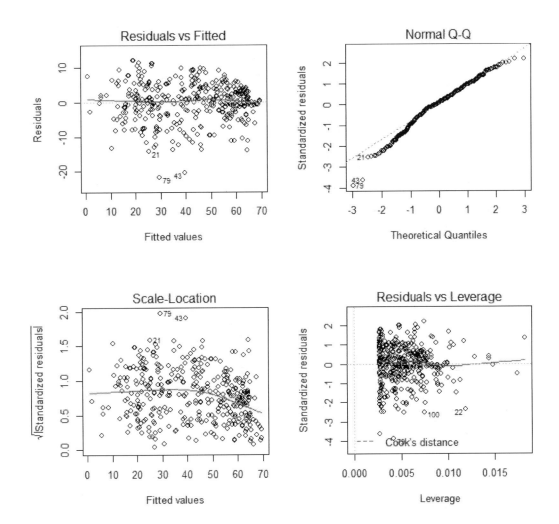

These plots are extremely helpful. They can tell us whether a linear model is appropriate, in large part by providing a useful way to help us analyze our residuals. From top left, to top right, to bottom left, to bottom right, here are the questions these charts help us to answer:

- Are the residuals randomly scattered around zero? If a linear model is appropriate, we definitely want the residuals scattered randomly around zero, and we don't want to see any patterns in this plot. S-curves, smiley faces, and any other pattern that looks like a pattern is *bad*, and indicates that a linear model may not be appropriate.

- In the chart on the top right: Are the residuals normally distributed? If they are, all of our observations will show up along the diagonal line. If they aren't, then a linear model may not be the most appropriate.

- On the bottom left, we get to ask the question: Is the variance pretty much consistent across the entire range of my x values? If not, then we have a case of *heteroscedasticity*, which is bad, and means that a linear model may not be appropriate for our data.

- On the bottom right, we ask: Are there any *influential points* in the dataset that might overwhelmingly influence the characteristics of the regression line? In the example above, it looks like points #100 and #22 are significant, and we should examine them to see if they tell us anything interesting or noteworthy about the data. (Sometimes, this chart has called out data points that were inaccurately entered into the dataset, so I find this one really useful in my analysis.)

Prediction and Extrapolation

Best fit lines are often used to predict values of y for a given value of x. But you have to be careful: don't try to predict values of y for values of x that are *well outside the bounds of the original data!* That's called extrapolation, and in general, extrapolation is very bad. Here's a silly and unreasonable example that will show you why.

Consider that we have a simple data set where x is a particular woman's age, and y is the total number of children she had at that particular age, whenever a new boy or girl (or twins) was born. Using `lm`, we can generate a new fit to predict the number of kids by (~) age. We can generate a scatterplot, and place the line of best fit on the graph:

```
age <- c(21,24,25,32)
number.of.kids <- c(1,2,4,5)
new.fit <- lm(number.of.kids ~ age)
```

```
plot(age,number.of.kids,xlim=c(20,50),ylim=c(0,15),
        main="Number of Kids by Age at Birth")
abline(new.fit)
```

The scatterplot, line of best fit, and summary of the details of the fit are provided on the next page. Notice that the linear model is pretty good: the coefficient of determination, R2, tells us that 81.38% of the variability in the data is explained by the model! Also notice that the equation of our best fit line can be read from the summary output, and it is y = 0.3538x - 6.0231. Given an age of the mother x, we can use this equation to predict how many children she should have at any time in her life!

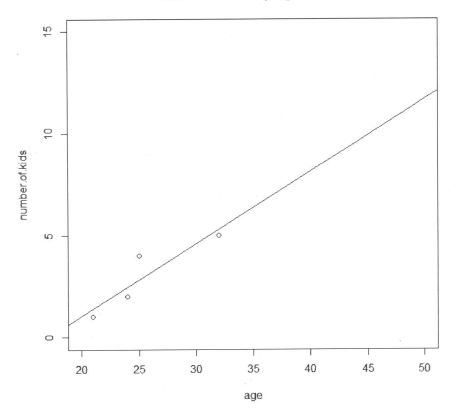

```
> summary(new.fit)

Call:
lm(formula = number.of.kids ~ age)

Residuals:
      1       2       3       4
-0.4077 -0.4692  1.1769 -0.3000

Coefficients:
            Estimate Std. Error t value Pr(>|t|)
(Intercept)  -6.0231     3.0893  -1.950   0.1905
age           0.3538     0.1197   2.957   0.0979 .
---
Signif. codes:  0 '***' 0.001 '**' 0.01 '*' 0.05 '.' 0.1 ' ' 1

Residual standard error: 0.9648 on 2 degrees of freedom
Multiple R-squared:  0.8138,    Adjusted R-squared:  0.7208
F-statistic: 8.744 on 1 and 2 DF,  P-Value: 0.09787
```

So let's do that. How many children would she have by age 50?

$$y = 0.3538x - 6.0231$$

$$y = (0.3538)(50) - 6.0231 = 11.6669$$

She should have almost 12 children by the time she's 50! It's clear to see that this is a ridiculous prediction, because there's no guarantee that she will continue having children at the rate she did in her 20's and 30's. Furthermore, it's physically impossible for women to continue having children past a certain age. This is considered extrapolating because we've gone *beyond the bounds of the original independent variable* - we have no data beyond age 32 - and yet we have attempted to make an out-of-bounds prediction using the linear equation that characterizes our best fit.

In conclusion, the bottom line on *extrapolation* in linear regression is... don't do it!

Other Resources:

- Here is an easy example of simple linear regression to predict height versus age in R: http://msenux.redwoods.edu/math/R/regression.php
- There is a great article on how to examine plots of residuals on R Bloggers at: http://www.r-bloggers.com/model-validation-interpreting-residual-plots/
- If you want to find out more about heteroscedasticity, the best explanation I've found is at https://www3.nd.edu/~rwilliam/stats2/l25.pdf.
- Here is a great discussion about R^2 versus the adjusted R^2 that explains both theory and how it works in R: http://thestatsgeek.com/2013/10/28/r-squared-and-adjusted-r-squared/

6.2 Multiple Linear Regression

Objective

Simple linear regression results in a model (equation) that can be used to predict one quantitative dependent (output) variable based on one quantitative independent (input) variable. As an extension of simple linear regression, multiple regression produces a model (equation) that can be used to **_predict one_** quantitative dependent (output) variable **_from two or more_** quantitative independent (input) variables. There are multiple (You can also use multiple regression if your two or more predictors are a mix of categorical and quantitative variables, but you will have to recode your categorical variables as "dummy variables" first. We will not be covering that method here but you can Google it.)

Background

The general form of the linear equation for our multiple linear regression case, with many independent variables (predictors) and one dependent variable (response), is:

$$y - \alpha + \sum_k \beta_k x_k + \epsilon$$

The total number of independent variables, or predictors, is k. Each one of those independent variables is an x. So this equation reads "we can predict y by adding together the intercept α (which is where the line crosses the y-axis), the sum of each slope-plus-independent-variable (βx) combinations for all k of our independent variables, and the error term (or residual) ϵ. We can expand this equation to actually see each of the terms for each of our k independent variables:

$$y = \alpha + \beta_1 x_1 + \beta_2 x_2 + \beta_3 x_3 + \ldots + \beta_k x_k + \epsilon$$

The goal of multiple linear regression is to model the relationship between independent variables (the predictors) and the dependent variable (the response). To do this analytically, you have to set up a system of simultaneous linear equations called the *normal equations* and solve for each of your regression coefficients. Then, you plug the solutions for the regression coefficients back into the equation for the line above. This can be a complex process, particularly if you have a large amount of data. As a result, we won't solve the normal equations analytically in this chapter, we'll just construct the multiple regression model in R.

For the rest of the examples in this chapter, I'm using the data frame of daily weather data reported throughout 2013 from the Shenandoah Valley Airport (SHD) near where I live in Harrisonburg, Virginia. Let's load the data directly from my repository on GitHub:

```
wx <-
read.csv("https://raw.githubusercontent.com/NicoleRadziwill/Data-for-
R-Examples/master/kshd-2013.txt",header=TRUE)
```

Now examine the header of the data to make sure it imported properly:

```
> head(wx)
  YEARMODA TEMP DEWP   STP VISIB WDSP MXSPD  MAX  MIN PRCP
1 20130101 43.3 25.8 971.2  10.0  5.4   8.9 47.8 37.8    0
2 20130102 38.5 29.4 973.3  10.0  1.5   5.1 42.3 32.0    0
3 20130103 32.0 19.2 978.0  10.0  1.4   7.0 42.6 21.9    0
4 20130104 34.6 17.4 978.5  10.0  3.6   8.9 45.9 26.2    0
5 20130105 36.0 17.9 981.0  10.0  3.4   8.0 48.2 25.9    0
6 20130106 40.6 26.9 976.8   9.9  3.8   9.9 47.1 31.1   NA
```

In the chapter on simple linear regression, we created a linear model to predict dewpoint (the dependent variable, or *response*, on the y-axis) from the average daily temperature (the independent variable, or predictor, on the x-axis). In this chapter, we will use *all* of the other variables (except the date) to predict the dewpoint.

Next, we'll eliminate the predictor variables one by one, until we're left with the minimum number of predictors that still effectively represent the variability in our dependent variable, dewpoint. With each elimination, we'll do a hypothesis test to see if the model is significantly different *without* the extra predictor variable. If it's not different, that means *we don't need that extra predictor, and we can eliminate it from the analysis.*

Performing the Multiple Regression in R

Now that the data is loaded, we can ask R to generate the first linear fit we'll try by calling the `lm` function (which stands for "linear model"). We want to predict the dewpoint temperature (`wx$DEWP`) by (~) the independent variables which are all located to the right of the tilde (~) sign, separated by plus (+) signs. Then, we ask for a `summary` of the linear fit, which will tell us more about the coefficients and how appropriate they are as predictors:

```
> fit1 <- lm(wx$DEWP ~ wx$TEMP + wx$VISIB + wx$WDSP + wx$MAX + wx$MIN +
wx$PRCP, data=wx)
> summary(fit)

Call:
lm(formula = wx$DEWP ~ wx$TEMP + wx$VISIB + wx$WDSP + wx$MAX +
    wx$MIN + wx$PRCP, data = wx)

Residuals:
     Min      1Q   Median      3Q     Max
-15.9742 -2.2366   0.1597  2.6872 11.0056

Coefficients:
            Estimate Std. Error t value Pr(>|t|)
(Intercept)  5.35717    1.93734   2.765 0.006021 **
wx$TEMP      0.88901    0.10993   8.087 1.30e-14 ***
wx$VISIB    -1.47676    0.18363  -8.042 1.76e-14 ***
wx$WDSP     -0.97402    0.12009  -8.111 1.10e-14 ***
wx$MAX      -0.13942    0.06423  -2.171 0.030706 *
wx$MIN       0.32946    0.06281   5.246 2.85e-07 ***
wx$PRCP      3.42481    0.88755   3.859 0.000138 ***
---
Signif. codes:  0 '***' 0.001 '**' 0.01 '*' 0.05 '.' 0.1 ' ' 1

Residual standard error: 3.953 on 318 degrees of freedom
  (40 observations deleted due to missingness)
Multiple R-squared: 0.9514,   Adjusted R-squared: 0.9505
F-statistic:  1037 on 6 and 318 DF,  P-Value: < 2.2e-16
```

Because the sampling distributions of the coefficients are t-distributions, there are t-tests performed for each of the model coefficients. What stands out about this model is that MANY of the predictor variables are significant (denoted by $***$ in the rightmost column). For most collections of data that you seek to find a linear model to represent, you won't see that many significant predictors. The next step is to reduce the number of predictors to find the simplest model that describes the variability in your data. Let's eliminate the maximum daily temperature (wx$MAX) and try again:

```
> fit2 <- lm(wx$DEWP ~ wx$TEMP + wx$VISIB + wx$WDSP + wx$MIN + wx$PRCP,
data=wx)
> summary(fit2)

Call:
lm(formula = wx$DEWP ~ wx$TEMP + wx$VISIB + wx$WDSP + wx$MIN +
    wx$PRCP, data = wx)

Residuals:
    Min      1Q   Median      3Q     Max
-15.6357 -2.3820   0.0971  2.4535  12.2644

Coefficients:
            Estimate Std. Error t value Pr(>|t|)
(Intercept)  3.78701    1.80764   2.095    0.037 *
wx$TEMP      0.67884    0.05235  12.967  < 2e-16 ***
wx$VISIB    -1.46280    0.18458  -7.925 3.85e-14 ***
wx$WDSP     -0.91712    0.11787  -7.781 1.01e-13 ***
wx$MIN       0.40621    0.05221   7.781 1.01e-13 ***
wx$PRCP      3.52183    0.89157   3.950 9.62e-05 ***
---
Signif. codes:  0 '***' 0.001 '**' 0.01 '*' 0.05 '.' 0.1 ' ' 1

Residual standard error: 3.976 on 319 degrees of freedom
  (40 observations deleted due to missingness)
Multiple R-squared:  0.9507,   Adjusted R-squared:  0.9499
F-statistic:  1230 on 5 and 319 DF,   P-Value: < 2.2e-16
```

This output shows us that each of the remaining predictors is still very significant (***) and the adjusted R^2, which tells us the proportion of variability in the data that is accounted for by the model, is still high (at 94.99%). This seems to be a good linear model for predicting the dewpoint temperature, and can be written by taking each `Estimate` and placing those values into the linear equation:

$$y = 3.787 + 0.679(temp) - 1.463(visib) - 0.917(wdsp) + 0.406(min) + 3.522(prcp)$$

Which Model is Better? Using ANOVA to Decide

But there's a problem: we have two comparable models to choose from (based on the adjusted R2), and would really like to know if `fit1` (with 6 predictors) is better than `fit2` (with 5 predictors). To make this determination, we can run an analysis of variance *between* the models:

```
> anova(fit1,fit2)
Analysis of Variance Table

Model 1: wx$DEWP ~ wx$TEMP + wx$VISIB + wx$WDSP + wx$MAX + wx$MIN + wx$PRCP
Model 2: wx$DEWP ~ wx$TEMP + wx$VISIB + wx$WDSP + wx$MIN + wx$PRCP
  Res.Df    RSS Df Sum of Sq      F  Pr(>F)
1    318 4969.6
2    319 5043.3 -1   -73.626 4.7112 0.03071 *
---
Signif. codes:  0 '***' 0.001 '**' 0.01 '*' 0.05 '.' 0.1 ' ' 1
```

Hypothesis Tests Performed in Multiple Regression

You will notice that in the output from the regression model, there are values for the test statistic t computed for each one of the model coefficients. However, there is also an F-statistic reported, along with a P-Value for that critical value of F. What's the difference?

- The F test describes the joint explanatory power of the regression model. It tells you whether your entire combination of predictors is significant.

- The t tests tell you the power of each predictor as an explanatory variable. If a predictor is not significant, you should consider dropping it from your model.

- If some of your t's *are* significant, it is unusual for F to *not* be significant. This makes sense: if one of your predictors seems noteworthy as a predictor, shouldn't your whole model be significant too?

For the F test, the null hypothesis is that *all of the coefficients of the linear model are zero.* That is, none of the predictor variables are important (because if they were, you'd want to multiply them by *something* - not a zero - so that they factor into your prediction). The alternative hypothesis is that one or more of the coefficients is *not* zero, meaning they are indeed important. As a result, we WANT to reject the null for the F test... because that means our model has some predictive value. How is F calculated? Like this:

$$F = \frac{Model\ SS/Model\ df}{Residual\ SS/Residual\ df}$$

"Model SS" is the total model sum of squares, and "Model df" is the total model degrees of freedom. "Residual SS" is the sum of squares of the residuals, and "Residual df" is the degrees of freedom of the residuals. You can verify the calculation of F in summary(fit) by using the information below. "Model SS" is what you get when you add up everything in the "Sum Sq" column, except for the bottom line (97270). "Model df" is the sum from the Df column, without the Residuals (6). "Residual SS" is 4970, and "Residual df" is 318, meaning F should be (97270/6)÷(4970/318) = 1037 (which it is, as per the earlier output).

```
> anova(fit)
Analysis of Variance Table

Response: wx$DEWP
             Df  Sum Sq Mean Sq  F value    Pr(>F)
wx$TEMP       1   91297   91297 5841.953 < 2.2e-16 ***
wx$VISIB      1    4047    4047  258.986 < 2.2e-16 ***
wx$WDSP       1     441     441   28.245 2.015e-07 ***
wx$MAX        1     741     741   47.441 3.041e-11 ***
wx$MIN        1     511     511   32.689 2.493e-08 ***
wx$PRCP       1     233     233   14.890  0.000138 ***
Residuals   318    4970      16
---
Signif. codes:  0 `***' 0.001 `**' 0.01 `*' 0.05 `.' 0.1 ` ' 1
```

How Good is the Model? Assessing R^2

For multiple predictors, R^2 is called the *coefficient of multiple determination*. It expresses what portion of the variability in the dependent variable is explained by the predictors. The adjusted R^2 is always smaller than multiple R^2. Because multiple R^2 is *biased*, the adjusted R^2 seeks to compensate for the estimate variability based on how many variables and how many observations are involved. The adjusted R^2 is useful because it lets you compare the explanatory power of different models with a *different number of predictors*. The multiple R^2 won't let you do that, because it doesn't consider how many predictors you are using.

Overfitting

Beware of **overfitting**! That's what happens when you use *too many predictors* to generate an explanatory model for one response variable. It's the "connect the dots" problem: with enough predictors, you could conceivably generate a linear model that passed through *all* of the data points. And this would be *great!* 100% of the variability in your data would be explained by the model. But you would have perfectly modeled random variability... rather than finding a real relationship between the variables. Think about what would happen if you used that "perfect" model with an R^2 of 100% to make predictions about a response variable, given a certain combination of values for predictors? Because you had captured all the random variation in your *sample*, you wouldn't effectively be characterizing the variability in the *population*. You would have overfit the model based on the limited information in your sample... making it perfect for right now, but woefully inadequate for any new data from the population.

Other Resources:

- This online book has extensive information about both simple and linear regression in R, with examples from the Hubble Space Telescope: http://cran.r-project.org/web/packages/HSAUR2/vignettes/Ch_multiple_linear_regression.pdf

6.3 Hypothesis Tests of Regression Coefficients

Objective

When you fit a linear model to a collection of (x, y) points where x and y are both continuous quantitative variables, it can be important to figure out *whether any of your regression coefficients are significant*. Why? Because you're generating a model from a *sample,* when in reality, you're trying to figure out the relationships between the variables in a *population.* If certain regression coefficients are *not* significant, then you should drop those terms in your linear equation... they are just not that important as predictors. In general, it's best to construct models that have as few predictors as possible. That way, you can characterize the variation of a whole lot of response variables (y's) more effectively.

To test whether a particular independent variable is a significant predictor, you want to make sure the regression coefficient (or slope) associated with it is *not* zero. Why? Remember that each slope (β_i) is paired with one independent variable (x_i). If the slope is zero, that means that no matter how much x changes, there won't be any change in y. You can make x infinitely large *and it still won't impact the corresponding value of y.* It's just not an important predictor:

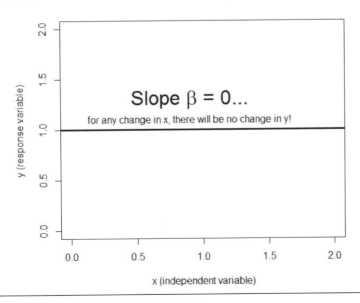

Here is the R code that produced the chart above:

```
> plot(1,1,xlim=c(0,2),ylim=c(0,2),col="white",xlab="x (independent
variable)",ylab="y (response variable)")
> abline(h=1,lwd=3)
> text(0.9,1.3,expression(paste("Slope ", beta, " = 0...")),cex=2)
> text(0.9,1.1,"for any change in x, there will be no change in y!")
```

This chapter shows you how to do hypothesis tests on each of the coefficients in a linear model, as well as for the y-intercept of the model. (From what I've discovered in practice, the tests on the slopes are far more important.) This will work for both simple linear regression and multiple regression... the only difference is *how many* coefficients you are evaluating.

Our Process for Inference Testing

We'll use Dr. R's 7 Steps in this chapter:

> **Step 0**: Check Your Assumptions
> **Step 1**: Set Null and Alternative Hypotheses
> **Step 2**: Choose α, the Level of Significance
> **Step 3**: Calculate Test Statistic (T.S.)
> **Step 4**: Draw a Picture
> **Step 5**: Find the P-Value
> **Step 6**: Draw Conclusion - Is the P-Value < α? If So, Reject the Null
> **Step 7**: Compute Confidence Interval & Double Check with R

We will solve the regression coefficients hypothesis testing problem *analytically* (meaning, using the equations and doing the calculations by hand) and *also by using R* to do our calculations. If you are doing research, it's always good to solve the problem both ways to check your work! That way, you have a better chance of being correct. If you are writing a research paper to document your study, be sure to include *all* of Dr. R's 7 Steps in your results section.

Step 0: Check Your Assumptions

Before beginning an inference test for regression, it's important to check and see if your data meets the assumptions and conditions for the test. If it doesn't, you either need to 1) explain why you're still doing the test in your limitations section 2) abandon the test entirely, 3) *transform your data* (e.g. take logarithms) so that you can perform the regression. Here are the essential assumptions:

1. **Observations are independent**: Do the values from one measurement influence the values in another measurement? If so, then it doesn't make sense to try and fit a linear model to your data to determine the relationship between the variables. For example, data that is collected over time can be autocorrelated, meaning that the observations will not be independent.

2. **Error terms associated with each observation are independent**: Do the errors (or residuals) associated with one measurement influence the values in another measurement? If so, then a linear regression is not appropriate.

3. **Relationship between the variables is linear**: This might seem obvious, but to fit a linear model, the underlying relationship between your variables must be linear. Fortunately, there are ways to find out if the relationship is not really linear, for example if a pattern appears in the plot of your residuals.

4. **The values for y vary normally around the mean of y**: Imagine this: you have a particular independent variable x, and you want to find out a corresponding response y, given that you know a relationship between the two (your linear model). The real values for those y's you should get should be normally distributed around your mean response, y-bar.

5. **Homoscedasticity**: The variance of y-values for any x-value should be *about the same* as the variance of y-values for any other x-values. (If you see that the variance changes, and that it's different in one portion of your x's than another, this is called heteroscedasticity. And it's bad for linear models.) There are two ways to check this: first, you could look at the scatterplot. If it looks like a megaphone, opening up to

either the right or the left, then your data is heteroscedastic. Second, you can try the R command `ncvTest` (non-constant variance test) which you apply on your fit, like this: `ncvTest(fit)`.

If your assumptions check out, which you can also verify by using the `gvlma` function in the `gvlma` package (which does all the work for you), then move forward with your regression. We will spend most of the time in this chapter reviewing the hypothesis tests on regression coefficients (slopes), but will quickly review the test for the intercept at the end.

For this example, we will use the Shenandoah Regional Airport (SHD) weather data for 2013. There are 365 observations, one for each day in the year. You can load it directly from my GitHub repository like this:

```
>  wx  <-  read.table("https://raw.githubusercontent.com/NicoleRadziwill/Data-
for-R-Examples/master/kshd-2013.txt",header=TRUE)
> head(wx)
   YEARMODA TEMP DEWP    STP VISIB WDSP MXSPD   MAX   MIN PRCP
1  20130101 43.3 25.8  971.2  10.0  5.4   8.9  47.8  37.8    0
2  20130102 38.5 29.4  973.3  10.0  1.5   5.1  42.3  32.0    0
3  20130103 32.0 19.2  978.0  10.0  1.4   7.0  42.6  21.9    0
4  20130104 34.6 17.4  970.5  10.0  3.6   8.9  45.9  26.2    0
5  20130105 36.0 17.9  981.0  10.0  3.4   0.0  48.2  25.9    0
6  20130106 40.6 26.9  976.8   9.9  3.8   9.9  47.1  31.1   NA
```

I'm only interested in creating a model from summer data, so let's take a subset of the data frame for weather, `wx`, which only includes data from May 31 to August 31, and leaves out the date in column 1 and precipitation in column 10:

```
> summer.wx <- wx[151:243,2:9]
> head(summer.wx)
    TEMP DEWP    STP VISIB WDSP MXSPD  MAX  MIN
151 72.7 57.0  978.8   9.8  4.1  13.0 88.0 55.6
152 75.0 59.7  974.8  10.0  4.9  11.1 87.1 61.2
153 74.1 60.4  971.2  10.0  6.0  13.0 82.8 66.9
154 71.7 59.9  969.9  10.0  3.7  13.0 80.1 65.7
155 65.7 47.6  975.2   9.8  3.4  12.0 75.2 55.6
156 66.3 50.5  977.5  10.0  2.7   9.9 77.4 55.6
```

Next, we will create two linear models. The first one will use simple linear regression (1 predictor and 1 response) to predict maximum temperature (MAX) from daily average visibility (VISIB). This is an interesting exercise because if the visibility is low (meaning there are clouds), the maximum temperatures should be lower because the clouds are inhibiting the warming of the Earth's surface.

```
> simple.fit <- lm(summer.wx$MAX ~ summer.wx$VISIB)
> summary(simple.fit)

Call:
lm(formula = summer.wx$MAX ~ summer.wx$VISIB)

Residuals:
    Min      1Q   Median      3Q      Max
-11.5316  -2.4915   0.0095   3.2730  10.8525

Coefficients:
                 Estimate Std. Error t value Pr(>|t|)
(Intercept)       76.9353     3.3970  22.648   <2e-16 ***
summer.wx$VISIB    0.6355     0.3846   1.652    0.102
---
Signif. codes:  0 '***' 0.001 '**' 0.01 '*' 0.05 '.' 0.1 ' ' 1

Residual standard error: 4.686 on 91 degrees of freedom
Multiple R-squared:  0.02913,   Adjusted R-squared:  0.01846
F-statistic:  2.73 on 1 and 91 DF,  P-Value: 0.1019
```

(The bold, underlined values are ones that you'll need to refer to later in this chapter - they will not show up as bold or underlined in the output on your R console, so don't be concerned if your output looks different.)

The second model uses multiple regression (8 predictors and 1 response) to predict maximum temperature from all of the other possible predictors. I'm using a slightly different notation here... instead of referring to the variable with reference to the data frame where it lives (summer.wx$MAX), I'm just referring to the variable name (MAX) and telling lm that I want to use the data contained in summer.wx. Also, I'm asking lm to produce a linear model to predict MAX using *everything else that's available*. (That's what the dot (.) after the tilde (~) means.)

```
> multiple.fit <- lm(MAX ~ ., data=summer.wx)
> summary(multiple.fit)

Call:
lm(formula = MAX ~ ., data = summer.wx)

Residuals:
   Min     1Q Median     3Q    Max
-5.090 -1.170 -0.188  1.024  6.773

Coefficients:
             Estimate Std. Error t value Pr(>|t|)
(Intercept) 22.09360   51.38221   0.430   0.6683
TEMP         1.53806    0.11607  13.251  < 2e-16 ***
DEWP        -0.10264    0.10966  -0.936   0.3519
STP         -0.01252    0.05262  -0.238   0.8125
VISIB       -0.42212    0.24639  -1.713   0.0903 .
WDSP        -0.51962    0.24699  -2.104   0.0384 *
MXSPD        0.12900    0.09869   1.307   0.1947
MIN         -0.43231    0.09016  -4.795 6.86e-06 ***
---
Signif. codes:  0 '***' 0.001 '**' 0.01 '*' 0.05 '.' 0.1 ' ' 1

Residual standard error: 2.175 on 85 degrees of freedom
Multiple R-squared:  0.8046,    Adjusted R-squared:  0.7885
F-statistic: 49.99 on 7 and 85 DF,  P-Value: < 2.2e-16
```

We will do a test for the slope associated with VISIB in the simple.fit model, as well as a test for WDSP in the multiple.fit model.

Step 1: Set Null and Alternative Hypotheses

The forms of the null and alternative hypotheses for the test of significance for regression coefficients (slope) are:

456

H_0: $\beta = 0$

H_a: $\beta > 0$ (one-tailed test)

$\beta < 0$ (one-tailed test)

$\beta \neq 0$ (two-tailed test)

Even though you could conceivably compare the slopes to a nonzero number (the value on the right-hand side of the null and alternative hypotheses), the test is typically performed to determine whether the slope is zero (meaning that a particular independent variable is not a significant predictor) or nonzero (meaning that a particular independent variable *is indeed* a significant predictor). The alternative hypothesis that I prefer is the two-tailed version, and that's what R uses as well.

Step 2: Choose α, the Level of Significance

The level of significance α is often set to 0.05, indicating that we're willing to *incorrectly reject the null hypothesis* one out of every 20 times we collect a sample and run this test. For this case, it means that 1 out of every 20 times we attempt to create a linear model from a sample of data, we will believe that a particular predictor is significant and important *when in fact it is not.*

This is acceptable for our current example because 1) the **cost** of collecting new observations is comparatively low, in terms of time, effort, and money, 2) the **risk** associated with drawing incorrect conclusions is also low (I'm just curious about the relationships between aspects of the observed weather in my local area, and not doing any serious research) and 3) there are no significant **ethical considerations** that I have to keep in mind based on how the results from my study may be applied by other people who read about or make decisions based on my study.

In contrast, if I were performing this study on behalf of an insurance company, and they wanted to know whether to change premiums for homeowner's policies based on my model, I might want to make my test more stringent, and set my level of significance α to 0.01, meaning I would only be willing to reject my null hypothesis and assert that *this predictor should definitely be included in my model* 1 out of every 100 times I collect data and perform the regression, due to sampling error.

Step 3: Calculate Test Statistic (T.S.)

For tests on regression coefficients, our test statistic will be a t. It is calculated like this:

$$t = \frac{\hat{\beta}_i}{s_e/\sqrt{SS_{xx}}}$$

Beta with the hat represents the slope that we estimate from our data. The summary statistics that I found from my sample of n=32 cars are a sample mean (y) of 33 mph, and a sample standard deviation of 5.6 mph. We can calculate the test statistic like this:

$$s_e = \sqrt{\frac{\sum Residuals^2}{n-2}}$$

$$SS_{xx} = \sum(x_i - \bar{x})^2$$

For the first case (testing the significance of the slope associated with the VISIB predictor), we can compute the test statistic t like this. Note that the computed value of t, 1.652, is *exactly* what we saw in the output from summary(simple.fit):

```
> iv <- summer.wx$VISIB   # Choose the right independent variable to use
> est.beta <- simple.fit$coefficients[2]
> ss.xx <- sum( ((iv-mean(iv))^2 ))
> se <- sqrt((sum((simple.fit$residuals^2)) / (length(iv)-2)))
> t <- est.beta / (se / sqrt(ss.xx))
> t
summer.wx$VISIB
        1.652239
```

Sometimes, it is easier to use a simplified form of the test statistic calculation. For the second case (testing the significance of the slope associated with the WDSP predictor in the multiple regression model), we can compute the test statistic t using this expression:

$$t = \frac{\hat{\beta}_i}{SE(\hat{\beta}_i)}$$

Here is the line that we look at from `summary(multiple.fit)` to find out how the test statistic is calculated:

```
WDSP          -0.51962    0.24699  -2.104    0.0384 *
```

The first value is our *estimate* of the regression coefficient (the numerator in the test statistic calculation). The second value is our standard error of the estimate (which will go in the denominator of the test statistic). When we plug the numbers in, we get:

$$t = \frac{-0.51962}{0.24699} = -2.104$$

The third value on that line, then, is the value of our test statistic (meaning that the fourth value is the P-Value that corresponds to our calculated t, which we'll use later).

Step 4: Draw a Picture

The t-distribution is used to determine areas under the curve for this test. Since the t distribution and the normal distribution have a similar shape, I'll use `shadenorm` to indicate what areas correspond to the P-Values in the tails beyond -2.104 and 2.104:

```
> source("https://raw.githubusercontent.com/NicoleRadziwill/R-
Functions/master/shadenorm.R")

> shadenorm(outside = c(1, 2, -1, -2.104, 2.104),col="black")
```

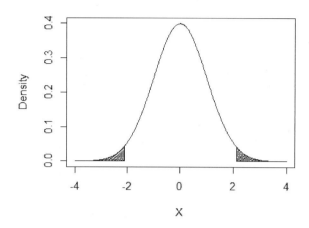

Step 5: Find the P-Value

The command to calculate areas under the t distribution in R is `pt`. Using the `pt` command, we can only find areas to the *left* of a particular t value. Since we want to find the area in both of the tails, we have to ask R to compute the area to the left of t=-2.104, and multiply it by 2 to capture both tails.

Here is how we do it for the simple regression case, where t=1.65:

```
> (1-pt(1.65,df=91))*2
[1] 0.1023906
```

And here's how we do it for the multiple regression case, where t=-2.104:

```
> pt(-2.104,df=91)*2
[1] 0.03813657
```

So our P-Value for the simple regression case, where we are exploring whether VISIB is a significant predictor, is approximately 0.102. For the multiple regression case, where we are exploring whether WDSP is a significant predictor, the P-Value is approximately 0.038.

Step 6: Is the P-Value < α? If So, Reject the Null

Now we have to ask ourselves: Are the P-Values we just calculated (0.102 and 0.038) less than our α of 0.05? In the first case, the answer is NO, but in the second case, the answer is YES. We REJECT our null hypothesis for the multiple regression case, but not for the simple regression case. Although WDSP is a significant predictor in the multiple regression model, VISIB is *not* an effective predictor in the simple regression model.

Steps 1 through 6: Hypothesis Test for the Significance of an Intercept

We'll come back to Step 7 shortly. First, check this out: you can *also* perform a hypothesis test for the significance of the y-intercept of a linear model. For this example, we will consider the simple.fit case where we made a linear model to predict max temperature (summer.wx$MAX) by visibility (summer.wx$VISIB). The null and alternative are:

H_0: $\alpha = \alpha_0$

H_a: $\alpha > \alpha_0$ (one-tailed test)

          $\alpha < \alpha_0$ (one-tailed test)

          $\alpha \neq \alpha_0$ (two-tailed test)

We are trying to figure out if the intercept from the linear model, α, is some value that we expect, α_0. The default test in R sets this α_0 to zero, and chooses a two-tailed test, so that we can tell whether the real intercept is zero or not. The test statistic t for the inference test on the intercept of a regression line is:

$$t = \frac{\hat{\alpha} - \alpha_0}{SE(\alpha)}$$

The standard error of the estimate, $SE(\alpha)$, depends on several other values that were defined earlier in this chapter:

$$SE(\alpha) = s_e \sqrt{\frac{\Sigma x^2}{n\, SS_{xx}}}$$

Fortunately, these values are easy to calculate in R when we have our dataset (summer.wx) loaded and our linear model, simple.fit, available for use:

```
> iv <- summer.wx$VISIB  # Choose the right independent variable to use
> est.alpha <- simple.fit$coefficients[1]
> ss.xx <- sum( ((iv-mean(iv))^2 ))
> se <- sqrt((sum((simple.fit$residuals^2)) / (length(iv)-2)))
> sum.xs <- sum(summer.wx$VISIB^2)
> t <- est.alpha/ (se* sqrt(sum.xs/(93*ss.xx)))
> t
(Intercept)
   22.64783
```

This calculated value for our test statistic t corresponds to a P-Value of about zero, even when we multiply by 2 to include the area in both tails!

```
> (1-pt(22.648,df=91))*2

[1] 0
```

Step 7: Compute Confidence Interval & Double Check in R

This is exactly the same information provided in the output from the summary(simple.fit) command, as you can see from the bold and underlined portions.

```
> summary(simple.fit)

Call:
lm(formula = summer.wx$MAX ~ summer.wx$VISIB)

Residuals:
     Min       1Q   Median       3Q      Max
-11.5316  -2.4915   0.0095   3.2730  10.8525

Coefficients:
                Estimate Std. Error t value Pr(>|t|)
(Intercept)      76.9353     3.3970  22.648   <2e-16 ***
summer.wx$VISIB   0.6355     0.3846   1.652    0.102
---
Signif. codes:  0 '***' 0.001 '**' 0.01 '*' 0.05 '.' 0.1 ' ' 1
```

```
Residual standard error: 4.686 on 91 degrees of freedom
Multiple R-squared:  0.02913,   Adjusted R-squared:  0.01846
F-statistic:  2.73 on 1 and 91 DF,   P-Value: 0.1019
```

You can also plot the confidence intervals on the scatterplot:

```
> source("https://raw.githubusercontent.com/NicoleRadziwill/R-
Functions/master/plotaddci.R")
> simple.fit <- lm(summer.wx$MAX ~ summer.wx$VISIB)
> plot(summer.wx$VISIB,summer.wx$MAX,pch=16,main="Max Temp vs. Visibility
(Summer)")
> plot.add.ci(summer.wx$VISIB,summer.wx$MAX,interval="confidence",
level=0.95,lwd=3,col="red")
```

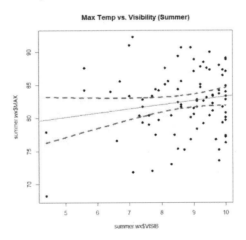

Other Resources:

- This resource goes into depth about inference on multiple regression models:
  http://www.uv.es/uriel/4%20Hypothesis%20testing%20in%20the%20multiple%20regression%20model.pdf
- Here is another great resource that talks about everything we discussed in this chapter, *plus* inference on prediction intervals, which can be useful:
  http://math.arizona.edu/~ghystad/chapter17.pdf

Appendix A: List of Variables and Acronyms

Here are the variables and acronyms that have appeared in this text, along with a description of what they represent whenever appropriate.

Variable	What it represents
α	The level of significance for hypothesis tests. Indicates what amount of risk you are willing to incur regarding false positives; for example, $\alpha = 0.05$ indicates that 1 out of every 20 times you collect a sample and run a particular inference test, you will be rejecting the null hypothesis when you really shouldn't have (that is, reporting a false positive).
API	Application Programming Interface. Helps us use software functions that other people have written, so that we can more easily interface with their systems.
β	Coefficients in an equation for a regression model OR the proportion of false negatives in a hypothesis test. In the first case, these variables often have subscripts (β_1, β_2, etc.) to help you distinguish them from one another.
C	Contingency coefficient. Describes the strength of association between two categorical variables.
CDF	Cumulative Distribution Function. Tells us the proportion of observations in a distribution that are less than or equal to a particular value.
CSV	Comma separated values. A file format that's easy to load into R. You can save your Excel (.xls and .xlsx) files as CSV.
D_0 or d_0	In tests for the difference between means or the difference between proportions, this is the value on the right-hand side of the null hypothesis that represents the nonzero difference we're comparing our observed difference to.
$\bar{d}$	A sample statistic: In a paired t-test, d-bar represents the mean of the *differences* between pairs in your two groups.
df	Degrees of freedom. Often, it's one less than the number of items in your sample, but it's calculated differently for things like contingency tables.
ε	The error term in regression equations.

e	A mathematical constant, approximately equal to 2.71828.
erf	The error function. A special mathematical construct that appears in the definition of some probability distributions.
F	A test statistic used for ANOVA and equality of variance tests. In ANOVA, it is computed by taking the Mean Square Between groups (MSB) and dividing by the Mean Square Within (MSW) groups. In the equality of variance test, it is the ratio of the variances between the two samples you are comparing (the bigger one should always go on top).
H_0	The null hypothesis.
H_a	The alternative hypothesis.
IQR	The interquartile range, or distance between Q1 and Q3. Represents where the middle 50% of the values in the distribution are located.
JSON	JavaScript Object Notation. A data format that makes it easier to encapsulate information as objects. Many online data archives provide their information in this format.
m	The slope of the regression line.
ME	Margin of Error. Represents one half of the size of the "net" that's the confidence interval, and computed by multiplying the standard error by a critical z or critical t.
n	*A sample statistic*: the number of items in your sample
$N(\mu, \sigma)$	This refers to the normal model with a mean of μ and a standard deviation of σ
μ	*A population parameter*: the mean of a quantitative variable
μ_0	*A population parameter*: the value you are assuming that the mean of a quantitative variable. Usually appears on the right-hand side of the null and alternative hypothesis.
π	3.14159... or, sometimes, how statistics textbooks will refer to the population parameter p. (Not in this one.)
PDF	Probability Density Function. Tells us the proportion of observations we can expect to have a particular value.
p	*A population parameter*: the true proportion of some characteristic ("successes") that is present in the complete population. These values can have subscripts (1, 2, etc.) if more than one group is being compared.

$\hat{p}$	*A sample statistic*: the proportion of some characteristic ("observed successes") that is observed in your sample. These values can have subscripts (1, 2, etc.) if more than one group is being compared.
P-Value	The area underneath a probability distribution in a particular region, typically in one or both tails.
Q1	The first quartile of a distribution. 25% of the values will be below this point, and 75% will be above.
Q3	The third quartile of a distribution. 75% of the values will be below this point, and 25% will be above.
q	*A population parameter*: the true proportion of some characteristic ("failures") that is present in the complete population. These values can have subscripts (1, 2, etc.) if more than one group is being compared.
$\hat{q}$	*A sample statistic*: the proportion of some characteristic ("observed failures") that is observed in your sample. These values can have subscripts (1, 2, etc.) if more than one group is being compared.
r	Correlation coefficient. Tells us the strength and direction of the linear relationship between two variables.
R^2	Coefficient of determination. Tells us what proportion of the variation in a linear regression model is explained by the model (the rest is contained in the residuals).
$SE(\overline{y})$	Standard error of one mean. There is a formula used to compute this.
$SE(\overline{y}_1 - \overline{y}_2)$	Standard error of the difference between two means. There is a formula used to compute this.
$SE_{pooled}(\overline{y}_1 - \overline{y}_2)$	The pooled standard error of the difference between two means. It's a simplification of the standard error that we can get away with *if* the two groups that produced the means have approximately the same variance.
$SE(\hat{p})$	Standard error of one proportion.
$SE(\hat{p}_1 - \hat{p}_2)$	Standard error of the difference between two proportions. There is a formula used to compute this.
s_p	The pooled standard deviation used in the computation of the test statistic t for the two sample t-test with equal variances.

s	*A sample statistic*: the standard deviation of the values in a sample, characterizing the dispersion of all the values
s^2	*A sample statistic*: the variance of the values in a sample, characterizing the dispersion of all the values in the sample.
s_x	Standard deviation of all of the x-coordinates in a dataset of (x,y) points.
s_y	Standard deviation of all of the y-coordinates in a dataset of (x,y) points.
s_{xy}	The covariance of coordinates in a dataset of (x,y) points.
σ	*A population parameter*: The standard deviation, characterizing the dispersion of all values in the population.
σ^2	*A population parameter*: The variance, characterizing the dispersion of all values in the population.
t	A test statistic that is computed for t-tests.
$t^*{}_{df}$	Critical t, which depends on the degrees of freedom (n-1) in your sample. Used as a scaling factor to determine the width of a confidence interval for means tests.
V	Cramer's V. Describes the strength of association between two categorical variables.
χ^2	Chi-square. A distribution (and test statistic) used to perform certain hypothesis tests.
x	*A sample statistic*: one of the quantitative values in your sample. Used to compute a z score for that value.
$\bar{x}$	*A sample statistic*: the mean of the quantitative variables within a sample. Also called the "sample mean".
$\bar{y}$	*A sample statistic*: the mean of the quantitative variables within a sample. Also called the "sample mean".
z (or z-score)	When using the normal model, z represents the number of standard deviations above or below the mean. It is also the test statistic that is computed for z-tests.
z^*	Critical z. The z score that corresponds to a particular area under the normal distribution, used as a scaling factor to determine the width of a confidence interval for proportions tests. For 90% CI z^*=1.645, for 95% CI z^*=1.96, and for 99% CI z^*=2.58.

Appendix B: Things to Tattoo on the Back of Your Eyelids

Background

I typically don't support memorizing formulas and expressions. (Really, who can remember all of them? Especially as you get older, have kids, and have all these different things competing for your brain space... memorizing anything becomes much less feasible.) What I do recommend is that each person build their own *formula sheets*, one for each statistical methodology or concept, and then refer to those formula sheets every time a problem must be solved. In fact, this is what I did to become an American Society for Quality (ASQ) Certified Six Sigma Black Belt (CSSBB).

Even so, you should COMMIT SOME THINGS TO MEMORY! I tell my students to "tattoo these phrases on the back of your eyelids, so that every time you close your eyes when you're thinking about a statistical problem, *you will see this stuff*." I try to keep my tattoo list as short and sweet as possible. But yes, memorize these things... and memorize them *exactly* as I have them listed. No flipping around the sign on P-Value question and stating something that's still perfectly logically sound, but is a different question.

I know it seems draconian, but *trust me on this*. Just memorize these things the **EXACT** way they are written below. You will be happy you did in 10 or 20 years.

Basics

- **Categorical** variables place observations in groups or categories, whereas **quantitative** variables are numbers that fall within a defined range. (Be careful! Sometimes people use numbers to represent their different categories.)
- When collecting data, **it's best to collect *quantitative variables* whenever you can**, because then you'll have much more flexibility later *creating* categorical variables - you can redefine the boundaries on the groups in any way that's necessary to explore your research questions (without committing sins like p-hacking).
- Each of our formulas and expressions contains population parameters, which represent the real values out there in the wider population (which is large, by

definition!) and sample statistics, which are the values you measure within the smaller samples you collect. Examples of population parameters are μ, σ, p, and q. Examples of sample statistics are x-bar, s, p-hat, and q-hat.

- **Independent Variables** (IVs) are the variables you use to PREDICT one or more **Dependent Variables** (DVs). The dependent variables DEPEND on your prediction. Plot IVs on the x-axis, and DVs on the y-axis.

Data Collection and Formatting

- When you think about collecting and preparing your data for analysis, picture a giant spreadsheet in your head.
- Each column should contain data representing *one and only one variable*. (The first column often, but not always, contains the observation identifier so you can keep track of individual observations.)
- Each column should have one and only one data type: either a categorical variable or a quantitative variable.
- Each row should correspond to one observation, or *case*. Your total sample size will be the *total number of rows* in your spreadsheet.

Confidence Intervals (CI)

- How do you interpret a confidence interval? **"We are [X]% confident that the TRUE value of the [population parameter] is between [lower limit] and [upper limit]."**
- The most common critical z* values for determining the size of the net that will be your confidence interval are **1.645** (for a 90% CI), **1.96** (for a 95% CI), and **2.58** (for a 99% CI).
- **If you have a SMALL SAMPLE (n ≤ 30), use the t-distribution** to figure out the critical t-value for determining the size of your net. Don't use z*.
- Any time you hear **LARGE SAMPLE**, think n > 30.

Hypothesis Testing

- **Is the P-Value Less Than (<) Alpha? If so, REJECT THE NULL!** You have detected what appears to be a significant effect.
- If the P-Value is NOT less than (<) alpha, **FAIL TO REJECT**. By examining your sample, you have noticed NOTHING out of the ordinary.
- The P-Value corresponds to an AREA under a probability distribution (often the normal or t distributions), and is DIFFERENT than the population parameter p, which is a proportion.
- The **level of significance (alpha)** is small, e.g. 0.01, 0.05, and sometimes 0.10.
- The **confidence level** is large, e.g. 0.90, 0.95, or 0.99.

Regression and Correlation

- Correlation coefficient r represents the *scatter or dispersion* of points characterized by the values of two quantitative variables (one on the x-axis, and one on the y-axis).
- The coefficient of determination, R^2, can be calculated by $r \times r$.
- The coefficient of determination, R^2, is the *percentage of variability* in the dependent (or response) variable *that is explained by the linear model*.
- $R^2\%$ of the variability within the data is explained by the model.

Decimal Places

- Use **no more than four** decimal places for your variables/probabilities, unless there's a compelling reason to do it differently! Round at the end, not in the middle.
- Also, consider what type of variable you are reporting. (Exam scores aren't reported to the 7th decimal place, so please don't report the average exam score as 71.4778982.)
- If a reported P-Value is less than 0.001 (1e-04) report it as "P < 0.0001".

Appendix C: Using R as a Lookup Table

Objective

You know all those tables at the back of a traditional statistics textbook? Well, once you get used to using R, you *never* have to carry them around with you again. In addition to being a fantastic analysis and programming language, R is also a compendium of any lookup table you could possibly want or imagine. Here are my most commonly used lookup utilities.

You have a/an...	You want to find...	How you get it
Area (or P-Value)	The **z-score** that is located at the position on the horizontal axis where that area is contained *to the left* of the z-score under the normal curve	`qnorm(`**`area`**`)`
Area (or P-Value)	The **z-score** that is located at the position on the horizontal axis where that area is contained *to the right* of the z-score under the normal curve	`qnorm(1-`**`area`**`)`
Area (or P-Value)	The **t-score** that is located at the position on the horizontal axis where that area is contained *to the left* of the t-score under the t distribution (must know degrees of freedom df)	`qt(`**`area`**`,df=`**`df`**`)`
Area (or P-Value)	The **t-score** that is located at the position on the horizontal axis where that area is contained *to the right* of the z-score under the t distribution (must know degrees of freedom df)	`qt(1-`**`area`**`,df=`**`df`**`)`

Area (or P-Value)	The **F value** that is located at the positive on the horizontal axis where that area is to the *left* in the **lower tail** (must know number of degrees of freedom df for both numerator and denominator)	$qf(\underline{\textbf{area}}, \underline{\textbf{df}}_{num}, \underline{\textbf{df}}_{den})$
Area (or P-Value)	The **F value** that is located at the positive on the horizontal axis where that area is to the *right* in the **upper tail** (must know number of degrees of freedom df for both numerator and denominator)	$qf(1-\underline{\textbf{area}}, \underline{\textbf{df}}_{num}, \underline{\textbf{df}}_{den})$
Area (or P-Value)	The **χ2 value** that is located at the position on the horizontal axis where that area is contained *to the left* of that χ^2 value under the Chi-square distribution (must know degrees of freedom df)	$qchisq(\underline{\textbf{area}}, df=\underline{\textbf{df}})$
Area (or P-Value)	The **χ2 value** that is located at the position on the horizontal axis where that area is contained *to the right* of that χ^2 value under the Chi-square distribution (must know degrees of freedom df)	$qchisq(1-\underline{\textbf{area}}, df=\underline{\textbf{df}})$
Desired **size for the confidence interval** (CI% expressed as a decimal, e.g. 0.95)	**Critical z** (or z*)	$qnorm(\underline{\textbf{CI}}+((1-\underline{\textbf{CI}})/2))$

Desired **size for the confidence interval** (CI% expressed as a decimal) *and* the number of degrees of freedom df	**Critical t** (or t*$_{df}$)	`qt(`**`CI`**`+((1-`**`CI`**`)/2),` `df=`**`df`**`)`
x or y	The **area (P-Value)** under the normal curve to the *left* of that x or y value, and you know the `mean` and the standard deviation `sd` of the distribution they come from	`pnorm(`**`x,mean,sd`**`)`
x or y	The **area (P-Value)** under the normal curve to the *right* of that x or y value, and you know the `mean` and the standard deviation `sd` of the distribution they come from	`1-pnorm(`**`x,mean,sd`**`)`
χ^2	The **area (P-Value)** under the Chi-square distribution to the *left* of that χ^2 value (must know degrees of freedom df)	`pchisq(`**`chisq`**`,df=`**`df`**`)`
χ^2	The **area (P-Value)** under the Chi-square distribution to the *right* of that χ^2 value (must know degrees of freedom df)	`1-pchisq(`**`chisq`**`,df=`**`df`**`)`
t-score	The area under the t distribution to the *left* of that t-score	`pt(`**`t`**`,df=`**`df`**`)`
t-score	The area under the t distribution to the *right* of that t-score	`1-pt(`**`t`**`,df=`**`df`**`)`

z-score	The area under the normal curve to the *left* of that z-score	pnorm($\underline{z}$)
z-score	The area under the normal curve to the *right* of that z-score	1-pnorm($\underline{z}$)

Examples

```
> # Find the area to the left of a z-score of -2
> pnorm(-2)
[1] 0.02275013
> # 2.27% of the area under the normal curve lies to the left of z=-2

> # Find the area to the left of x=2.9 in a normal model with
> # MEAN of 3.00 and a standard deviation SD of 0.01:
> pnorm(2.9,mean=3,sd=0.1)
[1] 0.1586553
> # 15.8% of the area under THIS normal curve lies to the left of x=2.9

> # Find the critical t (t*) for a 99% CI with df=9
> CI <- 0.99
> df <- 9
> qt(CI+((1-CI)/2), df-df)
[1] 3.249836

> # Find the critical t (t*) for a 99% CI with df=199
> CI <- 0.99
> df <- 199
> qt(CI+((1-CI)/2), df=df)
[1] 2.60076

> Find the critical z (z*) for a 98% CI:
> qnorm(CI+((1-CI)/2))
[1] 2.575829
```

Other Resources:

Here is a useful P-Value calculator that covers several of the different statistical inference tests: http://graphpad.com/quickcalcs/PValue1.cfm -- Note that these calculators USUALLY give you the area of the CLOSEST TAIL under the distribution you're working with! Because it's not always clear what convention each calculator is using, always be sure to draw a picture of the area you're trying to determine before using a calculator. Before you look up your critical values or P-Values, *guestimate* what the values might be. For example, if you know you're looking for an area (P-Value) that's greater than 50%, don't blindly accept an answer from a calculator that's less than 50%. *Trust your picture*.

Appendix D: Using Google as a Lookup Table

Objective

For all the lookup tasks covered in Appendix C, there are tables available that you can use to find the critical values and areas (P-Values). In fact, all statistics textbooks have these tables printed in the back. Even though you can look everything up in R, what if you have to do inference tests on a desert island where there is no internet (or maybe in a certification exam where you can't bring your R)? In that case, you should *print out the tables and bring them with you*. Google Image Search provides an excellent way to find these tables. Here are some links to ones that I have used.

Links

- This 10-page PDF file contains lookup tables for the normal, t, F, and Chi-square distributions: http://course.shufe.edu.cn/jpkc/jrjlx/ref/StaTable.pdf
- This 54-page PDF file contains lookup tables for normal, t, binomial, cumulative binomial, Poisson, Chi-Square, and F distributions, plus Correlation Coefficient: https://www.hawkeslearning.com/Documents/STATDataSets/STAT_Tables.pdf
- StatSoft has tables with little pictures that animate to remind you what you're looking up: http://www.statsoft.com/Textbook/Distribution-Tables
- There are some great interactive calculators on Richard Lowry's VassarStats page at http://vassarstats.net/tabs.html
- Stat Trek also has a nice selection of online calculators and lookup tables, with extensive discussions of the distributions in case you forget what you're looking at: http://stattrek.com/statistics/statistics-table.aspx

Remember, compare the picture in the table to the picture that you've drawn as you're trying to solve your inference problem. If you're looking for the *smaller* area, and the picture in the table shows the *larger* area, be sure to subtract whatever value you look up from 1 before using it.

Appendix E: Oh No! Troubleshooting Tips

Objective

I watch a LOT of people learn how to use R. And among other things, here's what I know for sure: you will *definitely* run into errors. You will *CAUSE* many of these errors yourself. When this happens, your goal will usually be to fix the error as quickly as you can, so you can move on to the next part of your computation. Your tendency may be to sit and stare at your screen, hoping the problem will fix itself. *It will not.* This section covers the most commonly encountered R-related panic attacks, based on my astute observations of the behavior of people in their first year of learning how to use R, and ways to fix them. If you have tried everything and still NOTHING works, go to the last two sections in this chapter.

`Error: could not find function`

There are a few possibilities here: 1) You're trying to use a function that is in a package you haven't installed yet. Type in `install.packages("the-name-of-the-package-you-need")` and R will get it for you. OR 2) You're trying to use a function that's in a package you *have* installed, but you've forgotten to use the `library` command to bring that package into active memory. Use `library(the-name-of-the-package-you-need)` to turn it on. Notice *no quotation marks in the library command.* If you have no idea what package the function came from, Google for the name of the function and the phrase, in quotes, "in R" - and the package name will probably be prominent in the first few search results.

`Error: unexpected '>' in ">"`

Were you copying in some code from this book, or maybe some code that you saw online (maybe at http://www.r-bloggers.com) and now you're mad because it didn't work??? Well... you're not supposed to put that leading caret (">") in front of your code. That's the R cursor. You type in all the stuff AFTER the caret. Every time you see that caret, you're seeing exactly what someone else saw on their R console.

Error: unexpected ')'

Count your parentheses. Every opening parenthesis needs to be paired with a closing parenthesis. If you count wrong, you will get this error. Also count your quotation marks, and make sure that each opening quote corresponds with an end quote. Or else, you could get this error. Also count your curly braces.

Error: unexpected **something other than > or) or (**

Were you cutting and pasting code into your R console again? If so, check to make sure you didn't accidentally cut and paste those *leading plus signs* at the beginning of each line. When someone is showing you the R code on their own screen, and some commands or function calls require multiple lines of input, R will insert a plus sign to indicate that the previous line is being continued. *This is R's job, not yours.* If you attempt to insert that plus sign at the beginning of the line, R will revolt, telling you that something was unexpected somewhere, and it can't interpret your code. Try again, without the leading plus signs.

Error in *** : object of type 'closure' is not subsettable

So here's what happened: you created (or loaded data into) some data structure, but it didn't quite work because whatever variable name you *think* contains data is ACTUALLY a function. R can't execute a `head` or `names` or `str` on a function. For example, if you *think* you have a data frame loaded up named `df`, try `head(df)`. You should see the first few lines of a function that makes no sense. What's the solution? Reload your data and recreate that data structure that you were trying to work with before.

Funky Quotation Marks

If you cut and paste code from the web (or a document, particularly a Word document) into your R console, you can get unexpected errors *if the quotation marks are not your standard, vertically-up-and-down, quotation marks.* What, you've never actually taken a really close look at your quotation marks? When you start coding in R, you will. If you get an error and notice that your quotation marks are tilted to the left or right on your input line, type the line again, entering the quotation marks manually using the SHIFT key and that quotation mark key just to the left of the Enter key.

You haven't mentioned my error message at all. NOW what I am supposed to do?

Your best plan of action is to <u>copy</u> *<u>that whole line or two where you got your error message</u>* in R, pop it into quotes, <u>and paste it into the Google search bar</u>. 99% of the time, someone will have gotten an error exactly like yours or very similar to yours, and they will have freaked out already and posted their request for support to Stack Overflow or Stack Exchange. Your situation might be different than what you see posted... you'll have to do your best to interpret what was said, and apply it to your own issue. If all else fails, have you considered sending an email to the person who wrote the package you're having problems with? The most beautiful thing about an open source community is that you can find the authors' emails in the package documentation. And I've found that often, they're happy to help you troubleshoot their package. They love it when people benefit from their work.

Not all packages are showing up on CRAN, and/or there is some just completely bizarre thing going on that's driving me absolutely insane and I've tried everything else possible and still NOTHING IS WORKING

I've found that *sometimes,* packages that you download via CRAN can be corrupt. If you're in the United States, I've found that the east coast repositories are much more intermittently problematic than the west coast repositories. If you are having a lot of problems with a particular package, you might want to try *deleting the current installation* and creating a new one. If you can't change your CRAN repository using the menu bar, do it manually.

This is a 2-step process. First, type `.libPaths()` on the R command line, which will tell you the directories where all of your packages are stored locally. You'll want to navigate to each of these directories, using Finder on Mac or Windows Explorer (the "Computer" selection on the Start Menu) in Windows, and manually delete the offending package. Once you've done this, type the following line into your R console:

```
options("repos"=c(CRAN="@CRAN@"))
```

Next, attempt to download the package using `install.packages("your-package-name")` which will require you to choose a new CRAN repository. (My advice is to pick one of the California repositories, since they seem to be more reliable.) Once the package downloads, you can use the `library()` command to activate it for your current R session.

Sometimes, the most up-to-date package is available on GitHub, but NOT on CRAN. (This is the case with the `twitteR` package at the time of this writing). Here's how you download a package directly from GitHub. To download the package you're interested in, be sure to replace the userid of the GitHub account hosting the package (in this case, `geoffjentry`) and the name of the package you want (in this case, `twitteR`).

```
install.packages("devtools")
library(devtools)
install_github("geoffjentry/twitteR")
```


I tried that too and still NOTHING IS WORKING!! Help!

Have you tried using the help functionality? You can request information about a particular command using `help`, or you can search for commands that contain information like what you're looking for with `help.search` (be sure to put your search string in quotes). Both ways, R will launch a web browser containing the results. For example:

```
> help(plot)
starting httpd help server ... done
> help.search("plot")
```

I tried THAT too and still NOTHING IS WORKING!! Help!

Maybe reinstall R and get a version that's more up to date? At this point, I really don't know without being able to drive your machine myself. Find a friend who also knows a little about R who you can commiserate with. Maybe they can help. Or, just take a break for a couple days, then go back to your computer and try whatever you were doing before *again.*

Have you ever heard the joke about the four engineers in the car that broke down? No? Well, there was this car that broke down, with four engineers in it. One was a mechanical engineer, one was an electrical engineer, one was a chemical engineer, and one was a software engineer. The mechanical engineer said "No problem! I can fix the car." He got out of the car, lifted the hood, and checked to make sure that all the moving parts were in working order. He checked the belts, the gears, and the connections, but everything seemed to be put together just fine. Defeated, he got back in the car. "Not to worry!" said the electrical engineer. "I bet it's just a power problem." He got out of the car and checked the ignition, the starter, and everything else having to do with the power. He even checked the fuses... but no luck. "It's got to be a problem with the fluids, then," the chemical engineer affirmed. He got out of the car, checked to make sure there was enough gas in the car, checked to make sure that they had used the right kind of gas, checked the oil, and even checked the antifreeze. No problems.

Everyone was really concerned now, because even though they were all really smart engineers, no one had a solution to the problem.

"I've got it!" said the software engineer. "How about we just all get out of the car, close the doors, open the doors again... then get back in and close the doors, and see if the car works again?"

The moral of this story is... sometimes, if you are having an R problem, things will work again if you shut down your computer, start it back up, and then try what you were working on again. Or, if you go to sleep for the night and try it again in the morning. You're right, this form of troubleshooting doesn't make sense. But it often works when nothing else will.

Appendix F: R Colors and Palettes

Objective

In many of the examples in this book, you will be able to *set the color* of your points, or bars, or fonts, or other element of a chart or graph. Although for printing purposes I've chosen very dull alternatives like "`gray`", "`lightgray`", and "`darkgray`", there are hundreds of choices you can use to make your on-screen plots exciting and fun.

Resources

Any place you are asked to specify "`col=`" in R, you can play with colors. You can refer to them in many different ways: by name, by hexadecimal color ID, or by color palette:

- My favorite listing of R color names was made by Tian Zheng, of Columbia University. It's at http://www.stat.columbia.edu/~tzheng/files/Rcolor.pdf.
- You can also use an interactive color picker to generate hexadecimal color IDs, like this one at http://www.w3schools.com/tags/ref_colorpicker.asp
- Or, you can have R pick colors for you, based on one of several predefined color palettes. All you need to do is specify the number of colors in the rotation, `n`.

Color Palette Name	What colors are included
`rainbow(n)`	A cycle through red, orange, yellow, light green, dark green, light blue, dark blue, purple and magenta. I've found that n=12 produces a nice range of colors.
`heat.colors(n)`	Reds, oranges, and yellows
`terrain.colors(n)`	Greens, yellows, beiges, and pinks
`topo.colors(n)`	Light and earthy blues, green, and yellows
`cm.colors(n)`	Pastel pinks and blues
`palette()`	The default color palette in R, which consists of `black`, `red`, `green3`, `blue`, `cyan`, `magenta`, `yellow`, and `gray`

There are additional color palettes in the `RColorBrewer` package too.

Appendix G: Typing Characters with Hats and Bars in Word

Background

I use Microsoft Word to prepare documents. I do not like Microsoft Equation Editor. And I have to type equations and expressions not often (like every sentence or every other sentence), but definitely regularly. This has led me to apply what I like to call "agile shortcuts" — basically, I'll write down the equation in my own handwriting, take a picture of it, and then use a paint program to crop and clean up my equation before inserting it into my document. This works nicely, and even though some people might think it's a kludge, I kind of like the ability to retain the personality of my own handwriting in my technical documents.

However, I don't want to be embedding images if all I have to do is make reference to a variable within a paragraph of text... and I've never had a good solution. UNTIL THIS MORNING when I really, really, really wanted to be able to use y-bar and p-hat in my paragraph, without having to do the even *kludgier* thing where you just call them "y-bar" and "p-hat" in the text. That doesn't feel good.

Even Arial Unicode MS, the behemoth of fonts (it even contains tons of Chinese, Japanese, and Korean characters) does not have essential statistical symbols. But turns out, it DOES have this very useful capability called "**combining diacritics**" — and here's how you can use it to type characters with their own hats and bars on them:

Process

1. Open up Microsoft Word

2. Choose "Arial Unicode MS" as your font

3. First, type in a letter that you want to adorn with a hat. Say, for example, p.

4. Next, go to Insert -> Symbol, drop down to "More Symbols", and in the window that pops up, make sure you have selected "Arial Unicode MS" as the font. In the bottom right, you'll see a text area and a dropdown. To the right of the text area labeled "Character code:" type in 0302. That's the code for a hat-on-top-of-a-letter.

Going further right, there's a dropdown that says "from:" and you'll want to make sure that you see "Unicode (hex)" selected in that box. Click "Insert".

5. Voila, your p has a hat!! Now, type a few spaces and let's do this again.

6. Only now, type in a letter that you want to adorn with a bar. Say, for example, x.

7. Next, go to Insert -> Symbol, drop down to "More Symbols", and in the window that pops up, make sure you have selected "Arial Unicode MS" as the font. In the bottom right, you'll see a text area and a dropdown. To the right of the text area labeled "Character code:" type in 0305. That's the code for a bar-on-top-of-a-letter. Going further right, there's a dropdown that says "from:" and you'll want to make sure that you see "Unicode (hex)" selected in that box. Click "Insert".

8. Voila again! Your x has a bar.

Fin

Here you go, in case you just want to cut and paste them from now on:

$$\hat{p} \qquad \hat{q} \qquad \bar{x} \qquad \bar{y}$$

Disclaimer

This doesn't work all the time under Windows 10.

Appendix H: The `shadenorm.R` Function

Many of the pictures of shaded areas under the normal distribution in this book were created using the `shadenorm` function, originally posted to the R Bloggers web site at http://www.r-bloggers.com/how-to-shade-under-a-normal-density-in-r/. To use it, 1) source the file into you R session using the first line of code below, 2) copy and paste the whole function below into your R session, or 3) copy and paste the whole function into a file called `shadenorm.R`, then put it into your R working directory and use `source("shadenorm.R")` to load the function into memory. An alternative to `shadenorm` is `polygon` on p. 73 and 400.

```
source("https://raw.githubusercontent.com/NicoleRadziwill/R-
Functions/master/shadenorm.R")
```

The `shadenorm` Function

```
# by Tony Cookson
# http://www.r-bloggers.com/how-to-shade-under-a-normal-density-in-r/

shadenorm = function(below=NULL, above=NULL, pcts = c(0.025,0.975), mu=0,
        sig=1, numpts = 500, color = "gray", dens = 40, justabove= FALSE,
        justbelow = FALSE, lines=FALSE, between=NULL, outside=NULL) {

    if(is.null(between)){
        below = ifelse(is.null(below), qnorm(pcts[1],mu,sig), below)
        above = ifelse(is.null(above), qnorm(pcts[2],mu,sig), above)
    }

    if(is.null(outside)==FALSE){
        below = min(outside)
        above = max(outside)
    }
    lowlim = mu - 4*sig
    uplim  = mu + 4*sig

    x.grid = seq(lowlim,uplim, length= numpts)
    dens.all = dnorm(x.grid,mean=mu, sd = sig)
    if(lines==FALSE){
        plot(x.grid, dens.all, type="l", xlab="X", ylab="Density")
    }
    if(lines==TRUE){
        lines(x.grid,dens.all)
    }
```

```
    if(justabove==FALSE){
        x.below    = x.grid[x.grid<below]
        dens.below = dens.all[x.grid<below]

polygon(c(x.below,rev(x.below)),c(rep(0,length(x.below)),rev(dens.below)),co
l=color,density=dens)
    }
    if(justbelow==FALSE){
        x.above    = x.grid[x.grid>above]
        dens.above = dens.all[x.grid>above]

polygon(c(x.above,rev(x.above)),c(rep(0,length(x.above)),rev(dens.above)),co
l=color,density=dens)
    }

    if(is.null(between)==FALSE){
        from = min(between)
        to   = max(between)

        x.between    = x.grid[x.grid>from&x.grid<to]
        dens.between = dens.all[x.grid>from&x.grid<to]

polygon(c(x.between,rev(x.between)),c(rep(0,length(x.between)),rev(dens.betw
een)),col=color,density=dens)
    }

}
```

Examples

You can use shadenorm to shade *regions between* two z-scores:

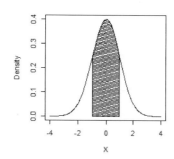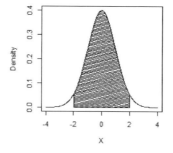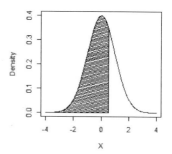

Here is the code that produced the three graphs above. Notice that the leftmost graph has the region between z=-1 and z=+1 shaded, the middle graph has the region between z=-2 and z=+2 shaded, and the rightmost graph has everything shaded from all the way in the left tail (z=-Inf) to z=0.537, about half a standard deviation above the mean. We've also chosen to change the default shading color from gray to black:

```
> par(mfrow=c(1,3))
> shadenorm(between=c(-1,+1),color="black")
> shadenorm(between=c(-2,+2),color="black")
> shadenorm(between=c(-Inf,0.537),color="black")
```

Or, you can use shadenorm to shade regions *between actual values of your own data.* For example, if you're modeling pulse rate in terms of beats per minute, and know that the mean pulse rate in a population of Americans between 18 and 24 years old is 78 beats per minute with a standard deviation of 8 beats per minute, you can use that normal model N(78,8) to create regions:

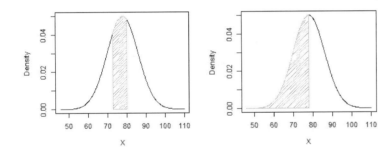
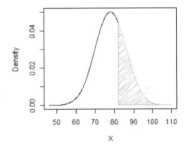

Here is the R code that created these three charts. Note that we've opted to keep the default shading color of gray:

```
> par(mfrow=c(1,3))
> shadenorm(between=c(73,80),mu=78,sig=8)
> shadenorm(between=c(-Inf,78),mu=78,sig=8)
> shadenorm(between=c(82,Inf),mu=78,sig=8)
```

There are more examples of `shadenorm` syntax in Chapter 1.8 on Z-Score Problems.

Appendix I: LaTeX Markup for Equations in this Book

Objective

To create images of equations that I can drag and drop into text, I use an online app to render images from LaTeX mathematical markup. Here is the LaTeX code for many of the equations in this book, if you need to include them in a research paper. All equations throughout this text were prepared using the Sciweavers online LaTeX equation editor at http://www.sciweavers.org/free-online-latex-equation-editor.

BASIC STUFF

```
\sigma^2 = \frac{1}{n-1} \sum\limits_{i=1}^n (y_i - \bar{y})^2
```

```
\sigma = \sqrt{\frac{1}{n-1} \sum\limits_{i=1}^n (y_i - \bar{y})^2}
```

SCATTERPLOTS

```
r = \frac{s_{xy}}{s_x s_y}
```

```
COV(x,y) = s_{xy} = \frac{\sum\limits_{i=1}^n (x_i-\overline{x})(y_i-
\overline{y})}{n - 1}
```

Z SCORE PROBLEMS

```
f(x) = \frac{1}{\sqrt{2\pi}} \hspace{  } e^{-x^2/2}
```

```
\frac{1}{\sqrt{2\pi}}  \int\limits_{-1}^{1} \! e^{-x^2/2} dx
```

```
= \frac{1}{\sqrt{2\pi}} \hspace{2} \sqrt{\frac{\pi}{2}} \hspace{2}
erf\frac{x}{\sqrt{2}} \hspace{2}
```

```
\Bigg| \right\vert_{-1}^{1}
```

SAMPLING DISTRIBUTIONS

```
\bar{X} \sim N\left(\mu,\frac{\sigma}{\sqrt{n}}\right)
```

```
 \lim_{n \rightarrow \infty} (SE\hspace{2}of\hspace{2}the\hspace{2}Mean) =
(SD\hspace{2}of\hspace
```

```
{2}the\hspace{2}Population\hspace{2}Mean)
```

```
\bar{X} \sim N\left( \mu_1-\mu_2,SE(\bar{y_1}-\bar{y_2}) \right)
```

```
\bar{x}   \sim N(d,\frac{\sigma_d}{\sqrt{n}})
```

ONE SAMPLE T-TEST

```
t = \frac{\overline{y} -  \mu_0}{SE(\overline{y})} = \frac{\overline{y} -
\mu_0}{s / \sqrt{n}}
```

```
\overline{y} \pm t_{df}^{*}SE(\overline{y})
```

```
\overline{y} \pm t_{df}^{*}\frac{s}{\sqrt{n}}
```

```
\overline{y} \pm z^{*}\frac{\sigma}{\sqrt{n}}
```

TWO MEANS

```
t=\frac{{\overline{y}}_1-{\overline{y}}_2-D_0}{SE_{pooled}{(\overline{y}}_1-
{\overline{y}}_2)}}=
```

```
\frac{{\overline{y}}_1-{\overline{y}}_2-D_0}{s_p
\sqrt{\frac{1}{n_1}+\frac{1}{n_2}}}
```

```
s_p =\sqrt{\frac{(n_1-1)s_1^2+(n_2-1)s_2^2}{n_1+n_2-2}}
```

```
(\overline{y}_1 - \overline{y}_2) \pm t_{df}^{*}SE(\overline{y}_1 -
\overline{y}_2)
```

```
(\overline{y}_1 - \overline{y}_2) \pm t_{df}^{*}{s_p
\sqrt{\frac{1}{n_1}+\frac{1}{n_2}}}
```

```
(\overline{y}_1 - \overline{y}_2) \pm C^{*}SE(\overline{y}_1 -
\overline{y}_2)
```

```
(\overline{y}_1 - \overline{y}_2) \pm
z^{*}\sigma\sqrt{\frac{1}{n_1}+\frac{1}{n_2}}
```

```
t=\frac{\overline{y}_1-\overline{y}_2-D_0}{SE({\overline{y}_1-
\overline{y}_2)}}=\frac{\overline{y}
```

```
_1-\overline{y}_2-D_0}{ \sqrt{\frac{s_1^2}{n_1}+\frac{s_2^2}{n_2}}}
```

```
df=\frac{\left(\frac{\displaystyle s_1^2}{\displaystyle
n_1}+\frac{\displaystyle s_2^2}
```

```
{\displaystyle n_2}\right)^2}{\frac{\displaystyle\left(\frac{\displaystyle
s_1^2}{\displaystyle
```

```
n_1}\right)^2}{\displaystyle n_1-
1}+\frac{\displaystyle\left(\frac{\displaystyle s_2^2}
```

```
{\displaystyle n_2}\right)^2}{\displaystyle n_2-1}}
```

```
(\overline{y}_1 - \overline{y}_2) \pm
t_{df}^{*}{\sqrt{\frac{s_1^2}{n_1}+\frac{s_2^2}{n_2}}}
```

```
(\overline{y}_1 - \overline{y}_2) \pm
z^{*}\sqrt{\frac{\sigma_1^2}{n_1}+\frac{\sigma_2^2}{n_2}}
```

PAIRED MEANS

```
t = \frac{\overline{d} - d_0}{SE(\overline{d})} = \frac{\overline{d} -
d_0}{s_d / \sqrt{n} }
```

```
CI: Estimate \pm Margin\:of\:Error\:(ME)
```

```
\overline{d} \pm t_{df}^{*}SE(\overline{d})
```

```
\overline{d} \pm t_{df}^{*} \frac{s_d}{\sqrt{n}}
```

```
\bar{d} \pm t_{df}^*\frac{s_d}{\sqrt{n}}
```

```
\bar{d} \pm t_{df}^*{SE(\bar{d})}
```

PROPORTIONS

```
z = \frac{\hat{p_1} - \hat{p_2}}{SE(\hat{p_1}-\hat{p_2})} = \frac{\hat{p_1}-\hat{p_2}}{\sqrt{pq

\hspace{2}(\frac{1}{n_1}+\frac{1}{n_2})}}

p = \frac{x_1 + x_2}{n_1 + n_2}

(\hat{p_1}-\hat{p_2})\pm\hspace{2}z^*\hspace{2}SE(\hat{p_1}-\hat{p_2})

(\hat{p_1}-
\hat{p_2})\pm\hspace{2}z^*\hspace{2}\sqrt{(\frac{\hat{p_1}\hat{q_1}}{n_1}+\frac{\hat

{p_2}\hat{q_2}}{n_2})}}

\frac{(2n\hat{p} + z^{*2}) \pm z^{*2}\sqrt{z^{*2} + 4n\hat{p}\hat{q}}}{2(n + z^{*2})}
```

CHI SQUARE

```
C = \sqrt{\frac{\chi^2}{n + \chi^2}}

V = \sqrt{\frac{\chi^2}{nt}}
```

REGRESSION

```
y =  \alpha + \sum\limits_{k}  \beta_k x_k +  \epsilon

y =  \alpha + \beta_1 x_1 + \beta_2 x_2 + \beta_3 x_3 + ... + \beta_k x_k + \epsilon

\hat\beta \pm t_{df}^* SE(\hat\beta)

SE(\hat\beta) = \frac{s_e}{s_x \sqrt{n-1} }
```

```
s_e = \sqrt{ \frac{ \sum {Residuals}^2}{n-2}  }

\hat\alpha \pm t_{df}^* SE(\hat\alpha)

SE(\hat\alpha) = s_{y.x} \sqrt{  \frac{1}{n} + \frac{\bar{x}^2}{SS_{xx}}  }

s_{y.x} =
\frac{Sum\hspace{2}of\hspace{2}Squares\hspace{2}of\hspace{2}Errors}{n-2}

SS_{xx} = \sum (x_i - \bar{x})^2

\beta  \sim N\left( \beta_1, \frac{\sigma^2}{\sum(x_1 - \bar{x})^2 \right)

t = \frac{\hat\beta_i}{s_e/\sqrt{SS_{xx}}}

t = \frac{\hat\alpha - \alpha_0}{SE(\alpha)}

SE(\alpha) = s_e \sqrt{ \frac{\sum x^2}{n\hspace{2}SS_{xx}} }
```

VARIANCE

```
SE(\sigma^2) - s^2 \sqrt{\frac{2}{n-1}}

\frac{(n-1)s^2}{\chi^2_{upper}}  \leq \sigma^2  \leq  \frac{(n-1)s^2}{\chi^2_{lower}}

\left(\frac{s_1^2}{s_2^2}\right)F_{lower} \leq \frac{\sigma_1^2}{\sigma_2^2}
\leq  \left(\frac

{s_1^2}{s_2^2}\right)F_{upper}

\chi_{df}^2 = \frac{(n-1)s^2}{\sigma^2} = \frac{(n-1) \times
{Sample\hspace{2}Variance}}{Reference

\hspace{2}or\hspace{2}Target\hspace{2}Variance}
```

Appendix J: Basic Probability

Objective

Pretty much everything we do in statistics depends on *probability*: that is, the proportion of the time that an outcome is observed once you look at many, many events over a loooooong period of time (the "long run"). Probability is defined as the *long run relative frequency* of a particular event occurring. There are several terms that you should recognize, and a few rules that help us know when we can manipulate probabilities to answer questions about what can happen as the result of a random process.

Definitions

Here are the most important definitions related to probability in random processes:

- **Trial**: Each trial results in one or more outcomes. If your trial is to flip one coin, you'll get one outcome (heads or tails). If your trial means flipping 10 coins at once, there will be one outcome recorded per coin.
- **Outcome**: A possible result of a trial. When flipping a coin, there are two possible outcomes (heads and tails). When rolling a 6-sided die, there are six possible outcomes (1, 2, 3, 4, 5 or 6). When choosing an M&M candy from the bag, there are six possible outcomes (Red, Green, Blue, Brown, Orange, Yellow).
- **Independent**: Two trials are independent if the outcome of one trial does not influence the outcome of another. For example, flipping heads on the first trial does not affect your likelihood of flipping heads on the second trial.
- **Event**: An event is something that *happens* as a result of a trial involving a random process. For example, "getting heads" on a coin flip is an event. "Rolling a 5 or 6" on the die is an event. "Choosing a Blue M&M" is an event.
- **Complement of an Event**: if event A is that you get a Blue M&M, the complement (A') is that you get a color of M&M that's *anything but* blue. The probability of an event plus its complement is always one: the probability of getting a blue M&M,

plus the probability of getting an M&M that's NOT blue, fills up the whole 100% of possibilities.

- **Sample Space**: The collection of all possible outcomes for an event, usually called *S*. For coins, the sample space is S = {heads,tails}. For six-sided dice, the sample space is S = {1, 2, 3, 4, 5, 6}. For M&Ms, the sample space is S = {Red, Green, Blue, Brown, Orange, Yellow}. For exam scores, the sample space is S = {$0 \leq x \leq 100$}. For exam *answers* where the exam has 2 questions and you can choose A, B, C, or D, the sample space is S = {AA,AB,AC,AD,BA,BB,BC,BD,CA,CB, CC,CD,DA,DB,DC,DD}.

- **Mutually Exclusive (or Disjoint)**: Two events are disjoint if they have *no outcomes in common*. When you roll one 6-sided die, the events A (rolling a 1 or 2) and B (rolling a 5 or 6) are *disjoint*, because they can't both happen. For employees at a company that are selected at random (like say there's a lottery for who's going to get a new computer), you can be both female and a manager, so event A (being female) and event B (being a manager) are not disjoint. Because they can very easily both happen at the same time!

- **Conditional Probability**: What's the probability that event A occurs, given that event B has *already* happened? (For example, what's the probability that a message in your email box is spam, *given that* you know it contains the word Viagra?) This requires Bayes' Theorem, which is best explained with Lego blocks, and tells how knowing about one event can inform us about what's going on with the other: http://www.countbayesie.com/blog/2015/2/18/bayes-theorem-with-lego

There are several relationships that help us work with outcomes and events:

Notation	What it means
A $\cup$ B = A or B	The **union** of sets A and B: what do you get when you join them all together? You can remember that this means *union* because the symbol looks like of like a capital U.
A $\cap$ B = A and B	The **intersection** of sets A and B. What outcomes do they share in common? If A and B are mutually exclusive, then P(A $\cap$ B) = 0.

P(A or B) = P(A) + P(B)	**The addition rule for mutually exclusive events**: the probability of *either* A *or* B happening is found by adding the probability that event A occurs, and the probability that event B occurs. For this to work, the events *have* to be mutually exclusive!
P(A and B) = P(A) x P(B)	**The multiplication rule**: the probability of *both* A and B happening is found by multiplying the probability that event A occurs with the probability that event B occurs. For this to work, the events *have* to be independent - what happens in one of them can't affect what happens in the other!
P(A or B) = P(A) + P(B) - P(A and B)	**The addition rule for events that aren't mutually exclusive**: the probability of *either* A or B happening is found by adding the probability that event A occurs, and the probability that event B occurs, and then subtracting off the probability that both events have happened together (that is, the ones you double counted by counting everything in A, and everything in B).
P(A|B) = P(A and B) ÷ P(B)	The **conditional probability** of event B happening, given that event A has already happened.

Examples

Here are a couple quick examples of the above principles in practice:

1) You're pulling M&Ms off the conveyor at the candy factory. Based on the distribution of M&Ms in the factory, you know there's a 12% chance of getting an orange, and a 16% chance of getting a blue. Because the colors are mutually exclusive (disjoint), he probability of getting an orange OR a blue when you pull one randomly from the bag is:

```
P(Orange OR Blue) = P(Orange) + P(Blue) = 12% + 18% = 30%
```

2) Considering that same conveyor of M&Ms, what's the probability that the first two M&Ms you pull will be orange? Because the events are independent, you can use the multiplication rule:

```
P(Orange AND Blue) = P(Orange) * P(Orange) = 12% x 12% = 1.44%
```

3) In your company, there are 84 employees. 52 are men, 46 are part-time, and 34 are men who work part-time. What's the probability that an employee randomly picked from this group is either male or works part-time? Because these events aren't mutually exclusive (you can be both male *and* work part-time), you can find the probability by applying the **addition rule** for events that aren't mutually exclusive:

```
        Event A = Person is male
      Event B = Person works part-time
    P(A or B) = P(A) + P(B) - P(A and B)
         = 52/84 + 46/84 - 34/84
              = 64/84
```

4) What's the probability of flipping heads on the second coin flip, given that you flipped tails on the first flip? Let's use the conditional probability rule to figure that out:

```
        P(A|B) = P(A and B) ÷ P(B)

  P(Heads|Tails) = P(Heads and Tails) ÷ P(Tails)
        P(Heads AND Tails) = 0.5 x 0.5 = 0.25
        P(Heads|Tails) = 0.25 ÷ 0.5 = 0.5
```

There's a 50% chance that you'll flip heads on the second flip, given that you know you flipped tails on the first flip. But hey, isn't there a 50% chance of getting tails *anyway*? Yes indeed, because these two events are *independent*. We can use the conditional probability rule to check for independence as well, as you can see.

Appendix K: Overview of Inference Tests

Type of Data

	Normal or Nearly Normal	Not Normal	Binomial (Proportions)	Variances
Compare data within one group to a standard, target, or recommended value	One sample t-test	Wilcoxon Rank Sum test	One proportion z-test (or Exact Binomial test)	Chi-square test for one variance
Compare data within two groups (where observations are unpaired)	Two sample t-test	Mann-Whitney U test	Two proportion z-test, Chi-square test of independence (or Fisher's Exact test if counts in cells < 5)	F Test for Homogeneity of Variances
Compare data within two groups (where observations are paired)	Paired t-test	Wilcoxon Signed Rank test	McNemar's test	Bonett's Test
Compare data between many groups	One-Way Analysis of Variance (ANOVA)	Kruskal-Wallis test	Chi-square test of independence (or Fisher's Exact test if counts in cells < 5)	Levene's Test (or Bartlett's if source data is normal)

Appendix L: Plotting Power Curves

Plotting Power Curves

One of the things I like to do when I am exploring my tradeoffs between Type I Error (that is, level of significance α, which I can *control*) and Type II Error (which I can *adjust* based on what power I choose for my test) is to plot the various sample sizes I will need to achieve a power of at least 0.80 for a range of α values. With sample size n on the horizontal x-axis, and power on the vertical y-axis, these tradeoffs become easier to see.

Here is some code to plot a power curve. Note that you will need a NEW power curve for each statistical test that you plan to do, and you'll have to change the effect size and the range of sample sizes you want to consider (based on your particular study):

```
# Set the effect size and range of n's to consider in your plot
library(pwr)
effect.size <- 0.3
n <- seq(10,400,10)

# Change these to reflect the TYPE OF STATISTICAL TEST you are doing:
pwr.05 <- pwr.t.test(d=effect.size,n=n,sig.level=.05,type="two.sample",
alternative="greater")
pwr.01 <- pwr.t.test(d=effect.size,n=n,sig.level=.01,type="two.sample",
alternative="greater")
pwr.1 <- pwr.t.test(d=effect.size,n=n,sig.level=.1,type="two.sample",
alternative="greater")

# Now Plot the Power Curve
plot(pwr.05$n,pwr.05$power,type="l",xlab="Sample Size
(n)",ylab="Power",col="black")
lines(pwr.1$n,pwr.1$power,type="l",xlab="Sample Size
(n)",ylab="Power",col="blue")
lines(pwr.01$n,pwr.01$power,type="l",xlab="Sample Size
(n)",ylab="Power",col="red")
abline(h=0.8)
grid(nx=25,ny=25)
title("Power Curve for Sample Size Estimation")
legend("bottomright", title="Significance Level",
c("sig.level=0.01","sig.level=0.05","sig.level=0.1"),
```

```
fill=c("red","black","blue"))
```

The plot below shows a prediction of power by sample size for least stringent (blue; topmost curve) to most stringent (red; bottom right-most curve) tests.

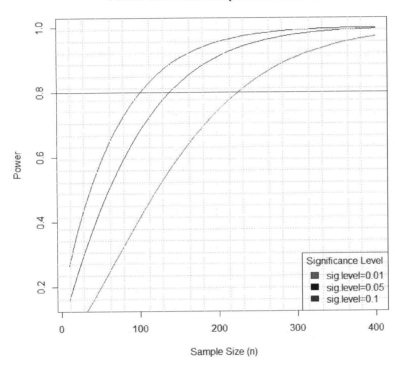

Power Curve for Sample Size Estimation

Conclusions

What sample sizes did you determine for each of your research questions? Now pick the *largest one* of all of those calculations you made. Choose that as your appropriate sample size, then move forward and *make great research*. (Props to Neil Gaiman on those words of encouragement.)

Index